WEAVING CONNECT

EDUCATING FOR PEACE, SOCIA

ENVIRONMENTAL JUSTICE

WEAVING CONNECTIONS

Educating for Peace, Social and Environmental Justice

EDITED BY

Tara Goldstein
& David Selby

SUMACH
PRESS

CANADIAN CATALOGUING IN PUBLICATION DATA

Main entry under title:

Weaving connections: educating for peace, social and environmental justice

Includes bibliographical references.

ISBN 1-894549-01-5

1. Education – Canada – Aims and objectives. 2. Educational planning – Canada.
3. Education – Canada – Curricula. I Goldstein, Tara, 1957- . II Selby, David.

LB41.W38 2000   370'.11   C00-932130-6

Edited by P. K. Murphy

Copyedited by Beth McAuley

Cover art by Helen D'Souza

Printed and bound in Canada

Published by

SUMACH PRESS

1415 Bathurst Street, Suite 202
Toronto Canada M5R 3H8
sumachpress@on.aibn.com
www.sumachpress.com

To educators everywhere working towards equity,
justice, peacefulness and earth awareness.

To Eva Lowitz, Audrey Lowitz Esbin, Rose Goldstein,
Lea Roback and Edgar Goldstein

— T.G.

To Stephanie Shields, a wonderful sister and
educator for social justice.

— D.S.

CONTENTS

ACKNOWLEDGEMENTS

We would like to acknowledge Sonia Hopwood, secretary, International Institute for Global Education, for her administrative expertise and unfailing support throughout the project; Liz Martin, of Sumach Press, for her initial interest in the project and her encouragement in getting the project off the ground; Lois Pike, of Sumach Press, for her helpful assistance in contract matters; P. K. Murphy for her commitment to clarity and her expert editing of the contributors' work; and Beth McAuley, of Sumach Press, for her insightful editorial guidance on the introduction and conclusion to the book and her excellent leadership during the final production stages.

Tara would like to acknowledge Margot Huycke for all her support during the writing of *Weaving Connections*.

David would like to thank his partner, Bärbel, for her constant support and encouragement as the idea of the book was born, transformed and then realized.

INTRODUCTION

Tara Goldstein and David Selby

DAVID: This collection of essays by Canadian educators seeks to achieve two important goals. First, it documents educational philosophies and approaches, developed over the past thirty or more years, that are directed towards equity, justice, peacefulness and earth awareness. These developments are now under serious and direct threat within an increasingly pervasive culture of compliance with what is useful for the marketplace. The second goal challenges these current directions in Canadian school reform — directions that promote "back to basics," a centralization of control, a conformist concept of citizenship, corporate intrusion, insidious deprofessionalization of the teacher, "doing more with less," "learning for earning" and performance measurability. The contributors in *Weaving Connections* explicitly and implicitly critique such orientations, which not only deny human potential but also dismiss humane values, exacerbate rather than heal social tensions, and deepen our estrangement from nature. In response to these unwelcome reforms, this collection recalls and celebrates some of the most positive developments in Canadian education in recent times.

The twenty-two writers featured here are all significantly involved in educational movements and initiatives that place a premium upon just and peaceful human relationships and social and environmental concern. They also value outcomes that can't be easily measured, such as active and democratic participation in the classroom, school and society. Some of the writers are university professors, some are school teachers, some are graduate students, some work as educational representatives of non-governmental organizations, some are active in social change movements. Some fit under two or more of these categories. Anglophone educators from Eastern, Central and Western Canada are represented. There are thirteen female writers and nine male writers. As editors, we tried with some success to ensure that the group of writers we brought together included people with a variety of backgrounds and identities.

TARA: *Weaving Connections* has been in development for several years. David, you and I first began working together because we thought it would be productive to trace the connections between our different educational interests. You were reading, writing and teaching global education, environmental and humane education and education for democratic citizenship while I was working in the areas of anti-racist education, sexual harassment and homophobia. However, very soon after we started looking for writers for this project, the Progressive Conservative government in Ontario introduced Bill 160. The educational reforms in Bill 160 centralized significant areas of decision-making and authority, redefined who was a classroom teacher and who was not, reconfigured official relationships between teachers and administrators, and substantially restructured the work of secondary school teaching.[1] At the time of the bill's implementation, public debate raged around what this shift of power might mean and whether or not it was desirable. Of the many issues raised during the province-wide protest of Bill 160, discussion of what the bill might mean for the pursuit of peace, environmental and social justice initiatives in our schools was almost non-existent. For both of us, this collection became an important way to, once again, look at how discrimination still characterized the world in which we taught and learned and how educational reform across the country was ignoring environmental and social justice issues in schooling.

While many provincial curriculum guidelines, including those in Ontario, outline the importance of providing students with an educational system that is "safe and secure" and "free from discrimination,"[2] current educational reforms are actually eradicating our potential to work towards reducing violence and discrimination in our schools. As Heather-jane Robertson writes, the new purpose of education in Canada involves producing and measuring "the skills to live in utility" rather than "the skills to live in liberty."[3] A phrase coined by Thomas Jefferson,[4] "the skills to live in liberty" include self-control, self-reliance as well as interdependence and responsibility towards others. To develop such skills at school, teachers and students need to understand the roots of the everyday violence and discrimination they experience. The authors in this anthology help us develop such understanding. They analyze social power relations and demonstrate how power imbalances of heterosexism (Tim McCaskell and Vanessa Russell in chapter 1), racism (Ouida Wright and Maxine Bramble in chapters 2 and 3), sexism (Lyndsay Moffatt in chapter 6), and colonialism (Louella Cronkhite and Susan Fletcher in chapters 5 and 13) affect us and create conditions conducive to violence.

DAVID: There is also a deep concern among many of the authors in this collection about the violence being done to the environment. They write about respect and reverence for the environment and all its life forms. They value the rich biodiversity of our planet which they rightly see as under serious threat from rampant consumerism and growth-oriented economics. The writers also have a desire to help young people confront environmental violence and break out of a felt disconnection with the natural world. In chapter 7, Connie Russell, Anne Bell and Leesa Fawcett discuss the many ways in which Canadian environmental educators are responding to and building upon those deep concerns. In chapter 10, I explore the field of humane education, which is about fostering an ethic of care and compassion for all living things, human and non-human.

TARA: Many of the authors write about the need for young people to respect diversity and difference inside the classroom. For Ouida Wright, Louella Cronkhite, Susan Fletcher, Lyndsay Moffatt, Tim McCaskell and Vanessa Russell, learning how to act responsibly towards others means learning how to negotiate differences of language, culture, race, gender, class, ability and sexual orientation.

DAVID: It is these themes of respect for diversity and difference, as well as for human rights and fundamental freedoms, that weave together the chapters in our collection. They are also themes that are woven through my own journey. I was involved in campus race equity and anti-apartheid movements in Liverpool, England, in the mid to late 1960s. But when I began my career in teaching, I didn't really make the connection between causes I had come to hold dear and what I taught in the history classroom. The entry point for me came in January 1972 in the wake of "Bloody Sunday," when British troops shot and killed thirteen Catholic citizens in Northern Ireland. At that time I was a young assistant lecturer in Education at University College, Cork, in the Republic of Ireland. The shootings not only appalled me but left me feeling more than ever personally complicit as an Englishman in a sorry history of centuries of oppression. Against a backdrop of widespread and justifiable public rage at the British actions, I vividly recall my nervousness as I went to lecture 150 student teachers on Irish Republican history of education only two days after the shootings. A more inflammatory mix I could barely imagine. After the lecture, student leaders came forward to assure me that, their hatred of the British military and establishment notwithstanding, they held nothing against me as an individual English person. It was a deeply catalytic moment. I saw the need for education that built connections across divides, that acknowledged accountabilities, responsibilities and complicities while forging new relationships built upon mutual respect.

Within weeks I had begun to address the question of how history teaching could contribute to intercultural and international understanding in my history method seminars and had helped instigate a school linking program between local schools and schools in England. I returned to England a year later and spent the next nine years as a school teacher developing integrated courses with an increasingly socially-critical dimension. These courses explored topics such as Anglo-Irish relationships, historical and contemporary racism in Britain, the dynamics of prejudice and discrimination, global North-South relations and environmental degradation. At the same time, my colleagues and I experimented with learning processes that acknowledged that the realization of equity also meant addressing a diversity of learning styles and needs and giving an authentic voice to students.

TARA: I began my work in the field of education as an English as a Second Language (ESL) teacher. Throughout the 1980s and early 1990s I worked with both adults and high-school students in a variety of settings. I taught ESL in universities, community colleges, settlement agencies and a number of workplaces. As I learned to develop curriculum that was relevant to my students' everyday language needs, I also learned about the everyday racism and linguistic discrimination my students faced and began to develop a critical consciousness. Having grown up with white privilege, I was often shocked at my students' experiences of discrimination. I realized that there were many things I took for granted that my students could not. For example, I took it for granted that when I needed to move I would be able to rent an apartment I could afford in an area I wanted to live in. Unlike some of my students of colour, I had never been told that an apartment that had been available for rent when I phoned the landlord was suddenly rented when I showed up to visit it. Nor had I ever been told that my job was in jeopardy unless I lost my "accent" (which linguist Rosina Lippi-Green says is impossible for adults to do in a consistent, enduring way[5]). Slowly, with the assistance and support of colleagues, I began to educate myself on the ways that racism and other forms of discrimination manifested themselves in my students' lives in Canada. Most difficult of all was learning to analyze the ways in which racism and linguistic discrimination — intentionally and unintentionally — manifested themselves in my own classroom. In chapter 2, Ouida Wright provides us with a history of the ways educators across Canada have begun to educate themselves on questions of diversity and racism through multicultural and anti-racist education policy development and initiatives.

DAVID: Since 1982, I've worked in global education curriculum development, research and teacher education centres within the university. The first was the Centre for Global Education at the University of York in England. I came to Canada and helped set up the International Institute for Global Education at the University of

Toronto in 1992. In the last eighteen years I have steeped myself within a holistic worldview and challenged myself to develop an educational philosophy and practice from within that worldview. I see global education as nothing less than a holistic paradigm of education, something that Graham Pike explores in chapter 8. Toh Swee-Hin and Virginia Floresca-Cawagas also offer a holistic vision from a peace education perspective in chapter 14. Significant influences have been eastern mysticism, writings on environmental philosophy and ethics, ecofeminism and, especially, writings that explore processes and relations in the sub-atomic world and their implications for self, society and the planet.[6] As I see it, western society is still heavily influenced by seventeenth- and eighteenth-century scientific thinkers who believed that, except for the human mind, everything in the world is a machine that is fully understandable by dividing it into its component parts. Everything is clockwork except for what is in our heads. This has led to our creating a hierarchy within ourselves (mind/reason above emotions and body) and to our locating ourselves outside and above nature. Such a worldview denies moral status to other life forms and environments (in that they are mindless machines) and, so, gives us license to exploit.

Also by emphasizing separation as a means to understanding, the mechanistic worldview has helped spawn countless false dichotomies including human/animal, reason/emotion, reason/nature, mind/body, male/female, culture/nature, self/other. These dichotomies lie at the root of oppression of humans. This is especially the case when the dichotomies are laid over each other. For instance, when the dualism reason/nature is superimposed upon the dualism male/female, a philosophical basis for patriarchal oppression comes closer (in that women come to be depicted as more natural and less rational). If a further false dichotomy — production/reproduction — is overlaid, in which the former is associated with male (and prized), and the latter with female/nature (and undervalued), the basis for oppression of both women and nature is further underpinned.[7] Mechanistic science, through Galileo, also gave us the dominant belief that what is measurable is worthwhile, and that what is non-measurable is of secondary significance. (So we have Galileo to thank for the current measurability trend in education!) But the mechanistic mindset holds much greater sway over the educational system and over educational theory and practice than the obsession with measurability. We still fail to educate the whole person and still separate body, mind, emotion and spirit in learning; we still divide a seamless world into disciplines; we still divide school from community; we still offer curricula built on the unquestioned assumption that humankind is separate from the environment and other life forms. These are some of the ideas that underpin my current courses at OISE/UT.

dichotomies in education

TARA: I joined OISE/UT a year after you. In my work with our pre-service teacher education program, my students and I learn about the ways our schools and communities are still divided by discrimination and about the ways we might challenge inequities through our work as teachers. For example, we know that sexism is still an enormous issue for high school students in Ontario. When researcher June Larkin asked sixty young women from four high schools in Toronto to describe their experiences of sexual harassment at school in 1994, here is some of what they said:

> I was sitting in class and the guys behind me kept flipping my skirt. When I turned around to tell them to stop the teacher yelled at me. I tried to tell her what they were doing but she told me to be quiet and stop interrupting the class.

> This one teacher always says horrible things about women. He doesn't think a woman can do anything.[8]

In chapter 6 on education for gender equity, Lyndsay Moffatt looks at the issue of sexism in schools and suggests ways to deal with this kind of harassment.

DAVID: An appreciation of gender issues and perspectives came late to me. I did not really begin to engage with feminism as a coherent and persuasive body of counter-cultural ideas until the early to mid 1980s. The trigger moment for me came in 1982 when feminist educator Yvonne Hennessy wrote a review article of a collection of essays, to which I had contributed, critiquing the absence of women's voices in the anthology even though the work was about "change, development, peace and justice." She began the critique with "David, Barry, Jim and Brian; Tony, David, Bill and Roger; Robin, David, Hugh and Charles have written a book ..."9 As women colleagues began to take the platform in conferences, workshops and classrooms, and as they came to be published more widely, my level of awareness, then understanding, grew. For me now, confrontation of patriarchy is crucial in and through education. I am especially interested in, and influenced by, ecofeminism. I very much build the principal strand of ecofeminist thought — the correlation of human and non-human oppressions — into my teaching and writing, and also work to give concrete expression in workshops to the call within ecofeminism for the rediscovery of relational, intuitive and experiential ways of knowing. These ways of knowing underlie the humane pedagogy I discuss in chapter 10.

TARA: My first encounter with issues of feminism and gender equity came earlier. I remember writing my first paper on the "changing role of women in our society" as a Grade 10 high school student in 1974. On the front cover of the paper, I pasted a magazine picture of a (white, middle-class) woman wearing a suit and a (white, middle-class) man wearing a housedress and carrying a mop. I took a minor in Women's Studies in my undergraduate program at Concordia University in Montreal and continued to read in the field throughout my graduate studies in education. As the field of Women's Studies developed, I, like many others, became interested and more informed about the intersections between sexism, racism and homophobia. This has been important for my work in teacher education since racism and homophobia are also enormous issues for high school students in Ontario. For example, when educator Doug Little asked Black high school students about their experiences of racism in school in 1992, right after the Toronto protest against racism in the aftermath of the beating of Rodney King in Los Angeles, here is some of what they said:10

> Eurocentrism goes further than just history or English. It's everywhere. Our math text has biographies and pictures of great mathematicians throughout it, but they are all white men! We are often told that maybe we shouldn't take math or science because

they are "hard subjects". They are also lies. Ancient Africa was very advanced in math. These things drive us out of math, but we know we will need it in the future. It has become so bad that when a Black kid does well in math even Black kids think they have cheated or something. We even take this inferiority into ourselves.

In chapter 3, Maxine Bramble examines the persistence of problems confronting Black education and the ways parents, students and teachers are working to address them.

A few years after the 1992 anti-racist demonstrations on Yonge Street, a Toronto television program called *Cable 10%* aired a documentary titled "Education" in which several gay and lesbian adolescents were asked to describe their experiences at high school.[11] Here is some of what they said:

> There was no atmosphere of support or understanding or anything. Or even any acknowledgment that there are gay people at our school. And there'd be people calling you names, whatever - "I'm going to beat those girls up if I ever catch one of them alone." They never did, but it was, like, a threatening atmosphere and I had to leave. I dropped out a couple of times.

What these young people's testimonies tell us is that discrimination is deeply embedded in the curriculum, the streaming system and in the attitudes and behaviour of teachers and students. In chapter 1, Tim McCaskell and Vanessa Russell write about the kinds of schooling initiatives that support gay, lesbian and bisexual youth in a world "rife with casualties of isolation, depression, substance abuse, prostitution, homelessness and suicide."

DAVID: We need to take account of the educational landscape globally. We should not forget that over the last half century the educations represented here have been legitimized in a succession of international conventions and declarations which Canada has signed. Recent documents of great significance include: the *Convention on the Rights of the Child* (1989); the *World Declaration on Education for All* (1990); *Agenda 21*, the Programme of Action for Sustainable Development, negotiated at the UN Conference on Environment and Development (1992); and the *UNESCO*

Declaration on Education for Peace, Human Rights and Democracy
(1995). These documents individually and collectively endorse the
educational approaches discussed in this anthology. They speak of
the need for education that is directed towards democracy and
encourages respect for human rights and fundamental freedoms.
These orientations are taken up by Mark Evans and Ian Hundey
(chapter 4) in their call for curricula and learning processes that
develop young people's capacities for active engagement in the civic
life of their communities. They are also addressed by Wanda Cassidy
(chapter 11) in her call to educators to help "cultivate a responsible,
proactive and compassionate citizenry literate in the law." The international documents also lay down that education can and should
help build a culture of peace. Toh Swee-Hin and Virginia Floresca-
Cawagas (chapter 14) elaborate on this concept, reminding us that
"dismantling a culture of war and violence also means creating
awareness and enabling humanity to avert all forms of violence,
whether it be social, economic, psychological, political or cultural."

The international documents emphasize, too, that education
should be directed towards achieving equity and social justice both
within and between nations. As we have discussed earlier, there are
several different educations for social justice within Canada included
in this collection. For example, Louella Cronkhite overviews development education, a field focusing upon the morality and economic, environmental and personal impacts of the North-South divide
and the growing disparities of wealth. It is important to note, too,
that the documents also emphasize the need to set students' understanding within the framework of an increasingly interdependent
world, an imperative fully addressed in chapter 8 by Graham Pike
in his essay on global education but also touched on by several other
authors. Another theme flagged in the documents is education for
environmental respect and protection, which is particularly taken
up in the chapters on environmental and humane education.

When the UNESCO *Declaration* of 1995 calls upon signatory
states and relevant parties within society to work to "achieve full
implementation of the objectives of education for peace, human
rights and democracy and to contribute in this way to sustainable
development and to a culture of peace," it pretty much sums up the

collective goals of our authors. If we take these international covenants and weave them together with a Canadian constitutional commitment to promoting a national culture of equality, human rights and multiculturalism as enshrined in the Charter of Rights and Freedoms (1982), we have a powerful backcloth of legitimization for what they are suggesting. The problem is that, Canada's signed adherence to these documents notwithstanding, current reforms of the educational system are undermining what these international and national documents stand for.

TARA: In spite of the direction of our current reforms, we have a vibrant history of Canadian educational initiatives that have engaged both teachers and students in what writer bell hooks has called "learning to transgress."[12] Learning to transgress involves moving beyond what is currently acceptable in order to create new visions of living and behaving. In chapter 13, Susan Fletcher talks about her own transgressive teaching practice of sharing a First Nations perspective of post-Contact history with non-First Nations teachers and students. Susan is often invited by teachers to visit their classes when their students are completing a unit on "native peoples." Among displays of cardboard totem poles, "Indian Villages" and "fierce looking masks," she begins the difficult work of teaching students a history of past injustices against First Nations people. For Susan, recognizing the legacy of injustice and its implications for the present and the future is a crucial first step towards an equitable relationship between First Nations and non-First Nations people in Canada. In answer to the question "What can teachers do in this current era of reform?" Susan, like many of the other authors in this anthology, maintains that transgressive possibilities do exist within public education. She suggests that teachers can begin by including First Nations subject matter in all areas of the curriculum and by expanding the study from the exclusive focus on the pre-Contact period to look in-depth at what has happened post-contact. Key to this work is the use of authentic materials written and produced by First Nations people.

Toh Swee-Hin's and Virginia Floresca-Cawagas's work is also clearly transgressive in their call for cultural solidarity, living in peace with the Earth, fostering inner peace and educating students to reflect critically on the future. Another way of learning to transgress is discussed by media educators Rick Shepherd, Barry Duncan and John Pungente in chapter 12. They discuss different approaches to deconstructing and understanding the media and argue that media literacy is central to learning how to critique and challenge unequal power relations.

DAVID: The transgressive educations discussed in our book can be likened to members of a community who have never quite completely come to terms with being a community. Proponents of each education have endeavoured to build legitimacy by securing sponsorship, developing a discrete and somewhat self-referential theoretical base, setting up networks, launching academic and professional journals and seeking to influence educational policy and practice through lobbying and the dissemination of noteworthy practice and classroom resources. Given the still marginal nature of each of the educations, this process helps ensure the fields stay at the periphery. It amounts to a "divide and be ruled" strategy. But a collective approach to the fields is not just a strategic issue. A sound case for viewing the educations holistically can be built upon conceptual considerations. Let me take new trends in health education to illustrate my point. Leading-edge health educators in recent times have transgressed and liberated their field from long-standing, tidy and fairly limited frameworks concerned with cleanliness, bodily functions, sex education and awareness of the health impacts of toxic substances. In doing so, they have begun to ask some very interesting questions of their students, such as:

- Am I a healthy person if my behaviours and lifestyle have a negative impact upon social and natural environments, upon other human beings and other species?
- Am I a healthy person if I am, in any way, part of an oppressive or abusive personal relationship?
- Am I a healthy person if I am prejudiced and discriminate against people of another culture, ethnic group, race, gender or sexual orientation?

• Am I a healthy person if I collude in a world economic system that operates against the interests of the majority of humankind?

Questions such as these, I think, begin to expose the profound way in which the educations are mutually enfolded. Health education, so conceived, folds into the anti-discriminatory educations, the development, environmental, human rights and peace educations. This is what Gale Smith and Linda Peterat in chapter 9 describe as a transformational approach to health education in which "health is broadly understood in social, political, and economic terms and health issues are fundamentally associated with justice, equity and peace."

TARA: Other authors who have linked their work in one field of education to other fields include Tim McCaskell and Vanessa Russell who draw on some of the principles of anti-racist education in their work in anti-heterosexist and anti-homophobic education. One such principle is that anti-homophobia education is not an add-on. It requires changes across the curriculum and in all subject areas. This is the principle that underlies Susan Fletcher's work on post-Contact history as well. Lyndsay Moffatt writes that we must commit to educating ourselves about the multiple ways that all of the "isms" affect our students' lives. In particular, she says we must look at how sexism and racism interact and reinforce each other and how homophobia and sexism are linked. Louella Cronkhite discusses the way school programs in development education evolved into global education programs that took in not only development education, but peace, human rights and environment education as well. Graham Pike offers a similar perspective on global education. While I agree that these links between different fields in education move our work forward, there are sometimes tensions between different approaches that need to be thought through. For example, I'd like to return to the question "Am I a healthy person if I am prejudiced and discriminate against people of another culture, ethnic group, race, gender or sexual orientation?" This question focuses on individual attitudes and behaviours towards other people rather than the systems of discrimination that people encounter in their everyday life. Sometimes individual action is not enough. Even though a student knows that it is unhealthy to tolerate sexual harassment and complains to a teacher or administrator, unless there is a school policy and set of procedures around what to do in case of a sexual harassment complaint, the students' complaint can be ignored or dismissed by those who have the power to intervene and challenge the harassment.

DAVID: I agree. I'd add that in any community, there are bound to be tensions. Many of the tensions are between different schools of thought within the one education. For instance, as Connie Russell, Anne Bell and Leesa Fawcett suggest, there are tensions between the many conservation-oriented environmental educators who view the environment as a resource and educators striving for an earth-centred formulation in which humans are seen as but part of the environment. They also point to the tensions between the many environmental educators across Canada who see their field as a subdivision of the science curriculum and those who question the dominance of science and who ask that equal weighting be given to cultural, ideological, political, social and spiritual dimensions of the environment.

TARA: There are similar tensions between educators who talk about multicultural education and "tolerance" for differences and those who talk about anti-racist education and moving beyond "tolerance." For many anti-racist educators, tolerance is associated with privilege, an acceptance of the *status quo* and only the slightest accommodations to difference in our schools. In her answer to the question, "How is antiracist education different from multicultural education?" Ouida Wright suggests that while both focus on making the school curriculum and environment more inclusive, multicultural education focuses on "intergroup harmony" while antiracist education focuses on "intergroup equity." The questions that educators ask themselves about working towards harmony (Do the students in my classroom all get along?) are different than those they need to ask about equity (Do all students in my classroom have equal access to what the school has to offer?). One way to begin to work through the inevitable tensions within and between different fields in education that have similar, compatible goals is to think about what kinds of questions are being asked and answered by writers and teachers who advocate particular approaches.

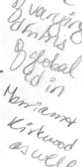

DAVID: One very clear divide running through this collection has to do with the fact that the majority of educational philosophies and approaches discussed here have tended to focus exclusively upon human relationships. Movements afoot in a few of these approaches, notably environmental, global and humane education, are proposing to recast the field in an earth-centred mould in which the human project is removed as the central focus. As I see it, crossing boundaries is easiest for those embracing a holistic conception of their field. For example, a peace educator whose working definition of peace is a broad one and involves negative peace (absence of war and physical violence), positive peace (absence of structural violence with consequent high levels of justice and equality), and Gaian (ecological) peace is likely to enjoy a good level of rapport with colleagues who, for instance, are working in anti-racist, anti-sexist, environmental, First Nations and development education. On the other hand, a peace educator limiting her or his attention to issues of war and other forms of direct violence is unlikely to feel such ready kinship.

TARA: Earlier you talked about how the still marginal nature of each of the educations discussed in this collection is reinforced by an inability or unwillingness to weave connections. In the chapters that follow, we hope readers will look for and find connections. In times of threat to what we value, educators need to coalesce and work together in multiple ways.

NOTES

1. Andy Hargreaves, "Teachers' Role in Renewal," *Orbit 29* (1998), 10-13.

2. Ministry of Education, *Ontario Secondary Schools Grades 9-12: Program and Diploma Requirements* (1999) (Toronto: Ontario Ministry of Education, 1999), 58.

3. Heather-jane Robertson, *No More Teachers, No More Books: The Commercialization of Canada's Schools* (Toronto: McClelland and Stewart, 1998), 34.

4. Stanley Arnowitz and Henry A Giroux, *Education Under Siege: The Conservative, Liberal and Radical Debate Over Schooling* (Boston, MA: Bergin and Garvey, 1985), ix.

5. Rosina Lippi-Green, *English With an Accent: Language, Ideology and Discrimination in the United States* (New York: Routledge, 1997).

6. Fritjof Capra, *The Tao of Physics* (London: Flamingo, 1983); Fritjof Capra, *The Web of Life: A New Scientific Understanding of Living Systems* (New York: Anchor/Doubleday, 1996); Danah Zohar, *The Quantum Self: A Revolutionary View of Human Nature and Consciousness Rooted in the New Physics* (London: Bloomsbury, 1990); Danah Zohar, *The Quantum Society: Mind, Physics, and a New Social Vision* (New York: Quill and William Morrow, 1994).

7. Valerie Plumwood, *Feminism and the Mastery of Nature* (London: Routledge, 1993).

8. June Larkin, *Sexual Harassment: High School Girls Speak Out* (Toronto: Second Story Press, 1994).

9. Yvonne Hennessy, "Global Perspectives and Vanishing Rabbits," *World Studies Journal* 4 (Autumn 1992), 32-33 The book she was critiquing was David Hicks and Charles Townley, eds., *Teaching World Studies: An Introduction to Global Perspectives in the Curriculum* (London: Longman, 1982).

10. Doug Little, "The Meaning of Yonge Street: What Do the Kids Say?" *Our Schools/Our Selves* 4 (1992), 16-23.

11. Roger Cable 10, Toronto, *Cable 10%*, "Education," 1995.

12. bell hooks, *Teaching to Transgress: Education as the Practice of Freedom* (New York: Routledge, 1994).

Chapter 1

ANTI-HOMOPHOBIA INITIATIVES AT THE FORMER TORONTO BOARD OF EDUCATION

Tim McCaskell and Vanessa Russell

L's Story

It was the early spring of 1992. L was a young man who showed up one day at the drop-in support group for lesbian and gay youth organized by the Toronto Board's Human Sexuality Program. For the first month, L always "passed" when it was his turn to describe his week. He sat hunched over, looking down, not participating in the conversation. He scarcely did more than announce his name to the group. But he kept coming back.

As time went on he began to relax a little and sometimes even took part in the conversations that skipped across the range of interests of the dozen or so in the group — conversations about relationships, parents, coming out, trying to find a place in an adult-oriented gay community.

Then one day L arrived visibly angry. When his turn came, he blurted out, "He did it again!"

"Who did what again?"

"He called me fag in the hall, in front of everybody."

"Who called you fag?"

We pulled the story out of him bit by bit. It was an account of four years of unremitting harassment. For some reason (L was not particularly effeminate or openly gay), another boy in his class was singling him out. He had whispered and shouted insults at L in class and in the hall, had told everyone who would listen that L was a queer and had left playgirl cut-outs of naked men on L's desk. He had been making L's life hell for L's entire high-school career.

We explained to L that he was a victim of sexual harassment and that he could make a complaint under the Board's Sexual Harassment Policy, which includes homophobic harassment. It would mean recording incidents, naming names and going to the school's administration, but he would have the support of a resource person trained in dealing with sexual harassment.

L said he'd have to think about it. What if it just made things worse? What about retaliation? What would happen if the principal knew he was gay? Would his parents find out? By the time he returned to the group the next week, he had made a decision. He would file a complaint.

The complaint was not handled perfectly by the school. The vice-principal asked L what L had done to "provoke" the situation, and he did not invite the sexual harassment resource person to the interview, despite the Board's policy that complainants had a right to an advocate of their choice when meeting with administration. On the other hand, the vice-principal did haul the harasser into the office and did tell him in no uncertain terms the consequences of his actions: any repetition would meet with suspension; with final exams approaching, suspension would be catastrophic.

The next week L returned to the group. He was different. No longer hunched over, he seemed to have grown two inches. He was beaming.

"It's stopped. I walked down the hall, right past his locker and he didn't say a thing."

The transformation in L was remarkable. A month later he spoke at a public hearing on Board programs for lesbian and gay youth. He became confident, centred, and enthusiastic about life. He graduated, went on to university, found friends, had relationships and became active in community work. L is a success story in a world of lesbian and gay youth rife with the casualties of isolation, depression, substance abuse, prostitution, homelessness and suicide.

Many elements contributed to L's success: a support group where youth could share their experiences under openly gay adult supervision, a Board policy against harassment that included homophobia, an administration that took that policy seriously and enforced it. Such elements are not the norm in secondary schools across the country. Nor do we know how long students of the Toronto District School Board can continue to count on support groups or on policies that protect their right to education that is free from harassment.

Times have changed for equity education at the current Toronto District School Board. At the time of publication it is unclear how equity work in general, or anti-homophobia initiatives in particular, will fare under this relatively new Board. In January 1998, the Ontario government, under Premier Mike Harris, legislated forced amalgamation of the Toronto Board with five other Metro Toronto boards to create the Toronto District School Board. The Ontario government also seized control of funding for education. School boards are now huge conglomerates, and trustees' positions are but part-time jobs. Local control of education has all but disappeared. As thousands of jobs are cut, social programs dismantled and public education itself jeopardized, a wave of despair is washing over students. Where it used to be relatively easy to organize students around equity, it is now much much harder. But it's important to understand how anti-homophobia education emerged as such an effective force so that maybe we can prevent its full dismantling.

LAYING THE GROUNDWORK

For generations lesbian and gay students have suffered silently — isolated, hidden in a system that ignored and denied their existence. That something was wrong and ought to be changed did not originate with the Toronto Board. Change came through the efforts of the assertive and visible communities of lesbians and gay men that emerged in Toronto in the 1980s to challenge the heterosexist and homophobic norms that had hitherto prevailed. As laws and institutions changed (human rights legislation, criminal law, the media), change in education became not only possible but inevitable.

The first attempts to set up an official Gay and Lesbian Community Liaison Committee on the Toronto Board took place in 1980. But these were swept away in the wave of reaction following the defeat of the progressive mayor of Toronto, John Sewell, and the massive police raid on the city's gay bathhouses in 1981. Homophobia did not re-emerge as a major issue for Toronto-area school boards until 1985, when a group of queer-bashing secondary school students killed Ken Zeller, a gay teacher working for the Toronto Board. Then in 1986, the addition of "sexual orientation" to the Ontario Human Rights Code raised the profile of lesbian and gay issues and led to the Board establishing a Human Sexuality Program to provide special counselling for youth who had questions around their sexual orientation. Finally, in the elections of 1991, John Campey, an openly gay New Democratic Party candidate, became the Toronto Board's first openly gay trustee. Campey emerged as the community's advocate and mobilized the generally progressive-leaning Board in support of some key policy changes. The Human Sexuality Program's gay counsellor position became a full-time one. A Consultative Committee on the Education of Gay and Lesbian Students was set up; it was comprised of representatives from the lesbian and gay communities, teachers' federations, Board staff and social service agencies serving lesbian and gay youth. The Board dropped policies that had effectively prohibited open lesbian and gay speakers from addressing classrooms. The lesbian and gay communities had won official recognition and access to the Board.

The moves were not unopposed. *Toronto Sun* headlines screamed that the Board was promoting homosexuality. A new homophobic group, Citizens United for Responsible Education (CURE), spearheaded a mass rally at the Board's offices and organized to intervene at local parents' meetings. But lesbians and gay men responded by setting up Education Against Homophobia (EAH), a coalition of lesbian/gay/bisexual students, staff and parents. EAH organized its own rally at the Board and successfully campaigned for the re-election of progressive school board trustees in the 1994 election. Lesbians and gay men were now a clear force in education politics.

CURRICULUM-WIDE CHANGES

After the Zeller killing, pressure mounted on the Board to produce a resource document on homosexuality that would outline class-room strategies for dealing with gay and lesbian issues. Since work around sexuality education of any kind has traditionally been the domain of physical education, the responsibility fell to the physical education consultants in the central Curriculum Department. The Department did not have strong links to the lesbian and gay communities or much experience in dealing with such issues, and the document became a political football between the lesbian and gay community and the homophobic right.

When the document was finally approved in 1992, it was far from perfect but was generally acceptable to the lesbian and gay communities. Because of the lack of material on homosexuality, it attracted interest among teachers from other subject areas and from other Boards. However, it had little to say about the curriculum for English, history or other subjects. Transforming subject-based curriculum to reflect the contributions and the history of lesbians and gay men remains a largely uncompleted task, and anti-homo-phobia education still tends to be an add-on. Furthermore, all who work in equity education meet resistance when they press for changes in the standard school curriculum.

That little had changed became emphasized when the student group Students of Toronto Against Racism (STAR) spent months analyzing English and history course outlines from all Toronto Board Secondary schools in 1994-1995. Not surprisingly, while STAR found excellent inclusive curriculum scattered throughout the system, progress was far from general, and lesbian and gay visibility was one of the weakest areas. Clearly, the inclusion of anti-homo-phobic, anti-racist and anti-sexist perspectives in the daily material of study throughout the system is key to transforming the education system. But how can it be achieved?

Several principles of anti-racist education, drawn from experiences in Canada, the UK and the US, provide a framework for guiding work in anti-heterosexist and anti-homophobic education.[1] To understand this framework, we need to start with definitions of key terms.

Homophobia literally means a fear of lesbians or gay men. More commonly it is used to describe the stereotyping, prejudice and discrimination gay people face. Since homophobia means fear (a feeling), heterosexism is often used to describe the more systemic aspects of this stereotyping and discrimination. From this point of view, homophobia is more like misogyny (a hatred of women) while heterosexism is more like sexism, which may not include hatred or dislike at all. Someone who is heterosexist may assume that heterosexuality is the superior or the only "normal" sexuality and that straight relationships are superior and the only "normal" relationships. A heterosexist person may assume that everyone is straight unless he or she declares otherwise and thereby ignore the existence of most lesbians and gay men. He or she may feel that it is "natural" to be straight, and that gay people are somehow "unnatural," "wrong" or "sick," even if it isn't "their fault."

Using these definitions, we can adapt the principles of anti-racist education to mould an anti-homophobia education that incorporates the following characteristics:

- Heterosexism and homophobia are deeply rooted in our culture but can be changed. They are not a natural response to "difference" as is sometimes claimed.

- The force for change lies in marginalized communities, in this case the lesbian and gay communities.

- Anti-homophobia education is not an add-on. It requires changes across the curriculum and in all subject areas.

- Anti-homophobia education requires a pedagogy that encourages and equips students and staff to understand power relations and to challenge unjust systems. It must be based on students' experiences and must be relevant to their lives.

- Anti-homophobia education must be system-wide. Hiring and promotion policies, assessment, discipline, school-community relations, social work and symbolic gestures all perpetuate heterosexism and homophobia, and all must be transformed. At the same time, special programs for students with special needs around issues of sexual orientation must be made available and promoted. The Triangle Program, for example, is Canada's only high-school program for gay, lesbian, bisexual and transgender youth and those victimized by homophobia.

- Anti-homophobia education must be willing to engage students in understanding other power relations (racism, sexism, classism), which will make their understanding of homophobia more acute.

We took these characteristics of anti-homophobia education and applied them to create an instructive and open-ended pedagogy through workshops and through system-wide initiatives. A key player in the implementation of this pedagogy has been the Equity Studies Centre.

The Equity Studies Centre was created under the former Toronto Board. It was once staffed by two co-ordinators, two consultants and four student program workers. Times have changed. Currently, the Centre has fewer staff to serve a constituency five times its original size. Nonetheless, the Centre continues to work within the Curriculum Department and in schools to put Board policy and programs on equity into effect. The Centre continues to provide leadership by raising awareness, increasing knowledge and developing the skills needed to challenge different forms of discrimination. Since its beginnings, Equity Studies Centre staff have created workshops for students, for inservice school staff requesting such programs and for union-organized professional development days.

The Centre is separate from the Toronto District School Board's Equal Opportunity Office, which works to ensure that the Board achieves equity in education with specific reference to visible/racial minorities, Aboriginal/First Nations Peoples and people with disabilities. The equity advisor[2] of the Equal Opportunity Office monitors and manages human rights complaints. The Toronto District School Board's human rights policy[3] provides protection against homophobic harassment by prohibiting expressions of bias in any form on the basis of sexual orientation such as derogatory comments, threats of outing, harassing letters or phone calls, and intimidation.

With all models of equity education, an effective pedagogy must start from the students' realities. It must examine systems of power and take students beyond their own histories so they might begin to empathize and make common cause with others, which creates the possibility for future coalition building. Finally, it must equip students to resist and challenge various manifestations of oppression. Anti-homophobia education is no exception. A look at the workshops regularly facilitated by staff of the Equity Studies Centre illustrates this point.

WORKSHOPS

To set the tone for the workshops, we begin with a brief explanation of the Toronto Board's Sexual Harassment Policy. This lets students know that there is some protection against homophobic harassment, not only for those who are gay and lesbian but also for those who are perceived to be homosexual. Unfortunately, this is news to many of our students. Many of them believe it is okay to call someone a "fag" if they're not really one."

There are many ways to respond to this perception, including drawing out what it means to be in a "poisoned environment," making connections between homophobia and sexism and pointing out that lesbians and gay men are likely an invisible minority in every classroom. The other advantage to starting with the Board's policy is that it creates the opportunity for us to state our expectations and for the class to set its own ground rules.

Once we set the tone, we briefly explore definitions. Talking about homophobia in the classroom is relatively new. Nonetheless, it is astonishing that so few students are clear about the meaning of the words homosexual, sexual orientation, homophobia and heterosexism. We find it useful to go over basic definitions and to draw the links among different forms of oppression. Together, we define *stereotype* (idea), *prejudice* (attitude) and *discrimination* (action), and talk about oppression as a system involving all three elements. Often, we ask the students to give examples of common stereotypes they hear at school or elsewhere about different marginalized groups (people of colour, women and girls, lesbians and gays). The lists are long and contradictory and can provoke interesting discussions. We may then ask the students to identify the stereotypes they have learned about a dominant group (white, attractive, rich, intelligent, straight, Christian businessmen). It takes them longer, and the stereotypes are never as damaging. That makes it easy to start a discussion about who gets stereotyped and who doesn't, and who has power and who doesn't. After exploring these commonalities among various forms of oppression, we begin to look at the unique ways homophobia manifests itself by using various interactive exercises. These exercises help students identify specific stereotypes about gays, lesbians and bisexuals, learn factual information, recognize themes and discover how sexism and homophobia work together to keep "real women/girls" and "real men/boys" within their prescribed roles.

Perhaps the most successful way to grab a group's attention is to have someone similar to them leading the group. Without exception, our most effective workshops are those we co-facilitate with gay and lesbian youth. However, such peer-facilitators must need to be skilled at speaking in front of a large group and at encouraging discussion. Over the years, we have developed a facilitator-training program for peer educators. For the most part, the les/bi/gay youth we work with are from Toronto Board secondary schools or from community-based youth groups.

One group that works closely with us is TEACH (Teens Educating About and Confronting Homophobia). TEACH is unique because some of its members are straight-identified. This sends out a powerful message to heterosexual students: homophobia and heterosexism affect us all and need to be challenged across all communities.

To counteract the pervasive stereotype that all homosexuals are white, middle-class and male, we make sure that facilitator groups are mixed in terms of gender, race, ethnicity and class. This also challenges students to make connections. For instance, a young, Black, Christian lesbian's experience may be very different from that of a South Asian, Muslim gay man. But if both come from an upper middle-class home, their experiences may be more alike. As students listen to a range of gay and lesbian experiences, we can help them unravel the complexities of multiple identities. Through such discussions, students can begin to recognize the parts of their social identity that are marginalized. Moreover, they might begin to think through the similarities and differences in the ways their communities and les/bi/gay communities deal with and resist oppression.

Working with gay and lesbian youth facilitators achieves another purpose. Because of the severity of homophobia and heterosexism in society, in general, and in educational institutions, in particular, there are precious few "out" students and teachers. Many people, especially younger students, believe that they have never met a gay man or lesbian. Having lesbians and gays speaking from their own experience and telling their coming out stories is a powerful way to put a human face on the effects of homophobia. As well, telling their stories is a profound experience for the les/bi/gay youth themselves. Nonetheless, it is essential that we debrief and support young facilitators at the end of a workshop because some may feel quite overwhelmed. As adult co-ordinators, we must always remember how difficult it is to risk sharing experiences.

In the last part of the workshop, we read out anonymous questions. While some students are assertive and confident enough to ask questions throughout the workshop, others are not. Anonymous written questions provide all participants with the opportunity to have their questions answered without being centred out. This is especially important for students who may be questioning whether they are gay or lesbian.

WORKSHOPS: WHAT STUDENTS WANT TO KNOW

PRIMARY SCHOOL

Generally, questions and comments during senior primary school workshops fall into several themes. There are questions about gender transgression: "Do you still like girl stuff like shopping and makeup?" (asked to a nineteen-year-old lesbian facilitator); "Did you go out with boys before you came out of the closet?" There are questions about discrimination: "Did you ever have a school mark go down on a paper by a teacher that knew the truth about you?" "What do you do when people call you names?" Students also want to know how people become gay and have worries about AIDS and STDs: "If you don't think this is too personal, please answer this question: Are you worried about catching any STDs?" "How do your friends cope with having AIDS?" Even in public school some students want to know "How do lesbians have sex?"

Then there are anonymous questions that reflect the struggles students are going through: "I think I'm bisexual. I'm attracted to males and females. Is this weird for someone my age? I'm scared to tell anyone. Please don't read this out." (Although the question is not read out loud, the facilitator can discuss the issues the question raises.) And there are comments that imply a lesson has been learned: "It's weird to think that gays are people beneath the stereotypes." "I think that what you are doing is very good. I think that everyone should get talked to about homophobia because as soon as people find out that someone is gay or lesbian, they think that they are weird or something. Keep up the good work."

And of course there are silly or immature comments: "I have no questions but take a long time to talk so we don't have to go to math." Clearly, the facilitators need to know what to expect and to be skilled enough to use each question as an opportunity to provide the students with age-appropriate information.

SECONDARY SCHOOL

Secondary school students display a similar range of knowledge, but for many reasons sometimes show more outright hostility. For example, shortly after the Triangle Program opened in September 1995, an incident between students in the program and other students from a nearby collegiate forced Triangle staff to complain to the principal of the collegiate. The collegiate in question draws most of its students from the largely working-class east end of the city, including the Regent Park Public Housing Development. Its student body is very racially mixed with strong represetation from Black and Asian students. The principal responded by making a call to us at the Equity Studies Centre and requested anti-homophobia workshops for the entire student body at the collegiate.

We needed to make sure that the teams running the workshops included openly gay Black and Asian facilitators. Several secondary school students from other schools and some older adults came as resource people. Because the workshops were organized in haste, in response to a crisis, we could not always guarantee that an equal number of women and men served as resource people. But the racial and age mix of the presenters was crucial to the participants' acceptance. The students were able to speak to the differences underlying the culturally based homophobia in the classes. In one very heated session, much of the discussion between the Black resource person and a group of young Jamaican-born men took place in Jamaican Creole and was unintelligible to most other participants. But the students' ability to express themselves in their first language and the resource person's ability to respond in kind allowed the group to make far more progress than would otherwise have been possible.

A similar program has been part of the curriculum for all Grade Nine students at a large west-end technical school since 1995. When teachers had complained of rampant homophobia in the new Grade Nine class, we organized teams to lead workshops in each class. Since then, more than two hundred students have attended workshops each year. The racial mix of the resource people reflected the racial mix of the school, and since the workshops were planned well in advance, we could make sure we had both male and female resource people in each session.

The questions students asked in these sessions reflect so many of the issues they face. The questions often start out expressing the fears and anxieties of young people facing sexual choices that are possible yet denied to them. "How do you know if you're gay or lesbian?" "Did you realize it all at once?" "Were you ever unsure?" "Do you ever think you will switch to the opposite sex?" "Have you ever had experiences with the opposite sex?"

The questions then move into relationships. "Do you feel the same way a girl feels for a guy or a guy for a girl?" "How do you find partners?" "If you like somebody how do you ask them or find out if they are gay?" "Have you ever felt bad because you were attracted to someone who was straight and you couldn't have them?" " How long have you been with your partner?" "Do you want to have children?" "Can you adopt children?" "Can you get married?"

Students want to know about coming out. "Does your family know?" "How did they react?" "How do they feel now about your being gay?" "Do your other relatives and grandparents know?" Coming out questions also touch on issues of cultural difference: "Do you think you would have come out if you had stayed in Jamaica or would you just have followed the crowd and got married?"

There are religious questions as well. "The Bible/Koran says it's a sin? Don't you believe in God? Aren't you afraid of going to Hell?" Many students ask about cures, reflecting the shift from notions of sin to notions of psychological illness: "Why can't you try to change and live a good life?" "If somebody could make you straight, would you do it?" Such questions also touch on ideas about the "cause": "Is it genetic?" "Is it inherited?" "Did you have a bad experience with a member of the opposite sex?" "Did you have a bad relationship with your father/mother?"

The questions also reflect one of the most widespread stereotypes today — that all gay men have AIDS. "Do all gay men have AIDS? Don't you worry about AIDS?" These questions let us remind students that all sexually-active people need to practice safe sex. Generally, however, questions around AIDS do not dominate the discussion. Worries about queer-bashing often do come up and may reflect increased fears about violence: "Have you ever been beaten up?" "Have you ever been threatened?" "How do you react when people call you names?"

Of course, there are questions about sex: "How do you do it?" "Do you masturbate?" "How does it feel to get it up the ass?" These questions, prohibited in other classroom discussions, can easily slide into open insult, especially when they are written and anonymous. For example, "All of you are big fucking gays. Why are you here you big nasties. Go suck a knob." "Why are you gay? That's bullshit. I think it's sick." Hostile comments such as these occasionally come up in secondary schools but very rarely in primary schools. There may be several reasons for this — primary students question "teacher authority" less often; the Board's anti-homophobia policies and programs are beginning to counter homophobic socialization among younger students; and primary school students are less likely to be in turmoil over an emerging sexual identity and therefore less likely to find it necessary to protect themselves, to project or to posture.

We do not usually read these outright insults aloud since it is important to protect younger resource people from abuse and to protect the invisible lesbian and gay students in every class. But we do read out most other questions and answer them as honestly as we can.

As can be seen from our discussion about anti-homophobia pedagogy, work to counter homophobia is not set up in competition with work to counter racism or sexism, or in competition with work to deal with issues of social class. The choice of facilitators and the open-ended discussions in the workshops provide the opportunity to deal with the wide range of issues the students raise. The same is true for workshops focusing on other equity issues. Workshop facilitators try to draw out the similarities between different forms of oppression and to draw students' attention to the differences in how such systems work. An honest discussion of similarities and differences averts dead-end debates about who is most oppressed or which oppression is worse.

SYSTEM-WIDE INITIATIVES

Workshops are one way to introduce anti-homophobia education into the curriculum. It is important, though, to implement system-wide initiatives that focus on the needs of students. If we lived in an ideal world where students' needs were met by a truly equitable system of education, special programs for les/bi/gay students and special system-wide efforts to challenge homophobia would not be essential. Students of all backgrounds, regardless of race, gender, class, ability and sexual orientation, would find themselves reflected in curriculum, supported by school staff and safe from harassment and violence. This is not the case. Realistically, anti-homophobia initiatives must not only help all staff and students challenge homophobia and heterosexism at the individual and institutional level, such initiatives must also support les/bi/gay students and staff.

Counsellors can provide much needed support. An openly gay counsellor in the Human Sexuality Program has been providing specialized counselling for lesbian, gay, bisexual and transgendered students, teachers and parents and their families since 1988. This counsellor makes classroom presentations and provides in-service training for teachers and other Board staff. In addition, the counsellor organizes a weekly support group for les/bi/gay students and has been key in the setting up of the Triangle Program, a high-school program for youth who find themselves forced to leave school because of the hostility and harassment they face.

More often than not, students will go to a trusted adult at their school when the harassment they endure is gender-based. However, equity workers have received many calls from students who have experience homophobic harassment. This is due, in part, to their embarrassment and because they fear being further gay or lesbian-baited if they are associated with lesbians or gays at school.[4]

Because homophobic harassment is so pervasive in the school system, equity activists at the Board set up the Triangle Program as a safe, harassment-free learning environment for les/bi/gay students. Since the fall of 1995, Triangle has served as a transitional program for students whose experience of homophobia in mainstream schools has forced them to drop out or has seriously effected their ability to work and learn. A "one-room school house," which is part of a larger alternative school and located in a local church catering to the lesbian and gay communities, the Triangle Program offers classes in English, history, personal life management, physical education, mathematics, keyboarding, geography, science and co-operative education. The curriculum has been specifically designed to include issues of sexual orientation, race, ethnicity, gender and class.

Generally, the students who end up in the Triangle Program cannot or will not choose to pass as straight. Many of them fit the stereotypes of cross-gender appearances. As a result, many have left or been forced to leave their families, live on the street and are on student welfare. Most of the students are courageous, articulate youth who have developed a repertoire of creative strategies to survive in a strongly homophobic and heterosexist society. The Triangle Program provides a safe haven where students can develop the necessary academic and emotional skills to re-enter mainstream schools or move on to post-secondary education or to the world of work.

Although, traditionally, most of the programs for gay, lesbian and bisexual youth have been open to both men and women, many young lesbians and bisexual women feel the need for a same-sex space to talk about issues specific to them as women. For example, some young women feel angry and harassed by some of the behaviour of young gay men who may "camp it up" and call each other "bitch" and "slut." When young women try to call them on their sexism, some slough it off as part of gay male culture. To address this issue, the Toronto Board's Equity Studies Centre and the East End Community Health Centre set up LABRYS, a support group for young lesbians and bisexual women. LABRYS was a ten-week closed group program that offered young lesbian and bisexual women the space to discuss violence in intimate relationships, harassment, coming out and lesbian history.

Staff in the Equity Studies Centre also developed a Lesbian and Gay Studies Course for Toronto Board staff and ran it several times in a variety of formats. Its purpose was to help educators explore the realities facing gay and lesbian communities and to make sure schools have resources in the event that education cutbacks destroy centralized equity work. The Equity Studies Centre has also produced several curriculum documents for elementary and secondary schools that include various equity issues including homophobia. These curriculum documents provide teaching staff with classroom strategies for dealing with issues of racism, sexism, homophobia and class-bias.

The Equity Studies Centre ran seven four-day residential programs (camps) for students on a variety of equity issues. One such camp focused on sexism. In the winter of 1996, a group of secondary students and two teachers who had participated in this program created an anti-sexist group in their school, which is situated about a block from Toronto's gay ghetto. The group wanted to challenge homophobia at school and contacted the Equity Studies Centre for help in creating an anti-homophobia program for Grade 9 classes. Students were paired with "out" gay and lesbian facilitators and with some TEACH members, and participated in a training session. This was the first time such a model was used. Students risked being gay- and lesbian-baited in their own school, which took enormous courage. Many straight-identified adults never challenge homophobia for precisely this reason. The workshops were successful and the original anti-sexist group became stronger.

Many senior elementary schools are now requesting assistance from equity workers in organizing Equity Activity Days. These are primarily in-school conferences. The Equity Studies Centre has done tremendous work to help these schools recognize that it's important to challenge homophobia. Equity staff include a selection of anti-homophobia activities in the conference kits and follow-up material and offer anti-homophobia workshops during Equity Activity Days.

The Equity Studies Centre also supported the publication of *Queer Voices*, a student-initiated and student-produced newsletter. The Centre invited gay, lesbian, bisexual and transgender students to submit letters, poems and articles about their lives. Several issues of the newletter were published and distributed to students, contact teachers and English department heads throughout Toronto Board schools in 1996 and 1997.

Since 1996, the Equity Studies Centre and the Toronto Centre for Lesbian and Gay Studies have also co-sponsored a student writing contest on the topic of homophobia. Several Toronto Board students have won awards for their submissions. English teachers throughout the Toronto Board secondary schools helped to gather submissions.

Finally, as a symbolic gesture, the Board participates in Toronto's Lesbian and Gay Pride Day celebrations. For several years now the Board has staffed a literature table to distribute information on its programs. In past years, the Board also rented a school bus and used the bus as its float in the massive Pride Day parade.

CHALLENGES AND DIFFICULTIES

The many requests for anti-homophobia work is, in itself, a strong indication that the former Toronto Board of Education made progress in responding to homophobia. Hopefully, this progress will not be eroded with the new amalgamated Board. We find that primary school students are more critical of homophobic behaviour than their secondary school counterparts are. In part, this may be because the Board prohibits sexual harassment and has done so throughout the students' short lives. It may also be because gays and lesbians are now more present in popular culture. Unfortunately, however, gay and lesbian studies are still not integrated into the regular curriculum. And, the Board is much less progressive than it once was.

All equity work poses many challenges and difficulties. Changing the way systems operate is seldom easy. Anti-homophobia educational programs present special problems, however, and those who wish to deliver such programs need to be prepared to face them squarely. Drawing on our experience, we can point to some of the difficulties that might be encountered.

LACK OF A MOTOR

If one argues, as we do, that leadership against oppression should spring from the oppressed community itself, then there is a major problem in working to combat homophobia in public education in many parts of the country.

A lively, vocal and focused gay and lesbian community was our motor force for change and guided our work during the time that most progress was made at the Toronto Board of Education. We also had an openly gay trustee at the Board. With the provincial government's forced amalgamation of Metro Toronto school boards in 1998, we lost that voice. We still have an openly gay co-ordinator for the Human Sexuality Program, two openly lesbian teachers in the Triangle Program (one full-time and one part-time), an openly gay student program worker in the Equity Centre and a smattering of "out" gays and lesbians sprinkled throughout our system. At the time of this writing, however, both the programs and the staff positions are in serious jeopardy.

Outside of a few major centres in Canada, however, lesbian and gay communities are far weaker and therefore far less likely to be effective in demanding changes in the local educational system. Nonetheless, the impact that a handful of organized and determined "out" individuals can have should not be underestimated. Education is a service, and, in most provinces, it cannot discriminate on the basis of sexual orientation. A failure to meet the special needs of lesbian and gay students can be understood as discrimination, and at last resort it may be possible to lay complaints under human rights legislation if a board of education is ignoring these needs.

A related issue is the question of gay and lesbian teachers in the system. Even the Toronto Board had but a handful of "out" teachers. Not only are most gay and lesbian teachers closeted, they are so afraid of being outed by their straight colleagues and students that very often they do not openly promote work that challenges homophobia. (Even sympathetic straight teachers may be reluctant to speak up out of fear of being "accused" of being lesbian or gay.) What makes this especially tragic is that there are so few role models for les/bi/gay students. Year after year youth tell us that their lives would be much easier if there were "out" teachers at school.

INVISIBILITY

Most gay, lesbian and bisexual students are invisible at school because the daily onslaught of homophobic harassment and violence keeps them closeted. As well, unlike other invisible parts of one's social identity (such as religion, class or ethnicity), sexual orientation is not transmitted through the family. In other words, while a child's race, religion, class and ethnicity generally matches that of his or her parents, a gay, lesbian or bisexual child's sexual orientation generally does not. For example, a Jewish or working-class student may choose to pass as Christian or middle-class to avoid being bullied at school. But that student is more likely to receive support, validation and protection from their family than a closeted gay student is.

Invisibility and lack of parental support means that homophobia is often seen as less pressing than discrimination and harassment aimed at visible minorities or a vocal minority in the classroom.

VISIBILITY

On the other hand, visibly lesbian or gay students may be so because they cannot, or will not, conform to gender expectations. Those who would like to be visible often find themselves being forced to conform to the two extremes of the "queenie fag/butch dyke" continuum, the most visible representations of the les/bi/gay community. While this may suit youth who fit the stereotypes, many youth do not want to be identified this way. At best, it limits their options for self-expression and at worst it scares them back into the closet.

Visibly lesbian or gay students are also likely to become outcasts. Often they leave or are forced to leave home and gravitate towards whatever open gay community structures exist. Often organized around adults, these communities are not the most appropriate places for young people. Youth in the communities may find themselves at risk of drug abuse, homelessness and prostitution.

ORGANIZED OPPOSITION

While vocal, organized hate groups promoting racism do not meet with wide public acceptance, homophobia remains widespread and open, making it useful for opportunists who hope to mobilize people into a malleable political force on the basis of common prejudices. CURE (Citizens United for Responsible Education) sprang up in the mid 1990s to oppose the Toronto Board's anti-homophobia initiatives. Although CURE tended to mobilize people with religious prejudices against homosexuality, the group's handbook instructs members to conceal their religious beliefs in order to appear more mainstream. Often such groups target other minorities as well. Those who wish to fight for change need to be prepared to organize the kind of grassroots educational campaigns that challenge prejudice and bigotry and reframe the issue in terms of justice and fairness. We must be willing to look for allies in such struggles.

ANTI-DISCRIMINATION POLICY

Many boards do not have an anti-discrimination policy that includes sexual orientation. Without such a policy it is difficult to mobilize people who may feel that the risks they run are too high. Although an anti-discrimination policy on its own changes very little, it is an important place to start. Without it, teachers, parents and students often feel too vulnerable to speak out.

LACK OF EXPERIENCE WITH OTHER KINDS OF EQUITY

Even if a board has something on paper, it may have very little experience in working towards equity. That the Toronto Board could build on its work to combat racism and sexism proved very important in taking up the challenge of homophobia. Establishing a strong alliance around a range of issues may be more effective than demanding change around homophobia alone. On the other hand, it is important to ensure that the alliance does not ignore homophobia or allow it to fall off the table.

FEAR OF PARENTAL REACTION

Although most anti-homophobia work has focused on secondary schools, more and more primary school teachers are requesting our help to challenge incidents in their classrooms. The request may sound something like this: "A bunch of grade fours are calling their teacher/classmate a 'fag' and we want you to do a workshop on sexual harassment without talking too much about gay and lesbian content."

Teachers and administrators do worry about the frequency and severity of incidents and the impact on students. But, there is also a pervasive fear about parental response, especially when doing direct work with younger students. Repeatedly, our challenge is to remind school staff of their responsibilities under Board policy and the Human Rights Code. Another challenge is to create a program that is interesting, age-appropriate and pushes students to think more openly.

It is even harder when teachers are expected to take on the work alone. Our office received a call several years ago from a second grade teacher who had been asked by a parent to read books that included all kinds of families, including gay and lesbian families. The school's administration supported the parent's request. But even with support, the teacher was terrified that if she read books like Leslea Newman's *Heather Has Two Mommies*, the majority of parents would go on a rampage. Unfortunately, her response is not uncommon. It takes a lot of work, support and patience to help some people reach the point where they can start doing basic equity work to address homophobia. It is comforting to know that when handled appropriately, fears of parental reaction are usually exaggerated, unless some politically motivated group is looking to take advantage of such an issue.

THE "BALANCE" ARGUMENT

We have found that right-wing homophobic groups attempt to co-opt the language of more mainstream institutions. They call on "inclusion" and "balance" as an excuse to suppress any positive discussion about gays and lesbians, claiming that heterosexuals don't get the same air time and don't "flaunt their sexuality in class."

The "balance" these groups propose is an interesting one. Often they insist that "if a gay or lesbian talks to a class or assembly about homosexuality, a former gay or lesbian (who is now straight, usually through religious conversion, or at least a person who believes that homosexuality should be condemned) must be allowed equal time and opportunity." In Toronto the use of "equal time" and "equal opportunity" and related language by CURE and other groups is strategic, since most people favour equality and fairness. In this context, however, the intent is oppressive and dangerous.

Lesbians and gay men are an oppressed group protected by both federal and provincial human rights legislation. Our society is homophobic. Our schools are social institutions and reflect this homophobia. CURE's interpretation of "balance" seeks to undermine the message that lesbians and gay men are entitled to the same rights and respect as others and encourages belief that homosexuality is terribly immoral and wrong, so much so that gays and lesbians can and should be encouraged to change their sexual orientation.

On the contrary, providing youth with the opportunity to hear from the gay and lesbian community is an effort to create some balance, for most of the time students are immersed in a heterosexist environment. Heterosexual students have a constant affirmation of who they are. Faced with enormous oppression, lesbian, bisexual and gay youth need "out" role models to affirm their lives, just as their heterosexual counterparts do.

Heterosexuals come out all the time in countless ways. Their heterosexuality is often wrapped around their fourth fingers for all the world to see. Youth need to learn that homosexuality is not just about what happens in bed. It's about who we are, who we spend time with, who we love, what movies we go to, what books we read, all the complexity and mundaneness of our lives.

NEW CHALLENGES, NEW RESOLVE

For any community to mobilize, it must believe that social justice is worth the fight and that positive change can be won. That belief is quickly being eroded in Ontario. It is remarkable that students still do find the courage to be themselves and even more remarkable that they still do take up community activism. For lesbian, bisexual and gay students, the stakes are even higher, the fight that much harder. E's story is a case in point.

E has just graduated from a downtown school not far from Toronto's gay ghetto. Her experience as a mixed-race young girl growing up in Toronto schools mirrored her coming out process. Throughout elementary school kids used to ask her, "Where are you from? What are you anyway?" E's mother is white and her father is African Canadian and Aboriginal. She never knew how to respond to their taunts and felt that she didn't fit in anywhere. E experienced similar feelings when coming to terms with her sexuality.

In high school, E began to surround herself with other mixed-race friends. It helped her to build a sense of community and figure out who she was in the world. Similarly, as she started to realize she was a lesbian, she wanted to meet other young lesbian and gays. At fourteen, she remembers telling a friend that she didn't like boys. For the next few years she had a female friend she used to kiss and hold hands with in public for "shock value." It wasn't until she turned eighteen that she realized that she was attracted to girls. She joined a lesbian and gay youth group run by Central Toronto Youth Services (CTYS) as she struggled to come to terms with herself. Her biggest fear going into the group was that because she had been sexually active with boys she might not be a "real lesbian," for "if you're not a lesbian and don't like guys, then what?"Around that time, she was working with the Department of Public Health as a peer educator, doing presentations in schools on teen sexuality. Her work provided her with a broad perspective on sexual health and sexual identity and helped her to understand that sexuality is fluid and variable. Still, at the end of the CTYS group, she didn't know where she fitted in and felt ill-equipped to deal with questions about sexual orientation or homophobic incidents during presentations. When such questions did come up, all she felt was a hot and immobilizing flash of rage.

At eighteen, E read about TEACH (Teens Educating About and Challenging Homophobia) and joined. Quickly things began to click into place. Her most powerful moment came when a TEACH member mentioned, during a presentation, that she was a "lesbian who occasionally slept with men." That comment gave the space to carve out a definition for herself, one that included her experiences during her early teens when she too was sexually active with boys. TEACH also gave E intensive facilitator training. E is an extremely creative young woman who has used the skills she learned to become an exceptional teacher, facilitator and presenter. She has led workshops throughout Toronto Board classrooms, including primary schools, and has participated in staff in-service training through the Lesbian and Gay Studies Course and has taken part in several conferences. Perhaps her greatest victory was coming out in her school newspaper. That article inspired another student at her school, a young man in the midst of coming out, to found *Queer*

Voices. E is currently finishing up her undergraduate degree in Women's Studies at Trent University.

E is a trail blazer who has eased the way for other queer youth at her school and beyond. But for students like E to approach their potential, a great deal of groundwork must be done. Without TEACH, without support from equity staff, without anti-harassment policies, without training, E's story would have probably been very different. Laying those foundations is the responsibility of all of us who are involved in education, wherever we are.

EPILOGUE

The pace of change due to forced amalgamation and underfunding continues undiminished at the TDSB. As a result, much of the organizational structure referred to in the present tense in this article no longer exists. The Equity Studies Centre has now become the Equity Department, with half as many employees and a fraction of its original budget. Because there are over 600 schools in the new Board, the ability of the six remaining employees to offer effective support for schools is seriously curtailed. The Equal Opportunity Office has been replaced by a new Human Rights Office, which is responsible for dealing with complaints of harassment by students, parents and employees. At present this office has a staff of three, down from eight recommended in the original Board report. As cuts continue as a result of decreased funding under the new provincial formulas, even these reduced levels of staffing are not secure.

On a slightly brighter note, facing a huge public outcry over its original proposal to pass an equity policy restricted to race and culture, the TDSB approved strong policies inclusive of all historically disadvantaged groups. The Equity Foundation Statement of June 1999 recognizes that the education system has poorly served minority communities, women and working-class people. In December 1999, five parallel implementation documents (Anti-racism and Ethnocultural Equity; Anti-sexism and Gender Equity; Anti-homphobia, Sexual Orientation and Equity; Anti-classism and

Socio-Economic Equity; and Equity for Persons with Disabilities) were passed outlining the Board's commitment to systemic change. In May 2000 the new Human Rights Policy, which outlined a complaints procedure on all areas covered by the Ontario Human Rights Code, was approved by the Board. It remains to be seen how the Board can possibly fulfill these extensive commitments in the absence of adequate staff for implementation.

TEACHER RESOURCES

Joanne Bacon, Alice Te, and Vanessa Russell, *Safely Out: Activities to Challenge Homophobia in School* (Toronto: The Equity Department of theToronto District School Board, 1997). *Safely Out* is a curriculum document that gives elementary and secondary school teachers hands-on lesson plans, conference models, staff in-service strategies and community resources for confronting homophobia in school. *Safely Out* also lists an extensive selection of books and videos for primary and secondary school students. Orders can be made through the Equity Department at the Toronto District School Board at (416) 397-3797.

Ellen Bass, *Free Your Mind: The Book for Gay, Lesbian and Bisexual Youth — And Their Allies* (Boston: HarperPerennial, 1996). Comprehensive, focused, readable handbook for adolescents and professionals, dealing with problems arising in the daily lives of lesbian, gay and bisexual youth in a variety of community contexts. Provides sensitive, effective suggestions for how to help.

Education Wife Assault, *Creating Safer Schools for Lesbian, Gay and Bisexual Youth: A Resource for Educators Concerned with Equity* (Toronto: Education Wife Assault, 1999). *Creating Safer Schools* helps teachers examine and create ways to include anti-homophobia work in equity initiatives. Orders can be made through Education Wife Assault at (416) 968-3422.

Gay and Lesbian Educators of British Columbia, *Counselling Lesbian and Gay Youth* (Vancouver: British Columbia Ministry of Education and British Columbia Teachers' Federation, 1995). This resource is designed to help counsellors assist gay and lesbian youth with coming out issues but is also a useful resource for anyone thinking about doing anti-homophobia education. The resource list contains articles, books and videos for further reference. Available from GALE BC, Box 93676, Nelson Park P.O., Vancouver, BC V6E 4L8.

Gerald Unks, ed., *The Gay Teen: Educational Theory and Practice* (New York: Routledge, 1995). Written by and for gay and straight teachers, these essays are designed to introduce and sensitize educators to the complexities of gay identity and set forth some of the issues besetting gay youth in schools, including alienation from peer groups, low academic achievement, violence, substance abuse and the absence of gay teacher role models.

CLASSROOM RESOURCES

Marion Bauer, *Am I Blue? Coming Out from the Silence* (Madison, WI: Demco Media, 1995). Sixteen short stories entertain but also dispel myths and provide information about growing up gay or lesbian or about gay or lesbian parents or friends.

Nancy Garden, *Annie on My Mind* (New York: Farrar, Straus and Giroux, 1992). Lisa and Annie are two secondary school students who meet by chance at an art museum and soon realize that their feelings for each other go beyond friendship. Both face conflicts in accepting their feelings, but the story captures the magic and intensity of first love.

A. Homes, *Jack* (Madison, WI: Demco Media, 1990). Jack discovers that his divorced father is gay and suffers harassment at school because of this. The book concerns both Jack's inner and outer struggles with having a gay parent.

Diana Weiler, *Bad Boy* (Toronto: Groundwood, 1997). A.J. struggles with the realization that his best friend is gay. Intense and dramatic, and touches on the issue of violence in sports. Winner of the Governor General's Award for Children's Literature.

MEDIA RESOURCES

Both of My Mom's Names are Judy (National Film Board). This 10-minute video presents a racially diverse group of children ages 7 to 10 talking about the love they feel for their families, how teasing and the classroom silence about lesbians and gay men affects them, and what they would like to see changed.

OUT! Stories of Lesbian and Gay Youth (National Film Board, 1993). An intimate look at the struggles and achievements of gay and lesbian youth in Canada. 79 minutes.

School's Out! (National Film Board, 1996). This 28-minute film provides an additional tool for anti-heterosexism educators. Five TEACH (Teens Educating and Confronting Homophobia) youth talk about their experience visiting classrooms and discussing homophobia, heterosexism and lesbian, gay and bisexual issues. Jane Rule contributes her wisdom and insights. For high school and college students, intermediate and secondary teachers. Discussion guide available.

ORGANIZATIONS

Central Toronto Youth Services: Supporting Our Youth Project
65 Wellesley Street East
Toronto, ON M4Y 1G7
(416) 924-2100

Equity Department
Toronto District School Board
155 College Street
Toronto, ON M5T 1P6
(416) 397-3345

Human Sexuality Program
The Toronto District School Board
155 College Street
Toronto, ON M5T 1P6
(416) 397-3755

Kids Help Phone
1-800-668-6868
Can make referrals to support groups in your area.

Lesbian, Gay and Bisexual Youth Line
P.O. Box 62, Station F
Toronto, ON M4Y 2L4
1-800-268-9688
(416) 962-9688
TTY: (416) 962-9688

Rainbow Classroom Network
252 Bloor Street West, 7th Floor
Toronto, ON M5S 1V6
(416) 923-6641, ext. 2467

A network of teachers and others across Ontario working to create gay-positive classrooms. They produce *The Rainbow Classroom: Inform-Support-Mobilize* newsletter.

Teens Educating and Confronting Homophobia (TEACH)
Planned Parenthood of Toronto
36B Prince Arthur Avenue

Toronto, ON M5R 1A9
(416) 961-0113, ext. 230

Triangle Program of Oasis Alternative Secondary School
c/o Steve Solomon
Human Sexuality Program (as above)
(416) 397-3755

NOTES

1. M. Francis, "Anti-Racist Teaching: General Principles" and "Anti-Racist Teaching: Curricular Practices," In *Challenging Racism* (London: All London Teachers Against Racism and Fascism); J. Goody and H. Knight, "Multicultural Education and Anti-Racist Teaching," *English in Education* 19 (Autumn, 1985), 3-7; E. Lee, *Letters to Marcia: A Teachers Guide to Anti-Racist Education* (Toronto: Cross Cultural Communications Centre, 1985); T. McCaskell, *Facilitators Handbook: Multicultural/Multiracial Residential Camp for Secondary School Students* (Toronto: Toronto Board of Education, Office of the Advisor on Race Relations, 1988); T. McCaskell, "Anti-Racist Education and Practice in the Public School System," in S. Richer and L. Weir, eds., *Beyond Political Correctness: Toward the Inclusive University* (Toronto: University of Toronto Press, 1995); A. Mukherjee, *From Racist to Anti-Racist Education: A Synoptic View* (Toronto: Toronto Board of Education, Equal Opportunity Office, 1988); C. Mullard, *Anti-Racist Education: The Three O's* (London: National Association for Multi-Racial Education, 1984); B. Thomas, "Principles of Anti-Racist Education," *Currents, Readings in Race Relations* (Fall 1984), 20-24.

2. Prior to 1994, there were three advisors — one for visible racial minorities, one for women and one for First Nations Peoples — who focused on system-wide policy development and the handling of complaints. Four student workers were cross-appointed to both the Equal Opportunity Office and the Equity Studies Centre. These three positions in the Equal Opportunity Office were cut back to one between 1994 and 1998.

3. In November 1997, the Toronto Board consolidated all its harassment policies into one, "Dealing with Human Rights in Schools and Workplaces." The policy, which includes all areas protected under the Ontario Human Rights Code, prohibits harassment, outlines remedies and provides a consistent approach to all harassment complaints. At the point of writing, it is still unclear what kind of harassment policies the new amalgamated Toronto District School Board will adopt.

4. While the Board has had a non-discrimination policy on the basis of sexual orientation in employment since 1980, it did not provide spousal benefits for the partners of lesbian and gay employees until 1995. The move had long been demanded by the Lesbian and Gay Board Employees Group, established in 1990. This group, while not a Board initiative, rapidly won recognition as a legitimate voice of employees and has intervened in a number of issues of concern to the community.

Chapter 2

MULTICULTURAL AND ANTI-RACIST EDUCATION

THE ISSUE IS EQUITY

Ouida M. Wright

CANADA'S POPULATION surged from a little more than some three and a half million in 1867 to more than thirty million 130 years later. Canadian society has become a sophisticated complexity of social mores, resulting from its peculiar geography and evolving history. Canada is a country of contrasts and reluctant diversity, a diversity which ebbs and flows with every crisis in our global village. Like its powerful neighbour to the south, Canada is a country of recent immigrants still striving to forge some sort of accommodation with the first inhabitants, the Aboriginal peoples. In the close to 400 years since the first French settled here, an increasingly varied population of diverse races, ethnicity, cultures, languages and religions have come from every quarter of the globe; people of every shade of colour and creed, of every economic and social class, have found refuge and hope in a country that offered unending vistas of opportunity, prosperity and advancement.

Canadians now hail from more than fifty countries around the world. The cultural mix is much greater than that identified in

Many Cultures, Many Heritages,[1] published in 1975. This source notes ten cultural groups but makes no mention of Chinese, Vietnamese or Koreans. Today, after English and French, Chinese is the most frequently spoken language in Canada. While each group has brought with it its own customs and lifestyles, each has been united with those which have come before by a set of universal principles embedded in the Judaeo-Christian values of the earliest immigrants. Even those professing the Hindu, Buddhist, Muslim or Baha'i faiths have found common ground in basic moral virtues such as honesty, integrity, reverence for a deity and honour for parents and elders.[2] These successive waves of immigrants from all over the world live in an uneasy peace with the doctrine of "the two founding nations" — the French and the English — and with the fiction of a mosaic, a concept based on a metaphor which seems to advocate separateness rather than togetherness. The turbulence of the last thirty years of the French sovereignty movement, in which Quebeckers are determined to become *maître chez-nous,* calls into question the much-wished-for concept of Canada as a country at peace with itself.

Add to this that, despite Canada's tremendous economic wealth and rich natural resources, there is great disparity in living conditions between an increasingly wealthy upper class (Canada, theoretically, has no class system) and an increasingly poorer majority. We talk of "equality," of treating everybody the same. If rigidly and insensitively applied, treating everybody the same can be considered a concept of dubious practicality, since it will inevitably lead to the inequity we are attempting to avoid.

The issue is equity. We must insist that all our people are entitled to certain services and benefits and set in place policies and practices that ensure that everyone has access to these services to the appropriate standard. This is no easy achievement. While it is fair to say that there is not enough money to achieve this standard of social and economic excellence, can we continue to find the resources to repair the damage due to lack of opportunity and wasted potential? Do we really want to keep mustering the fortitude to bear the physical, psychological and emotional pain resulting from inaction and faint-heartedness? As Rosalie Abella reminds us, "equity is defined as equality of outcomes ... [and]... sometimes equality means treating people the same, despite their differences, and sometimes it means treating them as equals by accommodating their differences."[3]

For the last thirty years, governments at all levels have promoted equity in Canadian society and encouraged and supported education authorities to persevere in this essential task. Two major policy directives inform these actions. The first is known as "multiculturalism" and multicultural education; the second, "anti-racism" and anti-racist education. These terms remain two of the most hopeful and, at the same time, two of the most divisive and controversial in the Canadian lexicon, depending on your point of view.

The drive towards multicultural and anti-racist education stems from different experiences and perceptions by one or more groups in our society. These can include:

- experiences and perceptions of exclusion from the systems of education or roles in society;

- experiences and perceptions of bias, prejudice or discrimination, which tend to exclude or demean; and

- the treatment of individuals or groups that results in disadvantage or harm to them.

The variation in the population of each province determines to a lesser or greater degree the emphasis placed on the initiatives that are proposed or implemented to address these experiences. These have ranged from a bilingual framework in New Brunswick, to religious pluralism in Newfoundland, to a human rights approach in Nova Scotia, to improved education for Aboriginal peoples in Saskatchewan, to using the arts as opportunities to combat racial prejudice in Prince Edward Island, and in Quebec, Ontario, Manitoba, Alberta and British Columbia,[4] to a wide array of initiatives to respond to the needs and concerns of more than fifty cultural groups.

HOW MULTICULTURAL EDUCATION BEGAN

Canadians tend to regard multiculturalism as either a unifying or divisive force. It is sometimes seen as creating a cultural mosaic with little interaction among the cultures, as a preservation of home cultures, or even as assisting people from cultural groups other than English or French to embrace the cultures of the "two founding nations." Almost daily, there are comments, letters or reports in the media which tend to support one or other point of view. We need, therefore, to recall where, at least, politically, the concept began.

THE ROYAL COMMISSION ON BILINGUALISM
AND BICULTURALISM

In 1963, on the recommendation of then Prime Minister Lester Pearson, a Royal Commission on Bilingualism and Biculturalism in Canada was set up. Its mandate was "to recommend what steps should be taken to develop the Canadian Confederation on the basis of equal partnership between the founding races, taking into account the contribution made by the other ethnic groups to the cultural enrichment of Canada and the measures that should be taken to safeguard that contribution."[5] Many groups made spirited submissions on their role in, and contributions to, Canada.

Economic factors have been the chief reason many people have come to Canada. Once in Canada, they have cherished and nurtured the traditions that enriched their lives in their homelands, even as they sought to adjust to the country that gave them the opportunity to make a fresh start and secure the advancement of their children. Those who came as refugees, particularly from Europe following two World Wars and later from Vietnam, Korea, Somalia, Chile and Nicaragua, left their home countries because of economic and harsh circumstances. Nonetheless, they have sought ways to accommodate the past and the present.

The Commission regarded our cultural diversity as an inestimable enrichment that Canadians could not afford to lose. The Commission's recommendations took pains to ensure that groups other than the French, English and Aboriginal peoples, loosely referred to as "other ethnic groups," not be seen as second-class citizens. The Commission rejected "race," "people" and "ethnic group" as the basis for multiculturalism. It also rejected "assimilation," which it saw as implying "almost total absorption into another linguistic and cultural group." Instead, it opted for "integration" on the basis of language and culture. Integration would be guided by three principles: the good of the individual, the good of the society he/she chooses and the good of the country as a whole. The expectation, in short, was that through integration Canada would achieve unity in diversity.

FEDERAL POLICY OF MULTICULTURALISM

Based on this hopeful view of multiculturalism, the federal government declared an official policy of multiculturalism in 1971. Six years later, in 1977, Parliament passed the *Canadian Human Rights Act*. In 1982, the Charter of Rights and Freedoms entrenched multiculturalism and equality rights in the Constitution, and, in 1988, Parliament passed the *Canadian Multiculturalism Act* "to preserve and enhance the multicultural heritage of Canadians while working to achieve the equality of all Canadians in the economic, social, cultural and political life of Canada."[6] The federal legislative support network for inclusiveness was therefore reinforced, and supported by provincial codes of human rights as well.[7]

While many Canadians endorse the government's policy on multiculturalism, many others do not. Divisions remain. Some members of the various cultural groups see it as an acknowledgement of their presence in Canada and as a recognition of their contributions. For them, multiculturalism affords the opportunity, as the flagship newspaper of the Toronto's Italian community puts it, to be "Fiercely Italian" yet "Proudly Canadian."

However, there are also those who fear that a policy of multiculturalism is divisive; that it stresses the differences among Canadians; that it will rob Canada of its chance to develop a Canadian identity; that Canada is now and will forever remain fractured into a community of communities, inhabited by groups of hyphenated people; that it implies equal status to all the cultures which make up Canada and so undermines the concept of the two founding nations.[8]

Canadians continue to wrestle with the meaning and implications of an official policy of multiculturalism. According to the

Canadian Consultative Council on Multiculturalism in its first report, issued in 1975, "multiculturalism may be viewed as the development of a consciousness of one's ancestral roots or ethnicity for creative purposes in the hope that a distinctive Canadian identity will emerge."[9] This definition of classic elegance leaves to each implementing partner the room to adjust and adapt policy to ensure the inclusion and participation of all groups in Canadian society.

PROVINCIAL MULTICULTURAL EDUCATION INITIATIVES

Since education is the purview of the provinces, provincial governments and boards of education, particularly those with a diverse population, found they needed to come to grips with multiculturalism and to set up structures and implement programs to help identify and support racial and cultural minorities living within their jurisdictions. Solutions developed in various ways across Canada.[10]

It is not surprising that Ontario, the province with the widest array of cultural groups and the centre for many active ethnocultural organizations and which has a long history of receiving frequent and successive waves of new immigrants and refugees, responded promptly to the federal initiatives. For example, the Ontario Ministry of Education began an energetic effort to embed multiculturalism in the educational system. The Minister announced in 1977 that "multiculturalism is a positive dynamic force, a philosophy that should permeate all curriculum ... Adoption of this philosophy of multiculturalism has implications for everything we do in schools. There are implications for curriculum, for teacher training, for learning materials, and really what we are reaching for in the schools is a general sensitivity and understanding of the great strengths of our multicultural character."[11] The Chairwoman of the Ontario Committee on Multiculturalism elaborated further: "It is an education in which the individual child of whatever origin finds not mere acceptance or tolerance but respect and understanding. It is an education in which cultural diversity is seen and used as a valuable resource to enrich the lives of all."[12]

Following the recommendations of the Ontario Committee on

Multiculturalism, the Ministry of Education launched several policies and projects. In its curriculum and policy guidelines (*P1J1, The Formative Years, Education in the Primary and Junior Divisions, Ontario Schools Intermediate and Senior Divisions*[13]), the Ministry set specific objectives for education at both the elementary and secondary levels to encourage in students respect for cultural diversity and understanding and an appreciation of points of view of ethnic and cultural groups other than their own. The goal was social harmony and personal enrichment as well as pride in Canada's national identity.

In a situation where appropriate staff is critical to the effectiveness of the action taken, the Ontario Ministry of Education appointed an Education Officer to take on the responsibility of multiculturalism.[14] Under her supervision, the Ministry began a program of assistance for teachers. It produced *Multiculturalism in Action,*[15] a document replete with ideas for curriculum, and assigned staff to assist school boards to provide in-service workshops, seminars and conferences. In addition, the Ministry offered a summer course for the Certificate in Multiculturalism in Education. The Ministry also targeted students through the Student Leadership Training Program, in which it collaborated with school boards in developing a residential week for racially mixed teams of high-school students on the topic of interracial relationships.

The Ministry set up a Learning Materials Development Fund to provide grants for individuals and for publishers to produce print and non-print materials relating to minority groups. It constantly scrutinized and revised *Circular 14,*[16] its list of approved textbooks, to ensure that unsuitable material was removed and that textbooks were accurate in their representation of, displayed respect for, and promoted understanding among Canada's cultural groups. Further, the Ministry and what was then the Ontario Ministry of Culture and Recreation worked with community groups to draw up a list of multicultural resource materials.

The Ministry put more funding into English as a Second Language programs and, in 1977, began to fund the Heritage Language Program. These optional classes for elementary school pupils, held outside of school hours or as part of an extended school day, offered instruction in languages other than English or French. This was and remains one of the most controversial programs to implement multiculturalism. While the Heritage Language Program promotes a sense of inclusion by encouraging more minority parents into the school and has done more to make both parents and students feel that their cultures are truly welcome and valued, the program has also caused considerable alarm among those who were concerned about the changing nature of their communities and their schools.[17]

Outreach to ethnocultural communities was one of the Ministry's most significant initiatives. The Minister and his education officers met with community groups and organizations across the province and encouraged their participation and suggestions. Work proceeded on every front and included curriculum to reflect the lives of Aboriginal peoples as well as those of Caribbean and African background. For example, one document entitled *English as a Second Language/Dialect*[18] attempted to provide suggestions to teachers as to how to deal with students whose first language was English but whose spoken language differed somewhat from Canadian English.

Ministries of education across the country drew up policies and set up programs to respond to the needs of the multicultural population. Those in British Columbia, Alberta, Manitoba and Quebec are particularly noteworthy. For example, one of Alberta's most important programs was the development of its bilingual language program. Up to 50 percent of the school day, in Grades 1 through 12, can be used for instruction in any language other than English. The languages range from Arabic to German, Mandarin to Hungarian, and include a variety of Aboriginal languages.[19]

MULTICULTURAL EDUCATION AT BOARDS OF EDUCATION

Some boards of education, such as those in major cities like Vancouver, Winnipeg, Toronto, Montreal and Halifax, took their cue from the obvious mix of their student populations and the dismal outcomes for some groups. They began to reflect, analyze and make changes, at times even before their own Ministries of

Education had set up specific policies. Vancouver, for example, required schools to submit action plans on race relations and multiculturalism to the Superintendent. The plans were to detail how the policies and guidelines would be communicated to staff, students and parents. Principals were asked to provide an explanation of how the school would expand and extend its work on race relations and multiculturalism in the next school year. As a result, a large proportion of the schools set up curriculum committees or sought parent involvement at some level, offered professional development programs and focused on multiculturalism in the form of planned teaching units. In some cases, multicultural workers were involved in various capacities. Home and school co-ordinators were provided to advise and counsel parents about their child's performance, to encourage parents to participate in the school, to provide interpretation when language was a problem and to explain the perspectives of ethnocultural groups to school staffs. Through a multicultural leadership program, students participated in a retreat to develop their leadership abilities by improving cross-cultural relations.[20]

In 1988, Winnipeg School Division No.1 outlined a general philosophy of "acceptance, respect and appreciation of all people in Canada and their cultures for their commonalities as well as their differences." The statement defined multicultural education as "the process of making education more responsive to the cultural and linguistic diversity that characterizes the Canadian society."[21] The Division also set goals for multicultural education and professional development, outlined the responsibilities of various levels of staff and made a commitment to staffing practices that reflect the multicultural nature of the Division.

The City of Toronto and its neighbouring municipalities are the most culturally, ethnically and linguistically diverse in Canada. It is therefore not surprising that these municipalities took decisive action in what was to become known as multicultural and anti-racist education. Area boards hired consultants to meet their priorities.[22] Often, local schools took the initiative. In 1978, North York's Downsview Secondary School, for example, set up a program designed to mobilize the power of the peer group in a positive and productive manner. This program helped diffuse tensions between

Black and white students and helped develop a positive attitude to the city's cultural diversity.[23]

The Board of Education for the City of Toronto set out on a deliberate identification and analysis of its student population, which led to one of the most extensive sets of initiatives designed to support its total school population and, in particular, to deal with almost every facet of school life to ensure access and equity for the students of the various multicultural groups. In 1970, the Board directed its Research Department to do a survey of the Board's secondary schools every five years. The first *Every Student Survey* revealed that more than half the students came from homes where neither English nor French was the first language, a finding reaffirmed by the second survey in 1975 — a finding which was destined to change significantly how Toronto schools would be run. Further, the surveys demonstrated that the children of non-British immigrants and those of low economic status were the most likely to be at a disadvantage in the Board's schools.[24]

The research led to changes or new initiatives in the curriculum, in in-service training for all Board staff, in student evaluation and reporting to parents, in program evaluation and evaluation of teacher performance and in a push to involve all parents in their children's education. There was an increased emphasis on how children think and reason, matching teaching styles to learning styles and on the teaching of French, English and international languages. The Board set up ESL programs, both in school and for adults, established reception and transition centres for new students, expanded its Guidance and Counselling Services to include a placement officer, and set up a Community Services Department. It even appointed a special community outreach advisor to assist the Director of Education.

The Board's issue paper, "The Bias of Culture," its research paper, "We are All Immigrants to this Place,"combined with the findings and recommendations of the "Draft Report of the Work Group on Multicultural Programs,"[25] helped provide a basis for making the Toronto school system truly accommodating of the many cultures that made up the city. The Board set up or expanded programs to serve a burgeoning multicultural population that had rapidly expanded through successive waves of immigration.

The Board's highly acclaimed Benchmark Program, on which the province's student evaluation program would later be modelled, was a direct result of the efforts to find methods of student evaluation that reduced stereotyping and cultural bias. Most important, the Board gave top priority to drawing up curriculum that was truly reflective of its students and to changing its personnel practices, with significant positive results. Its network of consultative committees and advisory groups included parents and the Board sent out newsletters in the eight most commonly spoken languages to ensure that all parents would be kept abreast of Board policies and programs.

For decades, the school day had opened with the Christian Lord's Prayer. The Board sought to show respect for other faiths. It invited religious organizations to work together with Board staff to compile a book of *Readings and Prayers for Use in Toronto Schools*.[26] It was a dynamic coming together of representatives from the traditional Christian faiths with those from faiths as varied as Jain, Baha'i, Muslim, Sikh and Hindu. The miracle was that they found common ground!

"Streaming," however, was the issue that most galvanized communities. It was obvious that Black children and children of other cultural minorities were vastly overrepresented in vocational and non-academic programs. That, and the unacceptably high drop-out rate for both, later confirmed in the Ministry of Education's own Radwanski report,[27] led to an overhaul of the options open to secondary school students and helped focus the debate on issues of race and ethnicity.

SUPPORT IN FACULTIES OF EDUCATION

The Faculties of Education at the major universities were quick to offer courses in multiculturalism education and, later, in anti-racist education to develop and expand programs to help their students become more sensitive to the issues. For example, the University of British Columbia (UBC) researched practical ways teachers could put multiculturalism into practice. For instance, staff developed strategies for responding to racial incidents through a curriculum approach. Discussions were designed to strengthen each child's self-esteem by giving value to each child's ethnic identity and to explore issues, understand them and stimulate positive action. The UBC research was used in the faculties of other provinces as well.[28]

The Faculty of Education at Simon Fraser University translated the growing diversity in the schools into a mandate to focus on multiculturalism in its teacher education programs. Faculty developed a Pre-Service Multicultural Teacher Education Module in which student teachers spent half of the semester in workshops and half observing in classrooms, which were socio-economically and culturally varied.[29]

York University developed an Access Initiative Program and hired a co-ordinator for the program, which was designed to recruit, retrain and support students from groups that have traditionally been underrepresented in teacher preparation programs. Initially, people of colour were one of the targeted groups, along with Aboriginal, refugee and differently abled students. Although the numbers enrolled have grown steadily, the long-term objective is to develop an admissions process that will eliminate the need for this special initiative. The York Faculty also initiated a field project with the neighbouring Westview family of schools in which university students and staff worked directly with school students. Their primary objectives were to increase the academic success of the students and increase the number of students entering and graduating from post-secondary institutions.[30]

At the University of Toronto multicultural education became a significant initiative and there was an attempt to include multiculturalism in many of the course offerings.[31] As well, the University of Toronto instituted a Transitional Year Program for adult students who had not completed their secondary education. The Program helped them qualify for entrance to university. Most of the students in the program grew up in communities in which few people had access to higher education. The program was intended as an equity provision and specifically targeted minority communities.[32]

TEACHER ORGANIZATIONS

Teacher organizations continue to play an active role in preparing and supporting teachers in multicultural education. These professional organizations have been cited time and time again for their advocacy and initiative in support of the culturally diverse school populations in every region of Canada. They worked closely with ministries and boards of education to provide in-service training for teachers and to develop curriculum materials. Indeed, recommendations from a conference of the Ontario Association for Curriculum Development in 1975 prompted the Ontario Ministry of Education to implement many of its own programs.[33]

In Manitoba, the provincial teachers' organization provided a booklet explaining the rationale for multicultural education and suggestions for how to put it into practice in the classroom. The Nova Scotia teachers' organization continues to work with the provincial government to provide training for teachers particularly to increase awareness of the educational barriers Black children face in that province. The Alberta Teachers' Federation and the Saskatchewan Teachers' Federation have promoted multiculturalism and Native education. Ontario's public and separate elementary and secondary school federations encouraged multicultural education by providing curriculum and offering professional development for teachers. Nationally, the Canadian Teachers' Federation (CTF) and the Canadian Education Association (CEA) carry out similar work.

NATIONAL AND COMMUNITY ORGANIZATIONS

Perhaps no other issue has so focused the energies of community, volunteer and quasi-professional organizations for, they see multiculturalism and anti-racism as inseparable. The national organization the Canadian Council for Multicultural and Intercultural Education (CCMIE),[34] for example, is comprised of provincial and territorial multicultural associations representing the diversity in Canadian society. The CCMIE encourages national dialogues that invite provincial and regional jurisdictions to share reports of their progress on issues of multiculturalism and anti-racism. CEA and the CTF work together and with government ministries, departments and agencies to encourage multicultural and anti-racist education. They, along with community-based groups, have produced materials, held conferences and workshops, written articles, published journals, issued reports and lobbied various levels of government.

The greatest impact of multicultural education was felt in the curriculum: the material prescribed for learning, the methods of instruction, in the school environment and, most of all, in the creation of an atmosphere of inclusiveness, both real and perceived, in every aspect of education. The perceptions, attitudes and behaviours of all persons involved in education from senior administration to custodial staff needed to change from beyond tolerance to acceptance of all cultural groups as worthy and deserving of respect and equity in educational institutions.

Despite the work of ministries of education and school boards, teacher federations, national and provincial organizations, and despite implementation reviews, there is little in way of hard research on whether the policies and programs have had the desired effect. Are schools now more inclusive, more likely to encourage all students to achieve than they were before the *Report on Bilingualism and Biculturalism*? Is Canada a more inclusive place? Our eyes and ears tell us "yes." But to what degree?

Clearly, multiculturalism means more than song, dance and food, more than costumes, festivals and special days of the month. Multiculturalism is being woven into the fabric of our society. The self-concept, self-esteem, self-confidence and ultimately the achievement of every student in our schools is influenced by it. We can see multiculturalism as a problem, or we can see our many cultures as rich resources that help to make Canada the best country in the world in which to live. The outpouring of grief at the death in September 2000 of former Prime Minister Pierre Elliott Trudeau, who vigorously advocated multiculturalism, speaks for itself.

ANTI-RACISM AND ANTI-RACIST EDUCATION

Just as ministries of education and school boards were beginning to congratulate themselves on putting multiculturalism into practice with relatively little distress, sections of society around them began to point out inequities that they attributed not only to prejudice, bias or discrimination but also to that ugly word racism. Parents from "visible minority" groups, a term which came into common use at this time, began to attribute their children's poor academic performance, at least in part, to the process of "streaming," which they contended was largely based on the assumption that persons from certain cultural groups need not or could not or did not wish to achieve academic excellence.

Racial minorities and other cultural groups were seen to be excluded from curriculum materials. Worse, when included, they were represented in a negative or disparaging manner. The South Asian community criticized books in *Circular 14 Textbooks,* the list of books which the Ontario Ministry of Education approved for use in its schools. The Canadian Society of Muslims requested that certain books be removed on the grounds that they were inaccurate and demeaned the image of Islam.[35]

Multiculturalism and by extension anti-racism differs from province to province according to the mix of the population and the priorities of that province. In Ontario, the most populous and diverse province, there are subtle differences among people of European descent, yet discrimination is felt most keenly among people of colour — people who are from Asia, the Indian sub-continent, the Pacific Rim, the Caribbean, Africa or who are of African or Aboriginal descent. Although there are variations from province to province, the theme remains largely the same, whether among the Aboriginal peoples in Saskatchewan or among Blacks in Nova Scotia. By the early eighties it became clear that multiculturalism was not enough; it was time to look the beast in the face and give it a name.

Even the language of multiculturalism had caused discomfort and friction. Words like ethnic, culture, multicultural and race proved to be more troubling than bias, prejudice, discrimination or stereotype. Euphemisms such as "culturally disadvantaged" or "culturally deprived" tended to distort or downplay the problem. Use of the word "ethnic" became troubling and divisive. Minorities and others agree that we cannot wait to get past the language before we attack the problem. Perhaps as we seek solutions, the language will take care of itself. Yet, unless we find common language and arrive at common understandings, it will be almost impossible not to be confounded and frustrated as we work to eliminate the problems.

WHAT IS RACISM?

Although educators had no difficulty defining and identifying multiculturalism, we are hard put to find definitions of racism in earlier Canadian educational materials. It is an extremely uncomfortable word. It does not fit with Canadians' sense of themselves. Racism does not happen here! It describes events that happen elsewhere: apartheid, ethnic cleansing, genocide, the Holocaust, slavery. At best the word is a reluctant addition to multiculturalism; at worst, some see it as a lame excuse proffered by those who will not or cannot make use of the opportunities this country offers to improve themselves and make a success of their lives.

In the last fifty years, Canada has become peacekeeper to the world, a role it bears with pride and distinction. Canada has given refuge to millions of people from all over the world who seek safety and a better life. Comprehensive legislation such as the Charter of Rights and Freedoms and human rights codes, both federal and provincial, protect individuals against discrimination. Some provinces also take into account the linguistic diversity of large sections of the community as well as recognition and preservation of Aboriginal languages. Canada has re-engineered itself into a country that is highly regarded for its humanity and fair play. Yet, there is still work to be done to ensure equity for all its people.

Like it or not, what we mean by racism is clearly evident in Canadian society and is a part of Canada's history. The media frequently refer to the Church's treatment of the First Nations, the Head Tax on the Chinese, the internment of Canadians of Japanese ancestry during the Second World War. We are still confronting the factors that contribute to the poverty and poor health among First Nations people on and off the reserves and the high suicide rate among Inuit teenagers.

The concerns of the Black community have been repeatedly expressed and reviewed. In January 2000, a national newscaster was fired for offensive remarks on air about Blacks, lesbians and people with disabilities because her comments sparked public outrage and controversy. The abuse and murder of a Somali youth by our own soldiers in 1992 led to an official inquiry. The history and experiences of people of African heritage in Canada as described in *The Blacks in Canada,* includes slavery and segregation. As well, incidents of anti-Semitism are often reported in the media. Abella and Troper in *None is Too Many,* rigorously document evidence of Canada's exclusion of European Jews during the Second World War.[36]

As documented by Michele Landsberg and Karen Mock, report after report highlight and confirm the sorry, heartbreaking story of racism. In 1977, Walter Pitman produced his report, *Now is Not Too Late,* for the Task Force on Human Relations for the Metropolitan Toronto Council. The report stressed the need to deal with growing racial tension in an increasingly diverse Toronto. In 1984, a federal parliamentary Task Force in its report, *Equality Now!* pointed out that racism was woven into the cultural, social and political structures of our society. In the same year, the federal Employment Equity Commission reported that systemic racism was pervasive in education, media, health services, criminal justice and employment across the country.[37]

In 1985, the Urban Alliance on Race Relations asked the question and published its report, *Who Gets the Work?* Their research found blatant discrimination in employment hiring practices and in the workplace. A 1987 report, *Access to Government Services in Ontario,* prepared by Masemann and Mock for the Ontario Race Relations Directorate, showed that differential treatment in Ontario appeared to be the norm, resulting in lack of equal access to services and the frustration, alienation and continued feeling of marginalization and helplessness among racial minorities. Dionne Brand's *No Burden to Carry: Narratives of Black Working Women in Ontario 1920s to 1950s* documents the triple jeopardies of race, sex and class as Black working-class women relate their aspirations and frustrations and how difficult it was for educated Black women to find well-paid jobs.[38]

Racism is commonly understood to mean bias, prejudice and discrimination or preference on the basis of race, ethnicity, country of origin, as colour of skin, facial features, texture of hair or linguistic accent — any of which can lead to stereotyping. Those who hold these stereotypes may deny to others employment, education and career choice opportunities and access to social services. In 1992, the Ontario Anti-Racism Secretariat of the Ontario Ministry of Citizenship defined racism as:

> A system in which one group of people exercises abusive power over others on the basis of skin colour and racial heritage; a set of implicit or explicit beliefs, erroneous assumptions and actions based upon an ideology of inherent superiority of one racial or ethnocultural group over another. Racism is manifested within organizational and institutional structures and programs as well as within individual thought or behaviour patterns.[39]

This definition of racism is commonly referred to as "systemic racism." The term, which came into general use in the early 1970s, carries the greatest degree of discomfort and tends to antagonize even some of those individuals who are willing to concede that racism does exist in our society. The discomfort may be because the definition moves beyond seeing racism as only the view or action of some individuals, rather it sees that racism exists within the structures of daily life. This, in turn, imposes the unwelcome conclusion that each of us is a party, reluctant or otherwise, to its existence.

WHAT IS ANTI-RACIST EDUCATION?

On the surface, anti-racist education would seem to be work that our elementary, secondary and post-secondary schools do to combat racism. As with multiculturalism, educators began to take action in the early 1970s. For example, Garnet McDiarmid and David Pratt, in *Teaching Prejudice: A Content Analysis of Social Studies Textbooks Authorized for Use in Ontario*,[40] provided strong support for those who saw negative stereotypes and misinformation in school textbooks. But it was an unassuming little book, *Letters to Marcia: A Teacher's Guide to Anti-Racist Education* by Enid Lee,[41] that really grabbed the attention of educators still preoccupied with implementing multicultural programs.

Letters to Marcia stated flatly that given that racism exists in our society, it follows that the school, as an institution of society, is influenced by racism. Enid Lee defined anti-racist education as education that "attempts to equip us as teachers and our students, with the analytic tools to critically examine the origins of racist ideas and practices, and to understand the implications of our own race and our own actions in the promotion of, or struggle against racism."[42]

Since then, educators have sought to clarify or augment this definition, with inconclusive results. For instance, anti-racist education has been defined as "a set of educators' attitudes, assumptions, expectations, interactions, and behaviours which work together with appropriate learning materials and environments to produce equitable outcomes for students of all ethnocultural communities, of various races."[43] Anti-racism education has also been defined as "an action-oriented strategy for institutional, systemic change to address racism and the interlocking systems of social oppression ... Anti-racism explicitly names the issues of race and social difference as issues of power and equity rather than as matters of cultural and ethnic variety."[44] The term "ethnocultural equity" sometimes replaces anti-racism. The educator who wishes to implement anti-racist education with objectivity and integrity is hard pressed to reconcile these definitions.

Further, how is anti-racist education different from multicultural education? Some critics suggest that it is a matter of emphasis.[45] But there are some essential distinctions. While both focus on making the school curriculum and the total environment more inclusive, multicultural education focuses on intergroup harmony and anti-racist education focuses on intergroup equity. George Dei, in his landmark analysis of the issues, suggests that it is also a matter of asking the right questions, different questions. Do all students have equal access to what the schools have to offer? What gets taught? What doesn't get taught? What do the textbooks, the curriculum overall, the opening exercises, extra-curricular activities, and so on, omit, negate, misrepresent?[46]

Anti-racist education calls for new ways of thinking about education. It means more than reforming the curriculum and teaching practices. It means examining the structure of education to ensure that those who make the decisions reflect the diversity of the community at large. It means transforming power relations in schools, in boards of education and in ministries of education. It means making room for knowledge that enhances the status quo.

Not surprisingly, it is much easier to talk about intergroup harmony, intergroup equity, even ethnocultural equity than anti-racism. As Canadians look at the world at the dawn of a new millennium, at the ugly events that have recently occurred in Europe, Africa and Asia, and as they consider their own diversity, they have reason to be proud of the harmony they have achieved. Yet, concerns related to cultural and ethnic diversity demand continuing attention. They won't go away even if we choose to ignore them, or worse, pretend that they do not exist.

PROVINCIAL ANTI-RACIST EDUCATION: POLICIES AND PROGRAMS

Anti-racism is a difficult topic to tackle. Yet, to their credit, the record shows that by the mid-1990s, every province, many large school boards and some universities had either drawn up anti-racism policies or had set up new departments, changed their administration or hired consultants to help carry out work to combat racism and promote ethnocultural equity and understanding. Provincial initiatives have been supported by the Council of Ministers of Education Canada (CMEC), which was established in 1967 to provide opportunities for ministries and departments of education to work collectively.[47]

The Government of Newfoundland and Labrador, in 1992, developed a policy statement titled *Multicultural Education Policy: Responding to Societal Needs.*[48] The province recognizes diversity as a unique characteristic of Canadian society and is a partner in the Atlantic Provinces Education Foundation, which developed a framework for essential components of education required for graduation. One of these was citizenship, which requires graduates to demonstrate an understanding of their own and others' cultural heritage and cultural identity, and the contribution of multiculturalism to society.

In 1985, Prince Edward Island, the smallest of the provinces, and the least diverse, developed a provincial multiculturalism policy. In 1989, Nova Scotia established an Office of Race Relations and Cross-Cultural Understanding. The Student Services Division provides leadership in race relations, anti-racist education, cross-curricula education and human rights issues. The Division is responsible for identifying and implementing policy, programs and activities relating to race relations and recognition of cultural differences. In 1990, the province established a Black Learners Advisory Committee to investigate and report on the education of Black Nova Scotians and to make recommendations for improvement in the provision of programs and services for Black learners. There is also specific provision for Mi'kmaq education. A Mi'kmaq studies course was implemented at the Grade 10 level in 1998.

In 1989, the Minister of Education of New Brunswick issued a Ministerial Statement on multicultural and human rights education that reiterated the provinces's aim to provide opportunities for success for every student regardless of gender, race, ethnic origin, language, economic or social status. In a province that officially recognizes the English and French linguistic communities within it, the challenge is to establish and implement policies, programs and practices that will encourage respect for cultural pluralism and encourage school boards through curriculum initiatives, in-service education and co-operative projects with community groups to promote tolerance, understanding and respect for all persons.

In 1997, the province of Quebec addressed the issues of ethno-cultural diversity in its policy proposal, *A School for the Future: Educational Integration and Intercultural Education,* which dealt aggressively with ideas for addressing issues of ethnocultural diversity in Québec. The writers advanced it as representing "a new step towards a more inclusive society ... a plan that involves education in a collective effort of society as a whole." In 1998, a *Plan of Action for Educational Integration and Intercultural Education 1998-2002* was developed to help the educational community carry out the guidelines described in the plan. The province approved additional funds to ensure its success. The goal is zero exclusion, and the Ministry of Education has developed a training unit for school principals to help accommodate religious and cultural diversity in schools.[49]

In 1992, the Ministry of Education and Training in Manitoba published a policy statement titled, *Multicultural Education: A*

Policy for the 1990's and appointed a Multicultural Education Research Collection Reference Officer within the Instruction Research Branch to ensure schools and educators had access to appropriate professional development resources. The Ministry's document, *Renewing Education: New Directions: A Foundation for Excellence,* outlines the province's commitment to a strong anti-bias and inclusive approach in curriculum development and educational renewal. In 1997, the Ministry released a resource on multidisciplinary approaches titled *Curricular Connections: Elements of Integration in the Classroom (1997),* a document which stresses curriculum integration and diversity of perspectives.[50]

Saskatchewan Education has supported cross-cultural and human rights education for over the past fifteen years and has taken several steps to ensure it is achieved. Again, because there is a large Aboriginal community in the province, provincial activity focuses on Aboriginal needs. Policy related to equity is contained in the document *Our Children, Our Communities and Our Future,*[51] which brings together ideas and goals, embodies a collective vision of and commitment to equity, and is a point of reference to be used towards achieving the goal of equity in education. It is significant to note that the definition of equity used in the policy framework is based on the understanding that the concept of equity goes beyond equality of opportunity where everyone is treated the same to fostering a barrier-free system in which individuals benefit equally.

In Alberta, as a result of the comprehensive report of a Committee on Tolerance and Understanding in 1984, the Ministry of Education, now Alberta Learning, adopted guidelines for tolerance and understanding that deal with age, race/ethnicity, religion, sex, functionally disabled and physically impaired, socio-economic status and political beliefs. The committee's report provided direction for many current policies and practices regarding multicultural education. One of these was the publication, in 1994, of *Bibliography of Learning and Teaching Resources to Support Cultural Diversity.*[52]

The British Columbia School Act ensures that all individuals who are of school age will have access to an education program regardless of their gender, race or place of origin. In 1990, the Ministry of Education created a Languages and Multiculturalism

Branch. The Branch took responsibility within the Ministry for supporting curriculum revisions and the review of learning resources as well as providing modest grants to support initiatives designed to address cultural issues in school districts. A statement related to multicultural and anti-racism education was included in each of its new curricula in all subjects and grade levels. In 1994, the Ministry of Education published *Multicultural and Anti-Racism Education: Initiatives in Schools and School Districts.*[53]

Ontario, together with its capital city Toronto, took concrete steps to adopt race relations and anti-racism and multiculturalism policies within the school curriculum and educational hiring practices. In 1980, with the assistance of a committee comprised of community leaders, representatives of school boards and publishers, the Ministry of Education published *Race, Religion and Culture in Ontario School Materials.*[54] This was the first time the word "race" rather than "multiculturalism" had been directly targeted in a Ministry of Education document, and it is interesting to note that neither "race" nor "racism" was defined.

The Ministry's policy on racism was voluntary. Boards and schools did not have to comply. Ministry-funded research in 1990 revealed that of the 124 Ontario school districts polled, thirty-nine had prepared race and ethnocultural equity policies, three had completed drafts of policies and twenty-two had begun a process of policy development.[55] The researchers recommended that anti-racist policies be mandatory, that the Ministry issue policy guidelines and that it direct funds towards programs to promote equity. Within the Ministry of Education, work to assist school boards develop their policies was begun.

Yet, although there had been compelling evidence of racism in society as documented by several reports and despite the years of organizing and pressure by community groups and education organizations, it was a riot erupting along Toronto's main thoroughfare, sparked, in part, by reaction to racial incidents in Los Angeles, which spurred the premier of Ontario to take decisive action. The premier appointed Stephen Lewis, Canada's former ambassador to the United Nations, as his Special Advisor on Race Relations. After a month of intense public consultations, in May 1992, Mr. Lewis submitted a report to the premier with recommendations dealing with issues of key concern to racial minority communities — especially the Black Community.[56]

The Lewis Report recommendations dealt with employment equity, the criminal justice system, education, community development and institutional change. It called for the effective development, implementation and monitoring of anti-racism and employment equity policies in school boards, curriculum revisions, de-streaming, consultation, protection of ESL/FSL programs, and teacher education. In response to the Lewis Report, the provincial government took immediate and comprehensive action. It set up the Ontario Anti-Racism Secretariat in the Ministry of Citizenship under the direct supervision of an Assistant Deputy Minister. It passed The Employment Equity Act and set up the Employment Equity Commission with specific responsibilities. It began race relations training for the police.

The Ministry of Citizenship launched "a comprehensive strategy" on Access to Professions and Trades and provided funding and worked with such varied organizations as the Association of Sri Lankan graduates of Canada, the Society of Vietnamese Canadian Professionals, the Organization of Black Tradesmen and Tradeswomen in Ontario and professional licensing bodies to work out ways to assess skills fairly. For some time, foreign-trained professionals and tradespeople had been reporting that they could not get accredited and therefore could not work at their professions and trades. The Ministry funded projects to help remove systemic barriers — such as licence and language testing, review and appeal processes, supplementary education and training, learning and credential assessment — faced by a wide range of professions and trade groups.

The Ontario Anti-Racism Secretariat took the lead in community outreach and worked with racial minority community groups and school boards to develop programs such as the Change Your Future Program,[57] which was to help reduce the drop-out rate among minority students, and developed a Community Youth Placement program to help provide job-related training. The Secretariat issued a number of publications in co-operation with other community organizations such as the Canadian Jewish Congress, the Chinese Canadian National Council, the Native Canadian Centre and Somali Immigrant Aid. The government also set up a Cabinet Committee on Race Relations that met with community organizations to discuss ways to ensure outcomes in the justice system, stimulate economic renewal and combat hate propaganda.

The work of the Ontario Ministry of Education and Training was far-reaching. An Assistant Deputy Minister of Anti-racism, Access and Equity was appointed in 1993 to oversee the implementation of the Ministry's anti-racism policies. The Deputy Minister was to set up a Ministry-wide policy on anti-racism and ethnocultural equity policy and mandatory in-house training for all Ministry staff and oversee the implementation of *Bill 21: An Act to Amend the Education Act in Respect of Education Authorities and Minister's Powers*, which required school boards to develop anti-racist and ethnocultural equity policies.[58]

The Ministry released two guides on anti-racist and ethnocultural education for use in all elementary and secondary schools: *Changing Perspectives: A Resource Guide for Antiracist and Ethnocultural-Equity Education and Antiracism* and *Ethnocultural Equity in School Boards: Guidelines for Policy Development and Implementation*. It sent out detailed procedures in *Policy Program Memorandum 119* for the development of the anti-racism and ethnocultural equity policies, and Ministry staff provided guidelines and other materials to help school boards develop their policies.[59] The Peel Board of Education, the York Regional School Board and other large school boards with a diverse school population and active community organizations set up comprehensive policies.

Further, the government set up an Implementation Committee for Bill 21 to ensure that boards complied with the legislation. In consultation with community organizations, the government moved to embed the diversity of the province in the newly developed *Common Curriculum* for the elementary school and revised *Circular 14,* the list of approved textbooks for use in the schools.[60]

Post-secondary institutions, particularly faculties of education, were changing, too. The Ministry of Education and Training launched eight initiatives and provided $1.4 million in funding over the next two years to create a more representative teaching force. The government sought to increase the number of teachers from racial and ethnocultural minorities by encouraging minority students to enter the field and by promoting the certification and hiring of racial and ethnocultural minority teachers trained outside Canada. Similarly, the government sought to bring more Aboriginal people into teaching. All Ontario post-secondary institutions were required to set up strong anti-harassment and anti-discrimination policies and adopt practices to make their governing bodies more representative of the population.

The initiatives undertaken by the post-secondary institutions often went well beyond what the government required. Every university and college sought, each in its own way, to address the realities and concerns of the community it served. For example, York University set up an Anti-Discriminatory Advisory Group in 1991, "with the long-term goal of advising the Dean in the development of comprehensive policies and programs to help eliminate the effects of racism and other forms of discrimination in education."[61]

In January 1995, the Royal Commission on Learning released its report with recommendations regarding public education in Ontario. The Report devoted considerable attention to the issue of equity and how to make the system "equitable." As with the Royal Commission on Bilingualism and Biculturalism a quarter of a century earlier, various minority and ethnocultural groups made submissions expressing their concerns. In response the Commission observed:

> The astonishing diversity that characterizes the people of Ontario, including its student body, is a phenomenon we celebrate with pleasure ... schools must welcome students of every background, faith, language, culture, or colour ... We see that ensuring equity for all students is a major Ministry responsibility.[62]

Apart from its recommendations regarding such matters as English as a Second Language programs and fair testing, the Commission made seven recommendations on equity, four of which dealt directly with racism. Specifically, the Commission expressed support for mandatory ethnocultural policies in schools and the review of the curriculum to ensure that it is unbiased and inclusive. Yet, despite the fact that the Commission's recommendations received all-party support in the legislature, none of the seven recommendations on equity has been implemented.

Ontario, once a leader in the development of policies and programs to combat racism and foster multiculturalism in all aspects of education, including staffing, hiring and promotion, no longer has the departments and staff to carry out the work. With the in-coming government in 1995, came sweeping changes. The Division of Anti-Racism, Access and Equity in the Ministry of Education and Training was dismantled; the unit on Anti-Racism and Ethnocultural Equity dispersed. Some staff retired; others were reassigned. Although some work continues, these comprehensive provincial policies and programs have largely disappeared to the extreme distress of the educators, school board trustees and parents who had spent the past quarter century pressing for changes that would ensure real equity for all the students. The government also repealed the Employment Equity Act and eliminated the Employment Equity Commission.

As we begin a new century and a new millennium, advocates hope that community and religious organizations, the Ministry of Education and Training, universities, colleges, boards of education, teachers' federations and the politicians will renew the dialogue regarding the place of multicultural and anti-racist education in the educational system of Ontario. There is hope that the educational system in Ontario will be seen to value the diversity of the society it serves, will build on what we have learned from the past, and that a new revitalized phoenix will arise from the ashes of the previous policies.

SCHOOL BOARDS' ANTI-RACIST EDUCATION

Many large school boards established separate anti-racism and multiculturalism policies or combined them into one. In Saskatoon, the Board of Education's Race and Ethnic Relations Policy stated outright "that the board condemn and refuse to tolerate any expression of racial ethnic bias in any form."[63] As with multiculturalism, the Toronto Board of Education, partly due to community pressure and partly in response to several instances of racial conflict in Toronto, was among the earliest to put in place anti-racist education and pursue anti-racist policy vigorously in every aspect of its operations. In 1979, after extensive consultation on its Draft Report, the Board approved the Final Report of its Sub-Committee on Race Relations and committed $1 million over five years to put its recommendations into effect. The Board's stated purpose was to "make sure that everyone in the system — students, their parents, staff, and trustees — understand clearly that we condemn any expression of racial bias and that we will use the authority we have to eliminate it."[64]

The Toronto Board report dealt with every sector of the educational system. As a result, the Board put structures in place to eliminate biased material from the curriculum and to incorporate material that reflected Toronto's diverse population, process assessment and placement and handle racially biased incidents in schools. The Board provided in-service training to promote system sensitivity, fair employment and promotion practices and its consultants on multiculturalism, race relations and equal opportunity worked with schools to put the report into practice. The Board also issued a number of support documents such as *Teaching Controversial Issues in the Curriculum* and *Handling Racial Incidents.*[65] In its *Fact Sheet on Race Relations,* the Board defined for its staff, students and the general public in very simple terms its position on racism:

> Racism is unjust behaviour shown against people simply because of their ethnic background, colour, religion or race. Racism can take on a variety of forms: racist jokes, name-calling, stereotyping, insults, bias in curriculum materials, discourteous and unfair treatment, the denial of equal employment opportunities and even physical violence. Racism is everyone's issue and everyone's responsibility to eradicate.[66]

Most telling, however, was the uncompromising statement, approved unanimously by the Board: "The Toronto Board of Education condemns and will not tolerate any expressions of racial bias in any form by its trustees, administration, staff or students." The Board's policy was, at that time, the most comprehensive in Canada.

Although the Board did issue reports on its progress in putting its policies into effect, it did not gather data that would permit it to analyze whether its goal for a change in attitudes was being met. Notwithstanding, students and staff did report changes for the better in the ambience in schools and greater diversity reflected in teaching materials. Board research also found that more teachers from racial minorities were being hired.

The newly amalgamated Toronto District School Board continues to work to set up policies that will accommodate the myriad concerns of its ethnocultural groups as well as those related to gender and sexual orientation. In 1998, the new Board set up a Task Group for Anti-racism and Ethnocultural Equity, which drew up a draft policy Anti-racism and Equity for All[67] for public comment and debate. In May 1999, twenty years after the original report on race relations, the Board approved the revised policy and the development of a foundation statement on equity in education. It is evident that the Board is seeking to find a meeting place which will promote equity among all its client groups; to find the place where, as George Dei and others put it, race, class, gender and anti-racism intersect.[68] It is important, Dei points out, that the social categories of race, class, gender and sexuality are not seen as competing for primacy. Classism, sexism and homophobia do not disappear because race becomes the central focus.

The Board's Equity Studies Centre and its Equal Opportunity Office continue to assist and support the system in promoting a system free of bias and in the hiring of an increasing number of racial minorities. Once again, in the province of Ontario, it is the school boards and their communities which lead the way in issues of equity in education.

THE ROLE OF TEACHERS' ORGANIZATIONS
AND COMMUNITY GROUPS

As with multicultural education, teachers' organizations in every province, aided by their national counterparts, have supported the work or taken the lead to help their members, boards of education and provincial governments make schools more inclusive. It is also important to note that the involvement of non-profit and community organizations, mayors' committees on race and ethnic relations as well as the considerable debate, editorials and information in the media created a climate that enabled schools to be more pro-active. Educational activities do not take place in a vacuum.

For example, Vancouver's non-profit Alternatives to Racism published a handbook to help enhance the multicultural climate of the school; the Council of Muslim Communities of Canada promotes multicultural and anti-racist education as does B'Nai Brith Canada; Toronto's Urban Alliance on Relations has published studies revealing the pervasiveness of racism; Toronto's Cross Cultural Community Centre published teachers' guides and bibliographies and its staff serve as consultants to school boards; Ontario's Black Educator's Working Group (BEWG) and the Anti-racist and Multicultural Educators' Network in Ontario (AMENO) promote multicultural and anti-racist education.[69] These are but a small sample of the many groups across the country carrying on the work.

Community organizations keep up their efforts but many worry at what they see as a withdrawal of support for equity. And they wonder if the withdrawal means, in effect, a turning away from the idea of "integration"as outlined by the Royal Commission on Bilingualism and Biculturalism and a turning towards "assimilation." A change in direction that will inevitably lead to the exclusion of communities and individuals that cannot physically assimilate.

There is continuing cause for concern but there is also a great deal to applaud. When this century began, who in Canada could imagine a new territory called Nunavut? Who could foresee the Nisga'a land claims settlement, or that those whose first language is

Cantonese or Mandarin would form significant segments of Canada's population? Who could foresee that the Lieutenant Governor of Ontario would be a Black person, or that eighty years after the *Komagata Maru* was turned away a man born in the Punjab would become premier of British Columbia, or that our Governor General would be of Chinese descent? Who could imagine that by the turn of the millennium Canada would become the most diverse country on earth? These are achievements of which all Canadians can be justly proud, yet there is still much work to be done as Canada continues to build an open society in which mutual understanding and respect are honoured, differences are respected and traditions are cherished.[70]

WHERE DO WE GO FROM HERE?

The beginning of a new millennium is a time for review, of introspection, for vision and vigorous action towards workable and unifying solutions. In a *Strategic Evaluation of Multiculturalism Programs,* prepared for the Department of Canadian Heritage, one contributor suggested:

> An emphasis on a culture of equal rights for all Canadians could be developed as the core of a new Canadianness. A patriotism based on the Charter of Rights would be more appealing than anti-racism, because it emphasizes the positive contributions towards justice to be made rather than negative behaviour to be penalized or ostracized ...[71]

This view strives for the "ideal solution," a situation in which everyone is "comfortable." Unfortunately, in the real world, sometimes it requires a certain level of discomfort for real change to occur.

In 1997, George A. MacBride, convener of the Education Committee of the Educational Institute of Scotland, stated, "If there is one theme, one concept, even one single word that characterizes Scottish education today, it is 'inclusiveness.'" To promote this inclusiveness the committee advanced the following policy:

- the equality of worth of all pupils;

- the pursuit of excellence for all pupils;

- the right of all pupils to an education which empowers them as individuals and as members of the communities to which they belong — local, national, European and world;

- a broad and balanced curriculum for young people to the age of sixteen in comprehensive schools;
- differentiation to meet the needs of all learners within a curriculum built on common principles;
- education that is in principle and practice anti-racist and anti-sexist;
- an education service which counters the class inequalities of our society;
- pedagogies that are based on co-operation, formative and diagnostic assessment, active learning, critical thinking, development of skills, knowledge, and attitudes, and the recognition of individual differences within a common curriculum.[72]

It is a model to which we might well give careful attention. As well, there is a growing number of practical aids for educators who wish implement anti-racist education practices.[73]

The evidence shows that the battle to promote equity has been joined in educational institutions across the nation. We must persevere to embed principles of intergroup harmony and intergroup equity in our curriculum, staff development, hiring practices and in every aspect of our educational system. The success and achievement of all our students demand it.

Community and religious organizations, universities and colleges, boards of education, teachers' federations and the people's representatives must continue or rekindle discussion on the place of multicultural and anti-racist education. Such discussion must focus on ways to value our diversity and the means to promote equity for all. There is also an urgent need to document the policies, programs and activities that have helped promote multicultural and anti-racist education across Canada since the report of the Royal Commission on Bilingualism and Biculturalism in 1969, not only to record thirty years of effort and achievement towards equity but also to serve as a basis for future planning and action.

Equity is not a consideration for minority groups alone. Racism affects society as a whole. Multicultural and anti-racist education is a means, not an end. It is a means to bridging the gap between rich and poor, between established communities and emerging ones, between visible minorities and others, between those who know how to get access to the system and make it work for them and those who do not. We need only recall the recent events in Somalia, Bosnia and Kosovo to recognize that only if we respect each other, can we forge harmonious relationships with persons of other cultures and countries.

Some will argue that policies promoting multiculturalism and anti-racism have not transformed education. These policies have, however, made a difference. There is much more to celebrate in our schools and communities than there was thirty years ago when the Commission on Bilingualism and Biculturalism submitted its report. As we watch the rainbow of potential and achievement unfold in our students and as we watch them succeed in meaningful careers, there can be little doubt that, despite its limitations, multicultural and anti-racist education contributes to their achievement; ultimately, this brings many advantages to our society.

The question today is how to promote harmony and equity in the face of cut-backs and budget restraints. The answers may be difficult to find, but there can be no compromise on the principle of equity for all. We have the blueprints; the execution remains.

TEACHER RESOURCES

Margaret Allen et al., *Reflections: Questions for an Anti-Racist Curriculum* (Toronto: Metropolitan Toronto School Board, 1996). Developed with the assistance of the Anti-Racism, Access and Equity Division of the Ontario Ministry of Education and Training, the video and handbook will help teachers from Junior Kindergarten to Grade 9 better understand the need for anti-racism and ethnocultural equity in education. As well, the video and handbook provide suggestions of how to protect racial and ethnocultural minority students against discrimination, suggest ways in which teachers can help every student learn to value and show respect for people from all racial and ethnocultural groups, and suggest ways the teacher can ensure that all students feel that they are part of the school.

Elizabeth Coelho, Bill Costiniuk, and Charis Newton, *Antiracism Education: Getting Started: A Practical Guide for Educators* (Toronto: Ontario Secondary School Teachers' Federation, 1995). This is a particularly useful resource for teachers in secondary and adult education. While it has practical suggestions for implementation, it is the authors' hardhitting analysis of the issues that captures the reader's attention. The authors discuss the curriculum, guidance and counselling services, Aboriginal education and human rights education. They also highlights the meaningful involvement of parents in the school and the education of their children. An extensive bibliography is included.

Louise Derman-Sparks and the Anti-Bias Task Force, *The Anti-Bias Curriculum: Tools for Empowering Young Children* 2nd ed. (Washington, DC: National Association for the Education of Young Children, 1991). This resource is designed for elementary school educators. It includes helpful suggestions for involving parents.

CLASSROOM RESOURCES

Enid Lee, *Letters to Marcia: A Teacher's Guide to Anti-Racist Education* (Toronto: Cross Cultural Communication Centre, 1985). This short paperback, 71 pages and five chapters, is presented in a letter and response format, illustrated with cartoons, diagrams and black and white photographs. It is chock-full of practical activities, definitions, questions, checklists, case studies and situations that dealing with identifying bias.

Enid Lee, Debra Menkart, and Margo Okazawa-Rey, *Beyond Heroes and Holidays: A Practical Guide to K-12 Anti-Racist, Multicultural Education and Staff Development* (Washington, DC: Network of Educators on the Americas, 1998). This guide is highly regarded by practitioners as perhaps the most comprehensive resource available. It presents discussion of the issues as well as practical suggestions and activities for implementation, and deals extensively with early childhood education.

Christine Rogriguez, Sherry Ramathan-Smith, Nancy Schniederwind, and Ellen Davidson, *Open Minds to Equality: A Sourcebook of Learning Activities to Affirm Diversity and Promote Equity,* 2nd ed. (Boston: Allyn and Bacon, 1998). Practitioners describe this resource as "superb" and "the best activity book available." It deals with all the issues including disabilities.

ORGANIZATIONS

The Canadian Teachers' Federation (CTF)
110 Argyle Avenue
Ottawa, ON K2P 1B4
(613) 232-1505
Fax: (613) 232-1886
E-mail: info@etf-sce.ca
www.etf-sce.ca

The Canadian Education Association
8-200, 252 Bloor Street West
Toronto, ON M5S 1V5
(416) 924-7721
Fax: (416) 924-3188
E-mail: cea-ace@acea.ca
www.acea.ca

The Canadian Council for Multicultural and Intercultural Education
124 O'Connor Street, Suite 200
Ottawa, ON K1P 5M9
Telephone: (613) 233-4916
Fax:(613) 233-4735
E-mail: ccmie@videotran.net
www.ccmie.com

The League for Human Rights, B'nai Brith Canada
15 Hove Street
Toronto, ON M3H 4Y8
(416) 633-624 or 1-800-892-264
Fax: (416) 630-2159
E-mail: league@b'naibrith.ca
www.b'naibrith.ca

Urban Alliance on Race Relations
642 King Street West, Suite 100
Toronto, ON M5V 1M7
Telephone: (416) 703-6607
Fax: (416) 703-4415
E-mail: uarr@uarr.org
www.interlog.com/~uarr

The Anti-Racist and Multicultural Educators' Network in Ontario (AMENO)
14 Dundurn Crescent
Toronto, ON M6C 1H6
(416) 653-4719
Fax: (416) 653-9685
E-mail: norahari@sympatico.ca

NOTES

The author is grateful that so many organizations and individuals sought to enhance the quality of life for racial and ethnocultural minorities in this country and acknowledges their vigorous, selfless advocacy of these difficult issues. She also wishes to express appreciation to those who directly assisted her in the preparation of this chapter by providing or verifying information. They include Dr. Karen Mock; Michele Landsberg; Dr. Stan Shapson; Professor Keren Brathwaite; Dr. Inez Elliston; Dr. Mavis Burke; Harold Brathwaite; Dr. Avis Glaze; Jasmin Zine; Myra Novogrodsky; Lloyd McKell; Elizabeth Coelho; Maisie Cheng; the staff of the Reference Library at the Toronto District School Board; Hari Lalla; Sylvia Lee; Diane Sibbett; Aline Petrie; and Michael Wright.

Staff of ministries and departments of education across Canada graciously forwarded copies of policy and resource documents. They include Dr. Shirley McBride; Sharon Adams; Dr. Craig Dotson; Gerald Farthing; Suzanne Dyotte; Kim Branch; Sylvia Parris; Dr. Patrick N. Kakembo; Patrick Balsom; Gloria Chalmers; and Karen Collin. The author is most appreciative of their prompt responses to her requests for documents and information.

1. Norman Sheffe, *Many Cultures, Many Heritages* (Toronto: McGraw-Hill, 1975).

2. Toronto Board of Education, *Readings and Prayers for Use in Toronto Schools* (Toronto: Board of Education, 1985).

3. Carol Agocs, Catherine Burr and Felicity Somerset, *Employment Equity: Co-operative Strategies for Organizational Change* (Toronto: Prentice-Hall, 1992).

4. B. Donahoe, "We Must Find Ways and Means — Together," in *Multiculturalism, Racism and the School System* (Toronto: Canadian Education Association, 1984).

5. Davidson A. Dunton and Jean-Louis Gagnon, co-chairs, *Report of the Royal Commission on Bilingualism and Biculturalism*, Book IV, *The Cultural Contribution of the Other Ethnic Groups* (Ottawa: Queen's Printer, 1969), 3.

6. Carol Tator and Frances Henry, *Multicultural Education: Translating Policy into Practice* (Ottawa: Multiculturalism and Citizenship, Canada, 1991), 35.

7. Karen R. Mock, "Twenty-Five Years of Multiculturalism — Past, Present and Future," *Multiculturalism* 18 (1997), 1-6. Dr. Karen Mock, National Director, League of Human Rights, B'nai Brith, has done extensive research to promote and advocate on behalf of multicultural and anti-racist education.

8. John W. Friesen, "Implications of Ethnicity for Teaching," in Leonard L. Stewin and J. H. McCann, eds., *Contemporary Educational Issues: The Canadian Mosaic* (Toronto: Copp Clark, 1993), 83-96.

9. Toronto Board of Education, "We Are All Immigrants To This Place," paper prepared for the IMTEC/OECD United States Bicentennial Seminar on Managing Change in Education. (Toronto Board of Education, 1976), 155.

10. Keith A. McLeod and Eva Krugly-Smolska, eds., *Multicultural Education: A Place to Start: A Guideline for Classrooms, Schools and Communities*, prepared for the Canadian Association of Second Language Teachers (Quebec: AGMV Marquis, 1997).

11. Sheilagh V. C. Dubois, ed., *Conference on Multiculturalism in Education* (Toronto: Ontario Association for Curriculum Development, 1977), 5.

12. Toronto Board of Education, "We Are All Immigrants to This Place," 54.

13. Ontario Ministry of Education, *Circular P1J1: The Formative Years* (Toronto: Ontario Ministry of Education, 1975), is the provincial curriculum policy for the primary and junior divisions of the public and separate schools of Ontario; Ontario Ministry of Education, *Education in the Primary and Junior Divisions* (Toronto: Ontario Ministry of Education, 1975); Ontario Ministry of Education, *Ontario Schools: Intermediate and Senior Divisions* (Grades 7-12/OACs) (Toronto: Ontario Ministry of Education, 1984).

14. Dr. Mavis Burke later became chairwoman of the Ontario Advisory Council on Race Relations and Multiculturalism and in 1988 became the Special Advisor on Race Relations to the Premier of Ontario, a position she held until 1991.

15. Ontario Ministry of Education, *Multiculturalism in Action: Curriculum Ideas for Teachers* (Toronto: Ontario Ministry of Education, 1977, 1981).

16. Ontario Ministry of Education and Training, *Circular 14 Textbooks* (Toronto: Queen's Printer, 1994).

17. Ouida M. Wright, *International Languages in the Elementary School: The Heritage Languages Program* (Toronto: Trebeel Consultants, 1997).

18. Ontario Ministry of Education, *English as a Second Language/Dialect* (Toronto: Queen's Printer, 1977). This document aroused some controversy and at times hostility among the parents of the students it was meant to benefit. There was considerable debate regarding the use of creoles, dialects and bilingualism as it affects those who speak standard English and either a dialect or creole.

19. Tator and Henry, *Multicultural Education*, 47.

20. Donahoe, "We Must Find Ways and Means," 28-29.

21. Winnipeg School Division No.1, *Multiculturalism* (Winnipeg: Winnipeg School Division No.1, 1988).

22. In Scarborough, for example, the efforts of Dr. Inez Elliston, an indefatigable and highly motivated consultant in multiculturalism provided leadership of similar activities in both multicultural and anti-racist education. Dr. Elliston became a chairperson of the Canadian Council for Multicultural and Intercultural Education and later Outreach Officer in the Division of Anti-Racism, Access and Equity in the Ontario Ministry of Education and Training.

23. Donahoe, "We Must Find Ways and Means," 29-30.

24. E.N. Wright, *Student's Background and its Relationship to Class and Programme in Schools, The Every Student Survey*, Research Department Report #91 (Toronto: Board of Education, 1970).

25. Toronto Board of Education, "The Bias of Culture," Issue Paper of the Work Group on Multicultural Programs (Toronto: Board of Education, 1974); Toronto Board of Education, "We Are All Immigrants To This Place"; and Toronto Board of Education, "Draft Report of the Work Group on Multicultural Programs" (Toronto: Board of Education, 1975).

26. Toronto Board of Education, *Readings and Prayers for Use in Toronto Schools*, 2.

27. George Radwanski, *Ontario Study of the Relevance of Education and the Issue of Dropouts* (Toronto: Ontario Ministry of Education, 1987).

28. The work of Drs. Stan Shapson, John Kehoe and Vincent D'Oyley and their colleagues significantly influenced the methodology of multicultural and anti-racist education. Similarly, Dr. Keith McLeod, one of the founding members of Canadian Council for Multicultural and Intercultural Education and a past president, profoundly influenced research, development and implementation of multicultural programs at the University of Toronto.

29. Stan M. Shapson, Vincent D'Oyley and Anne Lloyd, *Bilingualism and Multiculturalism in Canadian Education* (Vancouver: University of British Columbia Centre for the Study of Curriculum and Instruction, 1982), 77-94.

30. Stan M. Shapson, "Emerging Images for Teacher Preparation," in Vincent D'Oyley ed., *Innovations in Black Education in Canada* (Toronto: Umbrella Press, 1994).

31. Dr. Keith McLeod profoundly influenced research, design and carrying out of multicultural programs at the university.

32. Keren Brathwaite, who vigorously promoted the Transitional Year Program at the University of Toronto, is currently its English Co-ordinator. She was for many years the president of the Organizations of Parents of Black Children, which helped focus attention on the harmful effects of streaming which in turn led to the report of the Consultative Committee on the Education of Black Students in Toronto Schools.

33. Dubois, ed., *Conference on Multiculturalism in Education*, 3-18.

34. Canadian Council for Multicultural and Intercultural Education, *Multicultural and Anti-Racism Program Implementation. National Dialogue, '94: Summary of Proceedings* (Ottawa: Canadian Council for Multicultural and Intercultural Education, 1994). CCMIE also publishes a tri-annual periodical, *Multiculturalism*, now in its twentieth year.

35. Ontario Ministry of Education, *Race, Religion and Culture in Ontario School Materials: Suggestions for Authors and Publishers* (Toronto: Ontario Ministry of Education, 1980).

36. Robin W. Winks , *The Blacks in Canada: A History*, 2nd ed. (Montreal: McGill-Queen's University Press, 1997); Irving Abella and Harold Troper, *None is Too Many* (Toronto: Lester and Orpen Dennys, 1982).

37. Michele Landsberg, "Massive Discrimination Runs Rampant in Canada," *The Toronto Star,* August 2, 1992; Mock, "Twenty-Five Years of Multiculturalism"; Walter Pitman, *Now is Not Too Late* (Toronto: Metropolitan Toronto Council, 1977); Government of Canada, *Equality Now! Report of the Special Committee on Visible Minorities in Canada* (Ottawa: House of Commons, 1984); Rosalie Abella, *Report of the Commission on Equality in Employment* (Ottawa: Government of Canada, 1984).

38. Frances Henry and Effie Ginzberg, *Who Gets the Work? A Test of Racial Discrimination in Employment* (Toronto: Urban Alliance on Race Relations and the Social Planning Council of Metropolitan Toronto, 1985); Vandra L. Masemann and Karen R. Mock, *Access to Government Services by Racial Minorities, Phase I. Final Report,* prepared for the Ontario Race Relations Directorate (Toronto: Masemann and Mock, 1987); Dionne Brand, *No Burden to Carry: Narratives of Black Working Women in Ontario 1920s to 1950s* (Toronto: The Women's Press, 1991).

39. Ontario Anti-Racism Secretariat, *A Guide to Key Anti-Racism Terms and Concepts* (Toronto: Ontario Anti-Racism Secretariat, 1990).

40. Garnet McDiarmid and David Pratt, *Teaching Prejudice: A Content Analysis of Social Studies Textbooks Authorized for Use in Ontario* (Toronto: OISE Press, 1971).

41. Enid Lee, *Letters to Marcia: A Teacher's Guide to Anti-Racist Education* (Toronto: Cross-Cultural Communication Centre, 1985).

42. Ibid., 8.

43. Ouida M. Wright and Nora Allingham, "The Policy and Practice of Anti-Racist Education," *Orbit* 25 (1997), 4-6.

44. George J. Sefa Dei, *Anti-Racism Education: Theory and Practice* (Halifax: Fernwood Books, 1996), 25.

45. John W. Kehoe and Earl Mansfield, Earl, "The Limitations of Multicultural Education and Anti-Racist Education," *Multiculturalism* 15 (1993), 3-5.

46. Dei, *Anti-Racism Education,* 56.

47. In response to *The UNESCO Recommendation Against Discrimination in Education,* Francine Lecoupe prepared a report for the Council of Ministers of Education on the status in Canada, October 1997.

48. Government of Newfoundland and Labrador, *Multicultural Education Policy:Responding to Societal Needs* (St. John's, NFLD: Department of Education, 1992).

49. Quebec Ministry of Education, *A School for the Future: Educational Integration and Intercultural Education — Policy Proposal* (Quebec: Ministry of Education, 1997); Quebec Ministry of Education, *Plan of Action for Educational Integration and Intercultural Education 1998-2002: A New Direction for Success* (Quebec: Ministry of Education, 1998).

50. Government of Manitoba, *Multicultural Education: A Policy for the 1990s* (Winnipeg: Manitoba Education and training, 1992); Government of Manitoba, *Renewing Education: New Directions: A Foundation for Excellence*

(Winnipeg: Manitoba Education and Training, 1995); Government of Manitoba, *Curricular Connections: Elements of Integration in the Classroom* (Winnipeg: Ministry of Education and Training, 1997).

51. Saskatchewan Education et al., *Our Children, Our Communities and Our Future; Equity in Education: A Policy Framework* (Saskatoon: Saskatchewan Education, 1997). This policy framework was jointly produced by the Saskatchewan Teachers' Federation, the Saskatchewan School Trustees Association, the League of Educational Administrators, Directors and Superintendents, the Saskatchewan Human Rights Commission and Saskatchewan Education.

52. Ron Ghitter, *Final Report: Committee on Tolerance and Understanding* (Edmonton: Alberta Ministry of Education, 1984). The members of this committee included educators, business people, human rights and cultural representatives and a physician. The committee rejected stringent enforcement measures, penalties and jail sentences in favour of learning understand and enjoy each others' similarities and differences. See also Elizabeth Crump-Dumesnil and Anita Jenkins, *Bibliography of Learning and Teaching Resources to Support Cultural Diversity* (Edmonton: Alberta Education, 1994). This publication was prepared for Alberta Education and the Multiculturalism Advisory Council.

53. British Columbia Ministry of Education, *Multicultural and Anti-racism Education: Initiatives in Schools and School Districts* (Victoria: British Columbia Ministry of Education, 1994).

54. Ontario Ministry of Education, *Race, Religion and Culture in Ontario School Materials*, 40.

55. Karen R. Mock and Vandra L. Masemann, *Implementing Race and Ethnocultural Equity Policy in Ontario School Boards* (Toronto: Queen's Printer, 1990).

56. Stephen Lewis, *Letter to the Premier: Report on Race Relations in Ontario* (Toronto: Publications Ontario, 1992).

57. The Change Your Future Program, which began in 1991, was designed by the Ontario Anti-Racism Secretariat and the Ministry of Education and Training with the involvement of participating school boards. The program was successful in helping racial minority students achieve and overcome the challenges they faced in the education system through complementary learning experiences, access to job shadowing experiences, part-time and summer employment and career mentoring.

58. Ontario Ministry of Education, *The Lewis Report on Race Relations. Memorandum to School Boards and Minority Language Sections and Directors of Education* (Toronto: Ontario Ministry of Education, 1992); Ontario Parliament, *Bill 21: An Act to Amend the Education Act in Respect of Education Authorities and Minister's Powers* (Toronto: Queen's Printer, 1992).

59. Ontario Ministry of Education and Training, *Changing Perspectives: A Resource Guide for Antiracist and Ethnocultural-Equity Education* (Toronto: Queen's Printer, 1992); Ontario Ministry of Education and Training, *Antiracism and*

Ethnocultural Equity in School Boards: Guidelines for Policy Development and Implementation (Toronto: Ontario Ministry of Education and Training, 1993); Ontario Ministry of Education and Training, Policy/Program Memorandum No. 119 (Toronto: Queen's Printer, 1990).

60. Ontario Ministry of Education and Training, *The Common Curriculum 1-9* (Toronto: Ministry of Education and Training, 1995). This document has since been replaced by *The Ontario Curriculum;* Ontario Ministry of Education and Training, *Circular 14 Textbooks.*

61. Stan M. Shapson, "Emerging Images for Teacher Preparation," in D'Oyley, ed., *Innovations in Black Education in Canada.*

62. Monique Bégin and Gerald Caplan, *For the Love of Learning: Report of the Royal Commission on Learning.* Short Version (Toronto: Queen's Printer, 1994), 43-44.

63. Saskatoon Board of Education, *Race and Ethnic Relations Policy* (Saskatoon: Saskatoon Board of Education, 1983).

64. Toronto Board of Education, *Draft Report of the Sub-Committee on Race Relations* (Toronto: Toronto Board of Education, 1978), preface.

65. Toronto Board of Education, *Teaching Controversial Issues in the Curriculum: Suggestions For Teachers* (Toronto: Toronto Board of Education, 1988), and *Handling Racial Incidents: Information For Staff* (Toronto: Toronto Board of Education, Equal Opportunity Office, 1989).

66. Toronto Board of Education, *Race Relations: Fact Sheet 32: Information for Staff, Parents and the General Public* (Toronto: Toronto Board of Education, 1988).

67. Toronto District School Board, *Anti-Racism and Equity for All* (Toronto: Toronto District School Board, 1998). This policy statement is noteworthy because it sought to address the concerns of race, gender and class in one document and because it engendered public debate at a time when the reorganization of the Board itself was still uncertain.

68. Dei, *Anti-Racism Education,* 58.

69. Councillor Bev Salmon and Dr. Ahmed Ijaz of Toronto were two of the long-time advocates of anti-racism and anti-racist education and provided energetic leadership and support to the last two organizations mentioned.

70. Taken from the citation on the plaque erected in Vancouver to commemorate the seventy-fifth anniversary of the incident with the *Komagata Maru.* In 1920, 352 immigrants (Sikhs, Muslims and Hindus) from India were denied entry into Canada after a two-month wait in Vancouver harbour aboard their ship the *Komagata Maru.*

71. Department of Canadian Heritage, *Strategic Evaluation of Multiculturalism Programs: The Brighton Report* (Ottawa: Department of Canadian Heritage, 1996), 73.

72. George MacBride, "Achieving Inclusiveness in Scottish Education," *Phi Delta Kappan* 78 (1997), 635-639.

73. See Maisy Cheng and Avi Soudack, *Anti-Racist Education: A Literature Review.* Research Report No. 206 (Toronto: Toronto Board of Education, 1994); J. Banks, "Multicultural Education: Development, Dimensions and Challenge," *Phi Delta Kappan* 75 (1993), 22-28; Sandra Parks, "Reducing the Effects of Racism in Schools," *Educational Leadership* 21 (1999), 14-18.

Chapter 3

BLACK EDUCATION IN CANADA
PAST, PRESENT AND FUTURE

Maxine Bramble

THE EDUCATION OF BLACKS IN CANADA is marked by struggles against discrimination in school systems that fail to meet their needs. Historically, most Black students were educated in segregated schools. These schools were legally sanctioned or were unofficially imposed by white communities. In some cases they were chosen by Blacks, who wanted to avoid the discrimination in common or public schools and considered it in their best interest to attend their own schools. Ontario and Nova Scotia, the two provinces with the largest Black populations, passed legislation officially establishing segregated schools in 1859 and 1864, respectively. Both provinces already had segregated schooling so the legislation strengthened separate schooling for Black students and officially excluded them from common schools. While other provinces did not legislate segregated schools, such schools did exist, particularly in communities with a significant Black population. Segregated schools were inferior, ill equipped, underfunded and often staffed by underqualified, incompetent teachers. The level of education provided was limited; in some cases schooling was only available up to Grade 6.[1]

The struggles of Black communities against inequalities in the education system range from an 1811 petition requesting that a school be established in the community of Preston, Nova Scotia, to recent calls by parents in Toronto, Ontario, for Black-focused or African-centred schools. In the last three decades or so, Black parents, community organizations and teachers have put intense pressure on the school system to address the problems that Black students continue to face. These problems, a legacy of discrimination in education, include the streaming of Black students into non-academic programs, teachers' low expectations for and differential disciplining of Black students, and a lack of Black representation in the curriculum as well as in the teaching and administrative staff. These problems result in low academic achievement and high drop-out rates among Black students.[2]

In response to these problems, school boards and ministries of education across the country have conducted many studies and have set up committees to develop policies and make recommendations for change. Over the years, a plethora of recommendations have been made and a number of educational policies geared towards making the education system more equitable have been put in place. In the 1970s and 1980s, school boards across the country introduced multicultural and race relations policies. In the 1990s, some boards introduced policies that shifted towards an anti-racist education. These represent efforts to change the education system. However, while these policies may have brought some gains for Black students, many studies show that the problems persist.[3] For example, Stephen Lewis, in his 1992 report on race relations to then Ontario Premier Bob Rae, found evidence of systemic anti-Black racism. He concluded that "it's as if virtually nothing has changed for visible minority kids in the school system over the last ten years."[4]

The persistence of problems in Black education is due in part to the inadequacy of policies that focus on equality rather than equity. Equality policies are concerned with treating students the same and giving them equal opportunities, while equity policies are concerned with fairness and judge outcomes based on whether they bring about justice. Educational policies that are based on the idea of equal opportunity are not likely to effect change since equality of opportunity does not guarantee equitable outcomes.

BLACK EDUCATION TO THE MID-TWENTIETH CENTURY

The education that Black students received up to the middle of the twentieth century is linked to slavery in Canada[5] and to the ways schools were funded. Blacks were subjected to discrimination by every institution, especially schools.[6] While the experiences of Blacks varied largely because of where they lived and their numbers in the community, most Black students were excluded from common schools and segregated either by law or by custom, bearing the force of law, into separate schools. In Prince Edward Island and New Brunswick, where segregated schools had not been legislated, Black students were sometimes educated with whites, especially in areas where there were only a few Black families. In St. Andrews, New Brunswick, for example, Black students were enrolled with whites, but in St. John, where the Black population was larger, Black students were forced into separate schools. In communities with concentrations of Blacks, however, Black children were excluded from public schools and forced into segregated ones. In some communities, no schools were available to Black students. Where schools were available, Black girls were less likely to be educated than their male counterparts, since racism combined with sexism to deny them a formal education.[7]

Formal education in early nineteenth-century Canada was organized and administered primarily by Christian denominations and received little support from the government. The first schools to provide formal education for Blacks in Canada were set up by charitable religious groups funded by organizations such as the Society for the Propagation of the Gospel and the Associates of the Late Dr. Bray. These religious groups provided most of the early schooling for Blacks in the Maritimes. In Ontario, schools for Blacks also received support from the Associates of the Late Dr. Bray, from the Canada Mission and from other religious groups. Occasionally, such groups received government grants to help them provide education for Blacks. The objective of these church-run private schools "was to not create an integrated society, but a parallel society."[8] Blacks were seen as children of God, in need of spiritual guidance, but not equal to whites. Hence, church-run schools provided only a rudimentary education that focused on proselytizing and on the teaching of Christian values. Churches recruited Black preachers and community leaders as teachers for those early schools. The typical curriculum consisted of basic literacy, scripture and church music, with boys receiving the added benefit of instruction in arithmetic. Boys also received instruction in carpentry, while girls were taught needlework. This type of education "reflected the inherently racist [and sexist] ideas of white society"[9] and was geared towards preparing Black children not only for subordinate roles as adults, but for roles deemed appropriate for men and women.

Towards the middle of the nineteenth century, many provinces began to pass legislation to provide funding for free primary education. Ontario and Nova Scotia introduced this legislation in 1871 and 1865, respectively, but it did not make schools more accessible to Black students. The system of separate schools for Blacks remained largely intact in both provinces because school commissioners and trustees were permitted to create separate schools by race. The funding structure for common schools also perpetuated inferior education for Blacks. Provincial governments and local school districts shared the cost, but the school district had to raise its share through property taxes. Since school district boundaries were often determined on the basis of race, and many Black communities were segregated, Black or predominantly Black communities often lacked the tax base to fund schools or to staff and equip them properly. In some cases, Black communities in both provinces paid taxes to support common schools but Black children were still denied access to them.[10]

Most but not all Black students elsewhere in Canada were also educated apart from their white counterparts. The provincial legislation that permitted the setting up of separate schools gave Black students the right to attend common schools if their district had no Black schools. Black parents struggled to get their children into common schools and took those struggles to the courts. When they won the right to attend common schools, Black students faced discrimination and racism from both teachers and fellow students. In schools where Black students were integrated with white students, they received significantly less instruction time from the teachers and were seated on separate benches.[11]

The curriculum for Black public schools differed little from that for white schools; however, inadequate funding meant that Black students would not receive an education on par with their white counterparts. Schooled in "little Black school-houses"[12] built and maintained by Black community effort and with little government support, Black students were provided with a very basic education. In the Ontario of the 1850s, "separate schools for Negroes lacked competent teachers and attendance was irregular. Some schools met only three months in the year. Most had no library."[13] Many Black communities remained without schools in Nova Scotia; others could offer only limited grades or could open schools for only a few months of the year. This led to high drop-out rates among Black students in that province, most of whom dropped out before high school. Black girls, in particular, often dropped out of school to help support their families in tough economic times.[14] One Black woman noted: "I had to stop school when I got to grade two ... My father died before I was born ... I was the oldest and at age nine I had to work very hard to help support the family."[15] Black Nova Scotians were, for the most part, denied a high-school education because the province did not provide adequate funding for Black high schools, leaving them with few well-trained teachers.[16]

Throughout the nineteenth and early twentieth century, Black women set up a number of private schools for Black students. In addition to their duties as teachers, these women were also the schools' caretakers. Mary Bibb, a qualified teacher, operated a number of schools for Black students in Sandwich, Ontario, though the schools were open to students of all colours. Students paid to attend these schools, but the parents' inability to pay the small fees and the lack of government support led to their closure.[17] Mary Ann Shadd operated a private school in Windsor, Ontario, where she taught ten different classes in geography, history, botany, math, grammar and reading. Students whose parents could afford to pay were expected to do so, while those who could not afford the fees attended the school free of charge.

Although provincial legislation that enforced segregated schools remained on the books until 1954 in Nova Scotia and 1964 in Ontario, separate schools for Blacks all but disappeared by the late nineteenth century.[18] By 1917, most segregated schools in Ontario were closed, but one remained open in Colchester until 1965.[19] In Nova Scotia, segregated schools remained open longer because of residential segregation — in 1960, there were seven formal Black school districts and three exclusively Black schools that remained open. In Alberta, one Black school remained open until the 1960s.[20] Historian Robin Winks attributes the closure of segregated schools to the changing social and political context: "It was no longer good Christianity, good politics, good international affairs, good image-building, good human relations, or even good sense to discriminate openly against Negroes, especially in a nation which so prided itself on moral superiority to the United States."[21] But the closing of segregated schools would not signal an end to discrimination against Black students. Little was done to ensure that the integration of schools would be successful, and Black students continued to experience racism and sexism that frustrated their attempts to get an education.

CONTEMPORARY ISSUES IN BLACK EDUCATION

The history of segregated schools and inferior education would set the stage for contemporary Black education. Beliefs about Blacks' supposed inferiority have remained deeply entrenched, and teachers' attitudes towards Black students and a Eurocentric curriculum have been slow to change. As one Black student notes, "Some teachers right from elementary school give us subtle messages that being Black isn't so good."[22] Black students continue to experience serious problems in school even though many policies that were supposed to have solved those problems have been put in place. Over and over, researchers, community organizations, parents and students have identified key issues that need to be addressed if the promise of equity in education is to be fulfilled:[23]

- the streaming of Black students into non-academic programs
- teacher insensitivity and low expectations
- the lack of Black studies in the curriculum
- the high drop-out rates
- ineffective pedagogical approaches (for example, an over-reliance on lectures)
- the lack of role models and Blacks in teaching and administration
- the lack of race relations policies

For the last three decades, Black parents have pressured governments and school boards to deal with the systemic problems that plague Black students. In Nova Scotia, the 1970s marked a period of increased Black resistance against unequal education. Several class action lawsuits were filed against Nova Scotia school boards on the grounds of unequal school facilities; continuing and unchecked name calling and racist graffiti by white students; inappropriate behaviour by senior administrators; routine use of the RCMP to escort Black students from school grounds; and a pattern of suspensions for arbitrary reasons.[24] In Ontario, Black Caribbean parents and students have fought against many of the same problems. Many Caribbean parents came to Canada in search of better opportunities for themselves and for their children and saw education as the means to that end. When their children did not succeed in school, parents looked for answers. They refused to accept the schools' explanation that their children's low achievement stemmed from "adjustment difficulties" and "cultural differences." Instead, parents attributed the problems to systemic racism in the education system. Parents fought for change through community organizations and committees that often worked in collaboration with school boards and government officials. Black parents in the former Metropolitan Toronto took part in a government-community working group that drew up a plan to address the urgent needs of the Black community.[25] Black parents across Ontario made many submissions to commissions and task forces charged with studying the problems Black students face in school.

The problems Black students continue to face contribute to

their alienation and disengagement from school and ultimately to their high drop-out rates.[26] A Toronto Board study showed that 42 percent of Black students who were in Grade 9 in 1987 had dropped out by 1992. Studies from other school boards show that the problem is not unique to the Toronto Board but is common in other communities in Ontario.[27] In Nova Scotia, more than half of Black students drop-out of school by age seventeen, with 76 percent of them citing boredom or the inability to relate to school as their reasons for dropping out.[28] The situation is not much different in other provinces where racism is also widespread. A Manitoba study notes that of the more than 200 Black students interviewed, 81 percent reported experiencing racism as a major barrier impeding the integration of Blacks into the Winnipeg school system. The study concludes that racism is one of the major reasons behind the disproportionate dismissal and suspension of Black students.[29]

Community groups have emerged throughout Canada specifically to address the problems faced by Black students. Those groups are more common, however, in cities with a high concentration of Blacks. Their activities, which include tutoring programs, achievement awards and cultural programs, are aimed at countering the effects of systemic racism and filling the gaps in the curriculum for knowledge on Black history and culture. Through programs such as the Black Children's Cultural Camp in Saskatchewan and the Cultural Awareness Youth Group in Nova Scotia, Black children learn about their heritage. The Quebec Association of Haitian Teachers and the Ontario chapter of the Canadian Association of Black Educators help Black students through tutoring programs and remedial courses. In Nova Scotia, the Black Educators Association continues to work "to improve the quality of education for Blacks" and offers a summer math camp for Black students in Grades 7 and 8.

CONTEMPORARY RESPONSES TO CONTEMPORARY PROBLEMS

The first major institutional change in the education system was the introduction of multicultural education in the 1970s and 1980s. The change came about because of the Canadian government's adoption of multiculturalism as a national policy in 1971, and the subsequent passing of the federal *Multiculturalism Act* of 1988. A natural offshoot of official multiculturalism, multicultural education adopted the liberal underpinnings of the federal policy. At the heart of the policy were the beliefs that prejudice and discrimination stem from ignorance about others and that knowledge about one's own culture will lead to the acceptance of other cultures. School boards set up programs to teach tolerance and acceptance through "heritage studies," reading "multicultural literature," participating in "multicultural days" and going on field trips to "cultural communities."[30] These programs focused on celebrating cultural differences, especially differences in the food, costume and dress of non-white people. School boards across the country drew on federal funding to provide heritage language classes for students whose first language was neither English nor French, Canada's two official languages. Heritage language classes recognized the strong link between language and identity and classes encouraged students to take pride in their heritage.

The implementation of multicultural education has varied across Canada, depending on the ethnic and cultural make up of the province or local school board. Some programs sought to preserve language and culture while others focused on promoting good relations among students from different racial groups. In Alberta, Saskatchewan and Manitoba, multicultural education has meant offering instruction in several languages.[31] Given this orientation, it is not surprising that a 1987 study of multicultural education in Saskatchewan concluded that no one knew exactly what multicultural education meant and that it was unclear whether the schools or the public saw a "genuine and legitimate" need for it. In so far as Saskatchewan schools were promoting multiculturalism, that promotion was more likely to be through "passive displays than through active instruction."[32] In 1990, Quebec, a province that does not endorse multiculturalism, issued a policy on immigration and integration that espouses goals similar to those outlined in the federal policy. In place of multicultural education, however, the Quebec government pursued "intercultural education," a policy aimed at "remedial education for cultural communities."[33] Nova Scotia also concentrated on intercultural education, but unlike

Quebec, promoted "ethno-cultural awareness, equality of opportunity and equality of access, teacher sensitivity, curriculum reform, and the development of support services, program materials and resources."[34]

The varied ways in which multicultural education is understood and practised in school boards across Canada has not brought about the changes that Black parents seek. Parents argue that multicultural education celebrates cultural difference while at the same time perpetuating racist stereotypes. Their dissatisfaction with the inadequacy of such programs and with the programs' focus on very limited aspects of culture has led them to lobby for policies that would expressly acknowledge race as a crucial factor in education and racism as a systemic problem that prevents Black students from realizing their potential.

School boards in Ontario have responded to parents' criticism of multicultural education and their demands for change by implementing race relations policies and programs. The race relations approach recognizes race as a factor in student-student and student-teacher interactions, but limits the understanding of race to one of differences in colour and sees racism as attitudinal prejudices that result from ignorance. Ontario school boards' race relations programs include celebrating Black history month, inviting Black role models into schools and encouraging interactions between students in racially mixed groups.[35] In British Columbia, the Vancouver School Board put a race relations policy in place "to improve race relations and to increase cultural understanding in Vancouver schools." Schools in the Vancouver board are required to set up programs and use materials that portray racial/ethnic groups in a positive light.[36] Much like multicultural education, a race relations approach to Black education fails to address racism adequately and so maintains the status quo.

Little has changed for Black students, leading Black teachers and scholars to propose anti-racism education as a possible solution. The premise of anti-racism education is that racism is a structural problem and must be dealt with at that level. In other words, anti-racism locates racism at the heart of our social structures. One proponent of anti-racism education describes it as "an action-oriented strategy for institutional, systemic change to address racism and the interlocking systems of social oppression."[37] Anti-racism education looks at the ways in which racism is related to sexism, homophobia, classism and other forms of oppression, and devises plans to deal with them. This approach emphasizes the importance of centring students' experiences in the education process. Approaches to anti-racism education include anti-harassment and employment equity policies for schools, providing students with opportunities to look critically at their experiences at school and in the larger society, and promoting strong school-community relations. In theory, anti-racism education is radically different from either multicultural education or a race relations approach to education because it emphasizes equity as opposed to equality and aims to change the status quo.

Anti-racism education does not, however, receive the support given to multicultural education or race relations.[38] Ontario remains the only province to have attempted to put anti-racism education into practice. In 1992, the NDP government amended the *Education Act* to require school boards to develop anti-racism and ethnocultural equity policies, appointed an assistant deputy minister to oversee implementation of the new requirement and set up an anti-racism secretariat. Those initiatives quickly came to an end, however, with the election of a Conservative government in 1995. Within months of its election, the government dismantled the anti-racism secretariat and rescinded employment equity legislation.

Anti-racism education appears to have been supported by the Nova Scotian government. The government appointed the Advisory Group on Race Relations in 1991 in response to the Halifax "mini-riot," in which Blacks demonstrated their frustrations with systemic racism. The government began to implement some of the group's recommendations (a number of which deal with anti-racism education and employment equity), and appointed an African Nova Scotian as its education consultant for anti-racism policy development and Black education. That individual advises school boards on how to develop an anti-racism policy and trains them in anti-racism education. However, there is resistance to anti-racism education as several school boards are reported to be developing race relations policies, not anti-racism policies.[39]

Along with calling for anti-racism education, some Black parents, teachers and community groups in Ontario are calling for the creation of African-centred or Black-focused schools as an alternative to the mainstream school system.[40] Such schools would seek to "promote academic and social achievement by dealing with the educational issues contributing to the alienation, isolation and disengagement of students of African descent."[41] The curriculum for those schools would be similar to that of the public school system, but would focus on the knowledge, culture and history of people of African heritage. The use of African sayings, proverbs and traditional songs, and the inclusion of parents and community elders as teachers are envisioned as features of African-centred or Black-focused schools. Proponents of these schools do not see them as exclusively for Black students, nor do they think that only Black teachers and administrators should staff such schools. Rather, they see these schools as places that could foster Black students' success by "centering and sustaining Black and African-Canadian cultures in the school system."[42]

The need for alternatives to the regular school system and the potential of African-centred or Black-focused schools for fostering Black students' achievement gained recognition from the Royal Commission on Learning and the Four-Level Working Group on Metropolitan Toronto Black Community Concerns. The Commission recommended that demonstration schools be set up in areas with large numbers of Black students, and the Working Group recommended that one Black junior high school be set up in each of the six Metropolitan Toronto Municipalities as a five-year pilot project. These recommendations were not carried out, but in 1994 the former Toronto Board of Education[43] did set up Nighana, a Black Focus School, in collaboration with members of the Black community. Nighana closed for two years but re-opened in 1998 as a program at Eastdale Collegiate in Toronto. The Nighana program provides an Afrocentric curriculum and learning environment to African Canadian students ages fourteen to twenty who are experiencing difficulty in school. The program is geared towards reintegrating those students back into the regular school system. In January 2000, the Nighana program had an enrollment of about fifty students, most of whom are male.

THE CHALLENGES AND PROMISES IN THE FUTURE

Heading into the twenty-first century, the struggle for equitable education for Black students faces challenges of decreased funding for education, the implementation of standardized testing and curriculum and the dismantling of equity policies and programs. These circumstances threaten attempts to establish inclusive curriculum, since such curriculum initiatives often require funds to purchase new materials and to conduct staff development training. At the structural and fiscal level, advocates of equity in education face the challenge of building coalitions with other social justice groups to develop effective strategies. The development of such strategies would require a rethinking of current approaches to changing Black education, since many of the strategies used to address the problems Black students face in schools are not effective.

One reason for the ineffectiveness of these strategies is the way they identify and think about Blacks in general and Black students in particular. The tendency to think about race as a fixed category that is based on physical characteristics supports the view of Blacks as a homogenous racial group. This way of thinking marks people who look a particular way as Black and excludes others who do not bear certain identifying features. Such thinking puts all Blacks into one group and fails to take into consideration differences such as gender, class and sexual orientation. Grouping Black students into one undifferentiated category overlooks the multiple realities and experiences of those who fall under the category "Black" and erases the differences between them. For example, seeing Black students as a uniform group does not explain why Black girls tend to do better academically than Black boys and does not address the specific needs of Black boys and girls.[44]

The oversimplified use of the label Black overlooks the ambivalence that Black people often experience in relation to these terms and overlooks the limitations of labels. For example, a young Black woman notes:

> At one stage I thought of myself as a black person but that limits me because as a black person there are things I am supposed to be. So I had to shed that. I am not just black. I am also a woman,

and that limits me as well ... So "bust" being black and "bust" being a woman. That is a form of oppression because you are limited in those two little notches.[45]

Identification with the term "Black" is historically linked to the Black Power Movement that emerged in the United States in the 1950s and its championing of Black pride. Blacks in the United States and the Caribbean reclaimed the label "Black" and used it as a means of collective empowerment to resist centuries of racism. However, as the young woman points out, her identification as Black is at once empowering and limiting because of the multiple and contradictory meanings of being Black. She is ambivalent about the labels used to define her and the limitations such labels place on her. Current educational theory and future approaches to Black education need to deal with such tensions and contradictions.

The need to challenge undifferentiated views of Black students becomes even more critical in the current global context. The increased movement of people across borders and the displacement of people due to ethnic conflict around the world make Canada's population more diverse than ever. Schools, particularly those in urban areas, are reflecting this diversity in their student populations and the Black student population is no exception. Black students, more so than ever before, come from diverse backgrounds and experiences. Hence, the needs of those who are new immigrants are likely to be different from those who were born in Canada or whose ancestors have been here for generations. This is a crucial distinction that needs to be made when planning strategies for educational change.

Challenging a uniform view of Black students goes hand in hand with challenging fixed views of Black history and culture, especially in light of the need for inclusive curriculum. The tendency to see Black culture as a set of inherited attributes, customs and practices and Black history as an account of the contributions and achievements of Black people dominates thinking about Black inclusion in the curriculum. The inclusion of this knowledge is often framed in terms of presenting positive images to Black students and is based in the assumption that such images will give Black students a sense of pride in who they are. The expected outcome is that Black students' academic achievement will increase. While the need for positive images to counter the negative images of Blacks is important, it is equally important to provide room for engaging with what one theorist refers to as "difficult knowledge."[46] In this context, difficult knowledge refers to aspects of Black culture and history that may be hard to deal with. Engaging with difficult knowledge would mean, for example, confronting issues such as homophobia, sexism, classism and shadeism that often are perpetuated by Black people.

Discussion of role models is also crucial to debates on the future of Black education. Black parents and students continue to demand that there be greater numbers of Black role models in the school system, and schools often invite successful Black professionals to talk to students. The demand for role models is based on the idea of sameness, where race, read Blackness, is the common denominator. However, this demand often ignores the complex and contradictory positions the models embody.[47] For example, a successful Black professional embodies contradiction in that she or he reflects both what is possible and what is not possible for students. The fact that this person has achieved success reinforces the belief that Canadian society is meritocractic (that is, that promotion is always based on merit, therefore employment equity policies are unnecessary, if not unfair) and belies the racism deeply embedded in society. The use of role models also overlooks differences, especially class differences, between the models themselves and the students they are supposed to be models for; role models are often limited to successful or professional people. Although schools need to include diversity among their staff and students need to see teaching and administrative staff who look like them and who are likely to understand their perspectives, Black teachers and administrators are not automatically role models. The same is true for Black professionals. Students need a range of people from whom to choose their role models.[48] They may not necessarily see the professionals offered by their schools as role models.

For those who advocate changes that would provide equitable education for all students and those who are directly involved in educating Black students, the future of Black education presents many challenges but holds many promises. Cameron McCarthy's idea of non-synchrony can go a long way towards meeting the challenges and realizing the promises. Non-synchrony refers to the ways that class, race, gender and other factors produce social difference, mark people as different and affect how people experience racism in very different ways. Approaching Black education in ways that understand race as non-synchronous means being vigilant in addressing all forms of oppression and dealing with the complexity of the experiences of Black students. Like all students, Black students experience school differently, they compete with each other and receive different rewards, punishments and evaluations.[49] Black education must deal with the tensions that result from such different experiences. A non-synchronous view allows educators to see how race and racism change. Race is a fluid concept that is perpetually changing in response to challenges from political movements and others who dispute its premises.[50] Over the years, the meaning of "race" has changed from a supposedly scientific basis in biology to one based on culture, ethnicity and even language. Similarly, racism and the ways it manifests itself, changes constantly. Struggles for an equitable education for Black students must challenge racism's many forms, even as they change.

TEACHER RESOURCES

Ontario Ministry of Education, *Black Studies: A Resource Guide for Teachers Intermediate Division* (Toronto: Ontario Ministry of Education, 1983). This book is a valuable resource for teachers who are interested in integrating the Black Canadian experience in their classroom. It serves as a practical guide to teachers and students and provides a comprehensive list of resources and a framework for using them. The book highlights significant historical events in the development of Black Canadian communities and speaks about issues relating to the experiences of Black Canadians.

CLASSROOM RESOURCES

Almeta Speaks, *Hymn to Freedom* (Toronto: Almeta Speaks Productions Inc., 1994). In this four-part video, the history of the African-Canadian community is explored through the experiences and lives of four Canadian Black families whose survival depended on a unique set of skills. In Quebec, the Packwood family is part of the history of Lower Canadian slavery from the first documented sale of Oliver Le Jeune in 1626. In Nova Scotia, the Jones family is representative of the immigration that contributed to the formation of the province In Ontario, Reta Duvall-Cummings is the matriarch of a family that arrived via the Underground Railway. In British Columbia, the Collins family are descendants of the family who influenced the province to join Canada rather than the United States.

Bill Cosby and Willie Ruff, *Bill Cosby on Prejudice* (Santa Monica, CA: Pyramid Films, 1972). In a satiric diatribe in which a super bigot expresses hatred against all minority groups, actor Bill Cosby exposes the prejudices that are experienced by all.

Gurinder Chada, *I'm British But* (Toronto: Mongrel Media, 1990). Using Bhangra and Bangla music and the testimonies of young British Asians, this video uncovers a defiant popular culture that is part Asian, part British. An excellent tool for exploring fixed views of culture and identity.

Isaac Julien, *The Darker Side of Black* (London: BBC Television, 1994). Moving between New York City, New York; Kingston, Jamaica; and London, England, this film investigates the social and political influences of rap and reggae music, its proponents, fans, detractors and critics and explores the rough edges of the music: ritualized machismo, misogyny, homophobia and gun glorification, which increasingly dominate the images of Black popular culture. This film is and excellent tool to stimulate discussion about questions of Blackness and Black culture.

National Film Board of Canada, *Speak It! From the Heart of Black Nova Scotia* (Montreal: National Film Board, 1992). In the environment of their predominantly white high school, a group of Black students face daily reminders of the presence of racism, ranging from abuse (racist graffiti on washroom walls), to exclusion (the seemingly "innocent" omission of Black history from textbooks). The students set up the Cultural Awareness Youth Group, a vehicle for building pride and self-esteem through educational and cultural programs. With help from mentors, they discover the richness of their heritage and learn some of the ways they can begin to effect change.

NOTES

I would like to thank Gordon Pon and Carl James for their help in reading drafts of this paper and for offering suggestions.

1. Black Learners Advisory Committee, *BLAC Report on Education: Redressing Inequity — Empowering Black Learners* (Halifax, NS: Black Learners Advisory Committee, 1994); Robin Winks, *The Blacks in Canada: A History* (Montreal: McGill-Queen's University Press, 1971).

2. BLAC, *BLAC Report on Education*; George Dei, Josephine Mazzuca, Elizabeth McIsaac, and Jasmine Zine, *Reconstructing "Drop-Out"* (Toronto: University of Toronto Press, 1997); Keren Brathwaite and Carl James, eds, *Educating African Canadians* (Toronto: James Lorimer and Co., 1996); Toronto Board of Education, *Educating Black Students in Toronto Schools: Final Report of the Consultative Committee* (Toronto: Toronto Board of Education, 1988).

3. BLAC, *BLAC Report on Education*; Dei, Mazzuca, McIsaac, and Zine, *Reconstructing "Drop-Out"*; Brathwaite and James, eds, *Educating African Canadians;* Toronto Board of Education, *Educating Black Students in Toronto Schools.*

4. See Stephen Lewis, *A Report on Race Relations in Ontario.* The report, written as a letter to the Premier, is dated June 9, 1992. After what was described in the press and on the news as a "race riot" in downtown Toronto following a racist court decision in Los Angeles, California, Premier Bob Rae appointed Stephen Lewis as his special advisor on race relations. The premier asked Lewis to report within one month on the state of race relations in Ontario.

5. Although slavery was never as important an economic institution in Canada nor as widespread here as it was in the United States, enslaved Blacks began to arrive in New France as early as 1628, and slavery continued under British rule. Indeed, British Empire Loyalists fleeing the rebellious former colonies to the south brought 2,000 slaves with them. Abolition would not come to Canada until 1834, when the British government abolished slavery throughout the Empire. Blacks who came to Canada as freedmen were subject to discrimination like their enslaved counterparts. See Winks, *The Blacks in Canada.*

6. Historian James Walker notes: "The most important manifestation of colour prejudice in Canadian history is in education." See James Walker, *A History of Blacks in Canada* (Hull, QC: Canadian Government Publishing Centre, 1980), 107.

7. Winks, *The Blacks in Canada*; Bernice Moreau, "Black Nova Scotian Women's Educational Experience: A Study in Race, Gender and Class Relations" (PhD diss., Ontario Institute for Studies in Education, 1996).

8. Bridglal Pachai, *Beneath the Clouds of the Promised Land* (Halifax, NS: Black Educators, 1987), 53.

9. Walker, *A History of Blacks in Canada*, 114.

10. BLAC, *BLAC Report on Education;* Walker, *A History of Blacks in Canada;* Winks, *The Blacks in Canada.*

11. Daniel Hill, *The Freedom-Seekers: Blacks in Early Canada* (Agincourt: The Book Society of Canada Limited, 1981); BLAC, BLAC Report on Education.

12. Moreau, "Black Nova Scotian Women's Educational Experience."

13. Winks, *The Blacks in Canada,* 371.

14. Moreau argues that "it was the norm in the early 1900s when a Black family was experiencing acute financial difficulties to send the girls, at very young ages, into service because domestic type work was always available for them They rarely had a choice in the matter, since it was the duty of every member to help the family stay alive." See Moreau, "Black Nova Scotian Women's Educational Experience," 136.

15. Ibid, 135.

16. BLAC, *BLAC Report on Education.*

17. Afua Cooper, "Black Women and Work in Nineteenth-Century Canada West: Black Woman Teacher Mary Bibb," in Peggy Bristow, Dionne Brand, Linda Carty, Afua Cooper, Sylvia Hamilton, and Adrienne Shadd, *Essays in African Canadian Women's History* (Toronto: University of Toronto Press, 1994).

18. BLAC, *BLAC Report on Education;* Winks, *The Blacks in Canada.*

19. Paul Axelrod, *The Promise of Schooling: Education in Canada 1800-1914* (Toronto: University of Toronto Press, 1997).

20. BLAC, *BLAC Report on Education;* Walker, *A History of Blacks in Canada;* Winks, *The Blacks in Canada.*

21. Winks, *The Blacks in Canada,* 381.

22. Doug Little, "The Meaning of Yonge Street: What Do the Kids Say?" *Our Schools/Our Selves* 4 (1992).

23. Keren Brathwaite, "The Black Student and the School: A Canadian Dilemma," in Simeon Chilungu and Sada Niang eds, *African Continuities* (Toronto: Terebi, 1989); Four-Level Working Group on Meropolitan Toronto Black Community Concerns, *Towards a New Beginning: The Report and Action Plan of the Four-level Government/African Canadian Community Working Group* (Toronto: Government of Ontario, 1992); BLAC, *BLAC Report on Education.*

24. BLAC, *BLAC Report on Education,* 34-35.

25. The Working Group, *Towards a New Beginning,* vi.

26. BLAC, *BLAC Report on Education;* Dei et al, *Reconstructing "Drop-out";* Brathwaite and James, *Educating African Canadians;* Henry Codjoe, "Black Students and School Success" (PhD diss., University of Alberta, 1997).

27. *Royal Commission on Learning, For the Love of Learning* (Toronto: Queen's Printer, 1994), 93.

28. BLAC, *BLAC Report on Education.*

29. Barbara Thompson and Jean-Joseph Isme, *Needs Assessment of Newcomer Black Youths and Families,* (Winnipeg: Black Youth Helpline, 1993).

30. Carl James and Sandra Schecter, "Mainstreaming and Marginalization: Two National Strategies in the Circumscription of Difference," *Curriculum Studies* (forthcoming).

31. Andrew McAndrew, "Ethnicity, Multiculturalism, and Multicultural Education in Canada," in Ratna Ghosh and Douglas Ray, eds, *Social Change and Education in Canada* (Toronto: Harcourt Brace and Company, 1995).

32. John Lingard, "The Perception and Implementation of Multicultural Education: A Saskatchewan Study," in Sonia Morris, ed, *Multicultural and Intercultural Education: Building Canada* (Calgary: Detselig Enterprises, 1989), 122.

33. Ratna Ghosh, *Redefining Multicultural Education* (Toronto: Harcourt Brace AND Company, 1996), 23.

34. McLeod, cited in McAndrew, "Ethnicity, Multiculturalism, and Multicultural Education in Canada," 172.

35. Carl James, "Multiculturalism, Diversity and Education in the Canadian Context: The Search for an Inclusive Pedagogy," in C Grant and J. Lei, eds., *The Ideals and Realities of Multicultural Education in Global Contexts* (Mahwah, NJ: Lawrence Erbaum Associates Inc, 1999).

36. Donald Fischer and Frank Echols, *Evaluation Report on the Vancouver School Board's Race Relations Policy* (Vancouver: Vancouver School Board, 1989).

37. George Dei, *Anti-Racism Education: Theory and Practice* (Halifax: Fernwood Books, 1996), 25.

38. James, "Multiculturalism, Diversity and Education in the Canadian Context."

39. Agnes Calliste, "Anti-Racist Educational Initiatives in Nova Scotia," *Orbit* 25 (1994), 49.

40. Brathwaite and James, *Educating African Canadians*; Dei, *Anti-Racism Education*.

41. Dei, *Anti-Racism Education*, 107.

42. Ibid, 113.

43. In 1998, the Conservative government forced the amalgamation of six municipalities making up Metropolitan Toronto. The new Toronto District School Board comprises the former six local boards of education.

44. Rinaldo Walcott, "Beyond Sameness: Thinking through Black Heterogeneity," in Brathwaite and James, eds, *Educating African Canadians*. Indeed, the invisibility of Black girls in Canadian research and educational theory is a challenge that needs to be taken up.

45. Daniel Yon, "The Discursive Space of Schooling: On the Theories of Power and Empowerment in Multiculturalism and Anti-Racism," in Angela Cheater, ed, *The Anthropology of Power* (New York: Routledge, 1999), 38.

46. Deborah Britzman, "Beyond Role Models: Gender and Multicultural Education," in Sari Biklen and Diane Pollard, eds, *Gender and Education: Ninety-Second Yearbook of the National Society for the Study of Education* (Chicago: University of Chicago Press, 1993).

47. Ibid.

48. Carl James, "'You're Doing It For the Students': The Question of Role Modelling," in Carl James, ed, *Experiencing Difference* (Halifax: Fernwood Books, in press).

49. Cameron McCarthy, *Race and Curriculum* (New York: Falmer Press, 1990).

50. David Goldberg, *Racist Culture* (Cambridge: Blackwell Press, 1990).

Chapter 4

EDUCATING FOR CITIZENSHIP
IN CANADA
NEW MEANINGS IN A CHANGING WORLD

Mark Evans and Ian Hundey

EDUCATING FOR CITIZENSHIP continues to be a central goal of public education in Canada and other parts of the world. The citizenry and the policy-makers alike hope that public education will prepare young people for effective citizenship and, in doing so, strengthen the development of healthy civil societies. Yet how young people learn about citizenship for truly democratic settings remains a significant challenge.

Interest in educating for citizenship has escalated in recent years. This has been spurred by the growing concerns about the general lack of civic literacy among youth, changing realities of the late twentieth century and newly emerging ideas about citizenship. National studies in Australia and England, formal discussions in the "transitional democracies" of Central and Eastern Europe and a range of curriculum projects are being undertaken throughout the world as teachers, policy-makers and researchers attempt to understand and assess the complex processes by which young people learn about democratic citizenship.[1]

IDEAS ABOUT CITIZENSHIP

Citizenship in today's world usually encompasses three important elements: (1) a sense of "membership" or "identity" with some wider community, such as one's local community or one's nation; (2) a set of "rights" and "freedoms," such as freedom of thought or the right to vote; and (3) a corresponding set of "obligations,"' such as an obligation to respect the rights of others or a duty to obey the law.[2] In other words citizenship is the interplay of "legal, cultural, social, and political elements, and provides citizens with defined rights and obligations, a sense of identity, and social bonds."[3] Our understanding of citizenship continues to evolve and take on new meanings, depending on the contexts and circumstances in which we live, from the local to the global. And it continues to be "essentially contested."

In Canada, our understanding of citizenship is usually traced back to the traditions of Greece and Rome. Fundamental aspects of citizenship evolved from the classical works of Plato and Aristotle and the development of the "Twelve Tables" of Roman law. Early notions of citizenship emphasized various attributes and characteristics: the value of being a participating member in one's community, albeit in a limited and exclusive form; requisite civic virtues that contributed to the public good; and an individual's responsibility to the governance and operation of one's community (for example, military service and local decision-making). The emergence of laws explicitly delineated rights and responsibilities of citizenship.[4]

Liberal perspectives of citizenship began to take shape following the Middle Ages. The ideas of the Enlightenment, the democratic revolutions in France and America and the Industrial Revolution generated a shift in thought that emphasized science and reason and challenged traditional forms of authority. Political thinkers like Hobbes, Locke and Rousseau proposed new political theories and practices. They debated ideas about liberty, social fraternity, equality and democracy that raised many questions about "the possibility, desirability and justice of consolidating and broadening the realities of citizenship."[5]

Notions of citizenship underwent another fundamental shift with the development of individual rights and responsibilities. What was once an "exclusive" orientation to citizenship and governance shifted to an orientation that emphasized the rights of "all" people to participate in the governance of their communities and emphasized government's mutual responsibility to secure and protect these rights. This came to be known as "government by the people." Civil rights (for example, equality before the law and liberty of the person) and political rights (for example, the right to take part in elections and the right to serve in bodies invested with political authority) became central components to the understanding of citizenship in the countries of the West.[6]

Ideas about citizenship were also influenced by emerging perspectives that focused on social rights. The ideas of individuals like Marx and Kropotkin and the revolutionary experiences of the time further deepened and complicated notions of citizenship. While civic and political rights were being extended, there was also a belief that "privileges of rank and wealth maintained the wide gulf between the working classes and their superiors in the social hierarchy, the status of citizenship seemed to many unfulfilled if not a downright sham."[7] There was growing recognition that those persons with substantive wealth were in a privileged position and, as citizens, could have a greater impact on civic decision-making. Conversely, a person's capacity to fulfil the rights and duties more equitably in the civic life of one's community required a minimum standard of living as a necessary prerequisite.

During the nineteenth and twentieth centuries, we witnessed significant debate and protest in the West as governments and groups attempted to grapple with issues of social welfare and social inequality within and across countries. Individuals and groups continue to engage in activities to bring about social reforms that address social inequality and that help all people fulfil their rights and duties as citizens. How to do this, and to what extent, continues to be contested.

Interwoven into these ideas about citizenship was the connection to the nation-state. Rights, duties and citizens' identities, both personal and collective, were increasingly linked to the state. Citizens became "people of a particular sort, living in a particular space, united by common attributes, responsibilities, values and aspirations."[8] One's citizenship was "good" to the extent that it provided support for the nation as a whole and fostered its well being. Nationalism tended to promote uniformity, often at the expense of diversity, within nations. To nationalist advocates "the schools were the logical institutions to teach the requisite culture."[9] Today, nationalism continues to be an important force in defining citizenship throughout the world, however it is increasingly challenged by forces accentuating a more global orientation.

In the late twentieth century ideas about citizenship in democratic contexts exhibited both a growing complexity and multi-dimensionality as democracies proliferated throughout the world. While foundational criteria of modern democratic citizenship continued to find affirmation, contemporary perspectives of citizenship and how we educate for citizenship were tempered by contemporary forces of change, different social contexts, cultural traditions and varying stages of economic and social development in which they had evolved.

EARLY IDEAS AND PRACTICES IN CANADA

"The idea of educating people for their political as well as social roles was embedded in education in Canada even before Confederation" as a requisite to social and civil well-being.[10] Not surprisingly, this idea has revealed itself in varying patterns and practices since that time and is linked to the many historical forces and contextual factors that have shaped Canada's development.

Throughout the last half of the nineteenth century and the first half of the twentieth century, educating for citizenship in Canada tended to reflect a "social initiation" orientation: that is, a passing on of what were believed to be the core body of knowledge, skills, and values needed to be productive members of society.[11] Public education was viewed by many educational leaders of the time as a logical location for initiating young people to the principles and features of parliamentary government, to their freedoms and their responsibilities as "democratic" citizens and to the virtues of the nation state. Public education emphasized an acceptance of the authority of social institutions, values of loyalty and national pride and a belief that the role of society is to provide orderliness, protection and predictability for its members. This emphasis predictably led to an authoritarian style of teaching about citizenship. "Didactic thought, recitation, memorization, and largely passive learning remained the rule and by overwhelming agreement, the norm."[12]

Within the public school curriculum, educating for citizenship was primarily the responsibility of social studies and, as in other parts of the world, tended to emphasize nationalist intentions and the transmission of knowledge about structural, procedural and the legal aspects of political institutions.

> This meant that Canadian history, for example, was seen largely as the building of the federation ... History texts made it clear that nations were the work of exceptional individuals ... Canadian students learned that Confederation was the work of a handful of "fathers" ... Women rarely appeared in the pages of these texts and when they did it was usually doing what was regarded as women's work, such as teaching or nursing. Working people were similarly ignored. Native people were equally invisible.[13]

Predictably, the teacher was expected to direct learning and students were expected to receive it. Although there were some signs of a shifting emphasis as student councils and student-centred learning were gradually introduced in the 1920s and 1930s, learning that encouraged critical thought, collaboration, discussion of controversial issues or active participation had little priority. Despite the introduction of the *Canadian Citizenship Act* on January 1, 1947, educating for citizenship during the first half of the century was given a rather a low priority on provincial educational agendas.

The second half of the twentieth century unleashed an era of reform in education in Canada and elsewhere. Demands for higher quality teaching, more effective schools, more authentic and participatory forms of learning, more democratic educational practices and more equitable educational opportunities shaped a context of reform that continues today. Along with other new and innovative educational initiatives, a renewed interest in educating for citizenship emerged.

A. B. Hodgetts's publication of *What Culture? What Heritage? A Study of Civic Education in Canada* in 1968 sparked interest and debate in the area of educating for citizenship. Hodgetts emphasized the increasing multi-dimensionality of Canadian citizenship, its diverse cultural and pluralistic nature, its emerging global orientation and its conflictual character in democratic contexts, reflecting an important transition from earlier views.[14] A new Canadian Studies curriculum was developed that emphasized Canada's culturally diverse nature, French-English relations, Canadian-American relations and Canada's emerging role in the global community. This curriculum provided a context for further consideration and investigation of dimensions of citizenship. For the most part, however, explicit attention to educating for citizenship was largely neglected and remained a rather "invisible" dimension in the curriculum of most public schools.

In other parts of the world, educating for citizenship moved in different directions. Some spoke of "environmental competence" while others emphasized the "political literacy" and "multicultural" dimensions of citizenship education.[15] Implicit in these conceptions of what it meant to "educate for citizenship" was a focus on what were believed to be the "essential" learnings for effective citizenship. There was also growing attention paid to approaches in teaching and learning that were congruent with, and effective in, nurturing these intended learning outcomes.

CONTEMPORARY FORCES OF CHANGE

Today's world continues to be characterized by constant and significant change. We are becoming more aware and more appreciative of the global aspects of our everyday lives. We are increasingly cognizant of our interconnectedness with others throughout the world — politically, economically, culturally and technologically — and more fully aware that many of the issues and environmental stresses that we face transcend formal borders and boundaries. We are beginning to realize that solutions to world-wide problems require world-wide responses.[16]

In Canada, regionalism and nationalism already complicate the meaning of citizenship and the different identities entailed in that membership. Now, like people in many other countries, informed and conscientious Canadians see themselves not only as part of a local community, a province and a nation but also as part of a broader global community. Civic identities are being complicated by these tensions and contradictions that accompany diverse allegiances and the practice of community-based, national and global rights and duties.

The revolution in information technology, especially the development of the Internet, has fundamentally changed the scope and speed of communications and of acquiring, generating and sharing knowledge. Information technology allows Canadians to make instant and continuous contact with people around the world. Never before have we enjoyed "such immediate access to a wealth of on-line news sources, government documents, expressions of opinion, and other information sources from around the world. Increasingly, one can submit on-line contributions to, or simply read, the contributions made by interested citizens."[17] This access is influencing the nature and extent of civic participation, as reflected in the on-line civil rights, human rights and other solidarity campaigns.

While the potential benefits of the Internet are many, they are accompanied by questions and concerns. How do we respond to the volume of information and how do we rebut information that may be racist, sexist, violent, pornographic and hateful? How do we ensure access and equity? These are important considerations in any discussion about democratic citizenship. Furthermore, there is a widening gap between "information rich" and "information poor." In Canada alone, well-to-do households may have several computers while poorer households may have none. If access means power, then how do we respond to the fact that so many in Canada and in much of the world remain unconnected to the electronic village?

As well, we are witnessing the expansion and strengthening of a global economy that is building economic networks throughout the world. Economic policies, once developed locally or nationally, are now orchestrated by large transnational conglomerates. Economic relations, once conducted bilaterally or regionally, are now exercised within large trading blocs like the European Union, through trade agreements like the North American Free Trade Agreement (NAFTA) or directly shaped by international trade organizations like the World Trade Organization (WTO). While such connections often create strong economic links between nations, a range of disputes and concerns also emerge over tariffs and import quotas, where businesses will be located and which ones will be closed. These decisions have considerable impact on the distribution of wealth worldwide.

In Canada and elsewhere, public concern is moving beyond regulating branch plant companies or foreign investment within national boundaries. Now governments must react to economic and financial decisions being made by transnational corporations that operate at levels above national governments, by investors in the international money market and by international trade bodies like the WTO that make economic policy over which citizens have little direct control. Already, as the new century begins, concerned citizens are lobbying, protesting and rioting against WTO decisions, which, they believe, increase the gulf between rich and poor. Many would argue that citizens have little or no control over such organizations.

Changing migration patterns and growing contacts among peoples paint a picture of a world that is becoming increasingly diverse and pluralistic. In some contexts, this diversity is embraced. In other contexts, however, the close interaction sometimes generates discrimination and conflict, as diverse beliefs and traditions clash, sometimes violently.

The cultural diversity of Canada's population continues to increase. Canada continues to accept more immigrants in proportion to its population than any other country. While English is the primary language spoken, more than fifty languages are reported to be the mother tongue of more than ten thousand Canadians. Census statistics from 1996 indicate that visible minorities make up 11.2 percent of the population (3,197, 480 people) and that over 35 percent of the population (10.2 million) declared more than one ethnic origin on the census form.[18] Discrimination and conflict, motivated by diversity, are worldwide problems, and Canada is not been immune to them. If Canada's diversity is to be a source of vitality, citizenship means not only developing appreciation, respect and understanding of diversity but also developing capacities to work in a milieu of social difference, which can sometimes be conflictual.

Politically, there have been important forces at work as well. As nations and groups within nations strive for democratic forms of governance, strategic and economic security and the protection of human rights, they bring about important political shifts. Take, for example, the demise of Apartheid in South Africa, the fall of the Berlin Wall and the proliferation of democratic systems in Chile, Czechoslovakia, Hungary, Russia and Cambodia over the last two decades. There is also a growing recognition of and attention paid to the significant role civil society organizations play in building and sustaining democratic communities, roles that are distinct from the operation of formal governmental processes. These shifts are creating new opportunities for citizens to contribute both locally and globally.

In Canada alone, the are some 175,000 non-profit voluntary organizations, which provide community services, organize cultural, educational and supporting activities, and lobby for change on the political front.[19] These forms of engagement in civil society and activism, as well as the expanded opportunities for involvement afforded by technological advancements, are providing opportunities for citizens to exercise citizenship more effectively.

Internationally, while countries continue to conduct international relations through formal diplomatic channels, committed individuals and groups are making a difference, as in the case of the 1997 international treaty banning land mines. In speaking about the treaty, Canadian Minister of Foreign Affairs Lloyd Axworthy acknowledged the strength of "soft power." According to Axworthy, soft power, a non-coercive approach to international affairs, succeeded because "an ad-hoc but effective coalition of states and non-government bodies brought governments and international public opinion on side."[20]

These political, economic, technological, social, cultural and environmental forces are transforming modern societies in profound ways. They are reshaping how power is distributed and exercised and are also affecting how people view the communities in which they live. Contemporary notions of citizenship and how we educate for citizenship are taking on new meanings, reflective of these compelling forces of change and the diverse social contexts and cultural traditions in which they are being formulated.

STUDIES, DIRECTIONS AND POLICY INITIATIVES

In the last decade in Canada, we have witnessed a number of studies, the emergence of various theoretical directions and the introduction of assorted policy initiatives. The Citizenship Education Research Network (CERN) was created in the late 1990s under the leadership of Yvonne Hébèrt to bring together researchers, policy makers and educational practitioners interested in carrying out systematic long-term research and in developing a national capacity for research in citizenship education. Since its inception, the network has begun to investigate four main themes: citizenship conceptions and contexts; citizenship practices; citizenship values; and citizenship skills, knowledge, attitudes and behaviours. Educating for citizenship in today's world extends well beyond any "passport" status and requires a range of understandings and capacities if we are to fully exercise our rights and responsibilities in the communities in which we live. Earlier approaches, focusing primarily on knowledge acquisition, are quite simply no longer sufficient "unless [they are] linked with commitment and action. To adapt a well known maxim: it is one thing to understand the world, but the important task is to change it."[21] Below is an overview of these studies, theoretical directions and policy initiatives. It is interesting to note both the tone and multi-dimensionality with which new understandings of citizenship and educating for citizenship are being represented.

STUDIES

Three studies of particular interest are described here: *What Education For What Citizenship?* prepared by UNESCO's International Bureau of Education; *The Civic Education Study*, co-ordinated by the International Association for the Evaluation of Educational

Achievement; and *The Education Policy Study Project* from the University of Minnesota.

I. *What Education For What Citizenship?* explores images of democratic citizenship and educational practice among students and teachers in secondary education in over thirty countries. The first phase of this study, which began in 1994, offered three important preliminary findings:

1. That it is important to begin with the particular understandings (social representations) that the student has about democratic citizenship and to use constructivist learning approaches to deepen that understanding.
2. That citizenship awareness is linked to active involvement by students in civic-like activities in the school whether they be in specific subjects or across subjects.
3. That a student's involvement in school activities (for example, in decision-making and actions of the school, in conflict resolution situations, in participatory activities connected with the community) does seem to constitute a good precursor of civic commitment.[22]

II. *The Civic Education Study* has been in progress since 1963. Under the leadership of Judith Torney Purta of the International Association for the Evaluation of Educational Achievement (IEA), the researchers worked with students in twenty-four countries. The first phase of the study is now complete. It examined what students are expected to learn about their nation and citizenship. This phase is summarized in *Civic Education Across Countries: Twenty-four National Case Studies from the IEA Civic Education Project* (1999). The conclusions of the first phase are of particular interest:

> First, there is a common core of content topics in civic education across countries. Second, almost all of the authors of the 24 case study chapters express the belief that "civic education should be cross disciplinary, participatory, interactive, related to life, conducted in a non-authoritarian environment, cognizant of the challenges of societal diversity, and co-constructed by schools, parents, and the community." Third, there is a widely perceived gap between the goals for democracy expressed in the curriculum and the reality presented by societies and their schools. And fourth, everywhere diversity is a matter of concern; yet, there is

not much sense of the best direction to take in formulating programs.[23]

The second phase of the study, which focuses on students' understanding and skills, is now underway.

III. *The Education Policy Study Project* was a four-year, nine-nation study organized out of the University of Minnesota. It forecasts eight key characteristics that will be required of citizens for the twenty-first century and provides guidelines for educational policy makers based on these characteristics:

1. The ability to look at and approach problems as a member of a global society.
2. The ability to work with others in a co-operative way and to take responsibility for one's roles (and) duties within society.
3. The ability to understand, accept, appreciate and tolerate cultural differences.
4. The capacity to think in a critical and systemic way.
5. A willingness to resolve conflict in a non-violent manner.
6. A willingness to change one's way of life and habits of consumption to protect the environment.
7. The ability to be sensitive towards and to defend human rights.
8. A willingness to participate in politics locally, nationally and internationally.[24]

THEORETICAL DIRECTIONS

I. As analytic tools, theoretical models provide helpful frameworks deepening our understanding of citizenship, in principle and in practice. Theorists in the UK, Canada and the US are working on developing such models.[25] In Britain, Derek Heater has argued for "a globally relevant" framework that takes into consideration a "universal expression" of the citizenship principle and that respects the diverse historical traditions and contexts that have shaped the varying interpretations of citizenship. Heater's "Cube of Citizenship" includes three dimensions: elements, location and education. The elements focus on identity and virtue and on the legal, political and social aspects of the status of citizenship. Location identifies the range of levels in which citizenship is played out. These include civil society organizations, local government and global contexts. Education, which Heater views "not [as] an optional extra, but [as] an integral part of the concept," focuses on requisite knowledge, attitudes and skills.[26]

II. In the United States, Patricia Avery has outlined seven areas of learning that she expects will be necessary for effective political involvement now and in the future. These include:

> ... cognizance of the global dimension of many political problems and issues and an ability to see the complex relationships among these issues. Participants will need to work with others whose experiences and perceptions of the world are very different from their own. Political participation will require greater skills in listening, collaborating, compromising, and negotiating as we strive to find common ground among diverse viewpoints. The ability to deal creatively with conflict will be particularly important when citizens find common understandings elusive. If avenues of political participation are to be more inclusive, we will need to ensure that all participants have access to relevant and timely information ... Citizens will need skills in accessing and developing meaningful interpretations of massive amounts of data. Finally, we will need to recognize multiple forms of political involvement and to create new avenues of participation as the political sphere changes.[27]

III. In Canada, Alan Sears has constructed a framework for understanding and analyzing citizenship and citizenship education based on a continuum from "elitist" to "activist."[28] His Conceptions of Citizenship Model compares themes of sovereignty, government and citizen expectations, knowledge, values and skills within the elitist and activist perspectives. Central to Sears' organizing framework is the understanding that citizens are "expected, and enabled, to participate in the affairs of the state," and that the extent of this participation is guided by conceptions of citizenship that range from elitist to active.

The "good citizen" in the elitist conception is one who is "knowledgeable about mainstream versions of national history as well as the technical details of how public institutions function ... the highest duty of citizenship in this view is to become as informed as possible about public issues and, based on this information, to vote for appropriate representatives at election time." The activist conception assumes a significant level of participation by all citizens. The good citizens in this conception are those who participate "actively in community or national affairs. They have a deep commitment to democratic values including equal participation of all citizens in discourse where all voices can be heard and power is relatively equally distributed."[29]

POLICY INITIATIVES

A range of educational policy initiatives has also been introduced as international education agencies and governments worldwide attempt to understand and assess the complex processes by which young people learn about democratic citizenship.

I. UNESCO's *Learning: The Treasure Within: Education for the Twenty-first Century* identifies four pillars of education that should guide learning throughout life: learning to know, learning to do, learning to live together and learning to be. These pillars provide the mainstay for knowledgeable, competent, tolerant and autonomous learners and citizens and help inform curriculum initiatives pursued in this context.[30] In the United States, the National Council for the Social Studies Civics Standards has published *Essential Characteristics of a Citizenship Education Program*. This report describes the goal of citizenship education as one which prepares "young people to be humane, rational, participating citizens in a world that is becoming increasingly interdependent."[31] In Britain, the 1998 report of the Advisory Group on Education for Citizenship and the Teaching of Democracy in Schools stresses the role of the active citizen and lays out three central principles — social and moral responsibility, community involvement and political literacy.[32]

II. In 1994, the Canadian Committee for Effective Canadian Citizenship (a committee of the Canadian Association for the Social Studies, which is now inactive) issued a report entitled *Educating*

Canada's 21st Century Citizens: Crisis and Challenge. This report, with contributions from across the country, holds that "teaching methods and materials should emphasize the connection between citizenship education and students' personal lives. Students need to be active participants in, or engaged by, learning activities that address authentic issues and empower students as learners and citizens."[33]

III. Celebration Canada is a national organization promoting the celebration of Canada and the development of Canadian citizenship education in schools and the community. In 1998, it published *Components of Citizenship Education: Initiating Action,* which identifies three key aspects of citizenship education: (1) the traditional — knowledge of government institutions and law, and of Canadian history and geography; (2) the inclusive — anti-racism and human rights; and (3) the multidimensional — understanding the personal and social aspects of citizenship and developing decision-making skills.[34]

IV. Several policy papers have been initiated in Ontario. *For The Love of Learning: Report of the Royal Commission on Learning,* emphasized the importance of building the capacity for civic engagement. *The Common Curriculum* explicitly stressed the development of participation as a requirement of responsible citizenship. Most recently, the Ministry of Education and Training released the *Ontario Curriculum Grades 9 and 10* and *Ontario Secondary Schools Grades 9 to 12 Program and Diploma Requirements* (1999). These emphasize the importance of educating citizenship across the curriculum but also require that students complete a compulsory course in civics in order to graduate from secondary school. Both strongly emphasize a multidimensional view of citizenship education, reflecting an important shift in tone and emphasis from earlier policy emphases pertaining to educating for citizenship.[35]

These studies, theoretical directions and assorted policy initiatives reflect important shifts in thinking about what it means to educate for citizenship. They acknowledge the complexities of our fast-changing and interconnected communities, and they provide common ground to help us proceed. They raise important issues about how we might better study and understand citizenship, and they provide guidance about what might be considered the critical characteristics of citizenship as we move into the twenty-first century. And they grapple with the challenge of understanding *how* young people learn about citizenship. Together, they point to important learning goals and processes that are necessary if public school curriculums and educational programs are to address new understandings of educating for citizenship, reduce the gap between what is envisioned and what is experienced in the curriculum, and reduce the gap between the reality presented by societies and the schools.

EMERGING PEDAGOGICAL/SCHOOL-BASED PRACTICES

Educating for citizenship, which has remained largely "invisible" in the "enacted" curriculum in many public schools in Canada, is receiving more attention. School programs are gradually beginning to address their citizenship mandate. New understandings of citizenship are informing educators about the critical capacities required for meaningful civic engagement and for dealing with complex public issues of local and global proportions. New understandings about how we educate for citizenship are informing approaches to teaching and learning that can effectively achieve complex learning intentions.

Learning goals linked to effective citizenship include global and community mindedness, critical thinking, informed and ethical decision-making, collaboration, problem solving, non-violent conflict resolution, identity development and active participation locally, nationally and internationally. Increasingly, approaches to teaching and learning are weaving these many integrated capacities in cross-disciplinary, participatory and authentic ways. Knowledge is being constructed through personal and collaborative enquiries. Moral purpose and participation are being addressed through different types of complex problem-solving and decision-making learning strategies both within and outside classrooms as students address issues of local and global importance.

The following snapshots reflect some recent approaches being used in Canadian schools to educate for citizenship. Please keep in mind that these snapshots are neither representative nor widespread but rather reflect individual schools and classrooms where teachers and students are enquiring into issues of importance to civic life and exploring their capacities for civic engagement. As you read them, consider the following questions: How are the principles and practices of citizenship being *envisioned?* How are teaching and learning practices being *enacted?* How is learning being *experienced?*

RESCUE MISSION PLANET EARTH

At many schools, students take part in various international initiatives. Rescue Mission Planet Earth is co-ordinated by Peace Child International in England and involves young people worldwide. Students researched and wrote papers about environmental issues, exchanged information about Canada's environment with students from England, Poland, the Philippines and Tanzania, and took part in an international teleconference with Rescue Mission's Headquarters. They spoke at various functions in their communities, set up information booths at public gatherings and met with the local Member of Parliament and other officials on Parliament Hill in Ottawa to raise understanding about environmental issues.

MAKING A STAND AGAINST DISCRIMINATION

A group made up of students and teachers and known as STAND (Student/Teacher Action for Non-Discrimination) is active in a secondary school and its local community. The group's goals are to raise awareness about and acceptance of people as individuals and to promote unity through diversity. As a response to the growing concern about discrimination in Canadian society, the group participates in a variety of activities that increase awareness of and offer concrete solutions to discriminatory practices. The group has prepared educational kits for parents, set up booths that focus on other countries at an information fair, held a musical week to promote racial harmony and established exchanges with students in other schools to share their views about Canada and their diverse cultural backgrounds.

STUDENT TOWN COUNCIL

Each year, Grade 9 and 10 students studying local government and citizenship conduct their own Student Town Council meeting in the town's municipal council room. In preparation, they investigate the role of the local government, attend a real council meeting, job-shadow the town's elected councillors and department heads, and take part in workshops where they learn about decision-making, negotiating, debating and how to conduct a town council meeting. When they've completed their preparation, they hold a Student Town Council meeting. Students play the roles of mayor, councillors and department heads who meet to introduce, debate and vote on proposals for their town. Other students act as reporters, filing stories with the local press, and as a TV crew covering the event for a local community TV station.

MANIFESTO 2000 FOR A CULTURE OF PEACE AND NON-VIOLENCE

Secondary school students and teachers are studying the Manifesto 2000 for a Culture of Peace and Non-Violence, introduced by the United Nations General Assembly and co-ordinated by UNESCO. The Manifesto, drafted by Nobel Peace Prize laureates in celebration of the 50th anniversary of the Universal Declaration of Human Rights, stresses personal responsibility as a starting point for transforming the culture of war and violence into one of peace and non-violence. Students and teachers are using the Manifesto as a guiding vision for work in the school. To date, students have invited an expert in peace studies and a consultant on conflict resolution to speak about their work and conduct workshops, planned debates on nuclear disarmament and initiated an environmental restoration project.

Each of these snapshots is highly symbolic. Each touches on change, challenge and complexity. Each incorporates understanding, concern, responsibility, perspective and action — some of the important elements interwoven into new understandings of what it means to educate for citizenship. And each is part of a different school program that illustrates different approaches to citizenship education being undertaken within schools across Canada.

Canadian teachers, wishing to explore and integrate new under-standings of citizenship into classroom and school-based practices, are also finding a host of ideas to inform and guide their work both locally and internationally. One example is Ken Osborne's work that provides helpful guidance for teachers. He stresses that to become effective citizens, all students today should have an opportunity through their school curriculum to develop a deeper understanding of Canada and the world and to work collaboratively with one another. To achieve this, he suggests that teaching material be pre-sented as problems to be solved or questions to be answered and that the problems connect to the students' existing knowledge and experience with the outside world. This connection can create a classroom characterized by trust and openness so collaboration can take place. He also emphasizes the importance of developing the following innovative learning skills that will help students become active and participating citizens:[36]

- problem-formulating
- value-creating
- anticipation
- participation
- focus on the future
- autonomy
- critical judgement
- integration
- global orientation

The authors of this chapter have an informal catalogue of participatory citizenship activities that we have organized encour-aged both practising teachers and student-teachers to use and expand upon. These activities include involvement in school governance, political campaigns, community projects, public exhibits, letter writing campaigns, mock or model activities, inter-age projects, volunteer work, online Internet conferencing, food drives and environmental action. We have also encouraged the use of "authentic performance activities" to help address the multi-dimensional nature of citizenship education. There are five im-portant characteristics that guide the development of these activities:

1. Explore Substantive Public Issues
   • local issues
   • provincial or national issues
   • international issues

2. Develop the Skills of Practitioners
   • the skills of inquiry, research, communication
   • skills central to the discipline
   • skills used by real practitioners

3. Develop Capacities for Personal and Interpersonal Understanding
   • personal reflection and decision-making
   • co-operation and collaboration
   • respect for diversity and multiple perspectives
   • local and global mindedness

4. Contribute as Responsible Members of a Community
   • new knowledge shared with the community
   • community service
   • working with community member
   • participation in the political process

5. Operate in Real Life Contexts (actual or re-created)
   • the practitioners' environment
   • sense of purpose and reality
   • opportunities for insights into the work-place

Many others, both inside and outside Canada, are examining a range of different classroom and school-based practices that may be used both within and across public school curriculums to explore the new understandings of educating for citizenship. The use of case studies, international telecommunications linkages, peer mentoring, conflict resolution programs and the use of literature to teach civic virtues are a few of the learning activities and strategies being used. These classroom and school-based approaches provide a rich background for curriculum teachers and planners developing multidimensional approaches to citizenship education.

THE WAY AHEAD?

Educating for citizenship continues to be a focus of public education in Canada and other parts of the world. In assessing the
discussion and debate regarding educating for citizenship over the
last part of the twentieth century, it is clear that both significant new
directions and broad challenges have emerged. What remains
unclear, however, is what "essential capacities" young people are
going to need and how we will design and put into practice
curriculum and methodologies that attend to and are congruent
with the underlying values and principles of democratic living. We
close this chapter with a four important points to consider as we
look ahead:

1. Meanings of citizenship will need to be further clarified in ways
that respect its multi-dimensionality and that are also useful to
schools and their already over-burdened curriculum. These meanings will need to be sensitive to the contested and evolving nature of
citizenship. There is a general sense that widespread civic illiteracy
exists among young people today, but what does this mean? We will
need to address more carefully what civic literacy means and identify those "essential capacities" that will help young people contribute
effectively to their societies.

2. Models of teaching and learning that both attend to and are congruent with critical dimensions of democratic citizenship and that
are attuned to the developmental levels of the learners need to be
further investigated and developed. There is still significant evidence to suggest that approaches to teaching and learning citizenship remain largely didactic and passive. Participatory approaches
that move beyond traditional cognitive approaches. Furthermore,
how to design and, more importantly, implement participatory
learning methodologies and curriculum practices in citizenship education must be addressed.

3. Encouraging the practices of democratic citizenship in Canadian
schools influences a variety of educational experiences. We need to
examine the extent to which the structure and organization of
schools may either support or hinder the promotion of democratic

citizenship. There remains a wide gap between the goals for democratic citizenship expressed in the curriculum and the realities presented in schools. Restructuring schools in ways that more effectively encourage and support a citizenship focus requires careful thinking about school governance and relevant school-based programs.

4. Lastly, schools and educational systems have been slow to adapt to change and have had limited success in implementing change. More mechanisms are needed to help teachers and school systems respond to continuous change. At the same time, these mechanisms must respect our diverse historical traditions and contexts. As well, new and more effective approaches are required to manage and support changes within school systems and classrooms. For example, professional learning opportunities that honour teachers' needs and contributions are critical. The same top-down organization common to most schools dominates many of the options for teachers' professional learning in all areas, including citizenship education. Professional learning approaches that show the most promise are those integrating curricular, instructional and teacher development reforms and those that encourage citizenship capacity building through "change agency" and "moral purpose."

While the citizenry and the policy-makers alike look to public education to strengthen the development of healthy civil societies, it is clear that there is much to be done. Young people grow up in complex and varied contexts and face a diversity of issues, from the local to the global. How we choose to respond to the dilemmas and tensions raised by contemporary concepts of citizenship and how we choose to assist youth develop their capacities for active engagement in the civic life of their communities remain important challenges as we move into the twenty-first century.

TEACHER RESOURCES

Penney Clark and Roland Case, eds., *The Canadian Anthology of Social Studies* (Vancouver: Simon Fraser University Press, 1997).

Carole L. Hahn, *Becoming Political: Comparative Perspectives on Citizenship Education* (Albany: State University of New York Press, 1998).

Derek Heater, *What Is Citizenship?* (London: Blackwell Publishers, 2000).

Orit Ichilov, ed., *Citizenship and Citizenship Education in a Changing World* (London: The Woburn Press, 1998).

Alan Sears and Ian Wright, eds., *Trends and Issues in Canadian Social Studies* (Vancouver: Pacific Education Press, 1997).

Alison Van Rooy, ed., *Civil Society and Global Change: The Canadian Development Report* (Ottawa: Renouf Publishing and The North South Institute, 1999).

CLASSROOM RESOURCES

James Doyle, with contributions from Roland Case and Tom Morton, *Critical Challenges in Law and Government: Parliament in Session — A Simulation* (Vancouver: Pacific Educational Press, 1999).

Mark Evans, Rosemary Evans, Michael Slodovnik, and Terezia Zoric, *Citizenship: Issues and Action* (Toronto: Prentice Hall, 2000).

Ronald W. Evans and David Warren Saxe, eds., *Handbook on Teaching Social Issues Education for Development: A Teacher's Resource for Global Learning* (London: Hodder and Stoughton, 1996).

Tom Morton, with contributions from John Myers, *Co-operative Learning and Social Studies: Towards Excellence and Equity* (San Juan Capistrano: Kagan Co-operative Learning, 1996).

WEB SITES

The Citizenship Foundation (United Kingdom)

http://citfou.org.uk

The Citizenship Foundation encourages an understanding of the rights and duties of citizenship, the workings of the political, social and legal systems and the democratic process; it encourages participation in community and voluntary affairs and in public life at local, national and international levels; and encourages experiences that enable citizens to become caring, confident and effective members of society.

CIVITAS

http://www.civnet.org/civitas/civitas.htm

The CIVITAS site is an international consortium for civic education that aims to strengthen effective education for informed and responsible citizenship in new and established democracies around the world. CIVINET (http://civnet.org), published by CIVITAS, is a Web Site for civic education practitioners (teachers, teacher trainers, curriculum designers), as well as scholars, policymakers, civic-minded journalists and non-governmental organizations promoting civil society all over the world. It includes textbooks, lesson plans, original journal articles and book reviews, civic news headlines, events listings, organizational contacts and other resource material.

The Common Good Civics and Citizenship Education (Australia)

http://www.abc.net.au/civics/

The Common Good Civics and Citizenship Education site brings together a wide range of materials for schools and formal post-secondary study. The materials are drawn from ABC (AustralianBroadcasting Corporation) TV and Radio, as well as from a number of online productions created in collaboration with other organizations. One Project, One World — Many Democracies, provides a collection of collaborative international Internet projects for the schools sector.

Mightymedia "Youth in Action" Network

http://www.mightymedia.com/act/

The Mighty Media "Youth In Action" Network site is an interactive on-line service for youth, educators and organizations who want to learn about and participate in social action. This site offers opportunities for people from all over the world to come together to learn, communicate and take positive action on issues related to such topics as the environment and human rights.

The United Nations Cyberschoolbus

http://www.un.org/Pubs/CyberSchoolBus

The United Nations Cyberschoolbus was created in 1996 as an on-line education component of the Global Teaching and Learning Project, whose mission is to promote education about international issues and the United Nations. The Global Teaching and Learning Project produces teaching materials and activities designed for educational use (at primary, intermediate and secondary school levels) and for teachers' professional learning. The vision of this Project is to provide exceptional educational resources (both on-line and in print) to students growing up in a world undergoing increased globalization. Within the Cyberschoolbus site there are a number of activities and projects that teach students about global issues in an interactive, engaging and fun way.

NOTES

1. Carole Hahn and Judith Torney-Purta, "The IEA Civic Education Project: National and International Perspectives," *Social Education 65* (1999), 425.

2. Ken Osborne, "The Teaching of History and Democratic Citizenship," in Penney Clark and Roland Case, eds., *The Canadian Anthology of Social Studies* (Vancouver: Simon Fraser University Press, 1997), 29.

3. Orit Ichilov, "Patterns of Citizenship in a Changing World," in Orit Ichilov, ed., *Citizenship and Citizenship Education in a Changing World* (London: The Woburn Press, 1998), 11.

4. Derek Heater, *Citizenship: The Civic Ideal in World History, Politics and Education* (London: Longman, 1990), 2-23.

5. Ibid., 37.

6. Vernon Bogdanor, ed., *The Blackwell Encyclopaedia of Political Science* (Oxford: Blackwell Publishers, 1993), 94, 95.

7. Heater, *Citizenship,* 71.

8. Osborne, "The Teaching of History and Democratic Citizenship," 28, 29.

9. Keith McLeod, "Exploring Citizenship Education: Education for Citizenship," in Keith McLeod, ed., *Canada and Citizenship Education* (Toronto: Canadian Education Association, 1989), 6.

10. Ibid., 11.

11. Roland Case and Penney Clark, "Four Purposes Of Citizenship Education," in Clark and Case, eds., *The Canadian Anthology of Social Studies,* 17-27.

12. McLeod, "Exploring Citizenship Education," 11.

13. Osborne, "The Teaching of History and Democratic Citizenship," 31.

14. A. B. Hodgetts, *What Culture? What Heritage? A Study of Civic Education in Canada* (Toronto: OISE Press, 1968), 11, 12.

15. Osborne, "The Teaching of History and Democratic Citizenship," 33.

16. Patricia G. Avery, "The Future of Political Participation in Civic Education," *Social Science Education Consortium* (1997), 47.

17. Cynthia J. Alexander, and Leslie A. Pal, *Digital Democracy: Policy and Politics in the Wired World* (Toronto: Oxford University Press, 1998), 4.

18. Susan Girvan, ed., *Canadian Global Almanac* (Toronto: Macmillan, 1999), 46, 47.

19. Alison Van Rooy, ed., *Civil Society and Global Change: The Canadian Development Report* (Ottawa: Renouf Publishing and The North South Institute, 1999), i.

20. Department of Foreign Affairs and International Trade Press Release, March 2, 1998.

21. Ken Osborne, "Nationalism, Citizenship, and Curriculum," in *Our Schools/Our Selves* (1998), 55.

22. L. Albala-Bertrand, "The International Project. What Education For What Citizenship? First Lessons From the Research Phase," *Educational Innovation*, UNESCO International Bureau of Education, nos. 90, 8.

23. Hahn and Torney-Purta, "The IEA Civic Education Project," 425.

24. John J. Cogan, Patricia K. Kubow, and The CEPS Project Researchers from Nine Nations, "The Citizenship Education Policy Study Project: Final Report" (1997), 29.

25. Several other theoretical frameworks for citizenship and citizenship education have emerged in recent years including Ichilov's Multidimensional Model, Mclaughlin's Minimal and Maximal Model, Rauner's National and Post-National Model, and Indigenous Models.

26. Heater, *Citizenship*, 319.

27. Avery, "The Future of Political Participation in Civil Education," 48.

28. Alan Sears, "Something Different To Everyone: Conceptions of Citizenship and Citizenship Education," *Canadian and International Education Journal* 25 (1996), 6.

29. Ibid., 7, 8.

30. Jacques Delors et al., *Learning: The Treasure Within* (Report to UNESCO of the International Commission on Education for the Twenty-first Century, 1997).

31. National Council for the Social Studies, *Essential Characteristics of a Citizenship Education Program* (1983), 1.

32. Bernard Crick, *Education For Citizenship and the Teaching of Democracy in Schools* (London, UK: Advisory Group for the Qualifications and Curriculum Authority, 1998), 15.

33. The Committee for Effective Canadian Citizenship, *Educating Canada's 21st Century Citizens: Crisis and Challenge* (Ottawa: Advisory Group for the Canadian Association of the Social Studies, 1994), 1, 2.

34. Celebration Canada, "Components of Citizenship Education: Initiating Action," Submission to the Western Canadian Protocol for Social Studies, 1998.

35. Ontario Ministry of Education and Training, *For The Love of Learning: Report of the Royal Commission on Learning*, (1994), 4-5; Ontario Ministry of Education and Training, *The Common Curriculum*, (1995) 25-27; Ontario Ministry of Education and Training, *Ontario Secondary Schools Grades 9 to 12 Program and Diploma Requirements* and *The Ontario Curriculum Grades 9 and 10, Canadian and World Studies* (1999).

36. Osborne, "Nationalism, Citizenship, and Curriculum," 58.

Chapter 5

DEVELOPMENT EDUCATION

MAKING CONNECTIONS NORTH AND SOUTH

Louella Cronkhite

FIRST WORLD/THIRD WORLD, NORTH/SOUTH, developed/under-developed: what's in a name? Once it seemed relatively clear. First World countries were western, industrialized nations; and Third World referred to the former colonies of Europe. "Developed" countries were generally First World, and "underdeveloped" were Third World. However, with changing economies in Asia and Latin America, many formerly "underdeveloped" countries have become strong global players, while at the same time there is greater awareness of the pockets of poverty in so-called "developed" countries. First World/Third World and developed/underdeveloped both suggest a ranking that is defined by "us" and applied to "them." Imperfect as it is, North/South avoids this pitfall, yet it opens up other questions: Are nations of Eastern Europe, many struggling with economic collapse and civil war, part of the North or part of the South? Are New Zealand and Australia part of the South? There is no doubt that the field is open for the coining of a term that more accurately describes what we want to say.

The discussion over terminology reflects our changing perceptions and understanding of global dynamics — an appropriate example of the evolution of development education. Here, the term North will be used to refer to the post-industrial nations of Europe and North America, including Australia and New Zealand, while South refers to the countries of Asia, Africa, the Caribbean and Latin America — countries that continue to struggle under the legacy of colonialism.

ROOTS OF DEVELOPMENT EDUCATION

The roots of development education in Canada can be traced back at least to the end of the Second World War and to the shifts in the international scene that occurred in the years following.

Throughout the colonial period, powers such as England, France, Spain and Portugal held control over and reaped the benefits of their colonies' natural resources. Venezuela won independence from Spain in 1821. By the end of the nineteenth century, the rest of Spain's colonies in the Americas had won their independence, and Portugal no longer held Brazil. It would not be until after the Second World War, however, that colonies in Africa, Asia and the Caribbean would become independent. By the end of the war, many European powers had found themselves unable, or unwilling, to absorb the costs of holding on to their colonies while trying to rebuild war-shattered Europe. Still, some independence movements struggled for years. India, Ghana and Jamaica broke away from the British Empire in 1947, 1957 and 1962, respectively. Burkina Faso, Mali and Niger from France in 1960, Vietnam in 1954, and Algeria in 1962. Mozambique, Guinea Bissau and Angola broke away from Portugal in the 1970s.

The economic conditions in the newly independent countries opened the doors of development. An early World Bank report commented on the "need and potential for development" and noted that "the average income in the United States in 1947 was over $1,400. For more than half the world's population, however, [it] was less than $100 a person."[1] Reports such as this throughout the 1940s and 1950s would stress the gap between incomes in the USA and elsewhere. The figures cited would come to define whole peoples according to what they lacked, what others expected them to become and how they ought to organize their economies to accomplish that. When US President Harry S. Truman labelled most of the world "underdeveloped" in his inaugural speech in 1949, he made the doctrine official. With one word Truman reduced "the immeasurable diversity of the globe's South [its former colonies] into a single category — 'underdeveloped' ... all the peoples of the earth were to move along the same track and aspire to only one goal — development."[2]

No sooner had colonialism ended than a new form of intervention began. The powerful countries used economic and political pressures to control or influence events in other countries, particularly, but not exclusively, in the former colonies. The US government, anxious about what it saw as the prospect for communist revolutions in post-war Europe, set up the European Recovery Program commonly known as the Marshall Plan (so-named after Secretary of State George C. Marshall). From 1948 to 1952, the US offered European nations (including the USSR, its former ally, and other countries of Eastern Europe), some US$13 billion in aid. The Marshall Plan left it to European nations themselves to work out how to spend the funds.

The plan's success at rebuilding Europe and staving off revolution made it a model. The "First World" nations of the North — Western Europe, the USA and Canada — would soon set about "developing" the "Third World" nations of the South. Industrial production, new technology, better healthcare and education, as defined by the North, would create modern societies in the South. Whether the ideas and the aid destined to help put those ideas into practice fit with the history and cultures of the South did not come into question. All development needed was enough expertise and enough cash.

Canada took up that development model in 1949, with a modest contribution to the United Nations technical assistance program. In 1950, Canada played a prominent role in the Commonwealth Conference that launched the Colombo Plan, designed to put India, Pakistan, Sri Lanka (then Ceylon) and Malaysia on the path to development and to keep them in the western camp.[3] Loosely based on the Marshall Plan, the Colombo

Plan put a lot of effort into sending people from these former colonies to Canada, England, Australia and New Zealand for higher education. Laudable though that might seem, it created an educated elite, one with western views of progress and development and one which returned home committed to acting on these views. The stated goal of official Canadian aid was, as it would be for other countries in the West, humanitarian. The Cold War was on and Canada, like its allies, used aid to facilitate Canadian and American foreign policy and trade objectives.[4]

THE EARLY ORGANIZATIONS

By the early 1960s, some highly energetic, principled and idealistic Canadians were heading overseas as volunteers and workers. The Canadian University Service Overseas (CUSO, formed in 1961) is perhaps the best known of the non-governmental organizations with aid projects overseas. Many other secular and church-based organizations, however, also became active in development work and in what would become known as development education.

CUSO's first volunteers left for their two-year assignments overseas convinced of the wisdom of the development message: western technology, education and healthcare would solve the "problems" of the South. (Problems were defined within the development model.) But as volunteers began their overseas assignments, particularly in rural villages or with grassroots groups, they found themselves unprepared. First, there was culture shock. But more important, as volunteers worked with local people, they could see first hand the legacies of colonialism and they began to question the appropriateness of the western model of development. Why, they wondered, did once thriving societies now show such gaps between rich and poor? Why were almost all manufactured goods imported? Why should the children be studying British novels or European history rather than their own? And why did so many development projects fall apart after aid workers left? When these early volunteers returned to Canada, they hoped to share their experiences and their questions with other Canadians. To do so, they had to rely on producing their own slides and presentation materials. These volunteers spoke at small meetings held in church basements, libraries and university campuses across Canada, but they had no way of reaching the broader public.

In 1968, the Canadian Council for International Co-operation (CCIC) was formed to co-ordinate the activities of Canadian non-governmental organizations (NGOs), such as CUSO, working on international development. The CCIC funded the opening of the first "learner centre" in London, Ontario, to help co-ordinate CUSO volunteer orientation. The term "learner centre" itself reflected the philosophy that the orientation would be self-guided. Prospective CUSO co-operants (or volunteers, as they were then called) would come to the centre for a week or two to study development education before leaving for their postings. The volunteers poured over and debated books and articles, took part in role-playing and studied individually and in groups. "These learner centres became the foci for returnees and others interested in development education and social change, and bases from which a wide range of educational outreach programs soon developed."[5]

But as one writer long active in the field reminds us:

> This evolution of thinking did not occur in a vacuum. People were coming home to the liberal humanist policies of Trudeau's "just society", where money was being made available for a range of community and social programs. In Canada, too, people were developing and applying a structural analysis of underdevelopment, in order to better understand regional disparities, the chronic marginalization and poverty of certain sectors of the Canadian population and the impact of colonialism on Canadian Native people.[6]

CUSO's mobile learner centre travelled across Canada in 1972, stopping at cities and towns along the way. A dozen learner centres opened in its wake. In 1973, the learner centre in London hosted a national meeting for groups interested in setting up learner centres in their communities.

At the same time that CUSO and CCIC were being established, the first government organization was established by the federal government to support development education. In 1968, the Pearson government created the Canadian International Development

Agency (CIDA) to distribute official Canadian aid and to be Canada's voice for Third World development within the government. In 1971, under the Trudeau government, CIDA set up its Public Participation Program to help Canadians understand Canada's work in international development and to build support for public funding of foreign aid. NGOs and others working in development education could now apply to the program for dollar-for-dollar funding for that work.

In the early 1980s, the development education movement experienced a shift in perspective. Its perspective was becoming more critical and the volunteers began to ask deeper questions about the political and economic inequalities that left the countries of the South without real control over their own natural resources, put them at a permanent disadvantage in trade and left them without access to markets. By 1983, CUSO would describe underdevelopment, whether abroad or at home, as "ongoing, rooted in history, and maintained by political and economic structures. True development must ... also seek to change the structures at home or abroad [that block] real human development." Development, argued CUSO, should bring people the power to shape the decisions that affect their lives. Similarly, education, like development itself, is never neutral and should mean that the teacher and the learner work together towards new understanding based on action and reflection. Development education should seek to find an understanding that leads to new ways of thinking about development. This, in turn, will lead to action, which will lead to change, which itself will lead to yet a newer understanding.[7]

NGOs in Latin America were also redefining the meaning of development. In Latin America, participants in adult education programs often have little formal schooling, but they do have a great deal of knowledge — knowledge they often take for granted because it is what they must know if they are to survive. Brazil's Paolo Freire and his colleagues, for example, based literacy programs on bringing people together for discussion, group reflection, role-playing, popular theatre and the like, to encourage people to draw on what they already knew. Freire encouraged his students to use that knowledge to analyze, to see the connections between the way they lived and the economic, political and social forces that perpetuated those conditions. As Freire would say, people began to read their world.

In Latin America, Freire's "pedagogy of the oppressed" became key to organizing *communidades de base* — grassroots groups of the poor — often by priests and nuns who had committed themselves to what came to be known as liberation theology. Some of those priests and nuns were Canadians who would return to Canada with new ideas about education, development and poverty. Canadians who were working with NGOs in Latin America recognized the power of Freire's pedagogy to transform society and they too brought its principles back to Canada, where they adapted them to Canadian culture and reality.[8] Refugees of the military coup that toppled the Salvadore Allende government in Chile in 1973, including some who had worked with Freire in Brazil, also brought their knowledge to Canada and helped shape what development education would become.

At the same time, many Canadian groups working in development were focusing on adults, perhaps on the grounds that adults were better placed to work towards economic, political and social justice internationally. These groups published work on women and development, the new world economic order and poverty and hunger that could be used in high-school classes. But the publications tended to be heavy with statistics and were criticised for being "too weighty" or "too depressing" for use with younger students. Some groups did produce kits, slide-shows and booklets for use with high-school students, but distribution tended to be limited to teachers who held "radical" political views.

Meanwhile, the learner centres were basing their work on the strengths and needs of their local communities and initiating community projects. These projects focused on and celebrated national events such as World Food Day (October 16), International Women's Day (March 8), Ten Days for World Development (January-February, now called Ten Days for Global Justice) and, in time, CIDA's International Week.

CIDA AND GLOBAL EDUCATION

In 1988, CIDA offered significant funding to teachers' associations and ministries of education that wanted to promote development education. However, development education was now being referred to as "global education" — perhaps because those working in development education were seen as radical or perhaps because the term "development" itself was beginning to fall into disrepute. Global education now took in not only development education but also peace education, human rights education and environment education. Those working in global education made the same connections that those working in development education had made. Thus a discussion of poverty in a country in Asia, Africa or Latin America might draw on the link between the banning of organizing, the outlawing of peaceful assembly and poverty. The discussion might then look at how poverty often leads to slash-and-burn agriculture by those desperate for land to feed themselves and their families and how poverty propels villagers in search of work into already overcrowded cities. Another link might look at how activists in these countries organize demonstrations to protests against their particular country's scarce resources going to the military and how the activists find themselves facing an armed response.

Although development educators have made links between development and Canada as far back as the early 1970s, it became somewhat easier to do so under global education. Global education projects sprang up across the country and helped to shape all levels of the curriculum. CIDA had also begun to produce more material for classroom use, including the magazines *Somewhere Today* for elementary school students, and *Under the Same Sun* for older students. Global educators worked with their colleagues in development education and with others to create teacher-friendly materials based on the principles of popular education — materials that encouraged participation and co-operation. Global education projects encouraged teachers to create classrooms where students could explore ideas co-operatively through role-playing and simulation games, having guest speakers visit the classroom and looking at all subjects from a global perspective.

Development educators had been using these strategies for years, but global education projects lent legitimacy to their work, and many in the field now found themselves in greater demand. They were called on to organize classroom activities that encouraged participation, to run simulation games and even to hold professional development workshops at teachers' conventions. At the same time, more and more development educators were making the connections between what perpetuates inequity globally and what perpetuates it in Canada. Sexism, anti-racism, food production and distribution and trade policies (including the Free Trade Agreement between Canada and the United States, and eventually Mexico) became new areas of focus.

STRUCTURAL CHANGE VS PUBLIC AWARENESS

Development education or global education continued to deepen its analysis of the links between Canadian society and developing nations. In 1988, a CCIC Development Education Task Force reported that to promote awareness and transform Canadian social structures to better promote development education's goals would mean transforming many institutions. It would require a mass media that presents a fair, less culturally-laden view of global issues; a public education system that promotes critical thinking and debate on global issues; a business community that recognizes that strong economies in the South are mutually advantageous; and a broad range of ways for Canadians to take part in learning and acting on global issues.[9] Development educators argued that Canada was inconsistent, that it professed support for the poorest of the poor, but many of its bilateral government-to-government and multilateral (through international organizations such as the United Nations) projects perpetuated systems that kept the poor from gaining real control over their lives. For development educators, such criticism of CIDA and of Canadian foreign policy was no less than their duty as informed citizens of a democratic country. Not surprisingly, however, those under attack saw such criticism as biting the hand that fed development education.

Nonetheless, the National Advisory Committee on Development

Education returned from its consultation tour of Western Canada and Ontario with the following findings:

- The amount of development education work ... being done related to the money spent is enormous. It is diversified and is reaching an increasing number of people.
- The quality and dedication of the people involved in development education work is outstanding, which brings forth the human dimension of development education that the Committee ought not to overlook.
- Groups funded through CIDA's Public Participation Program (PPP) are at the forefront of the linking of issues, ie., of linking international development issues with environmental issues, human rights issues, etc.
- Development education workers also make the links between international development issues and local issues. The message of interdependence has to permeate in all development education thinking, not only in the message that is projected but also in the way development educators work. It is important to look at the commonalities between the situation here and overseas.
- All of the positive points just mentioned notwithstanding, it seems that the Canadian people still have very little idea of what this whole subject is about, very little idea of the globality involved, the integration of issues, the connection of Canada to this world of change. It is still seen in terms of foreign aid: we are aiding them.
- The development education message is being countered by an opposite message that comes through the media. Somehow the NGO and CIDA visions of the future and of change are not getting their message out.
- The shortage of resources is a big issue. Additional resources would make a big difference to how quickly we grow towards a critical mass that is sensitized in the Canadian population.
- Development education is long-term because it is a process that involves more than just transmitting information.
- Development education organizations are caught in a vicious

circle because at the same time as the resources, principally financial, available to them are being reduced, they are asked to increase their reach and to expand their activities. When they come up with new activities, they are told that no funds are available.[10]

The NACDE continued to promote development education in its 1990 Annual Report to the Minister for External Relations and International Development:

> The primary message of this report is that ... international development must continue to expand if the world is to become a safe and equitable place as the year 2000 approaches. The short-range blockage of development must give way to long-range vision. That is why development education must continue to be enlarged, not contracted just because certain assistance programs may have to be curtailed for the moment. The long-range development of greater public support in Canada for more resources to international development will depend in no small measure on the expansion of development education now.[11]

The committee continued to back development education and recommended in its 1991 Annual Report that the government place a high priority on development education when drawing up CIDA's policy on sustainable development, and that CIDA encourage discussion among those working in development education to ensure increased efficiency in the delivery of their programs. The committee also recommended that a national conference be held in 1992 to share ideas for more effective approaches, more efficient communications, and better tools for evaluation.[12] Although the minister responded favourably to each recommendation, it would be the committee's last report. The National Advisory Committee itself fell victim to federal budget cuts.

The committee had spoken to the ever-present tension between the objectives of NGOs, which wanted structural changes, and those of CIDA, the funder, which wanted NGOs to focus on public awareness. NGOs, particularly the learner centres, saw the tension as a healthy one. They argued that it was their responsibility to question how Canada carried out its development work and their responsibility to encourage public debate on our development practices.

The stance was principled; it was also naive. In 1986-1987, CIDA had granted some $11 million in funding to 300 or so development education projects run by 138 organizations, placing Canada as the second of fourteen members of the Organization for Economic Co-operation and Development (OECD) in the funding for development education, and fourth on a per capita basis.

In March 1995, CIDA announced it would no longer fund development education in Canada. Learner centres and global education projects lost CIDA funding they had come to count on. Many large NGOs, themselves strapped for funds and with reduced matching grants from CIDA, had already almost eliminated their development education programs. Many groups folded, and those that remained found themselves at least temporarily weakened.

CURRENT DEVELOPMENTS, INITIATIVES AND STRANDS

The massive funding cuts of 1995 sent the development education community reeling. At least half of the country's learner centres remain closed. In Saskatchewan, all are gone. Manitoba's International Development Education Association closed down, leaving the Marquis Project in Brandon. The latter is doing well, in part because it began to diversity its funding some years before the CIDA cuts.

Ontario groups have tried to make arrangements with other NGOs. Community coalitions are forming around local and global issues, although this tends to be done piecemeal by volunteers or by poorly paid staff. There are far fewer paid staff now, and volunteers and boards may not have the skills or the time to work on the many issues that are emerging.

Four of Alberta's six learner centres still run programs: Arusha in Calgary, the Centre for International Alternatives in Edmonton, the World Citizens Centre in Lethbridge and Unisphere in Medicine Hat. Both Arusha and the World Citizens Centre have shifted their focus to anti-racist education. Funding remains precarious from year to year.

In British Columbia, Vancouver's International Development Education Association concentrates on the distribution of films highlighting international development and human rights issues, and the Victoria International Development Education Association creates and distributes school materials.

Many working in development education looked at CIDA's cuts positively. For many years, there had been a tension between the guidelines for CIDA funding (which required centres to focus on international development issues) and what was seen as the softening, even the disappearance, of the we/they dichotomy between North and South. Rising globalization and crippling debt loads, not just in Africa or Latin America but in Canada too, meant the perpetuation of global poverty. The rising number of poor and dispossessed in Canada was becoming more obvious. The loss of CIDA funding meant that development education has had to find new ways of doing its work.

There have been murmurs, however, that Ottawa recognizes the draconian nature of the cuts and funding is once again available for development and global education through the new Public Engagement Program. Some development education projects continue to be funded through other routes, for example, through Ten Days for Global Justice, which CIDA funds through grants to the international development bodies of Ten Days' supporting churches.

Canadian NGOs, such as USC Canada and Oxfam, budget for development education. Although the material is often well done and backed up by videos, the challenge is to produce materials that teachers can fit into the programs of studies they must use. Otherwise, it will not be widely distributed.

Mathew Zachariah, a long-time development educator and recently retired member of the Faculty of Education at the University of Calgary, told me that Canadian development education groups, unlike their US counterparts, were always funded by government. There were always problems with such funding. For one, funding was tied to specific topics. And, while groups had to apply for funding each year, some became complacent that funding would always come. Now there is no room for complacency. Zachariah cites the example of groups in Kerala, India, which, except for specific small projects, refused to accept foreign or government funding on the grounds that acceptance would lead to dependency. That has certainly proven true in Canada. If we can, however, develop a sense of community, as Kerala did, we may regain some of the vibrancy of the grassroots development education movement. Part of regaining that vibrancy might lie in working, as Zachariah suggests, with those in multicultural and anti-racist education.

Zachariah notes several points where, for example, multicultural and development education intersect:

1. Poverty is a relative term; nevertheless, it has many harmful consequences for the poor as well as for the rich in nation states.
2. Widespread extreme poverty ... is the result of oppressive caste, race, class or gender relationships.
3. Poor people do the best they can, not necessarily because rich people help them but often despite such "help."
4. Rich people in poor and rich societies work in systems which are to their immediate but not necessarily long-term advantage.
5. Most poor people and poor countries are not looking for charity.
6. Attempts ... to create small-scale, caring communities out of concern for environmental pollution, alienation and others deserve our attention and support.
7. The problems of alleviating poverty and opposing oppression are immense, but that immensity should not stop us from doing what we can.[13]

THE ROAD AHEAD

Certainly the greatest challenge facing development education today is that it lacks the money to hire staff, produce new materials, maintain existing libraries and plan and carry out new projects. By its very nature, education is not self-financing. Education that challenges the status quo and the power structures that support only one model of economic development will always find funding hard to come by. The corporate world is unlikely to support such education, and development educators tend to reject corporate funding.

The federal government of Jean Chrétien cut funding to organizations that worked to raise the public's awareness of development issues. Such cuts mean that Canadians will find it much harder to find out about and to debate those issues. Already a well-insulated country, Canada may turn even more inward. Without a global context, we are unlikely to recognize global disparity and that its roots are connected to our own reality. If we rely solely on the mainstream media for answers to global questions, we will tend to slip even further into the belief that countries that dominate the global economy are somehow justified in exploiting the poorer nations of the world. Without an alternative vision of the future, how can we realize possibilities that lie in meeting our needs, not our wants? on creating sustaining communities, not free trade zones? in preserving cultures, languages, biodiversity, whole peoples?

Teachers have a key role to play in continuing the work of development education. First and foremost, teachers need to keep up to date on global issues and to continue to analyze global economic, political and social trends. Many approaches come to mind. For example, in their classrooms, teachers can focus on economic globalization and trace its roots to the Age of Exploration, colonialism and the transfer of resources from the South to the North. Critical analysis of globalization can also make links between the oil boom of the 1970s and the collapse of commodity prices in the 1980s; such an analysis can include the debt crisis and the International Monetary Fund's demand for "structural adjustment" and how that has furthered the rise of powerful transnationals, free trade and the dwindling power of nations to determine their own destinies. Such analysis would be valid whether the focus is on Nigeria or Canada.

For those working in environmental education, an examination of the "development" of the rainforests might draw out a complex picture of poverty. The link might connect an analysis of people losing their land to landlords who plant and grow export crops, a study of the traditional uses of rainforest products, the impact of cattle ranching, mining and timber production, and the work of social justice and environmental groups, which call for putting people over profits. Discussing the conflicts between indigenous people and land developers, exploring the different standpoints and competing value systems, might round out the picture.

Many teachers are already experienced at creating an atmosphere open to diverging opinions. They work to equip students with the skills they need to find out what they want to know, and they call on their own creativity to design activities that encourage students to think and reason. They make use of co-operative learning, role-playing, simulation games and debates to encourage students to take action on what they have learned, be it telling someone else, writing letters, starting a recycling program, twinning with a school overseas. Such teachers tend to say that teachers are role models and need to make choices consistent with educating for a sustainable future.

Development education need not be confined to the social studies classroom. A British Columbia teacher who volunteered through CUSO in a village in Kenya had his industrial arts class design a pump for a Kenyan village well. His students undertook the research to identify the most suitable pump and the most readily available materials, materials also easily replaced or repaired. As the class worked its way through the project, students learned a great deal about Kenya and the village and its people. The connections that students make from such a project can lead to an exchange of ideas and experience.

Activities in mathematics might include a study of global population trends. Students might explore population increases relative to food supply and distribution. Social studies students might look at the role education plays in determining population growth, particularly when women are educated and when that education gives them greater control over their lives. Former Rutgers University particle physicist Dr. Maurice Bazin teaches math and science to teachers in Brazil and has written workbooks exploring math in other cultures. Looking at math in other cultures also encourages students to consider other ways of knowing and doing.

Students of English might explore literature from Africa, Asia and the Caribbean and reflect on how literature reveals culture, world views and history. Students might compare oral traditions with the mass communication characteristic of North America, and explore the value systems that underlie each. A discussion of how Gutenberg's application of moveable type and the production of printed books influenced the oral traditions of Europe, or the role of libraries in the development of western thought, or the relation between moveable type, western thought and the Information Age, can push students to recognize that people create societies in response to their environment and history, and that people can and do shape the future.

In science classes, students can focus on the environment, water, food production, building styles and their suitability. Making links can help students understand why tens of thousands of children die each year from unclean drinking water, and how those deaths can be prevented. Students can explore a variety of ways to meet people's need for adequate food, or look into the nutritional value of the diets of people around the world, or ask whether money should be spent on new drugs to combat diseases such as malaria. There are no easy answers, but the resourceful teacher finds ways to incorporate development education in every subject.

Although the logical place to begin development education is in the schools, it did not begin there, and it is important to keep the principles of development education — the need for global social justice — before the public. Jeanne Moffat talks about the need to build networks in Canada and the need to forge partnerships around the world. Moffat says that a network for constructive social change must base itself on principles of justice: if we believe that those who are affected by a decision have a right to be part of making that decision, then it is up to us to ensure that it happens.[14] What might this mean for development education in schools and in the community? Given the trend towards thinking globally and acting locally, this might mean working in partnership with anti-racist education, for example, to forge connections between schools, First Nations groups, immigrant communities, teachers, students and people from around the world. When working with youth, it means encouraging them to help create the programs in which they take part. It means creating opportunities for reflection and action.

Effective action and advocacy means studying the issues from the standpoint of the South. The Canadian link must focus on

Canadian policies and practices towards the South. We need to centre our action around analyzing how we can change Canadian policies and structures for the benefit of the South and for the benefit of those subject to structural injustice at home.

Canadians are worried about their own lives. There is good reason to fear that we will forget about the rest of the world, even as the forces that lie behind the rise in global poverty are causing Canadians to feel uneasy about their own futures. Douglas Roche puts it well when he says,

> International development is about more than the old poverty-stricken areas or the new ecological refugees. It is about self-fulfilment and economic liberation, so that the financial and trading systems of the world begin to work for mutual advantage, East and West, North and South ... Canadians must be helped to see over and beyond the obstacles of the moment. The long-range interests of Canada demand a new sense of global citizenship.[15]

TEACHER RESOURCES

Rick Arnold et al., *Educating for a Change* (Toronto: Between the Lines, 1991). The authors explain the rationale for using popular education techniques, which originated in Latin America, and provide ideas on how to use them.

Jeffrey Atkinson, *Development Education in Canada: Increasing Awareness and Understanding of the Third World in a Western Society* (Victoria, Australia: Community Aid Abroad, 1989). Although this book was written for use in Australia, the author offers a succinct history of development education and learner centres in Canada.

Cecille DePass et al., eds., *New Challenges for Development Education in Canada in the Nineties* (University of Calgary: Canadian and International Education, 1991). These are the proceedings of the conference of the same name and provide a snapshot of development education thinking in the late 1980s.

GATT-Fly, *Ah-Hah! A New Approach to Popular Education* (Toronto: Between the Lines, 1983). A clearly developed explanation of how to encourage an analysis of local and global systems with a group of people working for social change. The book is based on popular education techniques from around the world and employs simple drawing to represent the forces at work in a given community or region.

Carrol Joy, *Believing is Seeing: Attitudes and Assumptions that Affect Learning About Development* (New York: National Clearinghouse, 1990). A clearly developed discussion of the evolution of development education, particularly in the United States. Useful for teacher training and for in-service training for practising teachers.

CLASSROOM RESOURCES

Barbara Maheu, David Hein, and Jody Osborne, *Global Interconnections: A Resource Handbook for High School Social Studies Teachers* (Edmonton: Alberta Teachers' Association, 1995). Available from the Alberta Teachers' Association, 11010 - 142 Street, Edmonton, AB T5N 2R1. This handbook, written to meet Social Studies program objectives, offers excellent activities under the topics Openers, Diversity, Disparity, Interdependence, Development, Quality of Life and Alternative Futures. There are also many good readings, suitable for Grades 9 to12.

Office on Global Education, *Make a World of Difference* (New York: Friendship Press, 1989). This kit is full of activities for use with community groups, clubs, study groups and classes from K-12. The activities are clearly laid out and easy to follow.

Jim Petrie, A *Two Way Approach to Understanding: Issues in Global Education* (Fredericton: Global Education Centre, 1993). This is an excellent compila-tion of 57 favourite development education activities and 15 international games, under the topics Trade, Poverty and Population, Refugees and Migrants, Aid, Food, Water, Literacy, Environment and Women. Activities are included for virtually every grade level.

Graham Pike and David Selby, *Global Teacher, Global Learner* (London: Hodder and Stoughton Ltd., 1988). This might more accurately be considered a book about global education, but the principles and ideas are consistent with devel-opment education, and the wide range of activities, designed specifically for the classroom, are excellent.

ORGANIZATIONS

While the 1995 cuts to CIDA's Public Participation Program resulted in the closure of half of the learner centres and all of the Global Education projects in Canada, there are many organizations that continue to work in development education. NGOs running projects overseas are still eligible for funding from CIDA for development education. Check with the organizations you support to see if they are producing materials.

CUSO
400 – 2255 Carling Avenue
Ottawa, ON K2B 1A6
(613) 829-7445
Toll-free for Canada: 1-888-434-2876
Fax: (613) 829-7996
www.cuso.org

USC Canada
56 Sparks Street
Ottawa, ON K1P 5B1
(613) 234-6827
Fax: (613) 234-6842
E-mail: uscanada@usc-canada.org
www.usc-canada.org

Several inter-church coalitions produce and distribute material on development issues:

Ten Days for Global Justice
Suite 201, 947 Queen St. East
Toronto, ON M4M 1J9
(416) 463-5312
Fax: (416) 463-5569
E-mail: tendays@web.net
www.web.net/~tendays

The Ecumenical Coalition on Economic Justice
Suite 208, 947 Queen St. East
Toronto, ON M4M 1J9
(416) 462-1613
E-mail: ecej@accessv.com
www.ecej.org

The Inter-Church Committee on Human Rights in Latin America
  (ICCHRLA)
129 St. Clair Avenue West
Toronto, ON M4V 1N5
(416) 921-0801
E-mail: icchrla@web.net
www.web.net/~icchrla

Inter-Church Coalition on Africa (ICCAF)
129 St. Clair Avenue West
Toronto, ON M4V 1N5
(416) 927-1124
Fax: (416) 927-7554
E-mail: iccaf@web.net
www.web.net/~iccaf

For more information about international development and
development education organizations, contact:

The Canadian Council for International Cooperation (CCIC)
1 Nicholas Street, Suite 300
Ottawa, ON K1N 7B7
(613) 241-7007
Fax: (613) 241-5302
www.fly.web.net/ccic

NOTES

The author would like to thank the following people who graciously
gave of their time and expertise in telephone conversations on this topic:
Marg Durnin, Dawn McLean, Linda Slavin, and Mathew Zachariah.

1. Wolfgang Sachs, "The Discovery of Poverty," *New Internationalist* 232 (June 1992), 7.

2. Wolfgang Sachs, "Development: A Guide to the Ruins," *New Internationalist* 232 (June 1992), 4.

3. William Winegard, Chair, "Discussion Paper on Issues in Canada's Official Development Assistance Policies and Programs" (Ottawa: House of Commons, Government of Canada, 1986), 6.

4. Ibid., 4.

5. Jeffrey Atkinson, *Development Education in Canada: Increasing Awareness and Understanding of the Third World in a Western Society* (Victoria, AUS: Community Aid Abroad, 1989), 8.

6. Jean Christie, "A Critical History of Development Education in Canada," *Canadian and International Education* 12 (1983), 10.

7. *Development Education: How to Do It!* (Ottawa: CUSO, 1983).

8. In Latin America, those working in adult education are often said to be working in educación popular, or "popular education," for they work directly with the people and not with those in power.

9. CCIC Development Education Task Force report, "A Development Education Strategy for Canadian NGOs," in Atkinson, *Development Education in Canada*, 64.

10. Douglas Roche, *We Journey Together, Preliminary Report to the Minister for External Relations and International Development by the National Advisory Committee on Development Education*, Ottawa (April 1990). Douglas Roche, former Progressive Conservative Member of Parliament and now a Canadian Senator, chaired the committee.

11. Douglas Roche, *Towards a Global Future, Annual Report to the Minister for External Relations and International Development by the National Advisory Committee on Development Education*, Ottawa (December 1990), 4.

12. Douglas Roche, *The Impact of Sustainable Development on Development Education, Final Report to the Minister for External Relations and International Development by the National Advisory Committee on Development Education*, Ottawa (1991).

13. Mathew Zachariah, "Linking Multicultural and Development Education to Promote Respect for Persons and Cultures: A Canadian Perspective," in James Lynch et al., eds., *Cultural Diversity and the School*, vol. 4 (London: The Falmer Press, 1992), 284.

14. Jeanne Moffat, "Networks Within Canada; Partnerships Abroad: The New Challenges for Development Education," in Cecille DePass et al., eds., *New Challenges for Development Education in Canada in the Nineties*, vol. 12 (University of Calgary: Canadian and International Education, 1991), 17.

15. Roche, *Towards a Global Future*, 5.

Chapter 6

EDUCATION FOR GENDER EQUITY

ORIGINS AND DEVELOPMENT

Lyndsay Moffatt

GENDER HAS BEEN a determining factor in our schools from the very earliest days of formal education in Canada.[1] Although schooling and later life have always been shaped by ability, class, fluency in English or French, geography and race, for much of Canadian history, whether children received any formal education at all, what they were taught and how has been greatly determined by gender. If you were a girl in Canada a hundred years ago, chances are you would have had little or no schooling. However, your brothers would likely have had some kind of schooling. Indeed, if they were of a certain class and white their education may have been fairly extensive.

That class, geography and race, among other factors, were and are very significant in terms of what kind of education a child received and receives cannot be emphasized enough. It was not until after the middle of the nineteenth century, with the spread of publicly funded schools and new laws making attendance compulsory, that many girls or boys received more than very limited schooling. Well into the twentieth century, schooling was often considered a luxury that could only be afforded to children who were not essential to the family economy. This consideration had a special impact on girls, for older girls were often responsible for the care of their younger siblings.

Evidence suggests that some working-class and immigrant families rotated school attendance among their children in order to give as many of the children as possible the chance to learn basic math, reading and writing. Evidence also suggests that some families by necessity required older brothers to take on some responsibility for childcare. However, for the most part girls did not attend school as regularly as boys did.[2]

An awareness of the importance of gender, though rudimentary, has also had a long history in Canadian education. Gender and class can be seen as a concern as far back as the 1640s when the Ursulines offered schooling for both poor and wealthy girls.[3] Similarly, in the nineteenth century, gender issues in education were evident when women fought for admission into universities and the professions. However, most attempts to deal with sexism in Canadian schools have been initiated only in the last thirty years.

Following the rise of popular feminism and in keeping with the widespread social justice movement of the late 1960s and early 1970s, women and men opposed to sexism began to examine how it was played out in educational settings, ranging from daycares to universities. The focus of this examination has varied throughout the years and various efforts to combat sexism in school has spawned many questions and much debate. Nevertheless, the general thrust has been and continues to be the creation of schools where all students can reach their full potential regardless of their gender.

THE EARLY YEARS:
TEXTS, STEREOTYPES AND ROLE MODELS

In the late 1960s and early 1970s, teachers, parents' groups and education students began to see school textbooks and children's picture books as reinforcing gender stereotypes. By the early 1970s, almost every province had conducted at least one study of sex-role stereotyping in texts approved by local school boards. Study after study found the materials used in schools to be rife with unequal depictions of girls and boys.

An extensive study commissioned by the Ontario Ministry of Education examined textbooks, literature, videos and educational kits and concluded that there was an unequal representation of girls and boys, women and men, in number and in kind in all of the materials.[4] In math, language, science and social studies texts females appeared as central characters only 11 percent to 40 percent of the time.[5] As well, as the grade level of the texts went up, the percentage of female characters dropped and the representation of women and men characters was found to be even more unequal than that of girls and boys. Social studies and science texts had the least numbers of females while health and French texts had the nearest to equal representation.[6]

Picture books, intermediate- and senior-level literature revealed similar patterns. In picture books, boy-centred stories were much more common, at a ratio of five to two, and girls appeared as central characters only 22 percent to 45 percent of the time. In anthologies of intermediate-level literature, females appeared as central characters in only 17.5 percent of the time. A survey of literature used in Grades 10, 11 and 12 found females were central characters only 22 percent of the time. The study did not, however, confine itself to tallying the percentage of male and female characters. It also examined the activities and occupations that male and female characters engaged in and found that male characters engaged in far more. The researchers noted, for example, that a 1975 North York study of primary readers found women engaged in fourteen occupations and men in 139. Similarly, a 1973 study found that a mere 17 percent of the women characters appeared to work outside the home.[7] Lest one think that these statistics reflected the reality of Canadian society at the time, keep in mind that in 1971 39 percent of all women over the age of fifteen were engaged in work outside their homes, and this number has risen steadily since that time.[8] The occupations most frequently ascribed to women in these readers were service sector jobs while positions in government were most frequently ascribed to men.[9]

In senior-level English literature, female characters occupied ten positions in society, while male characters occupied forty-nine. Women appeared, in order of frequency, as wives, servants, queens, lovers, mistresses, mothers, nurses, school girls, whores and countesses. Curiously, the most common occupation for male characters was that of soldier. Yet men also appeared, in order of frequency, as school boys, husbands, lovers, adventurers, professors, uncles, earls, doctors, farmhands, servants, kings, princes, clerks, lawyers, dukes, merchants, fishermen, fathers, salesmen, teachers, policemen, students, convicts, weavers, money-lenders, farmers, skinners, grooms, biologists, probation officers, supervisors, athletes, governors, slaves, monks, marquis, tramps, editors, organists, knights, priests, landlords, mayors, sailors, secretaries, racketeers, taxi drivers and ghosts.[10]

Male characters, more so than female characters, were more often shown as dominating, succeeding and being competent. Childcare and cooking, traditionally female domains, were also associated with male characters over 30 percent of the time. Driving, fighting, household repairs, gardening, reading, fishing, swimming and boating were also depicted as predominantly male activities. Also, somewhat curiously, more male than female characters were depicted crying, feeling helpless or feeling afraid. Thus male characters not only did more, they felt more too.[11]

To combat the stereotypes they saw presented in the available books, some teachers created their own materials that showed girls and women in a more positive light. Fortunately, small feminist presses were starting up in Canada and around the world, and some began to publish children's books that featured strong girl characters or recovered some part of women's forgotten history. More recently, mainstream publishing houses have begun to publish books that show girls and women as strong, capable, witty and intelligent. This shift is likely linked to the fact that teachers and parents have demanded such changes.

The early discussions of school textbooks and children's literature tended to focus on the depiction of girls and women. However, there was also an awareness of how gender stereotyping might affect boys and men. In an effort to encourage boys to explore non-traditional roles, some progressive teachers created materials that accentuated boys' ability to nurture and create, not just to compete. Some small feminist presses published similar works. Unfortunately, the larger publishing houses have rarely followed suit.

During the late 1960s and early 1970s, teachers, parents and researchers also began to examine the role models that students encountered everyday at school. In particular, they looked at who had authority in schools. What was most striking was that most elementary teachers were women, but most elementary principals were men.

Aware that the imbalance was not simply a matter of individual choice or natural capabilities, teachers who were challenging sexism began to name this imbalance as a problem. The disproportion of men in leadership roles reproduced the power dynamics of society as a whole and thus left elementary-school students with few female role models in positions of authority. This imbalance had economic repercussions for women teachers, for the salaries of principals and classroom teachers are quite disparate. Thus, for a number of reasons, women were encouraged to take leadership courses and apply for principal and vice-principal positions. Similarly, men were encouraged to become elementary teachers, for such men could provide students with positive role models of men in nurturing positions.

GENDER EQUITY IN SECONDARY SCHOOLS

During the early 1970s and into the 1980s, teachers at the intermediate and senior levels focused on bringing in textbooks that included more women and on balancing the number of women in positions of authority. However, they also began to look at how the curriculum shaped students' future employment prospects. Courses that had been closed to one sex, such as shop and home economics, were made co-educational and opened to all students, giving girls the chance to learn woodworking and shop and boys the chance to learn sewing and cooking.

As well, during the late 1970s and the early 1980s, secondary-school teachers, parents and guidance counselors began to look at the gendered patterns in course enrollment. Secondary-school students were given more choice in terms of the courses they took, but studies showed female students had significantly lower rates of enrollment in math and in most science courses than boys did. Specifically, young women appeared to avoid senior physics courses.

Studies in the 1970s in Newfoundland and New Brunswick, for example, reported that the number of girls enrolled in Grade 11 and 12 physics classes ranged from 8.6 percent in Grade 11 to 25.2 percent in Grade 12. In each study, the rate for boys' enrollment was two to three times higher. Studies of enrollment in mathematics courses also revealed a tendency for young women to drop math as they neared Grade 12. A 1979 sample of students in Ottawa found that the percentage of girls taking enriched math dropped from 56 percent in Grade 10 to 35 percent in Grade 12, while the percentage of boys taking enriched math dropped from 75 percent to 67 percent over the same period.[12]

These findings closely matched similar studies in the United States and the United Kingdom and were considered disturbing enough that the Science Council of Canada released a statement of concern in January 1982. The Council recognized that the lack of female participation in math and science would have an impact on the development of science and technology, on Canada's ability to keep abreast of international technological advances, on women's daily lives in an increasingly technological society, and on women's economic prospects.[13]

In recognition of the seriousness of the problem, many school boards set up programs to encourage girls to continue with math and science and to consider careers in those fields. For example, Rocky View School in Calgary, Alberta, began Operation Minerva to connect girls with mentors in science. Participants in the initial program shadowed a woman working in one of the sciences for a day. On the following day, they attended a conference at the University of Calgary, where they engaged in hands-on science workshops in engineering, forensic science, biomechanics and biology.[14]

Similarly, in the late 1980s, the Toronto Board of Education initiated a yearly conference that gave 500 young women in Grades

7 and 8 the opportunity to meet women working in science and technology. This city-wide event came to be known as the Horizons Conference and all schools with Grades 7 and 8 students were invited to send a teacher and twenty young women. By 1995, the Horizons Conference had grown into a program for *all* students and staff at participating schools. It not only encouraged young women to consider careers in math and science but also encouraged young men to consider traditionally female occupations such as nursing and childcare. The program included a three-week study unit, a full-day conference and workplace field trips.[15] It remains to be seen whether the recently amalgamated Toronto District School board will continue to fund this program.

During this period, teachers and parents weren't the only people pushing to end sexism in the schools. Secondary school students often raised the issues themselves. Some young women challenged dress codes that dictated what they could and could not wear to school. As well, beginning in the 1970s, young women began to demand the chance to play "boys" games, such as football, hockey and soccer. This demand had implications for extracurricular activities and for girls' status in physical education. Indeed, studies showed that girls' experiences in co-ed gym classes often mirrored their experiences in society in general, as their talents were often overlooked.[16] Girls worked with sympathetic teachers to demand a chance to play on boys' teams and to have their own teams.

SCRATCHING THE SURFACE:
THE ISSUES THAT WON'T GO AWAY

Concerned educators soon realized that sexism in schools would not be eradicated easily or quickly. By the late 1980s they knew that making women visible in textbooks and in the curricula, increasing the numbers of women in positions of authority, encouraging young women to continue their math and science courses and funding girls' sports teams would not be enough. As we head into the new century, research on how girls and boys experience school forces us to recognize that gender issues are far more complex and that sexist ideas are far more ingrained than we previously thought. Unfortunately, many of the more easily identified aspects of the problem remain with us, and many more have presented themselves during the last thirty years.

Young women continue to enter math, science and technology at a lower rate than young men. Although recent Canadian statistics on high-school girls' enrollment in math and science are not readily available, research on patterns of course enrollment in postsecondary education reveals that the gender gap in university math and science courses remains wide. As noted by Lorna Erwin, "[Canadian] women may now represent the majority of all undergraduates (53%), but they still account for a much smaller percentage of students in economics (33%), mathematics and science (28%) and engineering (18%)."[17] These findings are particularly troubling given current predictions for employment trends and the rise in poverty among women.[18]

It is difficult to say why young women and girls avoid these subjects.[19] Some researchers suggest that girls may suffer from math or science anxiety. Others point to sex differences in understanding spatial orientation. Further research has identified teachers attitudes and practices as remarkably significant in shaping girls and boys' ideas about math and science.[20]

The different expectations teachers have for girls and boys and the kind and amount of reinforcement that teachers give them may indeed create a self-fulfilling prophesy. Some studies of classroom practices found that teachers did not expect girls to be interested in math or science or to be skilled in either subject and thus did not give girls much attention during these classes. In contrast, boys were expected to be interested in these subjects and to be skilled at them and thus received more attention than girls did.[21]

What is also troubling is that the pattern of female underenrollment in math persists even though girls and young women appear to have as much aptitude for the subject matter as boys and men do.[22] The American Association of University Women's 1992 report on girls and education found that sex differences in mathematics achievement were "small and declining." However, the AAUW also reports that girls are more likely to doubt their capabilities in math than boys are, regardless of their competence. Girls are also more likely to attribute difficulty in the subject to personal failure. When boys drop math they say they don't like math because it's "not useful." When girls drop math they say they "can't do the work," regardless of the evidence that shows that they can. What is also interesting to note is that girls' experience a decrease in self-confidence before they experience any actual decrease in their academic achievement. These decreases seem to occur in or around the middle-school years.[23]

The statistics for science achievement tell a slightly different story. According to the AAUW report, sex differences in science achievement for nine-to-thirteen-year-olds rose between 1978 and 1986. The gap in science achievement was widest for boys and girls at age seventeen, and the differences did not change from 1978 to the time of the 1992 study.[24] However, as is becoming more and more evident, it is difficult to determine how much of the girls' lack of success during adolescence can be attributed to performance anxiety and how much is a consequence of stereotyping about aptitudes.

However, in light of the research we do have, many teachers and administrators continue to try to find new ways to encourage girls to stay with math and science courses. One of the most popular tactics has been to present girls and young women with a variety of strong role models of women in mathematics and science. For some teachers, this means drawing students' attention to women's contributions to math and science throughout the ages, either by decorating the classroom with posters featuring women mathematicians and scientists, or by making information about women in the fields readily available when they assign research projects. Some teachers also arrange for young women to meet adult women working in the fields.[25]

Apart from attempting to populate math and science with some female faces, much of the most interesting and most recent research focuses more on how math and science are taught and more particularly on how science is not taught in the elementary years. Some researchers suggest that girls have a hard time seeing science as something that women and girls do, in part because they so rarely see any real women doing it. Indeed, several studies suggest that science instruction is often entirely absent from many elementary classrooms, perhaps because most elementary teachers are women, many of whom did not have good experiences in their own science classes. Deborah Berrill and Keith De'Bell have created a science course for teachers-in-training that seeks to remedy negative associations with science and emphasizes female-friendly teaching strategies.[26]

These strategies, based on the work of feminist researchers such as Mary Blenkley and Carol Gilligan, suggest that many girls and women favour more "connected" approaches to learning, where group work, discussion and prior knowledge are recognized as important. Some of these strategies include giving students time to brainstorm collectively about specific problems, using a hands on approach where students help create physical models of specific problems, providing guided practice with scientific equipment that girls and women may not be familiar with, and creating a non-competitive classroom.[27]

Such strategies may also encourage boys who do not easily conform to the traditional teaching style of most math or science classrooms. In particular, many studies show that teaching that fosters competition tends to be of little value. Very few students appear to benefit from a competitive environment. Instead, a select few tend to monopolize the teacher's attention while the majority suffer in terms of motivation and actual learning.[28]

Most interesting is the suggestion that highlighting famous women mathematicians or scientists may in fact work against efforts to encourage women to enter these fields. As described by Pat Rogers, the "famous few" approach may present students with the idea that women who do math and science are an anomaly, or lead them to think that there are "winners and losers" in these fields which would further discourage and devalue those who enjoy working collaboratively.[29]

Another issue that has not gone away is the struggle to bring gender equity to physical education. Not much research has been done on gender equity in physical education. Although some suggest that progress has been made, this observation of a typical

Grade 5 co-ed gym class is very telling:

> Girls tended to be left out of game interactions by the boys. This
> was true even when the girls had a higher skill level than boys did.
> Additionally, both girls and boys regarded boys as better players
> even when the girls were more highly skilled. Boys preferred to
> pass a ball to an unskilled boy rather than to a skilled girl. Girls
> tended to give away scoring opportunities to boys. Unskilled girls
> were almost completely left out of game action. However, both
> skilled and unskilled girls received fewer passes than boys did.[30]

Girls' unequal experience of physical education may seem less
pressing than the need to address their avoidance of math or science.
However, in light of recent research that shows a marked decrease in
girls' self-esteem and an increase in depression during adolescence,
as well as the evidence of a strong connection between physical and
mental health, this issue should certainly be included in our
struggle for gender equity.[31]

GENDER EQUITY IN THE CLASSROOM

In recent years, those working for gender equity in the schools have
continued to pursue the goals of a non-sexist curriculum, an administration balanced between men and women and equal academic
and extracurricular opportunities for both female and male
students. They have also begun to look at more illusive and complex
aspects of schooling, particularly at how teachers and students
interact in the classroom.

Following the remarkable work of researchers Myra and David
Sadker, many teachers began to see the gross imbalance in the
gender dynamics of most classrooms. From the early 1970s until
Myra Sadker's death in 1995, the Sadkers conducted hundreds of
inquiries into gender relations in classrooms from primary schools
to universities. Their studies and others show that girls begin school
ahead of boys in terms of speaking, reading and counting, but that
as they move through school, girls' skills begin to fall behind the
boys'. The Sadkers also note that the attention girls and boys receive
in classrooms is often very different:

> Boys call out and demand their teachers' attention eight times

more often than girls and significantly, when teachers responded they tended to accept boys' answers and to correct girls' behaviour, advising that they raise their hands.[32]

In addition, girls generally receive less praise and less constructive feedback, are asked fewer complex and abstract questions, and are given less instruction on how to attempt a task by themselves.[33] Girls wait longer for the teacher's attention and when they do get it, the teacher is more likely to respond to them neutrally or negatively (although this varies somewhat, depending on the girl's race and class). When girls do get reinforcement, it is often for being passive or neat, not for having the right answer.[34]

In most respects, boys' experiences are the mirror opposite. Boys attract more negative attention than girls do and are more likely to be scolded or reprimanded in class, even when their behaviour is no different than the girls'. Boys are more likely to repeat a grade and more likely to drop out of high school.[35] Recent studies of special education programs also reveal that more boys than girls are deemed learning-disabled.[36] Studies repeatedly find that teachers do generally give boys more positive and negative attention than they give girls. It is interesting to note that women teachers are just as likely as men teachers to focus on boys' needs.[37]

Classroom dynamics have changed little in the thirty years since the Sadkers first began their work. Much of the primary school curriculum still seems designed, deliberately or not, to help boys catch up with girls.[38] The average school continues to allow boys to stretch and grow while it allows or encourages girls to let their abilities atrophy.[39] Attempts to correct this problem have ranged from making teachers and students conscious of the imbalance, to advocating same-sex classes or same-sex schools. Some schools have conducted workshops on the Sadkers findings and on devising strategies to equalize the kind of attention girls and boys receive. The recommended strategies include taking answers alternately from girls and boys in the classroom and discussing the research with students so they can become aware of who speaks and how often.

Yet for some teachers and parents, progress is too slow. Some argue that single-sex classes or single-sex schools are needed if girls are to have an equal education. Advocates of single-sex education cite studies that have found that girls fair better, particularly in math and science, and that boys fair no worse than in mixed classes.[40] Opponents of single-sex education say it is but a band-aid solution, and that it may very well run counter to the aims of gender equity in education. One fear is that single-sex education makes it very difficult to teach boys and girls new ways of behaving with each other and that boys and young men schooled separately from girls and young women will *not* learn that they have an equal right to an education, nor will girls and young women learn how to assert themselves in the presence of boys and young men. Single-sex schools offer no way for students themselves to face the issues on a day-to-day basis.

The American Association of University Women recently released a report on single-sex education. While the researchers admit that "single-sex programs produce positive results for some students in some settings," they also contend that there is "no evidence that single-sex education in general *works* or is *better* than co-education." On the contrary, they hold that "no learning environment, single sex or coed, provides a sure escape from sexism" and that "the long term impact of single-sex education on girls and boys is unknown."[41]

DIGGING DEEPER:
RECOGNIZING WHAT WE DON'T WANT TO SEE

Perhaps the most disturbing recent findings come from research on what could be called "hallway pedagogy" — in other words, what boys and girls learn from one another in halls, lunchrooms and school yards. Most significant is the evidence that sexual harassment is overwhelmingly commonplace at school. A 1994 survey by the Ontario Secondary School Teachers' Federation, the Ontario Women's Directorate and the Ontario Ministry of Education found that 80 percent of the female respondents had experienced sexual harassment at school. Many girls reported they received comments on their physical appearance, were grabbed, pinched and groped as routine experiences at school. An American study of 2,000 girls found that 89 percent had been subjected to inappropriate sexual comments, gestures and looks and 83 percent had been touched, pinched or grabbed. Forty percent said such incidents occurred daily at school.[42]

June Larkin and Pat Stanton's report, *Sexual Harassment: The Intimidation Factor,* helps to put a human face to these statistics, as Larkin and Stanton quote extensively from their young respondents. What is most revealing is how frightening sexual harassment is for the girls. Many of the young women in the study had seen minor incidents of harassment escalate into more extreme forms of violence. The girls' own recognition that seemingly minor harassment and larger acts of aggression can be linked appeared to influence how they felt they could respond to their harassers. As one girl wrote, "When guys at school pinch me I feel uncomfortable — scared, like what are they going to do next?"[43]

Girls reported that they avoided certain teachers and areas of school, dropped classes and even switched schools to escape sexual harassment from fellow students and from teachers. Some girls in Stanton and Larkin's study recognized that at times the harassment they experienced was racist as well as sexist when they heard such comments as "Black women are — " or "Asian women are — ."[44] The girls felt strongly that sexual harassment harmed their emotional well-being and their academic achievement.

It is easy to imagine how sexual harassment leads to a more narrow or restricted school experience for girls. As we uncover the pervasiveness of this kind of behaviour we must commit ourselves to eradicating it. This task is not easy, particularly because so much of it happens outside the classroom in common areas and hallways where teachers cannot easily intervene. Indeed, teachers often do not know how or when to respond to the incidents of harassment they witness. (Certainly, at times, the line between flirting and harassment may be difficult to distinguish among adolescents.) However, we must continue to challenge ourselves to address this behaviour when and where we can if we are truly concerned with gender equity in our schools. The work of Larkin and Stanton suggests that one of the most important things a progressive teacher can do to help students is to give them the tools to name harassment when they see it. In addition teachers can provide students with their board's policy on sexual harassment and the procedure for lodging a complaint.

When thinking about sexual harassment, it is important to remember that perhaps boys are at times victims of sexual harassment. It is commonly observed that less aggressive boys often suffer from bullying by more aggressive boys in both co-ed schools as well as in all boys' schools. "While boys appear to hold more power in classrooms, not all boys hold power. A hierarchy exists among boys: (usually) a few dominant boys intimidate and control other boys."[45] Yet this bullying is rarely described as "sexual harassment" even though it often entails unwanted comments about the victim's body, his sexual desires and his sexual orientation. While boys' experiences of sexual harassment may rarely be named as such, when one examines some of the bullying that boys experience one cannot help but recognize how much it has in common with girls' experience of sexual harassment.

That we do not name this kind of harassment as "sexual harassment" may reflect our commitment to preserving the term for the experience that women have traditionally had. Yet sexual harassment has had a broad range of interpretation during the last twenty years. Inappropriate comments about a woman's body that are often veiled as a "compliment" as well as hostile comments have both been considered sexual harassment. Similarly, unwanted sexual advances be they coercive or violent are both considered part of the continuum of sexual violence. That we have not traditionally seen boys' experience of homophobic harassment as sexual harassment may reflect how difficult it still is for us to recognize that sexual harassment, like rape, is not an expression of desire but a tool of control and intimidation. However, if we define sexual harassment as unwanted comments about one's body/sexuality we may see that "sexual harrassment" or at least "sexual intimidation" is an appropriate term for some of this behaviour.

Seeing sexual harassment as an appropriate term for the bullying boys experience is supported by what many researchers describe as a common practice for boys in all-male environments, namely, the boys choose the least "manly" boy to act as a "substitute girl":

> In an all boys' school a group of "not real boys" gets created. They are called the poufters and the sissies and are constantly likened to girls. The sexual hierarchy gets set up but some boys have to play the part that the girls would take in a mixed school.[46]

In Canada, of course "poufters" and "sissies" are called "fags." Thus, as noted by a number of researchers, the difference between boys' and girls' experiences of sexual harassment is that when boys are the victims of sexual harassment, the harassment is usually homophobic in nature and it is most frequently perpetuated by other boys.[47]

Some research suggests that boys who sexually harass girls or other boys may do so as much, or more, to impress certain male peers as they do to intimidate the girls or boys in question. It is as though this kind of harassing behaviour was a sure-fire way to assert their credentials as males. Researcher Michael Kaufman cites this as evidence that masculinity is a "fragile construct that (requires) constant nourishment for replenishment." As he notes:

> For most men, particularly when young, there is a running dialogue of doubt (in one's head) about one's masculinity. There is enormous terror that other boys will discover one's own fears. There is also enormous fear of ridicule and of violence at the hands of other boys. There is enormous fear of other males.[48]

Such fear of other males can also be deemed homophobic, whether the boys involved acknowledge that their actions are connected to a fear of homosexuality or not, for in essence they are afraid of censure from other males. Recognition of such patterns of behaviour forces us to think about how homophobia is connected to sexism:

> Boys have various means to deal with this combined fear of other males and fear of not being manly enough. Some are violent towards females and other males, some engage in self-destructive forms of behaviour, and some engage in forms of controlling and dominating behaviour that aren't normally considered violent — domination of classroom discussion, control of the hallways, conquest in sports and so on.[49]

If such aggression is connected to boys' deeply held fear of other boys, then when we work with boys to end sexism we must work within both a feminist and an anti-homophobic framework. If we hope to create equitible schools, we must draw our students' attention to their behaviour and work to eradicate all forms of oppression. Indeed, at this point students in many Canadian schools are far more likely to use homophobic name calling to intimidate other students than they are to revert to insults based on race or gender. Along the same lines, as we move into the next century and as more and more youth and staff begin to identify as gay, lesbian, bi-sexual, trans-gendered and trans-sexual we need to think about how these experiences fit into even our most basic notions of gender equity.

WHAT ABOUT THE BOYS?

It is important when thinking about boys in school to remember that boys who do act out may have very good reasons for doing so. Disruptive or demanding boys may be reacting to feelings that they cannot do the work assigned or may not understand the relevance of their academic work. They may have pressures at home or at school of which the teacher is unaware. All these factors need to be taken into account if we want to create gender-fair schools and a gender-fair society.[50]

Some acting out may have to do with how their academic skills develop. Boys enter school with fewer language skills than girls do, and certainly many more boys become identified as learning disabled.[51] Some of their acting out, however, may be in response to social expectations. Although relatively few researchers have explored how boys are made into men, the work of psychologist Terry Real and others give us good reason to think that being socialized to be a man is fairly traumatic in itself.[52]

Initial research on boys' culture suggests that "the pressure on boys to become 'male' is an enormous burden." Some researchers link boys' depressed reading skills in the years before adolescence to the social pressures boys face.[53] Boys learn stereotyped behaviour earlier and more harshly than girls do and boys who score high on "sex-appropriate" behaviour tests also score highest on anxiety tests. Preliminary studies suggest that at school, boys are more likely to engage in dangerous and risk-taking behaviour and are more likely to be targets of physical violence than girls are.[54] Yet, to truly understand boys' lives, we must also look at some of their experiences outside school. Research into parents' use of physical punishment and physical abuse, children's exposure to violence and the impact of exposure to violence on children's behaviour can shed some important light on why boys might behave the way they do.

Research on physical punishment and abuse reveals that physical punishment as a form of discipline is still widely used and that parents use of it usually peaks when their children are between the ages of three and four. Research has also found, that in general, boys are more frequently the victims of both minor and severe violence in the home. (In specific circumstances, namely when the father is the perpetrator and has a white-collar job, girls are more frequently the victims of very severe abuse.)[55]

A 1997 American study on the frequency in which children are exposed to violent episodes and the effects of this exposure on them found that eleven-year-old boys reported witnessing or hearing about violent episodes or being victimized far more frequently than girls of the same age did. As well, the study found that in general children who reported a higher exposure to violence in their communities were found to have higher levels of anxiety, depression, post-traumatic stress, dissociation and anger than other children.[56] In an earlier study of eleven-year-olds, researchers found that students who had been exposed to acute violence showed symptoms of post-traumatic stress disorder at school. Symptoms include avoidance, lack of concentration, sleepiness and aggressive behaviour. Boys outnumbered girls in these behaviours in all of the classes studied. In one of the classes they did so by nearly 4 to 1.[57]

It is difficult to know how many Canadian boys or girls are exposed to violence in their homes, schools or communities. As noted by the National Clearing House on Family Violence, reports of family violence have increased dramatically in the last decade. At the moment, our rate of child abuse appears to be less than that of our American neighbours. However, a 1996 random survey of 154 Canadian police agencies found children under eighteen made up 22 percent of the victims of all assaults. Children represented 60 percent of all victims of sexual assault and 18 percent of all victims of physical assault.[58] It is also telling that in a survey of 3,229 families throughout the United States, 90 percent used physical punishment with their children as a means of discipline.[59] Yet, for various reasons, many instances of family violence in Canada are still never reported. Thus we cannot know how many students are grappling with this kind of issue while they are attempting to learn all that we are trying to teach them.

Within our schools, teachers are often ignorant of their students' lives outside school and when faced with boys' inattentive or disruptive behaviour they often perpetuate the idea that the boys themselves are the problem. Similarly, teachers like other adults can easily stereotype this behaviour as "typically male" by expecting boys to be less interested in school or by expecting boys to "act out."[60] It is easy to see how this attitude would affect teachers' responses to boys' behaviour. Certainly, many teachers, under the pressure of delivering complex programs to large classes, often use punitive forms of discipline with boys who "act out." Admittedly, these methods do little to actually change a child's behaviour. As we begin to recognize how complex a boy's experience of masculinization is, it is essential that teachers and pre-service teachers question their own assumptions and strategies for dealing with these common behaviours.

WHAT LIES AHEAD: CHALLENGES AND RESOURCES

The lack of material that can help pre-service and working teachers reflect on how their own practices may influence their students and the relatively low-profile of equity issues at most faculties of education have come under scrutiny in recent years. In response to this, teachers' unions, school boards, education professors, graduate students and provincial women's directorates have produced a number of materials that can be used to raise awareness of gender issues among teachers and pre-service teachers. There are also some resources that can be used directly with elementary and senior students. However, to really advance the issues of gender equity, faculties of education must commit to using these materials and to encouraging critical thinking skills that help pre-service and working teachers question and reflect on their personal practices and assumptions about gender.[61] If these things happen, and if education is funded in such a way that teachers have time to really reflect on their day-to-day practices, we will have a body of teachers who are capable of confronting all of the gender issues we have identified — from girls' experiences of sexual harassment and neglect in the classroom, to boys' experiences of bullying and so-called "disruptive" behaviour.

Teachers must also continue to expand their understanding of equity. As has become more and more obvious over the last decade, there are multiple ways that the "isms" affect our students' lives. If we are truly concerned with creating classrooms where all students are given the opportunity to reach their full potential, we must look at how sexism and racism interact and reinforce each other and how homophobia and sexism are inextricably linked. As noted by Heather-jane Robertson, "we must refuse to buy into the current ideology of corporatism which forces us to parse ourselves into interest groups that seek only to gain more of what we believe others have."[62] In other words, we must refuse to limit our thinking to one "ism." We must refuse to see forms of oppression in isolation and must begin to see how all our struggles are linked. To do so also means that we must be willing to recognize that at times there may be factors that are even more significant than gender in determining school success and quality of life.[63]

If we do not do so, we run the risk of being inadvertently abilist, classist, heterosexist and racist. It is important to remember that there have been relatively few examinations of classroom interactions that also factor ability, class, sexual orientation or race into the observations of gender that we have noted. In fact, much of the work that does exist leads one to believe that class, more than any other factor on it's own, is the most significant predictor of school success.[64] Those concerned with gender equity have the challenge of incorporating their knowledge of other oppressions into their struggle against sexism. Or perhaps the real challenge that lies ahead of us is to learn to see how our struggle against sexism fits into the larger struggle for social justice.

TEACHER RESOURCES

Maurianne Adams et al., eds., *Teaching for Diversity and Social Justice* (New York: Routledge, 1997). This collection of activities is ideal for staff development and work with pre-service teachers around all of the "isms."

Allan Creighton, Battered Women's Alternatives, Paul Kivel, and Oakland Men's Project, *Helping Teens Stop Violence: A Practical Guide for Counselors, Educators and Parents* (Alameda: Hunter House, 1992). This guide contains thoughtful discussions and excellent activities about ablism, ageism, racism, sexism and anti-working class bias.

Teaching/Learning Gender Equity: An Overview of Three Education Partnership Projects (Toronto: The Ontario Women's Directorate, 1998). Available on the Ontario Women's Web Site at <http://www.gov.on.ca/owd>. This overview describes three remarkable projects developed in partnership with the Ontario Association of Deans of Education and the education faculties of three Ontario universities. The three individual teaching resources produced through this partnership are designed to promote gender equity education with pre-service teachers, faculty members, associate teachers and educational policy-makers. The University of Western Ontario produced two videos and two manuals entitled "Taking Action: Reworking Gender in School Contexts" and "Taking Action: Negotiating Power Relations in the Practicum." "Equality in Education: A Course Designed for Teacher Education," produced by Laurentian University, includes a Teacher's Guide and a Student Manual. The University of Ottawa produced "Words Can Change the World: A Gender Education Manual for Pre-service Teaching" and "Les mots peuvent changer le monde. Vidéo et guide d'utilisation." The *Overview* provides distribution information for these resources.

CLASSROOM RESOURCES

ELEMENTARY

Nancy Schniedewind and Ellen Davidson, *Open Minds to Equality: A Sourcebook of Learning Activities to Promote Race, Sex, Class and Age Equity* (Needham Heights: Allwyn and Bacon, 1998). This is the revised edition of a classic collection of activities for students between Grades 3 and 8.

The following titles directly address sexism and racism. They are ideal for classroom and school libraries:

Mary Hoffman, *Amazing Grace* (London, Frances Lincoln, 1991).

Lenore Keeshig-Tobias, *Bird Talk* (Toronto: Sister Vision, 1989).

Janice Schoop, *Boys Don't Knit* (Toronto: Women's Press, 1986).

Charlotte Zolotow, *William's Doll* (New York: Harper Trophy, 1985).

INTERMEDIATE/SECONDARY

A small wave of girl-positive material has been published for the intermediate and secondary school market. Check your local women's bookstore.

Susan Merritt, *Herstory, Herstory II* and *Herstory III* (Toronto: Vanwell, 1993, 1994 and 1998). Each volume contains short biographies of a wide range of interesting Canadian women from the time of Contact up to the twentieth century.

Metropolitan Toronto School Board, *Challenging Ourselves: Towards Gender Equity and Violence-free Relationships* (Toronto: Pembroke, 1996). This handbook provides countless practical resources for students and teachers in Grades 7 through 12.

Janese Swanson, *Tech Girl's Internet Adventures: An Adventurous and Fun Way for Girls to Learn about the Internet from Girl Tech* (Foster City, CA: IDG Books Worldwide, 1997). There are many girl-focused sites on the Web. This book can help you connect to some of the best.

Cool Women Cafe

http://www.coolwomen.org

This all-Canadian Web site focuses on women's history and has many articles on famous Canadian women and on Canadian women's issues. It offers a bulletin board for current events, chat threads and a search engine.

ORGANIZATIONS

Women's Directorates and Secretariats
Check to see what your provincial government offers by way of its women's directorate or secretariat.

The Ontario Women's Directorate
http://www.gov.on.ca/owd
Some of the OWD publications include
How Hard Can it Be? An Annotated Bibliography of Background Materials and Curriculum Resources to Encourage Girls and Young Women into Computer Technology, Engineering and Trades, Leadership and Entrepreneurship, Mathematics and Science.
In Our Own Words: A Workshop for Teachers on Gender Equity.
Policy on Full and Fair Access for Women and Girls in Sport and Physical Activity.
Raising Young Voices: A Discussion Kit.
Succeeding Young Sisters: A Guide to the Development of After-School Encouragement and Mentoring Programs for Young Black Women.

British Columbia
http://www.weq.gov.bc.ca/

Saskatchewan
http://www.womensec.gov.sk.ca/

New Brunswick
http://www.gov.nb.ca/sw_cf/index.htm

Nova Scotia
http://www.gov.ns.ca/staw/

Newfoundland
http://www.gov.nf.ca/exec/wpo/wpo.htm

Green Dragon Press
135 George Street South, Suite # 902
Toronto, ON M5A 4E8
(416)360-6006
1-800-305-2057
Fax: (416)360-6788
www3.sympatico.ca/equity.greendragonpress/

Green Dragon Press is a small publisher that develops and publishes feminist and educational resources. Some are appropriate for classroom use and others are designed to be teacher resources. Look for: *Black Women in Canada: Past and Present; Count Me In: Gender Equity in the Primary Classroom.*

Canadian Teachers' Federation
110 Argyle Avenue
Ottawa, ON K2P 1B4
(613) 232-1505
Fax: (613) 232-1886
E-mail: Info@ctf-fce.ca

The CTF has many resources on gender equity for teachers. One of the best is the Gender Equity Poster, which is quite large and illustrates all areas in a school where gender issues arise.

Canadian Men's Network for Change
infoweb.magi.com/~mensnet/
Although the Men's Network for Change is now dissolved, the Men's Site has many useful links and a library of articles for pro-feminist, gay-affirmative, anti-racist, male-positive men.

Our Schools/Our Selves
107 Earl Grey Rd.
Toronto, ON M4J 3L6
Phone/Fax (416) 463-6978
1-800-565-1975

Our Schools/Our Selves publishes *Our Schools/Our Selves: A Magazine for Canadian Education Activists* and a wide range of books on issues concerning progressive education in Canada. A year's subscription brings three issues of the magazine and three books.

Rethinking Schools
1001 E.Keefe Ave.
Milwaulkee, WI
USA 53212
(414) 964-9646
Fax(414) 964-7220
E-mail: Barbaramin@aol.com
www.rethinkingschools.org/

Rethinking Schools is a quarterly newspaper advocating the reform of elementary and secondary public schools. Its mandate is to promote educational equity, support progressive educational values and provide a voice for teachers, parents and students.

NOTES

The author would like to thank the women who have nurtured her intellect and her feminist sensibility throughout the years: her mother, Lesley Lang (teacher), her grandmothers Amy Lang (teacher) and Betty Moffatt (teacher), Susan Gerrard, Nora Peat, Marm Goldstein, Myra Novogrodsky, Christine Dunbar, Liz Martin, Kathy Bellomo, Leslie Chud, Susan Cole, Judy Wapp, Sheila Koffman, Heather Murray, Tara Goldstein and Elaine Mitchell. This chapter is dedicated to Molly Cole Chudnovsky for what will be, and to Alison Orrett for her emotional, physical and intellectual maintenance work.

1. This is true of informal education as well, particularly in post-Contact Canada. Informal education has also been remarkably important in Canadian history for people of colour, women and working-class people.

2. Alison Prentice et al., *Canadian Women* (Toronto: Harcourt Brace, 1988), 155-156.

3. Ibid, 57.

4. L. Fischer and J. Cheyne, *Sex Roles: Biological and Cultural Interactions as Found in Social Science Research and Ontario Educational Media* (Toronto: Queen's Printer, 1977), 46.

5. Ibid, 88. Fischer and Cheyne used the term "central characters" to include both fictional and non-fictional persons.

6. Ibid, 90, 91, 107, 112, 115. Curiously, the researchers found that the representation of females, while not equal was somewhat more favourable in textbooks during the 1950s than in the late 1970s.

7. Ibid, 116-118, 119, 120, 136.

8. Prentice et al., *Canadian Women*, 367.

9. Fischer and Cheyne, *Sex Roles*, 137.

10. Ibid, 141-142.

11. Ibid, 149.

12. Joan Scott, "Is There a Problem? Environment and Achievement of Girls in High School Science in Canada," *Who Turns the Wheel* (Ottawa: Science Council of Canada Publications, 1981), 24, 26. Studies of enrollment in biology courses showed that more young women than young men took biology. However, the difference may be linked to a genuine interest in the subject or because most school boards required students to take at least one science course, and biology is often perceived to be the least difficult of the sciences.

13. Science Council of Canada, *The Science Education of Women in Canada: A Statement of Concern* (Ottawa: Science Council of Canada Publications, 1982), 5-6.

14. Operation Minerva continues. It can be reached through its Web site <www.awsn.com/OPMIN/opmin.html>.

15. Myra Novogrodsky and Andrea Alimi, "Overcoming Sexism in Career Choices and Work," *Orbit* 28 (1997), 44-45.

16. Fischer and Cheyne, *Sex Roles*, 30.

17. Lorna Erwin, "Gender Subjectivity and Career Identity: The Construction/Deconstruction of Occupational Aspirations Among Female Undergraduates" in Carol E Harris, ed., *Proceedings from the Association for the Study of Women and Education Summer Institute: Advancing the Agenda* (St. Catharines, ON: Brock University, 1996), 237.

18. Lesley Harman, "The Feminization of Poverty: An Old Problem with a New Name," *Canadian Woman Studies* 12 (1992), 6-9.

19. Patricia Kenschaft has outlined fifty-five possible reasons, ranging from broad social traditions, to familial and educational customs, to subject-specific practices, in her article "Fifty Five Cultural Reasons Why Too Few Women Win at Mathematics," in P Kenschaft, ed., *Winning Women into Mathematics* (Washington, DC: Mathematical Association of America, 1991), 11-15.

20. Eileen Byrne, *Women and Science: The Snark Syndrome* (Washington: Falmer Press, 1993), 162-163.

21. Byrne, *Women and Science*, 163.

22. Judi Stevenson, *Gender Equity in Ontario Education: Giving Teachers the Tools to Contribute* (Toronto: Ontario Teachers' Federation, 1992), 15.

23. Carol Harris, ed., *The American Association of University Women Report: How Schools Shortchange Girls* (Washington, DC: The American Association of University Women Educational Foundation, 1992), 24-30.

24. Ibid, 26.

25. For a list of science programs and related initiatives, see Beth McAuley, *How Hard Can it Be? An Annotated Bibliography of Background Materials and*

Curriculum Resources to Encourage Girls and Young Women into Computer Technology, Engineering and Trades, Leadership and Entrepreneurship, Mathematics and Science (Toronto: Ontario Women's Directorate, 1997), available through the OWD Web Site at <wwwgov.on.ca/owd>. See also *Expanding Choices: Math and Science Programs for Girls and Women* (Halifax: Nova Scotia Women's Directorate).

26. Deborah Berrill and Keith De'Bell, "Strategies for Inviting Females to the Physical Sciences," *Orbit* 28 (1997), 50-53; Beverley Hardcastle Stanford, "Gender Equity in the Classroom," in D Byrnes and G. Kieger, eds., *Common Bonds: Anti-Bias Teaching in a Diverse Society* (Association for Childhood International, 1992) 96.

27. Berrill and De'Bell, "Strategies for Inviting Females to the Physical Sciences," 51-53; Pat Rogers, "Changing Women or Changing Mathematics," *Orbit* 28(1997), 33; Stanford, "Gender Equity in the Classroom," 96.

28. Rogers, "Changing Women or Changing Mathematics," 30; Stanford, "Gender Equity in the Classroom," 96.

29. Rogers, "Changing Women or Changing Mathematics," 31.

30. Barbara Houston, "Should Public Education be Gender Free?" in Lynda Stone, ed., *The Education Feminist Reader* (New York: Routledge, 1994), 123-124.

31. Christine McCauley Ohannessian et al,"Direct and Indirect Relations Between Perceived Parental Acceptance, Perceptions of the Self and Emotional Adjustment During Adolescence," *Science News* 5 (December 1996), 159-183; Bruce Bower, "Teenage Turning Point: Does Adolescence Herald the Twilight of Girl's Self-Esteem," *Science News* 139 (March 1991), 184-186; Patricia A. Schmuck and Richard A. Schmuck, "Gender Equity: A Critical Democratic Component of America's High Schools," *NASSAP Bulletin* 28 (January 1994), 22-31.

32. Stanford, "Gender Equity in the Classroom," 89.

33. Ibid, 87.

34. Houston, "Should Public Education be Gender Free?" 124. These patterns appear to hold or increase across race lines. Research on teachers working with Grade 1 girls found they gave more feedback to Black girls for their classroom behaviour than for their academic work. In assessing their students, the teachers similarly mentioned social skills more often for Black girls than for white girls or boys of either race. Linda Grant, "Black Females' 'Place' in Desegregated Classrooms," paper presented at the Annual Meeting of the American Sociological Association, National Institute of Mental Health, Rockville, 1982.

35. Stanford, "Gender Equity in the Classroom," 87.

36. S. Askew and C. Ross, *Boys Don't Cry: Boys and Sexism in Education* (Milton Keynes: Open University Press, 1988), 25; Beverley Stitt et al., *Building Gender Fairness in Schools* (Carbondale: Southern Illinois University Press, 1988), 4; Harris, *The American Association of University Women Report*, 19.

37. Stanford, "Gender Equity in the Classroom," 89.

38. Stevenson, *Gender Equity in Ontario Education*, 12.

39. Stanford, "Gender Equity in the Classroom," 87.

40. Elizabeth Sarah, Marion Scott, and Dale Spender, "The Education of Feminists: The Case for Single-Sex Schools," in E. Sarah and D. Spender, eds., *Learning to Lose: Sexism and Education* (London: Women's Press, 1980), 55-66.

41. Susan Morse, ed., *Separated by Sex: A Critical Look at Singe Sex Education for Girls* (Washington: American Association of University Women Educational Foundation, 1998), 2-3.

42. June Larkin, "Confronting Sexual Harassment in Schools" *Orbit* 28 (1997), 15.

43. Pat Stanton and June Larkin, *Sexual Harassment: The Intimidation Factor* (Toronto: Green Dragon Press, 1993), 19.

44. June Larkin, *Sexual Harassment: High School Girls Speak Out* (Toronto: Second Story Press, 1994), 26-28.

45. Linda Eyre, "Gender Relations in the Classroom: A Fresh Look at Co-education," in Jane Gaskell and Arlene McLaren, eds., *Women and Education* (Calgary: Detselig Enterprises, 1991), *196*.

46. Askew and Ross, *Boys Don't Cry*, 32-33.

47. Stevenson, *Gender Equity in Ontario Education*, 10; Spender as found in Askew and Ross, *Boys Don't Cry*, 32.

48. Michael Kaufman, "Working With Young Men to End Sexism," *Orbit* 28 (1997), 17.

49. Ibid.

50. Askew and Ross, *Boys Don't Cry*, 1.

51. Ibid, 25-26.

52. Ibid. See also Terrence Real, *I Don't Want to Talk About It: Overcoming the Secret Legacy of Male Depression* (New York: Simon and Shuster, 1997).

53. Stevenson, *Gender Equity in Ontario Education*, 10.

54. Stitt, *Building Gender Fairness in Schools*, 5.

55. Barbara Wauchope and Murray A Straus, "Age, Gender, and Class Differences in Physical Punishment and Physical Abuse of American Children," paper presented at the 1987 Annual Meeting of the National Conference on Family Violence Research, New Hampshire University, Durham, NH.

56. Pamela B. Miller, "Community Violence and Young Children: A Survey of Massachusetts Sixth Graders," paper presented at the 1997 Biennial Meeting of the Society for Research in Child Development, Washington, DC.

57. Beneita Dennis, "Chronic Violence: A Silent Actor in the Classroom" (n.p., 1994).

58. National Clearinghouse on Family Violence, "Sharing Information and Solutions" <www.hc-sc.gc.ca/hppb/familyviolence/news.htm>. September 1999.

59. Wauchope and Straus, "Age, Gender, and Class Differences in Physical Punishment and Physical Abuse of American Children."

60. Bob Meyenn, Judy Parker, and Katie Maher, "Come Along Then Naughty Boys: Perspectives on Boys and Discipline," paper presented at the 1998 Annual Meeting of the American Education Research Association, San Diego, CA.

61. For an example of some particularly fine work, see *Teaching/Learning Gender Equity: An Overview of Three Education Partnership Projects* (Toronto: Ontario Women's Directorate, 1998), which is available through the OWD Web site at <wwwgov.on.ca/owd>.

62. Heather-jane Robertson, "Must Girl-Friendly Schools be Girl-Only Schools?" *Orbit* 28 (1997), 4-7.

63. Some aspects of feminism have been taken up by mainstream culture, without changing the choices young women and young men have. For example, it has become the norm that all women work for wages. However, it is not nearly so common that men in heterosexual families take on half of the housework. And, although it is socially acceptable for a woman to stay home with her young children, men are not generally encouraged to do so. Similarly, traditional "women's work" such as childcare is still chronically underfunded and not given the status it deserves.

64. Bruce Curtis et al., *Stacking the Deck: The Streaming of Working-Class Kids in Ontario Schools* (Toronto: Our Schools/Ourselves Foundation, 1992); B. Levin, "Poverty and Education," *Education Canada* (Spring/Summer 1995); Mary Haywood Metz, *Veiled Inequalities: The Hidden Effects of Community Social Class on High School Teachers' Perspectives and Practices* (San Diego: American Educational Research Foundation, 1998).

Chapter 7

NAVIGATING THE WATERS OF CANADIAN ENVIRONMENTAL EDUCATION

Constance L. Russell, Anne C. Bell
and Leesa Fawcett

THE THREE OF US SET OFF on a journey of exploration, curious about the Canadian landscape of environmental education. Separately and together we have wandered this terrain for many years, in and out of elementary, secondary and university education systems, and along various environmental and community advocacy routes. Guided by those who have set out on similar journeys, we have grown increasingly aware and appreciative of the diversity of environmental education across the country and its everchanging and intermingled waters. We have been able to keep our bearings in large part thanks to other Canadian environmental educators who generously shared insights and information about the particularities of environmental education in their regions. This chapter reflects our travels so far, enlivened and enriched by the voices of those with whom we have learned and taught, and by the words of environmental educators across the country.

CONSULTING THE MAPS

Writing about environmental education in Canada is a daunting task. How can our partial, open-ended meandering do justice to the experiences of those on parallel yet different journeys? Environmental education is taken up in many sites (including schools, museums, parks, zoos, summer camps, community centres) and in countless ways (including instruction replete with courses, textbooks and exams, advocacy by environmental and community organizations, media programs, and ramblings in the woods). The focus of this anthology, however, is elementary and secondary school, and so we are concentrating our attention there. We recognize that in so doing we leave unexplored many significant currents in environmental education.

Even with the scope thus narrowed, the difficulty of accounting for the diversity of school-based environmental education practices across Canada remains. Nature study, outdoor education, conservation education, critical pedagogy, sustainability education and global education have all helped to shape environmental education; thus the lines between the fields are not strictly drawn.

School-based environmental education in Canada is less than thirty years old.[1] In 1990, Canada was said to have had no coherent national understanding of environmental education, in part because the country lacked "a Canadian journal of environmental education and an active, federally funded network ... in search of common perspectives," and in part because education falls under provincial jurisdiction. As a result, environmental education in each province and territory has tended to reflect the geographic, political, and cultural features of that area as well as the influence of long-standing provincial environmental education organizations.[2]

Whether or not the lack of national cohesion is a problem remains open to debate. Some suggest that federal initiatives, like the Green Plan, and concerted, co-operative national efforts can help create an "environmentally literate" citizenry.[3] Some also think the field should be paying more attention to the definitions, goals and objectives of environmental education nationwide and caution that without national standards and better communication, there is much reinventing of the wheel. Others fear, however, that efforts to standardize environmental education across the country might discourage new or alternative approaches; whose version of environmental education gets to count? Still others believe that questions of definition and purpose should be explored but not necessarily resolved. The point is not to find the one right answer, but to open up the discussion and to reflect more deeply on the meanings of our engagement.[4]

Certainly, the possibility of exploring environmental education in a more co-ordinated fashion is now within grasp, given the founding in 1993 of the Canadian Network for Environmental Education and Communication (EECOM), and the founding in 1996 of *The Canadian Journal of Environmental Education.* Two national arenas are now available in which to exchange information and ideas, and the combined (if not necessarily united) voices of Canadian environmental educators are beginning to be heard.

SCANNING THE HORIZON

As we work to define what environmental education means here at home, we would do well to remember that it is also a manifestation of an international movement. Environmental education is now an established area of study in many parts of the world. The approaches to and definitions of environmental education vary by culture, reflecting diverse relationships to their environments. The Treaty on Environmental Education for Sustainable Societies and Global Responsibility, drawn up at the Rio World Conference on the Environment in Rio de Janeiro, Brazil, in 1992, honours that diversity. The Treaty, written in four languages by non-governmental organizations and educators from five continents, is the most inclusive, democratic and comprehensive definition of environmental education to date. It outlines sixteen guiding principles, five of which we highlight here:

Principle 4: Environmental education is not neutral but is value-based. It is an act for social transformation.

Principle 9: Environmental education must recover, recognize, respect, reflect and utilize indigenous history and local cultures, as well as promote cultural, linguistic and ecological diversity. This implies acknowledging the historical perspective of native peoples as a way to change ethnocentric approaches, as well as the encouragement of bilingual education.

Principle 11: Environmental education values all different forms of knowledge. Knowledge is diverse, cumulative and socially produced and should not be patented or monopolized.

Principle 12: Environmental education must be designed to enable people to manage conflicts in just and humane ways.

Principle 16: Education must help develop an ethical awareness of all forms of life with which humans share this planet, respect all life cycles and impose limits on humans' exploitation of other forms of life.[5]

We support the Rio Treaty because it came about through a democratic exchange of ideas among people of many cultures. As well, it acknowledges that education is always value-laden, that cultural and ecological diversity are to be welcomed and protected, that movements for social and for environmental justice are interdependent and that the belief that humankind is at the centre of existence ought to be challenged.

The Rio principles resonate with the concerns and aspirations of a growing number of Canadian environmental educators whose practice is also shaped by critical pedagogy, popular education, feminism and eco-feminism, environmental thought, environmental justice, bioregionalism, holistic education or indigenous knowledges. Many examples of environmental education illustrate this overlapping of ideas. One project, for instance, brings feminism, popular and global education together in work that traces the path of a tomato from its beginnings, through the hands of farm and factory workers and multinational distributers, to the supper table. Elsewhere, those inspired by the Deep Ecology Movement and by bioregionalism are calling for a celebration of our connections to other life and for a reappraisal of fundamental societal assumptions.[6] Others, determined to highlight the connections between environmental degradation and social injustices like racism, sexism and classism, are infusing their practice with insights gleaned from the environmental justice movement and eco-feminism.[7]

Other environmental educators have adopted a holistic approach, recognizing that environmental issues are complex and require interdisciplinary responses. Typically, environmental education has found its home within the sciences or geography. Some secondary schools in Saskatchewan and Ontario, however, offer integrated environmental studies programs. Subjects are grouped together to make a four-credit package (for example, a combination of English, drama, physical education, leadership, environmental science or geography). Many integrated programs also offer one or two credits for co-operative education so that secondary students can teach elementary students about local environmental issues or apprentice in another job that has an environmental focus. These programs are based on a pedagogical approach more often used in primary and junior grades whereby these secondary students spend the full day with one group of peers and one or two teachers for an entire term. Experiential learning is emphasized so classes are usually conducted in the communities and natural areas adjacent to the school. Such integrated programs are lauded for promoting critical aspects of environmental education: grounding learning in authentic, "real world" experiences; demonstrating links between subject areas; fostering student responsibility; increasing student-teacher contact; and improving relations among students.[8]

Some environmental education programs draw on the traditions of different First Nations. For example, some Dene and Inuit students study the land, the animals, people's relations to the land and the essential relationships between land and culture.[9] One Ahkwesahshne environmental education project encourages students to develop a sense of place, to explore their relationships with the earth and cosmos, and to become comfortable traversing multi-cultural worlds. These approaches offer both a counterweight to mainstream understandings of human-nature relationships and a reminder that for many cultures, nature is sacred.[10]

Attention to the relationships between humans and nature is played out somewhat differently in the Green School movement.

Programs like Destination Conservation in Alberta and British Columbia emphasize waste and energy audits, while the national SEEDS Foundation, through the Learners in Action program, reward schools who participate in environment-related activities.[11] Many schools, often with the support of the Evergreen Foundation, also participate in schoolyard naturalization, where students transform paved or barren schoolyards into welcoming green spaces burgeoning with plant and animal life.

In Ontario, Green Schools are moving beyond traditional environmentalism to include development, equity, health, peace and rights. The seven schools in the Ontario Green Schools Project have taken a whole-school approach based on the following principles: (1) learning environments that promote equity, fairness, peace and social justice; (2) participatory democracy; (3) environmental responsibility; (4) valuing diversity while affirming commonality; (5) recognition of the inherent worth and dignity of every person; (6) safe school environments; (7) positive interpersonal relationships; and (8) congruence between principles and practices.[12]

Green Schools reveal the potential for wide participation in environmental education, engaging teachers, students, administrators, staff and members of the broader community (parents, college and university students, business people). Such participation, however, is the exception rather than the rule in environmental education. Far more often, one or two committed teachers bear the bulk of the responsibility alone. Their presence is the primary reason some schools have a strong environmental education program. This strength can become a weakness, for if a motivated teacher leaves a school, programs can wither.[13]

Not surprisingly, then, teacher training is essential for furthering the growth of school-based environmental education.[14] Environmental education remains on the margins of most teacher training, whether pre-service, in-service or graduate. It is strong only in institutions where there is a committed faculty member. Even then, with the exception of a few programs, environmental education at best is offered as a single course among many electives. At worst, some institutions do not offer even a single course.

It seems obvious that increased teacher training in environmental education throughout Canada is essential. Yet unless it becomes part of the bedrock of teacher training at all levels, many fear that it will become one more requirement for teachers who are already feeling overburdened. As one teacher wrote: "We want to make teachers passionate about computer literacy, and co-operative planning, and information processing and technology, and conflict resolution, and ... you get the point. We're all *extremely* overloaded."[15]

In many parts of the country, teachers must confront such chronic challenges as funding cuts, inadequate preparation time and large class sizes. Their time and resources are stretched to the limit, which has worrisome repercussions for the implementation of environmental education. Among other things, it can mean that environmental education is treated as an add-on, not deserving of the same attention and funding as "core" subjects. Committed teachers can find themselves put in the position of trying to subvert the curriculum to include environmental education. Being so stretched can also push teachers to lighten their load by relying on packaged materials generated by governments, consultants, industry and non-governmental organizations. American programs such as Project Wild, Project Learning Tree, and Earthkeepers are used extensively in Canada.[16]

Some in the field resist the lure of packaged curriculum materials on the grounds that environmental education should remain locally relevant. They advocate more active collaboration with grassroots organizations familiar with the intricacies of local, contemporary environmental issues.[17] This valuing of local context and content is also reflected in the continuing (and, in some cases, renewed) emphasis on natural history.[18] The growing popularity of such school-based initiatives as habitat restoration, energy and waste audits and bird and tree surveys seek to situate environmental education in the immediate life contexts of students and to acknowledge the intimacy of their relationships with other life.

Some of the most exciting environmental action in the schools is not a planned result of instruction but comes from "environmental clubs, recycling groups, student action committees ... leading whole communities — and often teachers — into new forms of environmentally responsible behaviour."[19] Students can and do act as catalysts for environmental change, initiating discussions and taking action on issues in concert with adults at school and at home and in the broader community.[20] Just as many education theorists are calling for more student involvement in the creation of knowledge generally,[21] a transformation of traditional teacher-student relationships appears to be underway in environmental education. With the aim of engaging students in personally meaningful, creative and critical learning experiences, more and more teachers are sharing their power by encouraging far greater student participation in decision-making.

Student participation is, however, a complex phenomenon. Often overlooked is how classism, racism, sexism and other forms of social injustice influence participation in a system that itself often reinforces such injustices. The culture of the school can also constrain students and teachers who want to focus more on eco-political work than on the "domestic" environmentalism of recycling and waste management.[22]

RIDING THE CURRENTS

Many currents stir and animate the waters of Canadian environmental education. We travellers must pick and choose among them, depending on the vantage points we seek, the pace we deem desirable, and the destinations we have in mind. The routes we wish to follow are seldom direct. They twist and turn while currents far more powerful than our canoes carry us along. Choices must be made, and we are grateful when the occasional eddy provides respite from the momentum forward. There is no single correct way of proceeding, and what we propose now is simply to pause for a moment to contemplate some of the directions that lie ahead.

HUMAN-ENVIRONMENT RELATIONSHIPS

There are many conceptions of "environment" and each has implications for definitions of and approaches to environmental education.[23] One of the most contentious and yet most common equates "environment" with "resources." That belief is part of the common heritage of people living in modern, industrialized societies where humanity is generally imagined to be not only different from, but superior to, all other life; the environment thus becomes our dominion, to be controlled and used solely for our benefit.[24] Within the context of environmental education, the belief is played out in curricula that advocate the rational or "wise" management of natural "resources," often according to the principles of sustainable development and equitable sharing.[25]

In contrast, indigenous knowledges make an important contribution to environmental education precisely because of a radically different premise that humans are part of, not separate from, environmental processes.[26] That premise holds more promise for educators who struggle with "resourcist" assumptions and seek to encourage the understanding that the dilemmas we face have deep cultural roots in modern industrial society's profound alienation from the "more-than-human world." Some are developing strategies that examine dominant and alternative conceptions of "human," "environment" and "nature." They seek to reawaken, validate and celebrate care, responsibility, participation and the sensory dimensions of being a human animal in constant relation with other life.[27]

The differences in opinion about what constitutes appropriate human-environment relationships have led to substantial disagreements in environmental education. For example, the relative merit of "sustainability" has been much discussed.[28] Some argue that environmental education is no longer a useful term and ought to be replaced with, or supplemented by, sustainability education which is said to move beyond a perceived narrow focus on natural environments by including greater consideration of human needs. Others maintain that broadening the discussion in that way simply allows for development to continue unabated and to place humans once again at the centre of life. These and other disagreements have led some commentators to speak of a continuum when they describe different approaches to environmental education, with "light" or "shallow" green representing a wise-use "resourcist" position and "dark" or "deep" green representing a position which sees intrinsic value in all life.[29] While useful for analysis, we suspect labelling some theories and practices as "shallow" and others as "deep" is divisive, for it can mask the complexity and contradictions inherent in environmental education.

SCIENCE AND TECHNOLOGY

Discussions about appropriate human-environment relationships are linked to, and reflected in, a burgeoning skepticism about the scientific/analytic paradigm. Environmental education is generally treated as a "subset of the science curriculum" and is presented with a highly technical bias.[30] In Atlantic Canada, for example, where environmental education falls under the rubric of science, the most recent draft curricula emphasize technology, trade and resources. Such an approach can lend itself to a fragmented understanding of environmental issues and leads some to equate environmental education simply with a decontexualized, isolated unit on rainforest conservation.[31]

A growing number of Canadians are calling into question environmental education's current emphasis on science in environmental education.[32] They hold that teaching about ecological processes and environmental hazards in a supposedly objective and universally valid manner belies the fact that knowledge is socially constructed and therefore partial. It conceals the values, beliefs and assumptions that underlie information and create an illusion of neutrality and anonymity. An emphasis on objectivity also works against the possibility of understanding plants, animals and other beings as experiencing subjects of a life. Such reservations, however, usually do not translate into an outright rejection of science in environmental education. Rather, much as many feminists urge, science ought to be placed in context so that its cultural and historical specificity can be recognized.[33]

ADVOCACY

Many in the field acknowledge the need for more critical approaches in environmental education. Teaching and learning involve far more than the mere transmission of facts. There are ethical and political dimensions to every aspect of education and to ignore that is to lose the very possibility of examining the assumptions under-pinning claims to knowledge. Recent debate in Canada and abroad has considered the merit of approaches to environmental education that openly challenge existing social arrangements. Concerned that a particular platform may run counter to the wishes of the majority, some prefer to distinguish clearly between the role of the teacher and that of the advocate. Teachers, they contend, must be wary of their power and careful not to abuse it. They must convey the complexity of the issues discussed, and not attempt to indoctrinate students.[34]

The task is not easy, given that "groups from all sides of the political spectrum can and do present their side as the only or cor-rect side of the story."[35] Teachers have little choice but to proceed thoughtfully. Many prefer to avoid the turbulent waters of politics and advocacy altogether, perhaps because they fear controversy or because they firmly believe that education can be neutral and objec-tive. Others caution that advocacy in the classroom places the onus for change on children, not on industry. Further, even if students do agree with their teacher's views, they may feel that they have no way to take action.[36]

Others look at advocacy somewhat differently. They say that environmental education has always sought to transform the societal values that promote environmental degradation. That revolutionary function runs counter to schooling's traditional purpose: "conserving the existing social order by reproducing the [dominant] norms and values." Whether environmental education does transform norms and values is an open question. For some, "much environmental education seems entrenched in 'business as usual' and explores only those topics which don't necessitate funda-mental changes."[37] Focusing on individual behaviour, like "Reduce, Recycle, and Re-use," may lead only to superficial reform and mask the need for collective action and profound structural change.[38] The increasing use of free, industry-subsidized materials adds to the concern. Some insist, then, that more eco-political work be brought to the fore in environmental education to "spark fundamental questioning and action on cultural assumptions and practice."[39]

Similarly, others call for environmental education to be grounded in the understanding that education always has an agenda, either implicit or explicit, whether it be to maintain the status quo, to move carefully towards reform, or to transform society radically.[40] We agree. One of our roles as teachers is to facilitate critical thinking about these and other positions.

DIVERSITY OF NARRATIVES

Traditionally, environmentalism and environmental education have represented the voice and the vision of the white middle-class, despite decades of activism by other communities.[41] The environmental justice movement links environmental degradation with social injustices like racism, sexism and classism and its insights vastly enrich the scope of environmental education. For example, environmental justice advocates point out that it is no accident that the working-class and people living in poverty and people of diverse ethnic, cultural, linguistic and racial groups often live within or beside toxic areas. These groups continue to be underrepresented in politically powerful circles, their voices ignored. The environmental education movement, generally, has mirrored this wider trend: "More often than not, other cultures and perspectives have been excluded, or played marginal or insignificant roles."[42]

Environmental education needs to come to terms with the "monoculturalism" that pervades it. Part of the challenge is to recognize that different cultures may value different bodies of knowledge and different ways of knowing. Another part of the challenge is to create spaces for a diversity of approaches to and understandings of teaching, learning and being.

One promising path is the Ahkwesahshne practice of examining "stories from many cultures, including scientific and biblical stories, in order to understand how the relationships modelled in them are reflected in the daily life of the societies they influence." The point is to ease the conflict between seemingly contradictory perspectives and to recognize "that we can live with ambiguity."[43]

Others suggest drawing attention to several of the dominant anti-environmental narratives that shape how and what students learn. The "Growth Myth," for example, assumes that there are no, and ought not be, limits to industrial and economic growth. Although rarely expressed bluntly, these anti-environment myths pervade textbooks and weave a tale of human dominance and ingenuity that is simply accepted as truth. Identifying and exposing such myths, putting forward contending points of view, and revising or replacing textbooks and the like accordingly is recommended.[44]

In many cultures, the actual telling of stories is a legitimate, often preferred, way of making and passing on knowledge.[45] Through storytelling we can express the particular and honour diversity. The three of us have found that stories of our individual and collective experiences, however muddy and messy, can move and inspire students far more than matter-of-fact presentations about environmental problems. Sharing anecdotes of our encounters with other animals in urban, rural and wilderness settings, for example, offers a starting point and sounding-board for discussing broader issues. Stories can also provide a glimpse of the vitality of the more-than-human world.[46] Storytelling by students themselves allows them to share, develop, and honour their own perspectives. We need only see the excitement in children's faces, listen to the quality of the questions or watch the activities that spring from hearings and tellings of stories, to appreciate the power of narrative.[47]

RAPIDS, ROCKS AND TAILWINDS

While rocks and rapids may add excitement to our journeys, they can leave us stranded too. Wind, likewise, can be a blessing if it is behind us, but it can hinder us if we meet it head-on. Learning to anticipate, read and negotiate these contextual features is crucial to navigation. It means learning to recognize advantages in one situation and disadvantages in another.

The diversity of approaches to environmental education in Canada is a case in point. If, on one hand, we regard our differences as a problem, they become stumbling blocks, impeding conversation and co-operation. If, on the other hand, we consider our differences as "fuel for critical reflection, discussion, contestation and evolution," our practice will be much richer.[48] We need to keep talking about what it means to live and teach environmental education.

Critical questions and challenges lie ahead. How are we to define environmental education? Who decides? Is there a distinctly Canadian approach to environmental education? How do we make room for cultural and ideological diversity? How will we handle the tensions that spring from differing opinions on appropriate human-environment relationships, the role of science and technology, the relationship between advocacy and education, and the calls for greater diversity in content and approach? How might we begin to better meet the need for more teacher training at all levels? What research needs to be done? How might we create room for more collaboration between academics and teachers in research, particularly in much-needed program evaluation? There are no simple answers. Instead, we see the need to continue the debate in Canada and beyond.

These ongoing conversations, we hope, will be grounded in both practice and theory. Practice allows us the opportunity to develop our understandings and grasp the complexity of environmental education firsthand. Theory places firsthand knowledge in diverse contexts, deepens insights, and provides for critical reflection. Insights from the multiple practices and theories of environmental justice, indigenous knowledges, feminism and ecofeminism, critical pedagogy, environmental thought, deep ecology, bioregionalism and the other educations highlighted in this anthology all have much to offer environmental education, just as environmental education can enrich the theory and practice of each. While not wishing to minimize the important differences and tensions between these movements and educations, each contributes to a diversity of voices, each is grounded in specific communities and experiences, and each combats injustice and works towards more inclusive politics and social change.

All of us who are deeply committed to environmental education have our own unique starting points, and our diversity inevitably leads to some tension. Nonetheless, when our paths do cross it would be refreshing to sit down together to share a fire and a meal, ready to talk and learn from one another. Together, we can consider the distance covered and contemplate the challenges and possibilities that lie ahead. There are many questions we might discuss as we evaluate our journeys. Have we ended up where we intended? Or are in some unknown, possibly unsettling place? Is it somewhere more interesting than first anticipated? Has everyone been sheltered and well cared for? Did we lose anyone en route? Did we forget to invite others who might like to join us in our upcoming journeys? If so, how do we accommodate their hopes, interests, and motivations? Perhaps we also need to consider joining others on their travels? If we speak from the heart and encourage openness, these conversations will sustain and inspire us on the journeys ahead. They will help to ensure that we do not repeat mistakes endlessly, that we fully appreciate good fortune, and that we continue to learn along the way.

TEACHER RESOURCES

Joseph Cornell, *Sharing the Joy of Nature* (Nevada City, CA: Dawn CA, 1989); *Sharing Nature with Children* (Nevada City, CA: Dawn CA, 1989); and *Journey to the Heart of Nature* (Nevada City, CA: Dawn CA, 1994). These books provide excellent outdoor education activities.

Michael Caduto and Joseph Bruchac, *The Keepers Series* (Calgary: Fifth House). This series of Native stories and environmental activities explore the perspectives of various Native North American nations. Each chapter begins with a story that provides a starting point for activities that reflect an interdisciplinary approach to environmental education. The four books in the series are *Keepers of the Earth* (1989), *Keepers of the Animals* (1991), *Keepers of Life* (1994) and *Keepers of the Night* (1994). Teacher's guides and audiocassettes are also available.

Sue Greig, Graham Pike, and David Selby, *Greenprints* (London: Kogan Page and World Wide Fund for Nature, 1989).

Kathryn Sheehan and Mary Waidner, *Earth Child: Games, Stories, Activities, Experiments and Ideas About Living Lightly on Planet Earth* (Tulsa, Oklahoma:

Council Oak Books, 1994). This book offers a wide range of activities that encourage connections with nature. Each chapter has a "Dream Starter," a simple story to help children imagine the life and feelings of another animal, insect, or plant. Each chapter also has many activities and recommendations for children's books. A Teacher's Guide, CD-ROM, and audio tape are also available.

Green Teacher
95 Robert St.
Toronto, ON M5S 2K5
(416) 960-1244
E-mail greentea@web.net
ww.web.ca/~greentea/
This is one resource that most environmental educators consider essential.

CLASSROOM RESOURCES

Schoolyards and adjacent natural areas are important resources for environmental education. In Canada and elsewhere, teachers are exploring the possibilities of teaching from and with a sense of place where they and their students live and work. Whether a rural community, a small town or a large city, place can serve as a basis for reflecting on relationships between humans and nature.

Orion Magazine, published by the Orion Society, regularly reviews children's environmental literature. The Society also publishes *Bringing the World Alive: An Annotated Bibliography of Children's Books With Nature Themes.* Order by phone at (212) 758-6475.

Richard Kool and Emma McMillan, *An Environmental Educators Guide to the Internet* (Ottawa: E Ecom, n.d.). This Guide lists many Internet sites of interest to teachers and students. It is available through EECOM.

ORGANIZATIONS

The Federation of Ontario Naturalists
355 Lesmill Road
Toronto, ON M3B 2B8
(416) 444-8419
1-800-440-2366
www.web.net/fon or http://gbr.org

The FON publishes many useful books, education kits, posters and activities.

Acorn Naturalists
PO Box 2423
Tustin, CA 92781
1-800-422-8886
www.acorn.group.com

The Evergreen Foundation
163 West Hastings, Suite 106
Vancouver, BC V6B 1H5
(604) 689-0766

355 Adelaide St. West, #5A
Toronto, ON M5V 1S2
(416)596-1495
E-mail: info@evergreen.ca
www.evergreen.ca

A non-profit registered charity with a mandate to promote and establish natural areas in urban areas through education.

The Canadian Network for Environmental Education and Communication
(EECOM)
P.O. Box 948, Station B
Ottawa, ON K1P 5P9

The North American Association for Environmental Education
(NAAEE)
P.O. Box 400
Troy, OH 45373, USA
(937) 676-2514
http://eelink.umich.edu/naaee.html

NAAEE is an umbrella organization with affiliates in Canada, the United States and Mexico. The Association sponsors an annual conference and publishes a bi-monthly newsletter, books and resources.

NOTES

The following individuals generously responded to our survey or read an earlier version of this chapter, or both, offering their insights on difficult questions: Pix Butt, Paul Hart, Bob Henderson, Ann Jarnet, Bob Jickling, Fay Katay, Rick Kool, Janet Pivnick, Claude Poudrier, Scott Slocombe, Sue Staniforth, Dan Stoker, Rosanna Strong, and one other who wished to remain anonymous. We also wish to thank Tara Goldstein, David Selby and P.K. Murphy for their comments on an earlier version. The standard proviso remains, however: the three of us together are responsible for our assertions and mistakes. Anne Bell gratefully acknowledges the financial assistance of the Social Science and Humanities Research Council of Canada.

1. Indeed, Paul Hart states that it has been only in the past ten years that environmental education has really become a part of the school experience See his article, "Problematizing Enquiry in Environmental Education: Issues of Method in a Study of Teacher Thinking and Practice," *Canadian Journal of Environmental Education* 1 (1996), 57.

2. For a good overview of the state of Canadian environmental education up to the late 1980s, see Paul Hart's article, "Environmental Education in Canada: Contemporary Issues and Future Possibilities," *Australian Journal of Environmental Education* 6 (1990), 45-66.

3. Rick Mrazek, "Seeing the Trees Through the Forest: Navigating Toward Environmental Citizenship in Canada," *Canadian Journal of Environmental Education* 1 (1996), 125.

4. Sue Staniforth, writing in response to our survey of Canadian environmental educators, June 1996; Environment Canada's Ann Jarnet, writing in June 1996 in response to our survey, agrees that developing a national framework for environmental education is a good idea, but she is concerned that "there might not be room for ideas other than those which are currently being expressed"; and Janet Pivnick, writing in response to our survey, June 1996.

5. United Nations Conference on the Environment and Development, *Environmental Education for Sustainable Societies and Global Responsibility: A Citizen's Treaty From the International NGO Forum of the UNCED, Rio de Janiero* (Rio De Janiero: UNCED, 1992).

6. See, for example, Deborah Barndt, "Tracing the Trail of Tomasita the Tomato: Popular Education Around Globalization," *Alternatives Journal: Environmental Thought, Policy and Action* 22 (1996), 24-29, and Deborah Barndt, ed., *Women Working the NAFTA Food Chain: Women, Food and Globalization* (Toronto: Second Story Press, 1999; now available from Sumach Press, Toronto); Bert Horwood, "Tasting the Berries: Deep Ecology and Experiential Education," *Journal of Experiential Education* 14 (1991), 23-26; Janet Pivnick, "Speaking From the Deep: The Problem of Language in Deep Ecology Education," *The Trumpeter: Journal of Ecosophy* 14 (1997), 53-56; Janet Pivnick, "A Piece of Forgotten Song: Recalling Environmental Connections,"

Holistic Education Review 10 (1997), 58-63; Diane Pruneau, Omer Chouinard, and Charline Arsenault, "The Cap Pelé Model," *Alternatives Journal: Environmental Thought, Policy and Action* 243 (1998), 28-31. See also the special issue of the deep ecology journal, *The Trumpeter: Journal of Ecosophy* 14 (1997), which was devoted to the topic.

7. Jennie Barron, "Shhh! Movement Afoot! Listening to the Voices in the Grassroots," *Pathways: Ontario Journal of Outdoor Education* 10 (1998), 22-25; Leesa Fawcett, dian marino, and Rebecca Raglon, "Playfully Critical: Reframing Environmental Education," in J. Baldwin, ed., *Confronting Environmental Challenges in a Changing World: Selected Papers from the 1991 North American Association for Environmental Education Conference Proceedings* (Troy, OH: NAAEE, 1991); Wanda Martil-diCastro, "Grounding Environmental Education in the Lives of Students," *Pathways: Ontario Journal of Outdoor Education* 11 (1999), 16-20; Constance L. Russell and Anne C. Bell, "A Politicized Ethic of Care: Environmental Education From an Ecofeminist Perspective," in Karen Warren, ed., *Women's Voices in Experiential Education* (Dubuque, IW: Kendall Hunt, 1996).

8. Council of Outdoor Educators of Ontario, *Inventory of Integrated Programmes* (Toronto: COEO, 1996); Bert Horwood, "Integration and Experience in the Secondary Curriculum," *McGill Journal of Education* 29 (1994), 89-102.

9. Rosanna Strong, writing in response to our survey, June 1996.

10. Mary Henderson, "A Mohawk Vision of Education," *Green Teacher* 49 (1996), 15-19; Lucy Wren, Marge Jackson, Harry Morris, Carol Geddes, Daniel Tlen, and Norma Kassi, "First Nations Perspectives: What Is a Good Way to Teach Children and Young Adults to Respect the Land?" in Bob Jickling, ed., *A Colloquium on Environment, Ethics, and Education* (Whitehorse: Yukon College, 1996).

11. Dan Stoker, writing in response to our survey, June 1996.

12. David Selby, "Towards the Darker Green School: Making Education for Sustainability Sustainable," *Orbit* 27 (1996), 41-45.

13. Pix Butt, writing in response to our survey, June 1996; Paul Hart, "Teacher Thinking and Practice: Environmental Education in Canadian Elementary Schools," a paper presented at the North American Association for Environmental Education Annual Conference, November 1996, Burlingame, CA.

14. Many of our 1996 survey respondents (Pix Butt, Paul Hart, Ann Jarnet, Rick Kool, Janet Pivnick, Claude Poudrier and Sue Staniforth) argued that teacher training was one of the most pressing needs in Canadian environmental education.

15. Pix Butt, survey response, June 1996.

16. Paul Hart and Bob Henderson made similar points in response to our survey, June 1996; Hart, "Environmental Education."

17. Fay Katay, Rick Kool, and Sue Staniforth each made this point in their survey responses, June 1996.

18. Anne Bell, "Natural History From a Learner's Perspective," *Canadian Journal of Environmental Education* 2 (1997), 132-144; Michael Quinn, "Knowing

Your Friends By Name: The Importance of Natural History in Interpretation and Outdoor Education," *Pathways: Ontario Journal of Outdoor Education* 7 (1995), 5-8.

19. James Raffan, "The Failed Curriculum," *Journal of Experiential Education* 13 (1990), 49.

20. Roy Ballantyne, Sharon Connell, and John Fien, "Students As Catalysts for Environmental Change: A Framework for Researching Intergenerational Influence through Environmental Education," *Environmental Education Research* 4 (1998), 285-298; William Hammond, "Educating for Action: A Framework For Thinking About the Place of Action in Environmental Education," *Green Teacher* 50 (1996), 6-14.

21. To name only a few, bell hooks, *Teaching to Transgress: Education as the Practice of Freedom* (New York: Routledge, 1994); John Miller, *The Holistic Curriculum* (Toronto: OISE, 1993); Ira Shor, *Empowering Education: Critical Teaching for Social Change* (Chicago: University of Chicago Press, 1992).

22. Cheryl Lousley, "(De)politicizing the Environment Club: Environmental Discourses and the Culture of Schooling," Environmental Education Research 5 (1999), 293-304; dian marino, *Wild Garden: Art, Education, and the Culture of Resistance* (Toronto: Between the Lines, 1997); Peter McClaren, *Life in Schools* (New York: Longman, 1989). For a discussion of the limits of schooling for environmental education more generally, see Anthony Weston, "Deschooling Environmental Education," *Canadian Journal of Environmental Education* 1 (1996), 35-46.

23. Nelleke Bak, "Green Doesn't Always Mean 'Go': Possible Tensions in The Desirability and Implementation of Environmental Education," *Environmental Education Research* 1 (1995), 345-352; Constance L Russell, "Approaches to Environmental Education: Toward a Transformative Perspective," *Holistic Education Review* 10 (1997), 34-40; Lucie Sauvé, "Environmental Education and Sustainable Development: A Further Appraisal," *Canadian Journal of Environmental Education* 1 (1996), 7-34.

24. David Abram, *The Spell of the Sensuous: Perception and Language in a More-Than-Human World* (New York: Pantheon, 1996); Neil Evernden, *The Social Creation of Nature* (Baltimore: Johns Hopkins, 1992); John Livingston, *Rogue Primate: An Exploration of Human Domestication* (Toronto: Key Porter, 1994).

25. Sauvé, "Environmental Education," 10.

26. Strong, survey response.

27. Bob Henderson, "Friluftsliv," *The Trumpeter: Journal of Ecosophy* 14 (1997), 93-94; Pivnick, "A Piece of Forgotten Song"; Michael Quinn and Jennifer Scott, "Of Mega-Malls and Soft-Shelled Turtles: Deep Ecological Education to Counter Homogeneity," *The Trumpeter: Journal of Ecosophy* 14 (1997), 53-56; Russell and Bell, "A Politicized Ethic of Care."

28. Bob Jickling, "Why I Don't Want My Children Educated for Sustainable Development," *Journal of Environmental Education* 23 (1992), 5-8; Sauvé, "Environmental Education."

29. Denis Mahoney, "Sharing Environmental Education Stories: A Critical Incident in a Canadian Community," *Canadian Journal of Environmental Education* 3 (1998), 136-155; Selby, "Towards the Darker Green School."

30. Rick Kool, "Directions for the Future: Environmental Education in British Columbia," in Jickling, ed., *A Colloquium on Environment, Ethics, and Education* , 168.

31. Butt, survey response; Selby, "Towards the Darker Green School," 42.

32. Barbara Bader, "Une vision socialisée des sciences au service d'une éducation relative à l'environnement socioconstructive," *Canadian Journal of Environmental Education* 3 (1998), 156-170; Anne Bell, Constance L Russell, and Rachel Plotkin, "Environmental Learning and the Study of Extinction," *Journal of Environmental Education* 29 (1998), 4-10; David Jardine, "'Under the Tough Old Stars': Meditations on Pedagogical Hyperactivity and the Mood of Environmental Education," *Canadian Journal of Environmental Education* 1 (1996), 47-55; Kool, "Directions for the Future."

33. Evelyn Fox Keller, *Reflections on Gender and Science* (New Haven: Yale University Press, 1985); Donna Haraway, *Simians, Cyborgs and Women: The Reinvention of Nature* (New York: Routledge, 1991); Carolyn Merchant, *The Death of Nature: Women, Ecology and the Scientific Revolution* (San Francisco: Harper and Row, 1980).

34. Pamela Courtenay Hall, "Environmental Education in a Democratic Society," in Alex Wellington, Alan Greenbaum, and Wesley Cragg, eds., *Canadian Issues in Environmental Ethics* (Peterborough: Broadview Press, 1997); Bob Jickling, "Why I Don't Want My Children Educated for Sustainable Development"; Bob Jickling and Helen Spork, "Education for the Environment: A Critique," *Environmental Education Research* 4 (1998), 309-327; Milt McClaren, "Education, Not Ideology," *Green Teacher* 35 (1993), 17-18.

35. Kool, in his survey response, was focusing on curriculum resources in this instance.

36. Jarnet, survey response.

37. Hart, "Environmental Education," 58-59; Pivnick, survey response.

38. Courtenay Hall, "Environmental Education"; Lousley, "(De)Politicizing"; Catriona Sandilands, "On 'Green' Consumerism: Environmental Privatization and 'Family Values'," *Canadian Woman Studies* 13 (1993), 45-47.

39. Stoker, survey response; Henderson, survey response.

40. CA.Bowers, *Education, Cultural Myths, and the Ecological Crisis: Towards Deep Changes* (Albany: State University of New York Press, 1993); Derek Hodson, "Politicizing Environmental Education," *Crucible* 23 (1992), 14-19.

41. Susan Lewis and Kathy James, "Whose Voice Sets the Agenda for Environmental Education? Misconceptions Inhibiting Racial and Cultural Diversity," *Journal of Environmental Education* 26 (1995), 5-12; Running-Grass, "The Four Streams of Multicultural Environmental Education," *Race, Poverty and the Environment* 6 (1996), 1-2; Noel Sturgeon, *Ecofeminist*

Natures: Race, Gender, Feminist Theory and Political Action (New York: Routledge, 1997).

42. Dorceta Taylor, "Making Multicultural Environmental Education a Reality," *Race, Poverty and the Environment* 6 (1996), 3.

43. Henderson, "A Mohawk Vision," 17-18.

44. Mark McElroy, "Paradigms Lost: And the Myths We Teach Our Children," *Green Teacher* 53 (1997), 6-10.

45. Sean Kane, *Wisdom of the Mythtellers* (Peterborough: Broadview Press, 1994); Joe Sheridan, " Twice Upon a Time," *Canadian Journal of Environmental Education* 3 (1998), 116-135.

46. Anne C. Bell and Constance L. Russell, "Life Ties: Disrupting Anthropocentrism in Language Arts Education," in Judith P. Robertson, ed., *Teaching for a Tolerant World, Grades K-6: Essays and Resources* (Urbana, IL: National Council of Teachers of English, 1999); Leesa Fawcett, "Animal Stories and the Struggle Against Forgetting," *Pathways: Ontario Journal of Outdoor Education* 11 (1999), 19-20; Zabe MacEachren, "Why and How I Tell Stories," *Pathways: Ontario Journal of Outdoor Education* 75 (1995), 6-9.

47. Courtenay Hall, "Environmental Education," 369.

48. Jarnet, survey response; Sauvé, "Environmental Education," 28.

Chapter 8

A TAPESTRY IN THE MAKING

THE STRANDS OF GLOBAL EDUCATION

Graham Pike

THE NEED FOR GLOBAL EDUCATION has never been more pressing. Globalization is creating a rapidly-changing global society, one whose citizens scramble to keep pace with change even as they work to build more just, more humane and more stable environments for all who live on the planet. A key outcome of globalization is connectedness: through the rapid movement of goods and information, countless opportunities are created for the sharing of ideas and experiences among communities worldwide. Distinctions between "local" and "global" have become increasingly blurred. Globalization, however, should not be confused with global improvement. Over the past thirty years, the divide between rich and poor — in Canada and worldwide — has widened considerably. National and regional conflicts continue to tragically waste human lives. The natural world, to which human life is inextricably connected, has suffered irreversible damage. Global education is a tapestry in the making: it weaves together the separate threads, such as economy, environment, society and technology, by which we currently make sense of the world. It is needed to help us fully realize our interdependence with all life forms, to understand that, ultimately, survival in isolation is neither desirable nor possible. What it might conceivably contribute to the twenty-first century remains unknown, but the dangers of education without a global perspective are starkly evident in the history of the twentieth.

Global education has a short history in Canada, but it has attracted considerable support. Many strands running through it can be traced to initiatives in the fields of development education and peace education, led by educators and social activists in the 1970s. The efforts of development educators, in particular, fueled the emergence of global education, which was, in turn, propelled by funding from the Canadian International Development Agency (CIDA), the federal agency responsible for Canada's official aid programs. The belief that schools were not sufficiently addressing global issues in the curricula prompted CIDA to invite ministries of education and teachers' associations in every province and territory to submit proposals for projects to promote global education in public schools. The first project opened in New Brunswick in 1987. By 1992, seven other of Canada's ten provinces — Alberta, British Columbia, Newfoundland, Nova Scotia, Ontario, Quebec, Saskatchewan — and one of the two territories of the time — the Yukon — were running global education projects. The Saskatchewan project closed in 1992. CIDA continued to fund the rest until 1995, when the Minister for Foreign Affairs suddenly and unexpectedly removed CIDA's financial support for both development education and global education. Since then, CIDA has funded some small-scale global education initiatives run by non-governmental organizations. The period 1987–1995 can therefore be regarded as the most productive in the weaving of Canada's global education tapestry. This period is the principal focus of this chapter.

A quick scan of the books and articles on global education in Canada reveals the field's willingness to adapt to Canadian needs many models, ideas and strategies that come from other countries, particularly from the United Kingdom and the United States. This does not mean that Canadian proponents have not determined the scope and direction of global education; rather, they have made use of theories that were developed elsewhere. One interesting point of note is that several of the most prominent writers on global education in Canada are immigrants and bring to their thinking and writing insights gleaned from living in other countries, as well as from the experience of immigration itself. Such influences have been so fundamental to the shaping of Canadian culture and identity over the past century that they are, in essence, part of being Canadian.[1]

This rich mix of influences might contribute, in part, to the difficulty in deciding on a generally accepted Canadian definition of global education. Ibrahim Alladin, who draws on American, British and United Nations sources, finds global education an important concept but one that "is vulnerable to loose definitions and vague interpretations."[2] Others agree that greater clarity is needed and adopt, or build on, established American models of global education. In so doing, Jim Petrie argues that clarity is required if global education is to avoid becoming the umbrella for every curriculum lobby group and thereby losing credibility with teachers.[3] In more recent writing, attempts to unequivocally define global education have given way to the painting of broader characterizations. Walter Werner and Roland Case identify four key themes:

(1) Interconnections: understanding links and interdependencies between countries and regions of the world and how global systems — cultural, economic, environmental and political — are also connected.

(2) Perspectivity: recognizing that individual perspectives are always partial and understanding the importance of seeking diverse viewpoints.

(3) Caring: acknowledging the necessity for a moral underpinning to teaching about the world.

(4) Alternatives: considering and promoting sustainable alternatives to the short-term policies and practices of today.[4]

My own exploration of how teachers address global education in practice reveals not a single method nor a common content but a range of overlapping approaches that generally encompass the key ideas of interdependence, connectedness and perspective. Connectedness has several senses for those working in classrooms:

the sense of connection implied in the sharing of common attributes by humans everywhere; the links perceived among contemporary global issues; the interlocking welfare of humans, other species and their environments; a desired relationship between education and the wider world; and the integration of subjects in the curriculum.[5]

It appears that global educators are now turning away from the search for a succinct definition and towards general statements of content and purpose that make room for the very diversity of perspectives and approaches that global education itself espouses.

SCOPE AND PURPOSE

One significant characteristic of global education in Canada, especially when compared with similar movements in the United Kingdom and the United States,[6] is the degree of consensus that global educators hold with regard to its scope and purpose. It is also characteristic, however, that few offer a critical appraisal of that scope and purpose, from either within or from outside the education system. As well, there appears to be little disagreement on key educational components in the emerging field of global education. These components are briefly reviewed here.

APPLIES ACROSS THE CURRICULUM

Despite its origins in development education and peace education, both often seen as perspectives within social studies, global education in Canada draws from many subject areas. Handbooks and journal articles on global education come from perspectives of the arts, history, home economics, the language arts, mathematics, science, social studies, special education and technology, as well as from cross-disciplinary fields such as citizenship education, environmental education and media education. In the elementary classroom, teachers illustrate how global education can be used to create a totally integrated curriculum built around global issues and themes rather than subjects.[7]

Two methods proposed for applying global education across the curriculum are infusion and integration.[8] Infusion entails enriching existing curriculum subjects with relevant global education knowledge, skills and attitudes. In mathematics, for example, students practice arithmetic skills using UN statistics on development, or explore geometric shape and symmetry through studying traditional patterns from various cultures. In language arts, students study universal themes such as conflict or justice in a selection of world literature, or use drama and role play exercises to explore the significance of non-verbal communication in their own and other cultures. The guiding premise of integration is the organization of learning in a way that reflects, and is easily transferable to, real-world situations. It emphasizes connections and relationships between different disciplines, resulting in a curriculum comprised of broad themes rather than subjects. For example, in a unit on population, students employ the skills of history and mathematics to graph world population growth since 1500 and make future projections, and they use insights from family studies and social studies to examine arguments on the rights of women to control their own fertility. Under the theme of water, students explore the scientific basis of pollution in the Great Lakes, and assess the significance of water scarcity as a catalyst for conflict in regions such as the Middle East.

FOCUSES ON GLOBAL ISSUES AND PROBLEMS

Though not necessarily categorized this way, educators' focus on areas of global concern include development, environment, equity, futures, peace, rights and responsibilities. These provide the substantive framework for, or organizing concepts of, global education, as distinct from focusing on specific countries or cultures (sometimes seen as the purview of multicultural education).

ENGAGES BOTH HEART AND MIND

Most models and definitions of global education move beyond an exclusive preoccupation with imparting knowledge and teaching skills to incorporate the development and refinement of attitudes and values. Many writers and classroom teachers stress the importance of changing attitudes if global problems are to be successfully addressed. They seek to encourage caring attitudes towards other people and other species; concern for the plight of the disadvantaged, for the poor and the oppressed; and they emphasize the need to challenge and expand insular views of the world.

ADDRESSES HOW WE LEARN, NOT JUST WHAT WE LEARN

Sometimes explicitly, at other times through examples of lessons or topics, global educators advocate learning that is student-centred, participatory and interactive, often couching their rationale in terms of the importance of maintaining harmony between the "medium" and the "message." They urge that concepts such as co-operation, equity, interdependence, justice, respect for rights, and self-esteem be addressed through teaching and learning methods that embody the essence of the message being conveyed.

ENCOURAGES ACTION

Although there are disagreements about the extent to which global education should promote social activism among students, there is no debate that it should empower learners to be more active in shaping their own futures. Thus, the purpose of global education is not simply to acquire knowledge about the world, but to enable students to be effective and responsible in applying that knowledge for the benefit of themselves and others.

The broad consensus on the scope and purpose of global education in Canada may be significant in understanding how it has had such an impact on education in a relatively short time. Research on educational reform suggests that an innovation of even moderate complexity takes from three to five years to develop from initiation to institutionalization (the point at which it gets built into the system), even if schools are dealing with only one innovation at a time.[9] Canadian schools have undergone multiple reforms since 1987, some of which are not at all compatible with global education.[10] Yet, by 1991, Robert Moore was claiming that the provincial global education projects had reached 300,000 teachers, or 90 percent of the teaching population. Tom Lyons reported that more than 5,000 teachers and sixteen school boards in Ontario had made "some kind of commitment" to the project in its first three years.[11] A 1992 survey of a random sample of 1,200 teachers found that two-thirds of the respondents thought that a global perspective in education was important and 40 percent had significantly altered their approach to teaching during the last two years to incorporate such a perspective.[12]

Examples of the institutional impact of global education can be found in the high profile it was afforded in *The Common Curriculum*, the Grade 1 to 9 curriculum guidelines developed under the Ontario NDP government (and subsequently scrapped by the Conservative administration), and in the setting up of "global schools." In Newfoundland, where global schools provided the framework for the provincial project, global education is seen as a vehicle for implementing many aspects of school improvement, including curriculum revision, staff development and community involvement. Nationally, support comes from the Canadian School Boards Association, which has published a model policy intended for use by school boards wishing to develop their own policies on global education.[13]

LACK OF CRITICAL DEBATE

Also characteristic of the consensus on the scope and purpose of global education is the lack of critical debate, from the movement itself and from other educators and the public. Opposition to global education from outside the field is rare in Canada, especially in comparison to the acrimonious attacks that religious fundamentalist and nationalist groups have launched in the United States.[14] But it does occur. For example, in 1994 the Canadian Christian Research Institute condemned the Alberta Global Education Project Conference for its "explicit anti-Christian bias and advocacy of new age and pagan religious practices."[15] In the previous year, an article in the Toronto Teachers' Federation newsletter criticized a "Federation Day" presentation on global education to Toronto elementary teachers on the grounds that global education is yet another educational experiment whose efficacy lacks scientific proof.[16] These are local and isolated examples and have not sparked serious or lengthy public debate.

Within the field itself, global educators rarely criticize each other's work or provide alternative theses. Again, the exceptions are remarkable, such as David Selby's two-part article on humane education that challenges global educators to explore the similarities between the two fields and to examine the tensions and conflicts between the two.[17] A sizable majority of those writing on global education in Canada are male, as were the original directors of all provincial projects, with the exception of Quebec. A feminist critique might be anticipated, particularly given that an Ontario survey found that women teachers were more likely to see global education as important and to alter their teaching accordingly. Contributions from women writers do appear in journals on global education, but the writers are frequently classroom teachers writing about their practice. An explicitly feminist perspective on global education, or an argument for including the perspectives of women in the analysis of global issues, is rare.[18]

Few Canadians in the field directly explore the relationship between the goals of global education and those of multicultural education. Matthew Zachariah argues that global education must encourage "fair and objective treatment of the cultures from which (Canada's) visible minorities originate," including recognition of the strengths and weaknesses of all cultures and the fact that, even in times of rapid change, there are elements of cultural continuity.[19] Elizabeth Parchment and Zubeda Vahed also argue that race is central to global education, but they acknowledge that their argument is not fully accepted in Canada. Ibrahim Alladin, however, makes a clear distinction between global education and multicultural education on two grounds: first, the former seeks to foster an international perspective, where the latter seeks to promote national unity out of cultural diversity; second, multicultural education focuses on domestic, multiethnic issues, where global education concerns itself with global issues and systems.[20] The Centre for Intercultural Education and International Co-operation (CEICI) in Quebec is unique among projects in Canada in including intercutural education and global education as two complementary but distinctive strands of education with a global perspective. The Quebec project's quarterly newsletter regularly features the two strands side by side.[21]

SOME UNSPOKEN TENSIONS

Research on global education in Canadian classrooms reveals that teachers share general agreement on its scope and purpose.[22] The research also suggests, however, that woven into the common strands are some subtle but significant differences of opinion on several of global education's more controversial goals, differences which can also be detected from a more critical exploration of the literature. Essentially, the diversity of viewpoint centers on four areas: global education's moral purpose; the interests of its constituency; its role in advocating change; and its stance on questions of citizenship.

MORAL PURPOSE

Writers in the field frequently refer, sometimes explicitly, to global education's underlying moral purpose. Walter Werner proposes that one of global education's key goals be that students discuss the moral questions that arise from exploring interdependent relationships in the global system. Kazim Bacchus and Jane Williams suggest that teachers have a moral obligation to help students understand that everyone bears responsibility for problems such as world poverty and injustice. Linda Darling proposes that global education is "a moral enterprise," that it goes far beyond providing knowledge about the world to developing "moral sensitivities and understandings," especially in terms of how students should relate to other people.[23]

For some, global education's moral purpose is grounded in a relatively non-controversial respect for, and empathy with, people in all situations and circumstances. For others, the moral purpose inevitably amounts to a critical analysis of western values and lifestyles. The "equitable new world order" advocated by Douglas Roche calls for the rich countries to give up their economic dominance and implies that Europeans and North Americans must consume less. David Ferns takes up the torch by attacking the concept of "sustainable development" as a bandwagon that allows the present, US-based emphasis on material development to flourish. That view of development, he argues, "is hollow, unfulfilling and lacking in any moral substance ... above all it is almost impossibly seductive."[24]

Global education's moral purpose, however, is not always couched within a seam of altruism. Roche also suggests that self-interest comes into play, that the motivation to find solutions to global problems is deeply pragmatic, if we are "to survive nuclear annihilation, the rich-poor gap in the world, environmental degradation and over-population."[25] In fact, pragmatism appears to be close to the heart of some perceptions of global education's raison d'être. Part of the rationale for the model policy of the Canadian School Boards Association is to help students explore global issues and take positive action to resolve global problems. But the policy also suggests that global education can help promote Canada's competitiveness in world markets by encouraging students to learn other languages, acquire teamwork skills and gain respect for cultural differences.[26] The idea of global education lending support to the national economy, popular in the United States where it is described as a "neomercantilist" view,[27] is not commonly found in Canada. For Brian O'Sullivan, however, the "global economic competitiveness" argument — the belief that competition and wealth are measures of success in the global marketplace and should therefore guide educational reform — poses a major threat to the institutionalization of global education. He contends that the power and influence of the global competitiveness constituency outside the education system, especially in the business community and the national business media, outweigh the power and influence of those in the global education movement. Furthermore, he suggests, while global competitivists capitalize upon people's self-interest and desire for material wealth, global educators appeal only to a sense of morality and responsibility. He urges the two divergent paradigms of educational change be reconciled, but notes with interest the marked absence of public debate on either.[28]

Not all global educators, however, appeal directly to a sense of morality. In sticking closely to the awareness-oriented goals of an American model of global education, Jim Petrie puts emphasis on understanding global issues and cultural perspectives, not on exploring relative values and morals. Roland Case extends the model to include a "perceptual dimension," within which he proposes values and attitudes such as "open-mindedness," "resistance to stereotyping" and "non-chauvinism." Case acknowledges that his account of a global perspective is not value-neutral but argues that "it does not prejudge for educators or students the particular view they should adopt on contentious issues such as the merits of maintaining the current world order."[29] That position is quite different from one that argues for an "equitable new world order," or one that attacks American-style material development.

CONSTITUENCY INTERESTS

Another angle on global education's moral purpose can be illustrated by asking the question: Whose interests are thought to be served through the implementation of global education? Not surprisingly, perhaps, given its roots in development education and significant funding from CIDA, much of the theory and practice of global education tends towards anthropocentrism. Visions of a new world order and a more caring, just and compassionate society centre on the needs and rights of human beings and on their obligations towards one another. A few writers in the field steep their work in a biocentric ethic, arguing that global education's links to ecology and cosmology are fundamental to an analysis of our present planetary crisis.[30] Susan Kiil proposes a new framework for the curriculum, focusing on "physical ecology, social ecology, creative ecology, integrated/whole systems and human technologies" in place of traditional subjects. In her vision of education, the needs of the planet as a whole, rather than the specific needs of humans, determine the intrinsic values of learning and the direction it takes. Tom Lyons decries the "anthropocentric arrogance" that leads human beings to aspire to "global perhaps cosmological dominance." In more dispassionate tones, David Selby contends that global educators have taken insufficient account of perspectives from the field of humane education, especially its insights into the relationship between animal rights and human rights. Selby calls for an ethic that respects life in all its forms and warns against the blinkered vision that comes from putting humankind at the centre of solutions to global problems.[31]

ADVOCATING FOR CHANGE

Underlying the "perceptual dimension" of a global perspective is a particular view of global education's role in fomenting social change. To the extent that students' behaviour does not meet certain expectations, the five elements of the perceptual dimension are oriented towards changing the behaviour of students. Roland Case, the author of this model, is not, however, explicitly critical of the global status quo, therefore he does not need to advocate social change. His pedagogical position is based on leading students "out of a naive, largely uninformed view of the world into a more enlightened view," without stating the principles upon which that enlightenment should be based.[32] This position is reinforced by Warner and Case who contend that the "classrooms are not platforms for launching children's crusades to save the world." They do accept, however, that "social action projects may be appropriate means (not ends)" for promoting students' intellectual, social and moral development.[33] Toh Swee-Hin's perception of the school's role in promoting change is quite different, in tone and objective: he proposes a "transformative paradigm of global literacy" which not only promotes critical understanding of global problems, but also encourages students and teachers "to act towards a more peaceful, just and liberating world." He presents this vision of education as a critical alternative to the "liberal technocratic paradigm" which, he contends, is predominant in Canadian textbooks and syllabuses and in the practices of otherwise well-intentioned teachers. Central to this latter vision of global literacy is not emancipation and justice but a passive respect for experts and ruling elites who promise to improve the lives of ordinary people.[34]

While most global educators are motivated by a vision of a better world, classroom teachers echo the different positions summarized above. A few are unequivocal in stating that their role is to educate for social change; many support the view that "there is a delicate balance to strike between education for citizenship and indoctrination for activism"[35] and encourage students to develop the skills of democratic participation but stop short of allowing schools to be used as launchpads for social reform. Often, the reasons for that restraint are more pragmatic than ideological, including fear of repercussions from principals, parents and school boards. Earl Choldin, director of the Alberta Global Education Project, expresses concern over the lack of "political action" he sees in local school initiatives that just raise awareness of social issues, or raise funds for worthy causes. He argues that teachers are missing valuable opportunities to teach students how to play an active role in a participatory democracy.[36]

CITIZENSHIP

For some, reconciling national and global interests is a major goal of global education. Ivan Head argues that humankind has largely created the global system, yet our understanding of interconnectedness is way behind the reality that makes us all "intimate neighbours." The resulting "mental insularity" leads, he suggests, to mutual vulnerability, particularly for the countries in the rich North.[37] Promoting the concept of global citizenship is one attempt to enhance our understanding of the interlocking nature of the contemporary world. Derek Heater, drawing on the concept of the "multiple citizen," proposes that we think of citizenship as "plural and parallel" and arising out of the "multiple identities and loyalties and the plurality of sources that define our sense of virtue and legal, political and social status."[38] Education for global citizenship suggests, then, that an expectation of exclusive loyalty to the nation state is nonsensical in an interdependent world, where anyone is likely to experience the pull of multiple loyalties to regional, national, international and transnational groups. Active participation is also critical: education for global citizenship "nurtures empowered students who view the world with enthusiasm." It fosters an attitude that challenges the "strident individualism which says 'me first, my country first.'"[39]

Others handle the idea of global citizenship a little more cautiously. Roland Case argues that fostering national interests is appropriate and desirable, but concedes that "attention to our own national interests must not obscure any moral obligations we have to the global community."[40] In Canadian schools, including "global schools," the persistence of nationalism suggests that "mental insularity" flourishes and may indeed be obscuring obligations to the global community. Curriculum courses continue to distinguish between "Canada" and "the world"; allegiance to the nation is commonly sworn, whereas allegiance to the planet — or even to the United Nations — is conspicuously absent; "other cultures" and "other countries" pop up as distinct entities in project work, as though global interdependence were merely a theory that had no meaning for our daily lives. The distinctiveness of global education in Canada, compared with dominant models in the United Kingdom and the United States, also lends credence to the view that national culture plays a significant role in how the field develops. A legitimate task for global education might be to "find a new language that will express our needs and concerns as common inhabitants of the earth" in order to acknowledge the reality that the nation is no longer the primary arbiter of our private fate.[41]

THE NECESSARY CHALLENGE

Despite global education's short history, and the tensions woven into its fabric, classrooms around Canada provide sufficient grounds for reasonable optimism about its future. The national soil is, after all, extremely fertile: Canadian's passion for internationalism,[42] coupled with a federal immigration policy that is diversifying and expanding the physical and cultural make-up of the country's population, indicate both a need for, and a receptivity to, the widespread implementation of global education. Individual schools and teachers continue, even without the support of CIDA-funded projects, to imbue their teaching with a global perspective and to contribute ideas and resources to the professional journals that have survived. The challenge now facing global educators, whether or not further federal support is forthcoming, is to translate the considerable grassroots achievements of the past decade into processes and products that will promote the institutionalization of global education in the nation's schools. This challenge is both timely and necessary: the history of educational reform suggests that innovation is unlikely to have long-term impact unless both bottom-up grassroots enthusiasm and top-down institutional support converge.[43]

Institutionalization requires the contemporaneous pursuit of several connected goals: more debate, more research, and more influence on curriculum development and teacher education. Of these goals, perhaps the most fundamental is to increase the range and the depth of the debate on global education. Current trends in globalization create, albeit inadvertently, a climate favourable to the spread of global education, yet those promoting a much narrower, more utilitarian philosophy of education for global economic competitiveness appear to have more influence in determining educational policy.[44] This may be due, in part, to global education's relatively low profile and the lack of clear understanding of its scope and purpose among educators and the broader public. This should not be interpreted as a call for a single, incontestable definition of global education. On the contrary, there is sufficient consensus for the field to move forward in relative harmony, always accepting that there will be degrees of difference in theory and in practice. In any case, to posit the existence or desirability of a single definition would run counter to global education's embrace of multiple perspectives. On the other hand, global educators do need to be able to clearly describe their work to those outside the field; many practitioners still find this conspicuously, and embarrassingly difficult.[45] Further discussion and debate — at conferences and workshops, in professional publications and at parents' meetings — would help clarify the key ideas and give them a broader audience. Such dialogue would also contribute to the development of the field, especially if it were to be conducted around the areas of tension noted earlier.

Complementary to the broader dissemination of its key ideas, global education requires endorsement from in-depth research and academic writing. In keeping with its beginnings as a grassroots movement, most writing on global education in Canada appears in professional journals. Whilst the emphasis on classroom practice is greatly valued by teachers, the lack of academic research is a significant weakness. Few have researched and published on the efficacy and impact of global education approaches in Canadian classrooms. The criticism that its methods lack scientific validation[46] is no more true of global education than it is of countless other innovations that influence education. Yet if global education is to survive as a real force for educational reform, it will need a solid platform of convincing research. In the United States, where a similar dearth of research activity has been noted, researchers have proposed research agendas[47] and they are now contributing a steady stream of conference papers and are publishing in respected journals.

A third necessary step towards the institutionalization of global education is the exertion of greater influence on curriculum development and on teacher education. The universities of Alberta, New Brunswick and Prince Edward Island, Memorial University and the Ontario Institute for Studies in Education of the University of Toronto offer graduate courses in global education, which are now more common in Canadian universities than at the beginning of the 1990s. Global education has made fewer inroads into pre-service teacher education, with notable exceptions being the elective streams offered at OISE/UT and UPEI. Effective professional development, for both beginning and experienced teachers, is critical not only to the successful implementation of global education in the classroom, but also to future curriculum and school development. As classroom teachers become increasingly involved in the writing of new curricula and the development of school-based initiatives, the presence of teachers with understanding and experience of global education can have a significant impact upon the directions taken. Indeed, my research confirms earlier findings that, after graduation, school colleagues generally have the most significant influence upon a teacher's professional development.[48] The research also found that the implementation of global education relies heavily on the local availability of suitable resources. Teachers consider many text books and curriculum guidelines inadequate or outdated, yet few have the time and energy to produce new materials. In the absence of funding for global education within the education system, non-governmental organizations involved in awareness-raising and action on global issues could make a very important contribution in this area, as they have done for more than twenty years in the United Kingdom.

Canadian global education is far from complete, yet it has rich potential. With due care and attention, it can offer a transformative model of education that both reflects global reality and deepens our understanding of the significance of global interdependence.

TEACHER RESOURCES

Charlotte Anderson, with Susan Nicklas and Agnes Crawford, *Global Understandings: A Framework for Teaching and Learning* (Alexandria, VA: Association for Supervision and Curriculum Development, 1994). This book offers a framework for integrating global education within the curriculum; it includes sample integrated units and has a useful section on performance assessment in global education.

Roland Case, Robert Fowler, and Walt Werner, eds., *Thinking Globally about the Arts in Education; Thinking Globally about Language Education; Thinking Globally about Mathematics and Science Education; Thinking Globally about Social Studies Education* (Vancouver: Research and Development in Global Studies, University of British Columbia, 1995). These four books make up the series called *Global Education Through School Subjects*. Each volume includes a collection of papers that explore the implications of global education for the respective subject area.

Graham Pike and David Selby, *Global Teacher, Global Learner* (London: Hodder and Stoughton, 1988). This is not a recent publication, but it is considered a classic in the field. It gives a rationale for global education through a four-dimensional model, examines appropriate approaches for teaching and learning and offers a wide range of K-12 activities.

Graham Pike and David Selby, *In the Global Classroom 1* (Toronto: Pippin Publishing, 1999) and *In the Global Classroom 2* (Toronto: Pippin Publishing,

2000). These two handbooks offer various strategies for putting global education into practice and have a broad selection of K-12 activities, organized by
key themes. The first volume features the environment, futures, health, interconnections, perspective and technology. The second volume focuses on citizenship, development, equity, media, peace and rights.

Kenneth Tye, *Global Education: A Worldwide Movement* (Orange, CA:
Interdependence Press, 1999). An interesting work with recommendations for
action, based on a survey of global education theory and practice in fifty-two
countries. The discussion of the relationship of nationalism to global education is especially useful.

Merry Merryfield, Elaine Jarchow, and Sarah Pickert, *Preparing Teachers to Teach
Global Perspectives: A Handbook for Teacher Educators* (Thousand Oaks, CA:
Corwin Press, 1997). A collection of case studies exploring practices in pre-
service and in-service teacher education, school-university partnerships, and
infusing global education into teacher education institutions.

Miriam Steiner, ed., *Developing the Global Teacher: Theory and Practice in Initial
Teacher Education* (Stoke-on-Trent: Trentham Books, 1996). Explores how
universities and non-governmental organizations in the UK have attempted to
incorporate global education into teacher education programs.

CLASSROOM RESOURCES

Dinny Biggs, *In Our Own Backyard: A Teaching Guide for the Rights of the Child*
(Toronto: UNICEF Canada, 1995). Innovative and interactive ways for helping students in Grades 1 to 8 explore the 1989 United Nations Convention
on the Rights of the Child.

Alanda Greene, *Rights to Responsibility: Multiple Approaches to Developing Character
and Community* (Tucson, AZ: Zephyr Press, 1997). A resource book for
Grades 4 to 9 that uses art, songs, stories and drama to aid in understanding
children's rights.

Susan Fountain, *Education for Development: A Teacher's Resource for Global Learning*
(London: Hodder and Stoughton, 1995). A UNICEF compendium of K-12
activities organized in five sections: interdependence; images and perceptions;
social justice; conflict and conflict resolution; and change and the future.

Bob Hill, Graham Pike, and David Selby, *Perspectives on Childhood. An Approach
to Citizenship Education* (London: Cassell, 1998). Activities for Grades 6 to 12
that explore the meaning of childhood, identity formation in childhood and
the rights of the child.

J. Johnson, J. Benegar, and L. Singleton, *Global Issues in the Middle School: Grades 5-8*, 3rd ed. (Boulder, CO: Social Science Education Consortium/Center for Teaching International Relations, 1994). Activities for the middle school, exploring the interrelated themes of human values, global systems, global issues and global history.

Graham Pike and David Selby, *Reconnecting: From National to Global Curriculum* (Godalming: World Wide Fund for Nature UK, 1995). Activities and approaches for infusing global education into separate subjects across the Grade 7 to12 curriculum.

ORGANIZATIONS

New Internationalist Publications
1011 Bloor St. W
Toronto, ON M6H 1M1
(416) 588-6478
www.newint.org
Publishes *New Internationalist* magazine (eleven issues per year), which features articles, briefings, reviews and organizations covering significant development and global issues.

American Forum for Global Education
120 Wall Street, S-2600
New York, NY 10005
(212) 624-1300
www.globaled.org
Publishes a bi-monthly newsletter, *Issues in Global Education*, publishes and distributes curriculum resources, and offers in-service programs.

ASCD Global Education Network
1161 Cardinal St.
De Pere, WIS 54115
(920) 983-0960
Publishes a bi-monthly newsletter, *Global TeachNet*, in collaboration with the National Peace Corps Association and organizes sessions at its annual conferences.

BC Teachers for Peace and Global Education
British Columbia Teachers' Federation
100-550 W. 6th Avenue
Vancouver, BC V5Z 4P2
Publishes a newsletter, *PAGES*, three times a year and holds a conference each fall.

Centre for Intercultural Education and International Co-operation (CEICI)
1665 rue La Fontaine
Montreal, QC H2L 1V3
(514) 521-8800
www.cam.org/~ceici

Runs a teachers' resource centre in Montreal, publishes a newsletter, *Liaisons CEICI*, four to six times a year and supports teachers and schools in the region.

International Institute for Global Education (IIGE)
Ontario Institute for Studies in Education of the University of Toronto
252 Bloor Street West, 10th Floor
Toronto, ON M5S 1V6
(416) 923-6641, ext. 2863

Runs BEd and graduate courses (MA and PhD) in global education; supports school and board initiatives in the region and operates a teachers' resource centre.

Ontario Council of Educators for a Global Perspective (OCEGP)
26 Iona Street
Ottawa, ON K1Y 3L7
(613) 722-0344

Publishes a semi-annual newsletter and organizes an annual conference.

NOTES

1. Michael Ignatieff, *Blood and Belonging: Journeys into the New Nationalism* (Toronto: Viking, 1993). American proponents include Lee Anderson and James Becker, Robert Hanvey, Willard Kniep and Steven Lamy. British influences include the writings of David Hicks, Sue Greig, Graham Pike and David Selby. See also Tom Lyons, Graham Pike, David Selby, Toh Swee-Hin, Mathew Zachariah.

2. Ibrahim Alladin, "Teaching for Global Awareness," *The ATA Magazine*, 69 (1989), 6. The magazine of the Alberta Teachers' Association.

3. Jim Petrie, "Global Studies in the Social Science Curriculum," *Orbit* 23 (1992), 20-21. See also Roland Case, "Key Elements of a Global Perspective," *Explorations in Development/Global Education, Occasional Paper #25* (Vancouver: University of British Columbia/Simon Fraser University, 1991). The models used are those of Robert Hanvey, *An Attainable Global Perspective* (New York: Global Perspectives in Education Inc.,1982), and Willard Kniep, "Defining a Global Education by its Content," *Social Education* 50 (1986),

437-446. Hanvey's five dimensions are (1) perspective consciousness; (2) "state of the planet" awareness; (3) cross-cultural awareness; (4) knowledge of global dynamics; and (5) awareness of human choices. Kniep offers four essential elements: (1) the study of human values; (2) the study of global systems; (3) the study of global problems and issues; and (4) the study of global history.

4. Walt Werner and Roland Case, "Themes of Global Education," in Ian Wright and Alan Sears, eds., *Trends and Issues in Canadian Social Studies* (Vancouver: Pacific Educational Press, 1997), 176–194.

5. Graham Pike, "Global Education: Reflections from the Field," *Green Teacher* 54 (1997), 6–10.

6. Graham Pike, "The Meaning of Global Education. From Proponents' Visions to Practitioners' Perceptions" (PhD diss., University of York, UK, 1997).

7. See Ronald MacGregor, ed., *Thinking Globally about the Arts in Education* (Vancouver: Research and Development in Global Studies, University of British Columbia, 1995); Russ McLean, "Global History or Globetrotting?" *Aviso* 6 (1990), 20; Joan Allen Peters, "The Global Curriculum in Home Economics," *Green Teacher* 30 (1992), 15–17; Gale Smith and Linda Peterat, *Developing Global/Development Perspectives in Home Economics Education* (Ottawa: Canadian Home Economics Association, 1992); Marilyn Chapman and James Anderson, eds., *Thinking Globally about Language Education* (Vancouver: Research and Development in Global Studies, University of British Columbia, 1995); Douglas Crawford, "Experiencing, Discussing and Reflecting on Global Issues Using School Mathematics," *Orbit* 23 (1992), 24-25; Douglas Crawford, "Mathematics," in Graham Pike and David Selby, *Reconnecting: From National to Global Curriculum* (Godalming, UK: World Wide Fund for Nature, 1995), 104–123; Gloria Snively and Allan MacKinnon, eds., *Thinking Globally about Mathematics and Science Education* (Vancouver: Research and Development in Global Studies, University of British Columbia, 1995); John van der Beek, "Global Perspectives in the Science Classroom," *Orbit* 23 (1992); Carla Spinola, ed., "Towards a Global Social Studies Education: Focus on Teacher Education," *Research and Development in Global Studies* (Vancouver: University of British Columbia, 1989); Petrie, "Global Studies in the Social Science Curriculum"; Robert Fowler and Ian Wright, eds., *Thinking Globally about Social Studies Education* (Vancouver: Research and Development in Global Studies, 1995); Werner and Case, "Themes of Global Education"; Gary Bunch and Angela Valeo, "Students with Disabilities and Global Education," *Orbit* 27 (1996); Martin Sterling, "Technology and Global Education," *Orbit* 23 (1992); and Helen Peterson, "A Global Perspective on Children's Literature," *Orbit* 23 (1992); Dinny Biggs, "Global Perspectives on Food and Agriculture. Grade 4/5/6 Classroom Themes," *Orbit* 27 (1996).

8. Graham Pike and David Selby, *In the Global Classroom 1* (Toronto: Pippin Publishing, 1999), 15–23.

9. Michael Fullan, with Suzanne Stiegelbauer, *The New Meaning of Educational Change* (New York: Teachers College Press, 1991), 49.

10. Brian O'Sullivan, "Reconciling Paradigms: Global Economic Competitiveness

and Global Education as Alternative Approaches for Constructing Curricula. A Review of the Current Debates as They Apply to Secondary Schooling in Ontario" (Doctor of Education diss., University of Toronto, 1995).

11. Robert Moore, "Education for Planetary Living. CIDA Initiatives," *Orbit* 23 (1992), 8–9; Tom Lyons, "Education for a Global Perspective," *Orbit* 23 (1992), 11.

12. David Kelleher and Gordon Ball, *OTF/CIDA Global Education Project: Final Report* (St. Anne de Prescott/ Oro Station, ON: Authors, n.d.).

13. See Ontario Ministry of Education and Training, *The Common Curriculum: Policies and Outcomes Grades 1–9* (Toronto: Ministry of Education and Training, 1995); Bertram Tulk, "Global Education Begins in the Bay: The Newfoundland and Labrador Global Schools Experience," in Graham Pike and David Selby, *The Global School* (in press); and *Education for a Global Perspective*, "CSBA Model Global Education Policy," *Education for a Global Perspective* 4 (1994), 3.

14. Ron Schukar, "Controversy in Global Education: Lessons for Teacher Educators," *Theory Into Practice* 32 (1993), 52–57.

15. Ron Galloway, "Global Educators Take New Age to Elementary Classrooms," *Christian Research Newsletter* 2 (1994), 1.

16. Angus Lloyd, "Confused? Concerned!" *Role Call* 16 (1993), 3.

17. David Selby, "Humane Education: The Ultima Thule of Global Education. Part 1," *Green Teacher* 39 (1994), 9-17, and "Humane Education: The Ultima Thule of Global Education. Part 2," *Green Teacher* 40 (1994).

18. Kelleher and Ball, *OTF/CIDA Global Education Project*, 7; Elizabeth Dodson Gray, "Choosing Life: Theology, Gender and the Earth," *Global Education-Global Literacy* 2 (1994), 9–18; Margaret Wells, "Bringing a Gender Perspective to Global Education," *Orbit* 27 (1996), 31–33.

19. Mathew Zachariah, "Linking Global Education with Multicultural Education," *The ATA Magazine* 69 (1989), 48-51; Mathew Zachariah, "Intercultural Understanding: Some Reflections," *Global Education-Global Literacy* 1 (1993), 42–44.

20. Elizabeth Parchment and Zubeda Vahed, "Opening the Closed Door: The Centrality of Race to Global Education," *Orbit* 27 (1996), 33–34; and Alladin, "Teaching for Global Awareness," 7.

21. CEICI, *Information File* (Montreal: Centre for Intercultural Education and International Understanding, n.d.).

22. Pike, "The Meaning of Global Education."

23. Walt Werner, "What is Global Education?" paper presented at the 1988 School's Role in Global Education Conference, BC Teachers' Federation, Vancouver. Cited in Smith and Peterat, *Developing Global/Development Perspectives in Home Economics Education*; Kazim Bacchus, "The Concept of Global Education," *The ATA Magazine* 69 (1989), 19–22; Jane Willms, "The Children Next Door: Bringing the Global Neighbourhood Into the

Classroom," *Orbit* 23 (1992), 14–16; and Linda Darling, "Solidarity and Strangers: Shifting our Global Perspectives," *Explorations in Development/ Global Education, Occasional Paper #26* (Vancouver: University of British Columbia/Simon Fraser University, n.d.), 2–4. In this paper Darling builds on the work of Jerrold Coombs, "Towards a Defensible Conception of a Global Perspective," *Explorations in Development/Global Education, Occasional Paper #1* (Vancouver: University of British Columbia, 1988).

24. Douglas Roche, "The New World Order. Justice in International Relations," *Global Education-Global Literacy* 1 (1993), 31–38; and David Ferns, "Director's Perspective," *New Perspectives* 3 (1992), 2.

25. Douglas Roche, "A Passion for the Planet," *The ATA Magazine* 69 (1989), 18.

26. Education for a Global Perspective, "CSBA Model Global Education Policy," 3.

27. Steven Lamy, "The National Interest or Global Interests?" *The ATA Magazine* 69 (1989), 40–46.

28. O'Sullivan, "Reconciling Paradigms."

29. Petrie, "Global Studies in the Social Science Curriculum"; Case, "Key Elements of a Global Perspective," 8–9.

30. Thomas Berry and Edmund O'Sullivan, "Global Education and Ecology: Moving Education into the Ecozoic Age," *Orbit* 23 (1992), 6–7; Edmund O'Sullivan, "The Need for a Holistic Global Perspective: In Anticipation of the Millennial Turning Point," *Orbit* 27 (1996), 3–5.

31. Susan Kiil, "Education for a Positive Future," *Education for a Global Perspective* 4 (1994), 1, 8; Tom Lyons, "Life Beyond Schooling" (Toronto: Education for a Global Perspective Project, 1995), 6; Selby, "Humane Education."

32. Case, "Key Elements of a Global Perspective," 19.

33. Werner and Case, "Themes of Global Education," 190.

34. Toh Swee-Hin, "Bringing the World into the Classroom: Global Literacy and a Question of Paradigms," *Global Education-Global Literacy* 1 (1993), 9–17.

35. McLean, "Global History or Globetrotting?" 20.

36. Earl Choldin, "Letter to Network Members," *Networks* 2 (1989), 2.

37. Ivan Head, "Knowledge in the Third Dimension: A World Turned Upside Down," *Global Education-Global Literacy* 2 (1994), 2-5.

38. Derek Heater, *Citizenship: The Civic Ideal in World History, Politics and Education* (London: Longman, 1990); David Selby, "Kaleidoscopic Mindset: New Meanings Within Citizenship Education," *Global Education-Global Literacy* 2 (1994), 20–31.

39. Earl Choldin, Preface, "A Note From the Editor: Educating for Global Citizenship," *Global Education-Global Literacy* 2 (1994); Roche, "A Passion for the Planet," 17.

40. Case, "Key Elements of a Global Perspective," 18.

41. Graham Pike, "Global Education and National Identity: In Pursuit of

Meaning," *Theory Into Practice* 39 (Spring 2000), 64-73; Darling, "Solidarity and Strangers," 2; and Michael Ignatieff, *The Needs of Strangers* (London: Penguin Books, 1984).

42. Moore, "Education for Planetary Living," 8.

43. Susan Greig, Graham Pike, and David Selby, *Greenprints for Changing Schools* (London: Kogan Page/World Wide Fund for Nature, 1989).

44. Brian O'Sullivan, "Reconciling Paradigms."

45. Pike, "The Meaning of Global Education."

46. Lloyd, "Confused? Concerned!"

47. James Leming, "The Influence of Contemporary Issues Curricula on School-Aged Youth," in Gerald Grant, ed., *Review of Research in Education* 18 (Washington, DC: American Educational Research Association, 1992), 111–161; Marilyn Johnston and Anna Ochoa, "Teacher Education for Global Perspectives: A Research Agenda," *Theory Into Practice* 32 (1993), 64–68; Judith Torney-Purta, "A Research Agenda for the Study of Global/International Education in the United States," paper presented at the 1989 American Educational Research Association Conference, San Francisco, CA.

48. Pike, "The Meaning of Global Education."

Chapter 9

READING BETWEEN THE LINES

EXAMINING ASSUMPTIONS IN

HEALTH EDUCATION

Gale Smith and Linda Peterat

HEALTH EDUCATION HAS BEEN PART of the public school curriculum in Canada since the late 1800s when children became the focus of efforts to improve society and ameliorate socials ills. Legislators, members of the clergy and others with influence were raising deep moral concerns about the working-class family, the health and welfare of working-class children and increasing the productivity of the workforce. The centre of production was changing from the farm and home-based crafts or trades to large factories in the cities. With parents, and sometimes older children, working in factories, younger children often remained at home or on the streets with nothing to do. Particularly in the cities, the family's role in educating and training children was diminishing and the extended family was beginning to disappear. At the same time, many immigrants and orphans arrived in Canada in poor health. Improper sanitation, inadequate housing, poor diets, high mortality rates among children, the spread of communicable diseases, criminal activity and child labour were key areas of concern. With the advent of compulsory education, reformers saw schooling as a means of "uplifting" the newcomers to Canadian standards of morality and industry,[1] and the school came to be seen as the logical place to protect and improve children's health and their social condition.

Egerton Ryerson, superintendent of education in Upper Canada from 1846 to 1876, was one of the most influential figures in education in the nineteenth century. In 1871, he was instrumental in making schooling free, universal and compulsory in Ontario. By the end of the century, most provinces had followed suit. Under Ryerson's direction, the 1871 curriculum included a course on hygiene, which combined physiology and temperance. (By 1887, there was even an authorized textbook in circulation, which was entitled *Public School Temperance*.[2]) The emphasis on temperance is an example of the influence the International Women's Christian Temperance Union had at the time. The WCTU actively promoted the teaching of temperance and hygiene worldwide.[3] Their approach to health education resembles modern anti-smoking and anti-drug campaigns that use fear and propaganda to rid society of a particular health problem.[4]

Hygiene was also the concern of those who lobbied for the teaching of domestic science or home economics in the belief that healthy homes — with better food, cleanliness, water, ventilation and clothing — would contribute to productivity. In Canada, Adelaide Hoodless led this campaign and wrote the first textbook on the subject, *Public School Domestic Science*, which was published in 1898. She also advised the Ontario government on domestic science.[5]

With the onset of the public health movement at the end of the 1800s, the health of Canadian children became a national issue. Public health physicians, nurses and sanitary inspectors led a campaign to make hygiene a compulsory subject in the schools. Their efforts included teaching sanitation and hygiene, providing vaccinations and health inspections. Teachers were often responsible for health instruction, especially in rural areas. In the cities, the school nurse was frequently the health instructor. *How to be Healthy*, written by a Winnipeg doctor in 1911 for Manitoba schools, was eventually adopted as the core textbook in seven other provinces to assist teachers with health instruction. *How to be Healthy* emphasized biological functions and how to preserve the body in a state of high efficiency. It was considered "much better than nineteenth century examples of the genre."[6] By the First World War, health professionals had succeeded in making the teaching of hygiene and physical education compulsory.[7]

Gradually the emphasis on hygiene gave way to health and health education, perhaps as a consequence of more positive approaches to hygiene and the emergence of progressive education.[8] In the 1920s, educators in Canada began to label their reform efforts "progressive," a loosely applied label that was widely used in the United States with both liberal and conservative dimensions.[9] On the one hand, it embodied the philosophy of John Dewey, who advocated for educating the "whole" child, respecting each child as a unique individual, and using active methods such as experiments, field trips, community study, problem solving and model making that related to real life experiences. Schools began to shift away from the mental discipline and academic tradition, which had dominated earlier thinking about schooling, to a more child-centred program, which embraced the teachings of child psychology. This "developed into a widespread interest in mental testing, which, ironically, tended to have the effect of solidifying the rigidities of the traditional school."[10] The changes, however, were relatively inexpensive to implement and the curriculum broadened to include more practical subjects such as domestic science, physical training and guidance, all of which included health. The development of health and character, and the effective and wise use of leisure time were prominent objectives of these new subjects.[11]

In the years following the First World War, the importance of furthering the cause of democracy became a new emphasis in education. The Canadian Red Cross began to infuse democratic ideals with its Junior Red Cross program, designed to promote good health, humanitarianism and international peace. The Red Cross materials included a monthly magazine and posters that were widely used by teachers, especially at the elementary level. The Red Cross is a good example of an outside interest group supplementing the formal curriculum.[12] Over time, the United Nations Children's Fund (UNICEF), the Canadian Lung Association, the Canadian Cancer Society, the Heart and Stroke Foundation and many other groups have produced materials to augment the health textbooks and other materials prescribed by provincial ministries of education.

In 1945, through the National Committee for School Health Research, the Canadian Education Association and the Canadian Public Health Association launched the first full-scale survey of the health conditions and the teaching of health in Canadian schools. The survey included items such as the mental health of teachers and the physical environment of the school, but concentrated on "the teaching of health, nutrition (food rules) and physical education."[13] The Red Cross was credited as being the most positive factor in the instruction of health. General health and cleanliness were found to be the chief emphasis in the classrooms. Few teachers had much training and the rote method predominated. The researchers recommended compulsory high school courses on marriage, parenthood and related topics as well more of the active learning methods promoted by progressivism.

By the 1950s, military preparedness for the Cold War predominated and physical fitness became a health priority. Health education, emphasizing physiology and healthy habits, was often combined with physical education. The 1960s brought greater affluence, leisure and the growth of the ideology of self-fulfillment, which fostered a shift to stressing lifetime sports in physical education, the inclusion of family life education and healthy choices in health education, which was now often referred to as "guidance."[14] While sex education and interpersonal relationships were part of the health curriculum, both were often too controversial and therefore sometimes not taught. The goal of sex education was to reduce teen pregnancy, sexually-transmitted diseases and abortion and encourage responsible behaviour. Some argued, however, that sex education led to sexual experimentation.[15] The "drug culture" of the late 1960s and the 1970s and the emerging AIDS epidemic brought the need for health education to the public's attention. This spurred reviews of school curricula in most provinces and support for health education nationally.[16] In the 1990s, violence in the schools and suicide prevention have gained prominence.

By the late 1980s, the effectiveness of health education was increasingly being questioned. Using health education as a means to address social ills continued to be widely believed, just as it had been at the turn of the nineteenth century, but single-issue approaches dominated, resulting in separate programs to address specific problems, such as smoking, drugs and HIV/AIDS. Many argued that dealing with health or social problems in isolation was not working. The curriculum was overcrowded and health education was not a priority. As a result, schools often "piggybacked" health education onto physical education or home economics, and trained health teachers were a rarity.[17] In 1988, the Canadian Association for School Health was formed. CASH is an umbrella group of provincial and territorial coalitions whose members are recognized by Health Canada as the national voice for school health. CASH advocates a comprehensive approach to health education that enables students enhance their health, develop their fullest potential and establish productive and satisfying relationships in their present and future lives. A comprehensive health approach involves school programs that include:

- health instruction by trained health teachers using adequate teaching materials and appropriate teaching methodologies;
- health services such as appraisal, treatment, counselling, and child protection;
- social support, for example, healthy public policy, staff wellness programs, role modelling and peer support; and
- healthy environments with adequate safety, sanitation, food services and air quality.

These are outlined in more detail in *A National Consensus Statement*, a document produced by CASH. In addition to the Consensus Statement, CASH has organized conferences to promote comprehensive school health, launched a campaign to publicize its comprehensive approach to leaders in health and education, taken part in national consultations on health issues affecting Canadian youth and compiled bibliographies on school health.[18]

In 1989–90, 1993–94 and 1997–98, Canada participated in the World Health Organization's cross-national study "Health Behaviour in School-Aged Children." A report on the 1993–94 study concluded that comprehensive approaches were needed to promote healthy living among young people, thus affirming the goals of CASH.[19]

Education in Canada is a provincial responsibility, but the federal government facilitates health education through the provision of consultant and advisory services to the provinces; stimulation and conduct of related research and other activities; preparation of educational materials; and assistance in the training of health professionals.[20] Health education curricula varies by province. Today, most provinces have some sort of mandated health curriculum from Kindergarten to Grade 9. Most provinces also require students to earn some health credits at the senior level. Health education also goes by different names across Canada. The subject may be called health or career and personal planning in British Columbia; career and life management in Alberta and New Brunswick; personal and social development in Quebec. Overlap with other subject areas continues. For example, family life educa-tion, home economics education and health education all include human and personal development, sexuality and interpersonal relationships.[21]

DIFFERENT APPROACHES TO HEALTH EDUCATION

This brief look at the history of health education in Canada demon-strates that what counts as health and the nature and purpose of health education has varied over time. As well, the meaning and purpose of health and health education are subject to political manipulation, redefinition by special interest groups and the tugs of conflicting ideologies. Even the term used to define health educa-tion has changed — hygiene, guidance, family life education and career and life management. Neither the changing nature and purpose nor the pressures brought to bear is unique to Canada. Not surprisingly, some claim that health education lacks both direction and a sound theory to back it up.[22] Others call for an analysis of the messages implicit or explicit in health education and of how the messages themselves influence how we select what to teach. Others decry the confused language or argue that the aims, rationale and expected results are often illogically diverse. [23]

In Figure 1, we categorize the major approaches to health education and tease out the underlying assumptions of each approach. In the following passages, we elaborate on each approach and explain how each would be used to teach health, using the topic of teen pregnancy as an example.

Figure 1. DIFFERENT APPROACHES TO HEALTH EDUCATION [24]

Assumptions About	Factual and Transmissive	Factual and Transactional	Interpretive and Transactional	Critical and Transformational
THE PURPOSE OF HEALTH EDUCATION	Health education prevents disease, reduces illness, and maintains physical well-being.	Health education regulates personal behaviour, develops socially responsible behaviour, and maintains physical and mental well-being.	Health education helps people live authentic lives. Health education maintains one's emotional, physical, mental, social and spiritual well-being.	Health education leads to critical awareness of the social conditions that need to change for there to be healthy living for all.

Assumptions About	Factual and Transmissive	Factual and Transactional	Interpretive and Transactional	Critical and Transformational
THE EMPHASIS	The emphasis is on changing or modifying behaviour and on prescriptions for self-care.	The emphasis is on constrained and formulated decision-making and on controlled choice.	The emphasis is on individual choice and individual freedom, dialogue, mutual growth and strengthening the sense of community.	The emphasis is on social relations, political processes, resource allocation, equity, peace and one's responsibility as a global citizen.
STUDENTS	Students are blank slates which unquestioningly accept facts and information, passive "consumers" of knowledge and a homogeneous group.	Students are detached, able to decide for themselves within limits, and capable of controlling themselves and of having interpersonal relationships.	Students are active, "in" the world, capable of thoughtful action, deliberation and purpose.	Students are knowledgeable, critical and reflective.
LEARNING	Reason and feeling are separate. Learning is unmediated by reality or by the needs and experiences of students.	Reason and feeling are not separate. Learning involves practice in simulated social situations.	Learning is social and comes about through shared meanings and authentic communication.	Learning comes from participating in and changing one's world.

Assumptions About	Factual and Transmissive	Factual and Transactional	Interpretive and Transactional	Critical and Transformational
KNOW-LEDGE	The content or subject is objective, and knowing has to do with the world "out there."	Knowledge is factual and should be applied to real situations, and knowing is about the world "out there" and about how to deal with that world.	Knowledge is open to interpretation, subjective, exists in many forms, and is always incomplete.	Knowledge combines action and reflection to improve individual and social conditions. Knowledge is personal and intuitive, not just rational.
TEACHING	Teaching means transmitting facts and information, controlling what students learn, and is didactic.	Teaching means giving students practice with the skills they need, while controlling what they learn, and involves telling, showing and doing.	Teaching means guiding the inquiry, stimulating students' thinking, should be inspiring and magical, includes students' experiences, and engages students in dialogue.	Teaching means encouraging critical inquiry, examining the basis of knowledge, equipping students to act for themselves and with others on behalf of the community, and means learning and acting.
LEARNING	Reason and feeling are separate. Learning is unmediated by reality or by the needs and experiences of students.	Reason and feeling are not separate. Learning involves practice in simulated social situations.	Learning is social and comes about through shared meanings and authentic communication.	Learning comes from participating in and changing one's world.

Assumptions About	Factual and Transmissive	Factual and Transactional	Interpretive and Transactional	Critical and Transformational
THE PURPOSE OF EDUCATION	Education is meant to transmit the society's accumulated knowledge.	Education is meant to help the student cope with what is risky or dangerous in society.	Education is meant to help in the formation of authentic and responsive individuals, and to encourage personal development.	Education is meant to encourage personal and social transformation.
SOCIETY	Society develops through its accumulated knowledge, and all should adopt existing norms and conventions.	Individuals are to adapt to society.	Society is constraining, to be tolerated, but its constraints can be overcome.	Society is a constraint on individual and community development. Society also influences and can be influenced by communities of individuals.

FACTUAL AND TRANSMISSIVE

The factual and transmissive approach to health education promotes health as hygiene and sanitary reform. This approach assumes that knowing the signs, symptoms, potential causes and cures of illnesses will improve health by changing behaviour and thus prevent epidemics and the spread of disease.[25] The factual and transmissive approach, which prevailed in Canada in the late 1800s and early 1900s, assumes that individuals are responsible for reducing illness and preventing disease. Hygiene became the "science of health," illustrating the tendency to formalize and "academicize" every subject. Although intended to meet a real social need, discussions of this approach was presented in textbooks in small print and without illustrations, and often was taught as a combination of "dogmatic dry-as-dust factuality and frightening propaganda."[26]

There were limitations inherent in the factual and transmissivie approach: it marginalized individual autonomy through its emphasis on experts and information-giving; used didactic methods of instruction; tended to blame the victim; denied health as a social product; and failed to substantiate the claim that knowledge does change behaviour.[27] Critics today point out that this approach may result in "overly zealous health educators who are so convinced [that they know] how people should behave, that they program people — as computers are programmed ... to behave in ... predetermined ways."[28] Such programming results in the loss of some measure of control by the student and serves to maintain the prevailing power structures.

A health program following this approach would include the topic of teen pregnancy. Its inclusion would be based on the assumption that teenagers become pregnant because they are ignorant and that once they have the right information they can behave correctly, thus the health "problem" of too many teen pregnancies will be prevented. Programs of this nature are characterized by the study of facts about teen pregnancy (for example, statistics on the number of teen pregnancies, the percentage of teens who choose abortion, adoption, marriage and single parenthood), by an analysis of the options for teens who become pregnant, and by information about how pregnancy occurs and how to prevent it. The program would be considered successful if at the end students could identify various body parts, explain the ways and means to prevent pregnancy and outline the options for pregnant teens.

FACTUAL AND TRANSACTIONAL

A second approach to health and health education began to appear in Canada in the 1940s with the emergence of guidance education. This approach focuses mainly on decision-making. We have labelled it factual and transactional. It broadens the meaning of health to include the functioning of body and mind, and broadens health education to include the development of reasoning. It assumes that health education can improve an individual's decision-making and problem-solving skills and that the information will be used to promote the well-being of body and mind. Self-responsibility, not blaming the victim, is emphasized.[29]

This approach stresses active learning and the uniqueness of the individual. Some consider the do-it-for-yourself emphasis problematic because it ignores that the economic, political, social and cultural roots of ill health that often lie beyond the control of the individual.[30] Free choice is implied, but the real interest would seem to be in controlling and disciplining the individual, thus maintaining the status quo and ensuring that the next generation contributes to the economy by becoming active members of the work force.[31]

Health programs that fall into the factual and transactional category often come about because a community and its politicians perceive a need. The assumption is that the "problem" is reaching epidemic proportions and that education can solve it. Programs of this nature are often deemed "teacher proof," and are packaged to make the teacher the deliverer of the program. In the case of teen pregnancy, such a program would probably consist of clearly outlined lessons on biology and anatomy, combined with a decision-making model and some assertiveness training. In some areas, birth control methods would be included; in others abstinence would be promoted. How well students answer questions and role-play certain situations would determine whether the program is a success.

INTERPRETIVE AND TRANSACTIONAL

The interpretive and transactional approach implies that health is a social construction in as much as it is informed by the philosophies of humanism and self-improvement. Since health is seen as dynamic, constructed by humans, influenced by personal interpretations and relative to the interaction of individuals with their cultural and physical environments, there is an openness to cultural variation on the meanings of health and health care.[32] Health education, then, concerns itself with developing the skills and abilities to overcome frustrations caused by socialization.[33] This approach includes values clarification, assertiveness training, developing communication skills and social and emotional learning.[34] Health education aims to help students understand themselves, make healthy decisions and "handle" social and environmental constraints on choice. While this view of health and health education has the potential to encompass social action, its emphasis on the individual largely ignores the economic, social and political roots of ill health.

In programs based on the interpretive and transactional approach, the underlying assumptions would be that teen pregnancy results from lack of understanding about sexual health, poor decision-making and problem-solving skills, low self-esteem, poor communication and social skills, alienation and a lack of support. Thus the topic would be covered within the context of improving the students' self-esteem, social communications and decision-making skills because that would allow the students to be more responsible for their health. Teaching strategies would tend to be more learner-centred, offer more opportunity for discussion and dialogue and pay attention to feelings and emotions. Case studies, role playing and cooperative learning might be used along with some research, particularly into the community resources and support networks available to students with "problems." The success of the program would be determined by the ability of students to make decisions, solve problems and empathize with, and interpret, various circumstances that give rise to teen pregnancy.

CRITICAL AND TRANSFORMATIONAL

The critical and transformational approach to health education is based on seeing good health as dependent on social transformation. Health is broadly understood in social, political and economic terms and health issues are fundamentally associated with justice, equity and peace.[35] While it can be argued that this conception has been around since 1948, with the declaration of Human Rights and the founding of the World Health Organization, it has not been widely evident in schools with the exception of some materials produced or distributed by organizations such as the Red Cross, Oxfam and UNICEF.[36] This approach has become more popular, however, with the rise of the environmental, development, feminist and social justice movements which have brought greater attention to poverty, power and unequal distribution of resources as underlying causes of poor health. The purpose of health education, then, is to prepare students to engage in social criticism and transformation, so they not only see themselves as part of society but also as influential in changing society. The major emphasis involves "recognition of the social and economic determinants of health and illness; the need for collective action and mutual support; the importance of combining education, service and political action; and the primacy of people and their immediate needs."[37] Thus, fostering the development of knowledgeable, critical, self-directed learners who discover how to participate in transforming the world is paramount.[38]

The work of Paulo Freire, particularly his concern for the development of critical consciousness, informs this approach. It has also been described as emancipatory or "empowerment" health education.[39] The critical and transformative approach emphasizes the importance of raising students' awareness of the social and political conditions that give rise to inequalities that cause ill health so they can challenge and even change the systems. Its proponents argue that "school health education in Canada supports a primarily conservative agenda grounded in Western, patriarchal, abled, middle-class, heterosexist assumptions" that ignore or distort the lives of Native peoples, people of colour, people with disablities, lesbians and gay men.[40] This approach challenges the western medical model of health and healthcare and shows an openness to exploring and investigating alternatives. The approach is often deemed controversial because some do not agree that social criticism and ethical questions should be part of education. Other critics question whether the social, economic and political problems posed may be too complex for students.[41] As well, the expectation that health education can change society may very well be unrealistic, given the social and political constraints on education.

Programs that fall under this approach would assume that the "problem" of teen pregnancy stems from a broader social and political context and that an understanding of the problem must include that broader context. Teachers in these programs would ask questions about teen pregnancy: Why is it deemed a problem? by whom? What social, economic and cultural conditions give rise to this health "problem"? Is teen pregnancy linked to oppression? to poverty? to the unequal distribution of power? In what ways? How should communities respond to teen pregnancy? What are the implications of the various responses? Teachers would encourage open inquiry and critical thinking into these questions. Students would be assessed on their awareness and knowledge of health issues, on their ability to articulate and reason about them, on the actions they suggest or take and the justifications they give, and on their ability to reflect on the process.

As we move from the factual and transmissive to the critical and transformative approach, there is a gradual shift in emphasis from the individual, to the individual in society, and from maintaining the status quo, to changing social structures and processes, but the approaches are overlapping, not mutually exclusive. Nor is one approach necessarily preferable to another. Each represents different interests and purposes. It is entirely likely, for example, that a concern for behaviour modification is both relevant and appropriate in some contexts, while in others, a more critical approach is required. To be able to read between the lines in health education publications and to articulate and engage in dialogue about the assumptions inherent in health education can only encourage greater consistency between practice and intention. This will also encourage more informed decision-making about a program's appropriateness for particular audiences and in specific contexts and encourage a more informed dialogue and better justifications for school health education.[42]

CHALLENGES FACING HEALTH EDUCATION

EXPANDING THE MEANINGS

The meaning of health has expanded from the early concentration on health as absence of disease and the preservation of biological integrity, to a state of complete physical, mental and social well-being offered by the World Health Organization in 1948, to the inclusion of spiritual health[43] in the 1990s. New focuses continue to expand the concept of health. Correspondingly, the meaning of health education has expanded from a technical approach with the goal of improved hygiene and temperance, to interpretive approaches of decision-making for healthful living and for understanding the meanings people make of health, to more critical approaches involving transforming society for the healthy living of all.

Increasingly, it has become clear that health is inextricably linked to the environment: global warming, to name only one example, could lead to more deaths from high heat, from infectious diseases spread by flooding and insects, from skin cancers, and from famines caused by desertification.[44] We need to understand the role that the environment plays in human health and become involved in actions that avert the threats to health that come from the degradation of the environment. Some argue that sustainable development should be fundamental to how we understand health.[45] Linking the health of individuals to the health of the planet means that health educators must make connections with environmental education and development education.

Considerable agreement exists internationally about the prerequisites for health, as pointed out in the UN's Declaration on Human Rights:

> Everyone has the right to a standard of living adequate for health and well-being of himself and his family, including food, clothing, housing and medical care and necessary social services, and the right to security in the event of unemployment, sickness, disability, widowhood, old age or lack of livelihood in circumstances beyond his control.[46]

The World Summit for Children in 1990 stressed the need to create the conditions that allow children to thrive. But poverty, particularly among children, is the greatest threat to children's health and is on the rise in Canada[47] and elsewhere. The rights to the prerequisites for a healthy life and well-being links health education with human rights education.

Reactions to globalization and calls for the recognition of, and respect for, ethnic diversity are challenging the ethnocentrism of the school curriculum, this creates a demand for health education to make connections with multicultural education, Native education, media education and global education.

A greater awareness about violence — whether physical or verbal, at school or in Canadian society at large — has brought calls for conflict-resolution and bullying-prevention programs[48] and for linking health education with peace education.

We are also challenged to envision a school health education "that celebrates diversity of human sexuality, counters heterosexism and homophobia, politicizes lesbian and gay issues and legitimizes the experiences of lesbian and gay students and teachers."[49] This means making connections with anti-racist education, education for gender equity and sexuality education and closely examining the curriculum materials we use for bias.[50]

DEALING WITH CONTROVERSIAL ISSUES

Sexuality (including abortion, sterilization and contraception), death and medical priorities are examples of controversial topics in health education.[51] Parents and students may strongly object when they do not agree that such topics should be part of the school curriculum, or when they do not agree on the approach used.[52] In British Columbia, a group of parents accused the Ministry of Education of "misuse of power" and of "indoctrinating children into politically correct beliefs"[53] when the Ministry made health-related program Career and Personal Planning mandatory from Kindergarten to Grade 12. Also in British Columbia, controversy over whether three story books that dealt with gay and lesbian families ought to be used in elementary schools ended up in court when the decision of Surrey School board to ban the books was challenged.[54] These examples highlight the need for health educators to be well prepared in dealing with sensitive topics and controversial issues.

PREPARATION OF HEALTH EDUCATION SPECIALISTS

Many people are involved in health education. Nurses, physicians, nutritionists, social workers, counsellors and psychologists educate people about health in the community and sometimes in schools. Elementary generalists, physical educators, home economics teachers, science teachers, and family life educators are often charged with doing bits and pieces of health education. Teachers working in the public school system who identify themselves as specialists in health education are few and far between. There is a strong need for teachers with specific preparation in health education and a professional commitment to the subject area.[55] The professional preparation of health educators should include a philosophical and knowledge base, competence in health education teaching techniques, and an awareness of ethical questions that relate specifically to health education. Ethical questions have a broad range: Does the program help or harm people? Does it arbitrarily or unfairly discriminate? Is the topic age-appropriate? Does it place too much emphasis on individual choice when other factors (such as genetic predisposition, poverty and environmental pressures) relevant to health are present? Does it focus on changing individuals rather than the social environment that supports and maintains unhealthy lifestyles? [56] At present, most teacher education programs across the country offer some courses in health education, some also have diploma programs and master's degrees. But there is little incentive to specialize in health education when it is not a priority in schools.

*

Health education is not really a "new" education in Canada. It has been around since public schooling was initiated in this country. However, partial approaches, inadequate resources and lack of support limit the effectiveness of most health education programs. The comprehensive school health movement with its focus on formal and informal instruction in schools, support services from health and social agencies, social support from parents, policy-makers and the community, and healthy physical environments in schools, homes and neighbourhoods offers a place to rethink the purpose and practice of health education. Lack of political will and poor funding have meant that comprehensive school health has yet to reach its potential, but it remains an excellent starting point to make links and connections with the "new" educations outlined in this book.

TEACHER RESOURCES

Roger Hart, *Children's Participation: The Theory and Practice of Involving Young Citizens in Community Development and Environmental Care* (London: Earthscan Publications, 1997) is recommended for those teachers who believe that sustainable development is key to healthy communities and healthy citizens. It has some wonderful examples of children's action research projects that help them better understand and take action on a variety of issues, including health-related topics of clean water, safety and access to food. Available from UNICEF regional offices or UNICEF Canada, 442 Mt. Pleasant Rd., Toronto, ON M4S 2L8.

Paul M. Insel and Walton T. Roth, *Core Concepts in Health,* 7th ed. (Mountain View, CA: Mayfield, 1994) is a basic text that provides a good overview of the key concepts. It is available at most university and college bookstores.

The provincial health curriculum guides are essential to anyone contemplating teaching health. They can be obtained from the Ministry of Education in your province.

Health Canada/Santé Canada has produced several publications, including *What is Comprehensive School Health?* , *Workplace Health System- Student Model, School Health Lesson Protocols, Health Behaviours in School Aged Children Survey,* and *Health Promoting School Environments.* Contact Health Canada in Ottawa (613) 957-2991, or through the regional office in your area. The Health Canada Web site is <www.hc-sc.gc.ca/english/about.htm.>

Health Promotion Online

www.hc-sc.gc.ca/hppb/psd/index.html

This bilingual Web site was established by Health Canada. It offers resources on a variety of topics including aging and seniors, cancer, diabetes, family violence prevention, HIV/AIDS, nutrition and workplace health.

Health Canada and the Canadian Society for Exercise Physiology
www.paguide.com
Promotes awareness about physical activity.

There are two recommended journals, both are American publications but contain research, thought pieces, teaching ideas and resource reviews.

Journal of Health Education
Published by the American Alliance for Health, Physical Education, Recreation and Dance
1900 Association Drive
Reson, VA 22091
(703) 476-3400
Fax: (703) 476-9527
www.aahperd.org

Journal of School Health
Published by the American School Health Association
P.O. Box 708
Kent, OH 44240
(330) 678-1601
Fax: (330) 678-4526
www.ashaweb.org

CLASSROOM RESOURCES

Because of the controversial nature of many of the topics in health education, we recommend that teachers use resources that are listed as prescribed or recommended in the provincial Ministry of Education Curriculum Guides. It is also important to learn about individual division or school board policies regarding what resources are allowed and the procedures for getting resources approved.

For the secondary level we recommend Cathy Beveridge, *Wellness* (Toronto: McGraw-Hill Ryerson, 1994). Part of a series called the Issues Collection, this is a collection of readings that includes short stories, poetry and articles designed to engage secondary students in the issues of health and wellness. There is an accompanying teacher's guide.

ORGANIZATIONS

Canadian Association for School Health
2835 Country Woods Drive
Surrey, BC V4P 9P9

(604) 535-7665
Fax: (604) 531-6454
E-mail: schoolfi@netcom.ca

Canadian Public Health Association
1565 Carling Ave., Suite 400
Ottawa ON K1Z 8R1
(613) 725-3769
Fax: (613) 725-9826
www.cpha.ca

Canadian Society for International Health
1 Nicholas St., Suite 1105
Ottawa ON K1N 7B7
Tel: (613) 241-5785
Fax: (613) 321-3845
www.csih.org

Canadian Red Cross continues to produce resources for teachers and provides guest speakers for classes. Contact your provincial division.

NOTES

1. Douglas Lawr and Robert Gidney, eds., *Educating Canadians* (Toronto, ON: Van Nostrand Reinhold, 1973), 15–48, provide a collection of documents that illustrate the assumptions and goals of education of the time. Neil Sutherland, *Children In English-Canadian Society: Framing The Twentieth Century Consensus* (Toronto, ON: University of Toronto Press, 1976), 40–42, outlines the influence of the public health movement and its objective of improving children's health. George Tomkins, *A Common Countenance: Stability and Change in the Canadian Curriculum* (Scarborough, ON: Prentice-Hall Canada,1986), 27–50, provides a comprehensive overview of the beginnings of public schooling in Canada.

2. Tomkins, *A Common Countenance,* 88.

3. Ronald Laura and Sandra Heaney, *Philosophical Foundations of Health Education* (New York: Routledge, 1990), 181.

4. Tomkins, *A Common Countenance,* 88.

5. Linda Peterat and Mary Leah deZwart, *An Education for Women: The Founding of Home Economics Education in Canadian Public Schools* (Charlottetown, PEI: Home Economics Publishing Collective,1995), 22–32.

6. Sutherland, *Children in English-Canadian Society,* 53.

7. Tomkins, *A Common Countenance,* 101.

8. Laura and Heaney, *Philosophical Foundations of Health Education,* 181-182.

9. Tomkins, *A Common Countenance,* 189-200; Lawr and Gidney, *Educating Canadians,* 212–213.

10. Lawr and Gidney, *Educating Canadians,* 213.

11. A. Doucette, "The Philosophy Back of Progressive Education," in Lawr and Gidney, *Educating Canadians,* 216.

12. Sutherland, *Children in English-Canadian Society,* 87; Tomkins, *A Common Countenance,* 159–160.

13. Tomkins, *A Common Countenance,* 403.

14. Ibid., 403–404.

15. Diane Shymko, "Quo Vadis? Family Life Education in Canada: Past, Present and Future," *Canadian Home Economics Journal* 28 (1978), 48–53.

16. Peterat and deZwart, *An Education for Women,* 225.

17. See for example, Hélène Cameron, Gordon Mutter, and Nancy Hamilton, "Comprehensive School Health: Back To The Basics in the 90s," *Health Promotion* 29 (1991), 2–5, 10; Canadian Association for School Health (CASH), *Comprehensive School Health. A Framework For Co-operation: A National Consensus Statement* (Ottawa, ON: National Consultation Meeting, 1991); Cathy McLean Stearns, Colleen Grover, and Kacy Chow, "Comprehensive School Health In Action: A Pilot School Experience," in *Proceedings of Canadian Symposium III: Issues and Directions for Home Economics/Family Studies Education* (Ottawa: Canadian Home Economics Association, 1995), 99–108.

18. CASH, *Comprehensive School Health.*

19. Alan King, B. Wold, C. Tudor-Smith, and Y. Harel, *The Health of Youth: A Cross-National Survey* (Ottawa: Health Canada and World Health Organization Regional Publications, 1996). A report of the Canadian results from the 1997–1998 study, *Trends in the Health of Canadian Youth,* is available at the Health Canada Web site: <www.hc-sc.gc.ca/english/archives/releases/99118ebk2htm>.

20. Marc Lalonde, "The Health Field Concept In Canada," in *Health Education Addresses Presented at the IX International Conference on Health Education, Ottawa Canada 29 August–3 September* (Washington: Pan American Health Organization Regional Office of the World Health Organization, 1976).

21. Ministry of Education, Province of British Columbia, *Active and Health Living: A Dialogue on Teacher Preparation* (Victoria: Ministry of Education, 1988); Linda Peterat and Jennifer Khamasi, "Current Directions and Future Possibilities for Home Economics Curriculum in Canada," in *Proceedings of Canadian Symposium III: Issues and Directions for Home Economics/Family Studies Education* (Ottawa: Canadian Home Economics Association, 1995), 186-187; Jane Thomas and Margaret Arcus, "What's in a Name? Home

Economics Education, Health Education or Family Life Education," *Journal of Home Economics Education* 31 (1992), 3–8.

22. See for example, Thomas and Arcus, "What's in a Name?" and Thomas C. Timmerec, Galen E. Cole, Gordon James, and Diane D. Butterworth, "Health Education and Health Promotion: A Look at the Jungle of Support Fields, Philosophies, and Theoretical Foundations," *Health Education* 18 (1991), 23–29.

23. Derek Colquhoun, "Economic Rationalism, Healthism and School Health Education," *Health Education Journal* 49 (1990), 15-16; Russell Caplan and Ray Holland, "Rethinking Health Education Theory," *Health Education Journal* 49 (1990), 10–12; and P. Lynch, "Adolescent Smoking — An Alternative Perspective Using Personal Construct Theory," *Health Education Research* 10 (1995), 95–106.

24. This chart is a modification of one we developed with Jane Thomas for a workshop called "Reading Between the Lines: Examining Assumptions in Health Education Programs," presented at Living School Health: A Provincial Conference on Learning for Living, Naramata, BC, May 1992. Our goal was to articulate different orientations to health education curriculum that health teachers could use to evaluate health education materials. We derived some of the terminology from our readings in curriculum theory, particularly John Miller and Wayne Seller, *Curriculum: Perspectives and Practice* (Toronto: Longman, 1990).

25. See for example, David J. Anspaugh, Gene Ezell, and Karen Nash Goodman, *Teaching Today's Health* (Columbus: Charles E. Merrill, 1987), 2–16; Joseph E. Balog, "An Historical Review and Philosophical Analysis of Alternative Concepts of Health Education" (PhD diss., University of Maryland, 1978); John Fodor and Gus Dalin, *Health Instruction: Theory and Application* (Philadelphia: Les and Febijer, 1989), 1–12; Janet Holland, Caroline Ramazanoglu, and Sue Scott, "Managing Risk and Experiencing Danger: Tensions Between Government AIDS Education Policy and Young Women's Sexuality," *Gender and Education* 2 (1990), 125–146; and Joseph Rittman, "On Health Education Becoming a Pedagogy of Global Health," *Health Education* 28 (1987), 8.

26. Tomkins, *A Common Countenance,* 88.

27. See for example, David Mace, "The Long, Long Trail From Information Giving to Behavioural Change," *Family Relations* 30 (1981), 599–606; Vicki Taylor, "Health Education-A Theoretical Mapping," *Health Education Journal* 49 (1990), 13-14; and Mohammad Torabi and Nangnoy Nakornkhet, "Smoking Among Teenagers: Educational Recommendations and Resources," *Journal of Health Education* 27 (1996), 40–43.

28. Jerrold Greenberg, "Health and Wellness: A Conceptual Differentiation," *Journal of School Health* 55 (1985), 405.

29. See for example, Joseph E. Balog, "The Concept of Health and the Role of Health Education," *Journal of School Health* 51 (1981), 461–464.; Holland et al., "Managing Risk and Experiencing Danger," 130–132; Meredith Minkler,

"Health Education, Health Promotion and the Open Society: An Historical Perspective," *Health Education Quarterly* 16 (1989), 17–30; Marion B. Pollock and Kathleen Middleton, *Elementary School Health Instruction* (St. Louis: Times Mirror/Mosby College Publishing, 1989), 4–16; and K. Allison, "Health Education: Self-Responsibility vs. Blaming the Victim," *Health Education* (Spring 1982).

30. For further discussion see Minkler, "Health Education, Health Promotion and the Open," 18–22; Taylor, "Health Education — A Theoretical Mapping," 13–14; and Keith Tones, Sylvia Tilford, *Health Education, Effectiveness, Efficiency and Equity* (New York: Chapman and Hall, 1994).

31. Cameron, Mutter, and Hamilton, "Comprehensive School Health," 8.

32. Balog,"The Concept of Health and the Role of Health Education," 461–462, argues for conceptual clarity recognizing that notions of health are human constructs. For futher reading on sensitivity to cultural diversity in health education, see Collins O. Airhihenbuwa and Odette Pineiro, "Cross-Cultural Health Education: A Pedagogical Challenge," *Journal of School Health* 58 (1988), 240–242; Collins O. Airhihenbuwa, "Culture, Health Education and Critical Consciousness," *Journal of School Health* 65 (1995), 317–319; Jane Victoria Ward and Jill McLean Taylor, "Sexuality Education in a Multicultural Society," *Educational Leadership* 54 (1996), 62–64; and Markella L. Pahnos, "The Continuing Challenge of Multicultural Health Education," *Journal of School Health* 62 (1992), 24–26.

33. Caplan and Holland, "Rethinking Health Education Theory," 12, refer to this as encompassing theories of radical change whereby individuals organize with others to change conditions which cause a sense of powerlessness, isolation and low self-esteem; Taylor, "Health Education — A Theoretical Mapping," 14, refers to this as a radical humanist perspective.

34. Tones and Tilford, *Health Education, Effectiveness Efficiency and Equity,* chapter 8; Maurice J. Elias and Jeffrey S. Kress, "Social Decision-Making and Life Skills Development: A Critical Thinking Approach to Health Promotion in the Middle School," *Journal of School Health* 63 (1994), 62–66. For further reading on social and emotion learning for teachers of all subject areas, see Maurice J. Elias, Joseph E. Zins, Roger P. Weissberg, Karin S. Frey, Mark Greenberg, Norris M. Haynes, Rachael Kessler, Mary E. Schwab-Stone, and Timothy P. Shriver, *Promoting Social and Emotional Learning: Guidelines for Educators* (Alexandria, VA: Association for Supervision and Curriculum Development, 1997).

35. Rittman, "On Health Education Becoming a Pedagogy of Global Health," 9; Mike Nelson, "A Global Challenge: Health Promotion for People and the Planet," *Health Promotion* 28 (1989), 2–7.

36. For example, the Red Cross has produced a secondary teaching resource, *Tomorrow's World,* with teaching activities for several health-related concepts; *World Day Handbook,* which suggests several activities for World Health Day on April 7; and the *Road to Health Game.* OXFAM has taken over the work of the World Food Day Organization and each year produces a *World Food Day*

Kit for teachers with activities related to food security, poverty and social justice. They have also published, with the assistance of Victoria International Development Education Association, Susan Gage, *Thinking Aids Globally* in 1993. UNICEF distributes, Roger Hart, *Children's Participation: The Theory and Practice of Involving Young Citizens in Community Development and Environmental Care* (London: Earthscan Publications, 1997).

37. Minkler, "Health Education, Health Promotion and the Open Society," 28.

38. R. A. Walker and D. Bibeau, "Health Education As Freeing — Part I," *Health Education* 16 (1986), 4–8.

39. Colquhoun, "Economic Rationalism, Healthism and School Health Education," 16, claims to have coined the term Emancipatory Health Education and describes a major feature to be a critique of ideology and how ideologies penetrate the school curriculum; Nina Wallerstein and Edward Bernstein, "Empowerment Education: Freire's Ideas Adapted to Health Education," *Health Education Quarterly* 15 (1988), 379–394; John Lord and D'Arcy McKillop Farlow, "A Study of Personal Empowerment: Implications for Health Promotion," *Health Promotion* 30 (1990), 2–8.

40. Linda Eyre, "Compulsory Heterosexuality in a University Classroom," *Canadian Journal of Education* 18 (1993), 273.

41. Ibid., 283–284.

42. Many authors have argued for conceptual clarity in health education. Balog, "The Concept of Health and the Role of Health Education," 464, states that "without a clear view of the end of health education, health education is at risk of becoming an ended profession." Similar comments can be found in Caplan and Holland, "Rethinking Health Education Theory," 10; Kate Lorig and Janette Laurin, "Some Notions About Assumptions Underlying Health Education," *Health Education Quarterly* 12 (1985), 231–243; and Keith Tones, "Why Theorize? Ideology in Health Education," *Health Education Journal* 49 (1990), 2–6.

43. Robert Bensley, "Defining Spiritual Health: A Review of The Literature," *Journal of Health Education* 22 (1991), 287–290; Nancy Goodlow and Patricia Arreola, "Spiritual Health: Out of the Closet," *Journal of Health Education* 23 (1992), 221–226; Patrick Pietroni, "The Return of the Spirit," in Alan Beattie, Marjorie Gott, Linda Jones, and Moyra Sidell, eds., *Health And Well Being: A Reader* (London: MacMillan, 1992); Brian Seaward, "Spiritual Wellbeing: A Health Education Model," *Journal of Health Education* 23 (1991), 166–169.

44. Ronald Labonté, "Econology: Integrating Health and Sustainable Development," *Health Promotion International* 6 (1991), 49–64, describes twelve principles that can be used to guide sustainable development decision-making such that the fullness of human health is nurtured.

45. See for example, Nelson, "A Global Challenge: Health Promotion for People and the Planet," 2–7, and Labonté, "Econology: Integrating Health and Sustainable Development," 49–64.

46. UN, *Declaration on Human Rights*, Article 25 (San Francisco, 1948).

47. The Canadian Council on Social Development has been researching the effects of poverty for a number of years. David Ross and Paul Roberts, *Income And Child Well-Being: A New Perspective on the Poverty Debate* (Ottawa: Canadian Council on Social Development, 1999), challenge Canadians to make producing healthy children the main objective of anti-poverty efforts.

48. See for example, Randy Page, Susan Kitchin-Becker, Donna Solovan, Tracy Golec, and Deborah Hebert, "Interpersonal Violence: A Priority Issue for Health Education," *Journal of Health Education* 23 (1992), 286–291.

49. Eyre, "Compulsory Heterosexuality in a University Classroom," 275.

50. For an example of this, see Mariamne Whatley, "The Picture of Health: How Textbook Photographs Construct Health," in Elizabeth Ellsworth and Mariamne Whatley, eds., *The Ideology of Images in Educational Media: Hidden Curriculums in the Classroom* (New York: Teachers College Press, 1990), 121–140.

51. These have been identified by John Odom, "The Status of Ethics Instruction in the Health Education Curriculum," *Health Education* 19 (1988), 10. Examples of other controversial topics are reproductive technologies and sexual orientation.

52. See Jerry Collins, "Reading, Writing and Sex: Parents Fight Graphic 'Health' Material in B.C. Schools," *British Columbia Report*, February 12, 1996, 20–23.

53. *The Vancouver Sun*, 23 October 1997, B4.

54. The provincial court ruled that the books could not be banned. For differing views on the decision see Ian T. Bensen and Brad Miller, "Lamentable Lack of Reason: True Charter Values are Undermined by a BC Court's Surrey Book Ruling," *Alberta Report* 26 (February 1999) 31; Larry McCallea, "BC Supreme Court Rejects Book Ban: Ruling on Surrey School Board Leaves Aside Intellectual Freedom Issues," *Quill and Quire* 65 (February 1999), 6.

55. As authors of this chapter, we strongly identify with health education, but our backgrounds are in home economics (Peterat) and physical education, elementary education and home economics (Smith). In 1986, Clint E. Bruess and David L. Poehler wrote "What We Need and Don't Need in Health Education — 1986," *Health Education* 17 (1986/1987), 32–36. Their number one point under "What We Don't Need" is people who are not trained in health education thinking they are health educators.

56. David A. Birch and Susan D. Scherpereel, "Examining Ethical Issues in School Health Education: Activities for Professional Preparation," *Journal of School Health* 25 (1994), 121–123; L. Lieberman, M. Clark, K. Krone, M. Orlandi, and E. Wynder, "The Relationship Between Cognitive Maturity and Information about Health Problems Among School Age Children," *Health Education Research* 7 (1992), 391–401; and Kenneth R. McLeroy, Daniel L.Bibeau, and Terrance C. McConnell McLeroy, "Ethical Issues in Health Education and Health Promotion: Challenges for the Profession," *Journal of Health Education* 24 (1993), 313–318.

Chapter 10

HUMANE EDUCATION
WIDENING THE CIRCLE OF
COMPASSION AND JUSTICE

David Selby

HUMANE EDUCATION has arguably the largest ambition, the longest pedigree and the least visibility of the fields discussed in this anthology. It is perhaps the most ambitious in that, through the fostering of humane attitudes and behaviours towards animals, it seeks to promote peace and social justice among humankind and a constructive relationship with the planet. "The humane education movement is a broad one," wrote Sarah Eddy in *Friends and Helpers* in 1897, "reaching from humane treatment of animals on the one hand to peace with all nations on the other."[1] "Humane education," claimed the US National Parent-Teacher Congress in 1933, "is the teaching in the schools and colleges of the nations the principles of justice, goodwill, and humanity toward all life. The cultivation of the spirit of kindness to animals is but the starting point toward that larger humanity that includes one's fellow of every race and clime. A generation of people trained in these principles will solve their international difficulties as neighbours and not as enemies."[2] "Humane education," writes Cindy Milburn, "is a vast subject area covering our treatment of animals, each other and the Earth we live on. Its objective is to achieve compassionate change which challenges the selfish and anthropocentric [human-centered] attitudes that have encouraged exploitation of each other and the world to the point where we are now threatening our very survival on the planet."[3]

Sarah Eddy's quote from 1897 indicates that humane education has a long history. In Canada it emerged in the 1870s as humane societies, including some but not all branches of the Society for Prevention of Cruelty to Animals (SPCA), were formed. The original mandate of these early humane societies often encompassed both animal and child protection, a mandate that was reflected in their mission statement. The 1894 Constitution of the Guelph, Ontario, Humane Society, for instance, identified the fostering "of humane public sentiment towards neglected, abandoned and orphaned children, and towards animals by purely educative influences in schools" as a primary goal.[4] The early humane societies, then, at least implicitly, acknowledged the connection between cruelty to animals and family violence, a link that would often be disregarded later on as child-specific welfare societies became established and humane societies consequently relinquished their child-protection role. As we shall see, a hundred years later the wheel has almost come full circle and the correlation between human and non-human abuse and oppression is becoming increasingly acknowledged.

Its long history notwithstanding, humane education has had perhaps the least success of any of the progressive educations in influencing mainstream education. Ministries of education do not grant it formal recognition, schools boards give it relatively little acknowledgement or support and proponents must fight for a foothold in the schools, especially at the secondary level. The field has been described as the "Ultima Thule" of progressive education — a far-away, unknown region, barely if at all recognized by Canadians working in related fields such as environmental, human rights, peace and anti-discriminatory education.[5]

This chapter explores the myriad currents and strands within humane education in Canada. It is based in part on the responses to an August 1996 questionnaire. The responses are from educators working for humane societies that have been at the fore in promoting humane education. Some of the fourteen respondents completed the questionnaire in a personal capacity, some as representatives of their organization. The questionnaire asked respondents to explain the goals and themes of humane education; to identify appropriate humane education content for different grade levels and school subjects; to describe the educational mission statement, work, publications and partnerships of their organization; and to reflect upon controversies, tensions and critical challenges facing humane education in Canada. Many of the quotations referred to in this chapter are drawn from these questionnaires.

FROM NARROW TO HOLISTIC EXPRESSIONS OF HUMANE EDUCATION

The Education Division of the British Columbia SPCA[6] introduces its program to teachers with this statement:

> Animals — and our relationships with them — are at the heart of Humane Education. By teaching children about the behaviour, needs, and care of animals, Humane Education provides gentle yet powerful lessons in compassion, responsibility, and respect for others.

The statement itself suggests that those working in humane education have lost none of the vision of their Victorian forebears. It remains an article of faith for those working in the field in Canada that humane education encourages caring, compassion, empathy, kindness, non-violence, respect, responsibility, sensitivity and resistance to injustice and oppression. These attitudes and behaviours can be applied not only animal welfare but also to larger scale environmental and human-related concerns and issues.

The field is divided, however, over the extent to which the realization of an unfractured compassion and seamless sense of justice extending to all humankind, individual animals and all species and ecosystems is worked into curricula, learning and teaching programs, educational initiatives and projects. Efforts to plan for and achieve this seem limited to a handful of leading humane societies that have a strong educational mission and to a few academics. For many organizations, the correspondence between the field's broad goals and the learning/teaching programs they offer is less than complete.

At the narrow end of the spectrum are the humane societies, many facing budgetary pressures, where education is something of an afterthought in the wake of a policy shift away from the apprehension and punishment of those who perpetrate animal cruelty and towards violence prevention through community development. Their education programs tend to focus, in some cases exclusively, on responsible pet purchase and care. Topics include choosing an appropriate pet (adoption and purchase), kindness and responsibility to pets, pets' needs and comfort, caution and safety around pets (especially dogs), pet overpopulation, spaying and neutering and pet euthanasia (a topic discussed with senior-level students). Programs often include talks by a veterinarian, a visit to a local animal shelter and an account of the humane society works. In some cases, and especially where programs stretch beyond the primary grades, the focus on pets broadens to include an exploration of the similarities between animal and human needs, concern for wild animals (especially those found in the neighbourhood and endangered species), an appreciation of animals that often provoke fear or distaste (such as spiders, snakes and wolves), a comparison of the needs of domestic and wild animals, animals in entertainment and farm-animal welfare. The fulcrum of the program, however, remains the pet.

Pet-centred education tends to act as an entrée into primary and junior schools (where working with pets is common), but an over-association with pet-specific issues may be one important reason for resistance from intermediate and secondary schools (where pets are viewed as a less age-appropriate topic). Most questionnaire respondents reported that secondary schools remain relatively inaccessible arenas for their work.

Further along the spectrum are those who hope to build upon the pet-oriented programs of the early grades by introducing topics at the intermediate and secondary levels that directly confront the human exploitation of animals and that promote wider ecological awareness. Topics discuss the treatment of farm animals (including a consideration of vegetarian and vegan diets); the pros and cons of aquariums, circuses, dolphin aquariums, manageries and zoos; animal experimentation, biomedical research and dissection in schools; ecology, biodiversity and humanity's impact on the natural environment; the pros and cons of fishing, hunting and trapping; and the international trade in animals. The Regina Humane Society's high-school resource manual *Humans and other Animals* includes sections on "Animals in Research," "Animals in Entertainment," "Animals as Luxury Items" and "Animals in Agriculture." It calls on students to discuss and determine their personal value position on the issues raised.[7] This approach is also used in programs that ask students to use checklists, which are provided from Zoocheck Canada or sister organizations, to investigate the morality of maintaining zoos.[8]

Those working at the broad or holistic end of the spectrum address similar topics but do so in ways that directly express the all-embracing aspirations of the field. Their expression is strategic, not simply a matter of faith. As education officers of the British Columbia SPCA put it:

> The study of cruelty to animals extends naturally to an examination of violence in society; the threat to individual species' survival leads to examination of forces which combine to extinguish life; the efforts to emancipate farm animals parallels in some ways the classic struggles opposing the exploitation of women.

To promote a holistic understanding of humane education, classroom activities point out how animal and human prejudices and oppressions feed from and reinforce each other. For instance, senior elementary or high-school students might spend a week on a media search recording occasions when animal formulations are used to describe people's character, habits or behaviours. Some examples are "Silly old cow!" "You bitch!" "They live like pigs!" Students then pool their findings and analyze them for ageist, classist, racist, sexist and homophobic allusion.[9] Holistic humane educators also share a certain conviction with their colleagues in environmental education (especially those working within a deep ecological or ecofeminist framework) and with global educators — that the well-being of humankind, other lifeforms and the planet are inextricably connected and that an expanded and permeable conception of Self, one divested of atomistic notions of individuality, will emerge from deeper sensitivity to our interconnectedness. As Stephen Huddart of the BC Human Education Society expresses it:

> In emphasizing our vital links to other species, we acknowledge their inherent value and right to exist, and in the process, modify our view of ourselves as a species and as individuals. As we teach and learn not to crush spiders underfoot, for example, we contribute to specific spiders, to spiders as invertebrate species, to our environment, and to our humanity. In simply observing or touching an animal, we enliven the quiet space within ourselves where we find the capacity for wonder, compassion and reverence. While it may sound odd, humane education involves animals teaching people.[10]

Calls for alliances with other progressive educational movements have most naturally emerged from the holistic end of the spectrum. A 1991 survey of Canadian animal advocates by Canadians for Health Research found that animal advocates "were likely to be involved with other movements: the environment (98%); civil rights (88%); anti-apartheid (86%); feminist (83%); anti-war (83%); students rights (70%); and gay rights (58%)."[11] In keeping with those findings and because of the close proximity of the two fields, those in humane education see a close "family likeness" in environmental education. The Kindness Club in Fredericton, New Brunswick, "teaches humane education combined with environmental education as it is difficult to separate the two when it comes to talking about all creatures great and small." Jane Tarn, one of the questionnaire respondents and who served as executive director of the organization from 1989–2000, notes, however, that "many environmentalists do not seem to acknowledge that humane education is connected to environmental education." Behind this coyness on the part of environmentalists lies not only a fear of being tarred with the same "crank" or "extremist" brush that is often applied to animal liberationists but also a reluctance to marry a primary focus upon ecosystems, per se, with a concern for the rights and welfare of non-objectified individual members of a species. This reluctance finds concrete expression in the still common environmental education practice of capturing creatures from the wild (tadpoles, insects) for classroom observation, a practice deplored by many humane educators (and, it should be added, radical environmental educators). The Fredericton Kindness Club, for instance, arranges and encourages class nature walks but lays down that "nothing is collected or intentionally harmed."

Proponents of other (generally anthropocentric) progressive educations also show a marked reluctance to acknowledge the "family likeness" they share with humane education. The use of animals for military testing and for bomb delivery, the structural violence implicit in humanity's treatment of animals and the renewed and increasing importance placed within humane education on the links between animal and family violence suggest peace education as a natural ally, but the latter stops short of applying the analysis of power, domination and aggression to human-animal relationships.[12] Animal liberationists' challenge to the species exclusivity of "human rights" suggests grounds for a dialogue between human rights and citizenship educators on the one hand and humane educators on the other, but this has not occurred to any great extent.[13] Similarly, the vegetarian solution to world hunger and malnutrition (that is, promoting vegetable production because it yields far more food per acre than meat production and because a diet not containing meat is healthier) provides grounds for a productive but, so far, virtually non-existent dialogue with development and health educators.[14] Humane education's linking of non-human and human oppressions and its insistence that concern and compassion for all forms of life should coalesce also speaks to the need for a coalition with anti-racist and anti-sexist education. There appears, however, to be marked reluctance, even resistance, to exploring shared concerns (and airing likely tensions) save amongst some ecofeminist educators.[15] In short, humane education remains something of a hapless suitor. A reciprocated courtship would, at the very least, challenge assumptions, sharpen understandings and open up a rich new vein of controversial issues for the classroom agenda of each education involved.

Educators working in other fields might also benefit from humane education's very catholic understanding of subject appropriateness. Respondents to the questionnaire tend to situate humane education across the curriculum, giving no primacy to particular subject areas. This is in marked contrast to, say, environmental education which, especially at the secondary level, remains dominated by the natural sciences despite the efforts of some in the field to give greater profile to the cultural, economic, social, political and spiritual dimensions of human/environment relationships. It is in some contrast, too, to the tendency of proponents of many of the fields discussed in this anthology to situate their work primarily in the social studies.

SOME CURRENT DEVELOPMENTS TOWARDS A HUMANE PEDAGOGY

Until recently humane educators have tended to concentrate on their field's importance for curriculum content. There has been little active reflection upon the learning process implications of a humane ethic. The debate on the nature of a humane pedagogy has now begun as proponents consider how the core "messages" of humane education — such as compassion, empathy, kindness, respect, responsibility, intrinsic value and equal consideration — should be reflected in the climate, ethos and quality of the relationships in the classroom. In practice this means emphasizing dialogue between students and between students and teachers. Such dialogue will value the contribution all can make to the learning process, cooperative learning, a decentralization of power, decision-making and initiative-taking in the classroom and sustaining a commitment to building self-esteem and group bonding.[16] The importance of building self-esteem and a positive self-image is twofold. First, learners with high self-esteem are more prepared to take risks in their learning and to share and confront opinions on the challenging and often controversial topics that frequently figure in humane education curricula. Second, a negative self-image is often expressed in negative attitudes about other people, animals and environments while a positive one often finds expression in pro-social attitudes such as caring and a readiness to stand against injustice.[17] The importance of building self-esteem is a significant factor behind initiatives to introduce animals into classrooms.

Humane societies with a clearly formulated education mission have begun to set up learning programs and produce materials designed to foster active and democratic learning.[18] Significant in this regard is the Canadian Federation of Humane Societies' annual national humane education workshop. The workshop, held in a different parts of Canada each year and principally attended by representatives of humane societies, uses and promotes interactive learning. The International Institute for Global Education at the University of Toronto has also been key in promoting new approaches to learning through its workshops and consultancies, and its graduate students are beginning to contribute to the theory and practice of humane pedagogy. There is, however, clearly much to do. A review of the returned questionnaires suggests that much of the work Canadian humane societies do in the schools remains rooted in traditional lectures, presentations and school assemblies.

The humane teacher's ability to recognize and then respond to the "subtle indicators of energy and compassion" in young people[19] by providing them with real-life opportunities to become involved in social action is also being recognizd as a hallmark of the humane classroom. "Voluntary participation in a school-based program," writes one respondent, "can provide opportunities to research animal issues, volunteer at animal shelters, carry out advocacy campaigns and special events and link up with students working on similar issues around the world." Teaching that encourages students to work for personal and social change (including change of a transformative nature) is inevitably controversial. What kinds of action project are acceptable? What are not?

What if a "Cuelty-Free Science" (student) group opposed to animal experimentation chooses to demonstrate against a visit to school by a careers representative of a pharmaceutical firm involved in such research? What if the same group trains its sights on a local branch of the firm where many parents are employed? ... Is the school prepared to "walk the democratic talk" of its mission statement and stand firmly by the core procedural values of freedom, toleration, fairness and respect for truth and reasoning, [or] to engage in constructive dialogue with the students and to allow the issue a full airing in both the school and community? [20]

For most educators in the field, the achievement of a humane pedagogy in natural science classes means the elimination of animal dissection or at least a student-choice policy on dissection.[21] While the outcry against dissection in schools has not been as vociferous or sustained as it has been in the United Kingdom or the United States, several humane societies condemn the practice and encourage schools to find other means for students to study animal anatomy. The Toronto-based Animal Alliance of Canada, for instance, offers a video and factsheets opposing dissection, and Digital Frog International of Puslinch, Ontario, has published an interactive frog-friendly CD-Rom, *The Digital Frog*.

ANIMALS IN THE CLASSROOM

Closely linked to the issue of humane pedagogy is that of introducing animals into the classroom. Having children take care of and be responsible for animals has been shown to have a number of important benefits. Animals can offer companionship that is non-threatening, non-judgemental, non-verbal, yet highly tactile. This relationships can be vital in enhancing a child's self-esteem, alleviating anxiety and depression, overcoming shyness, encouraging recovery from abuse, improving social skills, overcoming difficulties in expressing emotion, promoting empathy and fostering verbal and non-verbal communication.[22] Classroom animals can help boys strengthen their capacity to nurture. Classroom animals can also complement violence prevention programs by providing a calming presence and by helping children understand non-verbal cues. "In a school setting, classroom animals can foster a caring atmosphere while imparting lessons in practical stewardship. In some respects, this parallels and complements the goals of the schoolground naturalization movement."[23]

Pioneering efforts to introduce animals into the classroom, as visitors or as long-term residents, have flourished in British Columbia under the auspices of the British Columbia SPCA. The Society offers clear practical guidelines on choosing and looking after classroom pets and is insistent that its support for the introduction of animals into the classroom is contingent on teachers and children being thoroughly prepared and briefed.[24] In 1994–95, three Grade 7 classes at Westmount Public School in London, Ontario, undertook a two-month research project to explore the possibility of having a classroom animal. Their report detailed deliberations with parents, veterinarians and representatives of humane organizations (who were asked to participate in the classes' sharing circles). Only upon completion of the research did each class decide to adopt a pet rabbit. Their teachers reported that the self-esteem, confidence and articulateness of some students rose dramatically. As well, group cohesion was high as the classes exercised self-discipline in accordance with caring-for-animal checklists and according to democratically-negotiated class codes of students' rights and responsibilities. Furthermore, students frequently expressed unsolicited concern for human and non-human victims of cruelty and oppression when they met in their sharing circle throughout the year.[25]

Not all agree that animals should be in the classroom, however. Some, such as the officers of the British Columbia SPCA, recognize the dangers and drawbacks but, on balance, agree that the drawbacks are outweighed by the benefits. Others, such as officers of the Toronto Humane Society,[26] stand against classroom pets on the grounds that there are more drawbacks than benefits. They cite problems of supervision on weekends and during vacations, dangers to the pet through incorrect handling, the lack of peace and quiet for sensitive animals, and the fact that classes break up during a pet's life and the students cannot carry through on their commitment. While recognizing the validity of these objections, Steven Koebel argues that the risks can be contained by a school board animal policy. His survey of the fifty school districts in British Columbia revealed, however, that only two districts had written policies for animals in schools.[27] No policy can allay the more radical objection that the animals-in-the-classroom approach is anthropocentric, instrumentalist and meant to benefit people not animals.

ANIMAL ABUSE AND FAMILY VIOLENCE: RECOGNIZING THE LINKS

Within North American humane organizations over the last twenty years, recognition of the relationship between pet animal abuse and other forms of family violence has been growing. Most of the lead-ing-edge research comes from the United States, but it is beginning to influence the policy and practice of humane societies in Canada and has important repercussions for humane education.

Researchers have identified animal abuse as potentially predictive of violence against humans and as symptomatic of a dysfunctional family.[28] As well, a 1985 study of criminals and non-criminals looked at the relationship between cruelty to animals during childhood and aggression towards humans later in life and found that aggressive criminals were much more likely to have a record of early cruelty to animals than non-aggressive ones.[29] A subsequent study in 1986 found that certain features of cruelty to animals during childhood are much more accurate predictors of future aggression towards other humans. The predictors include direct involvement in an act of cruelty (rather than being a bystander), lack of self-restraint and remorse, a variety of cruel acts, the number of species victimized and acts directed against socially-useful animals.[30]

Of twenty-three families the British Royal Society for the Prevention of Cruelty to Animals investigated for animal neglect or abuse, 82 percent had been identified by social services as having children at risk for neglect or abuse.[31] A study of fifty-three New Jersey families who were known to have neglected or abused their children and who also owned pets revealed that 88 percent also abused the pets.[32] Several studies note that threats to give a pet away, or the torture or killing of pets, are used as means of coercion in families where women and children are being sexually abused or otherwise subjected to assault. [33]

The cumulative impact of such studies has created coalitions among such professional groups as social workers, animal cruelty investigators, doctors, veterinarians, teachers and police. The aim of such coalitions is to help us better understand and break the cycle of animal and family violence.[34] Strategies include joint conferences, cross-training, cross-referrals and inter-agency case-sharing. Canadian humane societies are beginning to draw up multi-disciplinary intervention strategies. In October 1996, the Canadian Federation of Humane Societies, together with the Calgary Humane Society and the Alberta SPCA, organized a seminar entitled The Tangled Web of Abuse. The seminar was offered to professionals in social services, mental health, education, the judicial system, law enforcement and animal protection. In September 1999, the Ontario SPCA sponsored The Link Between Animal Cruelty and Human Violence conference at the Toronto Police Association Conference Centre.

In schools, these developments are translating into learning programs that make the connections between animal abuse and violence against people, attempts to form local "humane coalitions" against violence, and calls for clear policies on reporting and following up on observed or reported instances of animal abuse by children or within families.[35]

In recent times, the Ontario SPCA has been at the fore of both the community and school level in raising awareness and building inter-agency coalitions around the link between animal abuse and family violence.[36] The OSPCA has published the *Violence Prevention Kit* and regularly updates the contents in response to specific requests from different sources (teachers, police, community groups). They are developing an educational unit for senior secondary students on violence prevention that makes a strong and explicit connection between animal abuse and human violence. Another initiative is a young offender program under which the offender is given the responsibility of an abused animal at an animal shelter prior to its adoption. The offender's role is to work with the animal to help it overcome the effects of trauma and to help it learn that not all humans are abusive. Early evidence suggests positive outcomes for both animal and offender, the latter experiencing a marked rise in self-esteem and in the capacity to care. The OSPCA has also begun to work closely with women's shelters. Many abused women are reluctant to leave the familial home, fearing for their pet's safety. Given that most women's shelters are unable to care for animals, the OSPCA is making arrangements to look after the pets until the women have re-established themselves and can take the pet back into their care.

POST-SECONDARY EDUCATION

Courses that teach prospective and practising teachers about humane education have been restricted to one-shot pre-service and in-service events that are facilitated by educators attached either to humane societies or to the International Institute for Global Education of the University of Toronto. No Canadian university faculty of education offers a course in humane education for pre-service teachers.

The first Canadian college-level course in animal welfare began in the spring of 1998 when the University College of the Cariboo in Kamloops, British Columbia, launched a Certificate Program in Animal Welfare. It is a distributed learning program[37] at the general and advanced levels, each taking six to eight months to complete and including a one-week practicum. While specifically geared to equipping participants to work in animal shelters and related services, sections on humane education are included at both levels. In January 1997 the University of British Columbia founded a Chair and Department of Animal Welfare. A third-year interdisciplinary undergraduate course, Animal Welfare and the Ethics of Animal Use, is intended to inform science students, some of whom become science teachers, of the humane implications of applied science. Education officers of the British Columbia SPCA are working closely with both initiatives.

The International Institute for Global Education has offered a graduate course on the theory and practice of environmental and humane education since January 1997 and, through its Global Education Interdisciplinary Focus, has become a magnet for master's and doctoral work on humane education. Graduate research projects include an impact study of a Grade 4 humane education curriculum,[38] the development and evaluation of an intermediate-level art unit in which students analyze human-animal relations through the art of successive periods, and women as change agents within the animal rights and humane education movements.

SOME DEBATES, DILEMMAS AND TENSIONS

LIBERATION VERSUS WELFARE

Broadly speaking, individuals protecting animal welfare hold that it is morally defensible to use animals for human ends as long as their well-being is, as much as possible, ensured at all stages of their lives. The compassionate treatment of animals, they would add, is essential for the well-being and sense of worth of humans individually and collectively. Those who advocate animal liberation label the claim to specifically human rights as "speciesist." Animal liberationists take the intrinsic value of each sentient being as their starting point and embrace the right of animals to a life free from suffering. They condemn society for being predicated upon the abuse and exploitation of animals, which gives their theory and activism a sharper edge, one more critical of the status quo.[39]

Some humane organizations are self-proclaimed animal rights organizations. The Animal Defence League of Canada, for instance, began as an anti-vivisection society and acquired charitable status before it "evolved into an animal rights organization." In the questionnaire returned from the ADLC, they write, "In 1992, our charitable status was annulled by the government. Our understanding is that this action was taken in response to pressure on the government by the food, fur and biomedical research industries." Those who are more oriented to concerns of animal welfare fear that animal liberationists and the activism associated in the public mind with animal rights is blocking the acceptance of humane education. One questionnaire respondent complains of "holier than thou activists who can't compromise to create change." Such feelings were voiced by several respondents. It needs to be said, however, that the liberationist and welfarist waters are very muddied. Many individuals, organizations and publications manifest a rather kaleidoscopic and hybrid mix of positions amounting to a pragmatic mix or fudge between animal welfare and liberation.

In many of the responses from those who wrote in a personal capacity there is the sense that they had to censor themselves because their organization's leadership, sponsors or funders were animal welfare advocates. One respondent wrote that "vegetarianism is divisive and politically risky." It appears that it is not uncommon for humane educators who want to produce materials that tap into the increasing interest in vegetarianism amongst youth to find their work vetoed because their organization "cannot afford to be anti-meat when it administers an act under the authority of the Ministry of Agriculture, and must maintain credibility with farmers." One respondent characterized the tensions as caused by "the generation gap between older and younger staff." "Each decade we move towards the more humane end of the spectrum, but we must still deal with our elders who are frozen in positions they adopted in their teens." Top-downwards palace revolutions are not unknown in humane societies were the "old guard" redirects or overturns the efforts of those whose educational work is critical of the status quo.

Ecofeminists criticize the animal welfare position for being essentially anthropocentric and for failing to espouse non-exploitative stances, such as vegetarianism. They also criticize the liberationist position for its basis in rationalistic, scientific theories of knowledge, its embrace of an abstract and atomistic theory of rights, and for its dismissal of emotion, sentiment, empathy and spiritual sensibility as valid bases for guiding our relationships with non-human animals.[40] For the most part, however, ecofeminism's criticisms remain peripheral to the humane education debate in Canada.

URBAN VERSUS RURAL

Intersecting with the animal welfare advocates-liberationist split is the rural-urban divide. I recall long discussions in the early 1990s with the then co-ordinator of a CIDA-funded provincial global education project who deeply feared what impact my teachers' handbook on humane education, *Earthkind*, would have on his work in what was a predominantly farming/trapping constituency, given I was known as a global educator. The humane organizations offering a socially critical and holistic rendition of humane education are based in the Greater Toronto Area and in Vancouver. In smaller towns and cities, humane education caters to a rural hinterland and more often than not focuses on domestic pets and animal ecology and downplays animal exploitation. "Hunting, trapping, farming and fishing and also lumbering are big "industries," writes one small city respondent. "Many parents are involved in jobs related to these industries. We do not discuss such issues, but information or stories showing the problems that arise from these issues are printed." Predicts another: "The split between rural and urban concerns about animals will remain a challenge for some time to come. There are many examples of human/animal economies which go unchallenged because they are held to be 'normal' — so it is easier to denounce Chinese use of bear gall bladders, for example, than to oppose bear trophy hunting by wealthy Americans who pay hefty fees to local guide-outfitters."

One way for schools to help bridge the divide between the rural and urban conceptions of human education might be to link urban and rural children in a discussion on animal issues through the Internet. More fundamentally, those working in humane education (and in environmental education) might do well to follow the example of some ecofeminists and environmental justice advocates and seek to find common ground with those working in and representing resource-based industries.[41] Humane education recognizes, at least in its holistic expression, the similar dynamics and intersection of a diversity of oppressions and should be in the business of building shared understandings and shared strategies for change that are inclusive in nature. Craig Naherniak, the director of the British Columbia SPCA Education Division, describes a new progam that offers promise:

> As we proceed, we have been able to move producers, retailers and governments to look carefully at "accepted practices" and [to] consider alternatives. The messages are couched in language that they can relate to. We are careful to [use the] less threatening "we want to work with you for the benefit of both the farmer (and his/her lifestyle and commitment to sound husbandry practices) and the animals" language.[42]

HUMANE EDUCATION IN A MULTICULTURAL CONTEXT

Humane education in an increasingly multicultural society has become a major dilemma for those working in the field. So has the question of confronting latent or manifest issues of race and ethnicity woven through many current animal-related topics and themes. Working with a wide range of ethno-cultural groups requires sensitivity to cultural and religious practices and taboos — a reluctance to touch or be close to a pet animal, for instance, or a fear of or distaste for certain animals usually viewed positively within western cultures — and it also draws the humane educator into the controversial debate on cultural and moral relativism versus moral interculturalism and universalism.[43] Are traditional and legal non-western practices involving animals off-limits to discussion and criticism? Or are they valid subjects for open intercultural debate? Is it always appropriate to encourage all students, irrespective of culture, to perceive and treat pets according to western ideas? A few questionnaire respondents report making some adjustment of classroom programs in response to the multicultural classes they work with. Others report that ethnic minority children readily participate in animals-in-classroom programs. Stephen Huddart and Craig Naherniak of the BC SPCA write that "some of the most enthusiastic responses to our classroom animal programs come from schools with large numbers of immigrants. We speculate that this may be due to the levelling quality of an animal's gaze, providing recognition irrespective of race or culture."[44]

Humane educators take an equivocal stance on the First Nations. On the one hand, they find inspiration in the varied traditional sustainable material cultures of Aboriginal groups across Canada and their deep reverence for animals and nature. Humane education materials for students often propose First Nations' perspectives on nature as ones that should be adopted by all Canadians. On the other hand, they oppose the First Nations' participation in the fur trade and in the seal and whale hunts, including current revivals of "cultural" whale hunting of threatened whale species. Locally, humane societies say that pets receive poor care on some reservations. Some respondents report successful humane education programs in First Nations schools, and others write that they intend to build bridges with bands through networking with First Nations educators and by establishing First Nations' advisory committees. Whether, and what extent, the successes reported are regarded as such by the First Nations' communities concerned remains unclear as does the extent to which those working for the humane societies were sensitive to, and sought means of neutralizing, the unequal power relations involved.

CRITICAL CHALLENGES AT THE DAWN OF A NEW CENTURY

The signs are that humane education is now coming of age. Since 1994 the Canadian Federation of Humane Societies has published a national newsletter for humane educators, *The Humane Educator.* The widely-read journal of environmental and global education, *Green Teacher,* now regularly publishes articles on humane education. *Earthkind* is one of the first comprehensive handbooks on humane education.[45] A graduate education program is up and running at the Ontario Institute for Studies in Education at the University of Toronto, and the Canadian Federation of Humane Societies holds an annual national workshop for humane educators. What, then, are the critical challenges facing the field in Canada in the early twenty-first century?

THE NEED FOR CANADA-WIDE DISCUSSION

We need a more coherent and cohesive understanding of the theory and practice of humane education among its proponents and an open discussion on definitions, goals, objectives and outcomes. This is not to suggest, as one respondent did, that a unified understanding across Canada should be the aim. It means that we need deeper, continuing and more purposeful debate about all aspects of the field while respecting and celebrating diversity of opinion and approach. Our priorities need to include encouraging networking, providing more opportunities for conferences and publishing a national academic journal to complement the national newsletter.

MORE FRENCH-LANGUAGE MATERIALS

There are very few resources for students and teachers on humane education written in French. Until this changes, there cannot be a truly Canada-wide discussion within the field. The Canadian SPCA in Montreal is now engaged in translating SPCA materials from the United States into French. The SPCA in the Eastern Townships, based in Sherbrooke, Quebec, also has a translation project under-way and is translating Canadian materials written in English into French. We need to both increase the output of materials available in French and to promote the publication of home-grown materials throughout the French-speaking regions of Canada, materials that are consonant with the local culture and that meet the demands of the provincial curriculum.

CULTIVATING PARTNERSHIPS

Humane education, one respondent writes, should "play a role in a broadly-based movement towards a humane and sustainable future." Another writes of the need "to co-operate and join forces with all groups [that] espouse equality and a reverence for life." While some respondents report their organization's successful par-ticipation in local and national partnerships on specific initiatives, the need remains for a wide range of continuing partnerships at many levels. This chapter has discussed the need for partnerships with those working in related fields and the need for coalitions that can build a more comprehensive approach to preventing violence. Questionnaire respondents also report on, or express interest in, forming partnerships with the media, publishers, businesses, groups representing the disabled, research institutes and universities. We lack, however, a clearing house through which to share information about successful partnerships and about experiences that have proven to be effective agents for change.

VISIBILITY AND SECURITY IN THE CURRICULUM

The importance of securing a place in curriculum guidelines at the ministerial level is emphasized by several respondents. So, too, is the need to raise human education's profile among teachers and teacher educators. One respondent wrote of the importance of explaining "to Ministries of Education Canada-wide the need for and positive value of utilizing Humane Education programs." Another insists that "[h]umane education must be included in Canada's school system. It should be part of the curriculum, taught by regular teachers." To fulfill these ambitions, we need a multi-dimensional strategy that can help us achieve the following: lobby school boards and provincial ministries of education; build academic credentials of humane education through university-based research and development work; provide strong pre-service and in-service teacher education programs; train teacher educators; raise public awareness by taking the initiative with the media and in community outreach; and produce high quality home-grown learning materials and programs (several respondents ruefully note a continued over-reliance on foreign, especially US, materials).

There are, unfortunately, many obstacles in the way of achieving these ambitions. One is the tendency, noted by several respondents, for humane education to be seen as "an expendable frill" by many humane organizations. There are also budgetary pressures facing many humane societies, not to mention the incredible volume of animal- and environment-related materials put out by agribusiness. "Lack of money is a problem for many humane societies and animal welfare groups [wanting to publish materials]," worries one respondent, "whereas industry and government have money to get their messages out. Industry and government have designed some wonderful school programs that encourage hunting, fishing, trapping, eating meat, lumbering, etc."

There are also the ever-present reservations about giving attention to animals when so many humans are suffering. Recognition of the "systemic iniquities that threaten humans and other animals alike"[46] is not widely shared among decision-makers in education or by the public at large. Nor are the therapeutic benefits of contact with animals widely appreciated. But there is a strong case to be made, as Richard Stanford points out:

> When I protest against factory farming, I am not only condemning the treatment of animals, I am also condemning the

degradation of the environment and the loss of the small family farm caused by agribusinesses. When I protest against vivisection, I also condemn the bad science which suggests that evidence extrapolated from animal research can be applied to humans. [47]

Or as a respondent explains:

> In some of the most challenging of circumstances, among badly abused children, or in inner-city schools rife with the dire effects of poverty and cultural dislocation, we have seen animals acting as remarkable catalysts for healing, learning and co-operation.

Making humane education mainstream education is made more difficult by the deep budgetry cuts in education that began in the early 1990s and by the now-dominant right-wing climate of "back to basics" and "education for global competitiveness." But, as one respondent reminds us, "The most critical challenge facing humane education in Canada is the shift in focus away from environmental and humane values to a self-involved focus on people." That shift to greater self-involvement, "makes our job as educators tougher yet more important than ever."

TEACHER RESOURCES

American Humane Association, *Protecting Children and Animals: Agenda for a Non-Violent Future* (Englewood, Co: American Humane Association, 1992). This is an important booklet on the interrelationship between violence against humans and against animals. Copies are available from AHA at 63 Inverness Drive East, Englewood, CO 80112, USA.

Stephen Koebel, *Animals, Children and Related School Board Policy in the Elementary School* (Vancouver: British Columbia SPCA, n.d.). Discusses the benefits and practicalities of having animals in the classroom and offers sample school district animal-in-school policies.

Jacqueline Pearce, *Greenscape: An Annotated Bibliography of Canadian Children's Literature with Environmental Themes* (Vancouver: British Columbia Humane Education Society (now the British Columbia SPCA), 1993). This bibliography lists fictional and non-fictional elementary-level works that are classified according to age and quality, revealing a wealth of home-grown environmental and humane literature for children.

David Selby, *Earthkind: A Teachers' Handbook on Humane Education* (Stoke-on-Trent, UK: Trentham, 1995). A Comprehensive guide to both the theory and practice of humane education. A wide range of classroom and teacher education activities suitable for all grade levels. Available from Green Brick Road and British Columbia SPCA (see below).

CLASSROOM RESOURCES

Barbara Pulling, ed., *How I learned to Speak Dog and Other Animal Stories* (Vancouver: Douglas and McIntyre, 1995). This anthology of fifty-four stories celebrates the presence of animals in the lives of British Columbians.

The Digital Frog (Trillium Place, ON: Digital Frog International, n.d.). An interactive CD-ROM offers high schools a humane alternative to dissection. The three modules cover dissection, anatomy and ecology and for students in standard level, Grades 9 to 11, and advanced level, Grade 12 to College. Available from Digital Frog International, Trillium Place, RR#2, Ontario N0B 2J0. (519) 766-1097.

ORGANIZATIONS

British Columbia Society for the Prevention of Cruelty to Animals
322-470 Granville Street
Vancouver, BC V6C 1V5
http://www.spca.bc.ca

A leading light in humane education in Canada. Its publications include *H.A.W.K.s (Humans Acting with Kindness) Teacher's Guide* and accompanying newsletter *Kids are H.A.W.K.s* (on animals visiting the classroom); *The Coyote Kit: An Urban Wildlife Curriculum Unit*, an intermediate level unit; *Kindness Count: A Teacher's Guide to Humane Education;* and the *Humane Leader*, a three-times-per-year newsletter. The SPCA also offers classroom presentations, and pre-service and in-service teacher education workshops, and has a resource centre open to the public.

Canadian Federation of Humane Societies (CFHS)
102-30 Concourse Gate
Nepean, ON K2E 7V7
(613) 224-8072

The Federation has published the semi-annual newsletter *Humane Educator* since 1994; it holds an annual national humane education workshop and has audio-visual and printed classroom materials for purchase. The Federation is well-placed to provide the national platform and clearing house for humane education envisaged in this chapter.

Canadian Society for the Prevention of Cruelty to Animals
5215 West Jean-Talon
Montreal, QC H4P 1X4
(514) 735-2711
www.spca.com.
The CSPCA volunteers to bring dogs into elementary classes to build students' comfort level with and trust of animals as an entrée to discussing responsible pet ownership and cruelty to pets. Involved in translating humane education materials into French.

SPCA of the Eastern Townships
1139 Queen North Boulevard
Sherbrooke, QC J1J 4N5
(819) 821-4727
www.spaestrie.qc.ca
This organization is also involved in translation projects.

International Institute for Global Education (IIGE)
Ontario Institute for Studies in Education of the University of Toronto
252 Bloor Street West, 10th Floor
Toronto, ON M5S 1V6
(416) 923-6641 ext. 4540
IIGE offers master's and doctoral programs in humane and global education and related fields, leads institutes, seminars and courses across Canada, and undertakes curriculum development and research projects. Publications list and flyer available. IIGE publications are distributed by The Green Brick Road, Toronto, ON 1-800-GREEN38.

The Kindness Club
65 Brunswick Street
Fredericton, NB E3B 1G5
(506) 459-3379
Publishes a quarterly newsletter that is sent to all English-speaking and First Nations schools. It offers a liaison teachers' program to 100 schools, classroom visits, professional development days for teachers, and loans videos.

Kindness Club Foundation
35 Acheson Boulevard
Scarborough, ON M1C 3C4
(416) 282-2658.

Seven full-time teachers volunteer to conduct 45-minute "Values Through Humane Education" presentations for Grades 1 to 8 classes in the Greater Toronto Area. The organization also offers presentations exploring links between humane education and the Ontario Common Curriculum.

L'association Inter-Canada Jane Goodall
5165 Sherbrooke Street West, S-408
Montreal, QC H4A 1T6
(514) 369-3384

This is the Canadian branch of the international organization, Roots & Shoots, that began in Tanzania in 1991 as a result of Jane Goodall's research with chimpanzees. Roots & Shoots clubs encourage students to undertake activities that promote peaceful conflict resolution, environmental protection and concern for animals. Members receive Roots & Shoots guidelines and a Grades 3 to 7 curriculum. Guidelines for starting Roots & Shoots clubs and for teacher training are available.

Ontario Society for the Prevention of Cruelty to Animals
16586 Woodbine Ave., RR#3
Newmarket, ON L3Y 4W1
(905) 898-7122
www.ospca.on.ca

Publishes a free *Violence Prevention Kit*, containing brochure and articles. The OSPCA is developing an educational unit for senior high school students on violence prevention and the links between familial violence and animal abuse. Teachers wanting to know more about OSPCA programs and initiatives should contact Christa Chadwick, Manager of Education, by e-mail at cchadwickj@ospca.on.ca.

Regina Humane Society
Box 3143
Regina, SK S4P 3G7
(306) 543-6363

The RHS publishes *Sharing our Earth,* an education manual distributed annually to all elementary schools in Regina. The manual lists suggestions and activities for incorporating humane education into the curriculum. The RHS has also published *Humans and Other Animals,* a high-school resource manual. The Society offers programs for schools, invites visitors to the Society's animal shelter and has a resource centre for teachers.

Toronto Humane Society
11 River Street
Toronto, ON M5A 4C2
(416) 392-2273
www.humanesociety-ca.org

The largest humane society in Canada, the THS offers presentations to schools on safety around dogs, responsible care, wildlife and the city, and the role of the humane society in the community. Animal shelter tours arranged.

NOTES

Officers of the following organizations kindly responded to my questionnaire on humane education: Animal Defence League of Canada, Toronto; Antigonish SPCA, Nova Scotia; British Columbia SPCA, Vancouver; Calgary Humane SPCA; Gander and Area SPCA, Newfoundland; Grand Praries SPCA, Alberta; Guelph Humane Society, Ontario; Humane Society of Ottawa-Carleton; The Kindness Club, Fredericton, New Brunswick; Kindness Club Foundation, Scarborough, Ontario; Shelby County SPCA, Nova Scotia; Swift Current SPCA, Saskatchewan; and Yarmouth SPCA, Nova Scotia.

I would like to thank Connie Russell for undertaking the initial analysis of questionnaire returns and for carrying out a range of follow-up research tasks. Connie also commented on the first draft of this chapter as did Stephen Huddart and Craig Naherniak of British Columbia SPCA, and Judita Pamfil, doctoral student attached to the International Institute for Global Education, Ontario Institute for Studes in Education of the University of Toronto. The opinions expressed here remain exclusively my responsibility.

1. Sarah Eddy, *Friends and Helpers* (1897), cited in National Association of Humane and Environmental Educators, *KIND Workshop Leader's Guide* (East Haddam, CT: NAHEE, 1991), 2. Sarah Eddy was a pioneer humane educator in the US.

2. Cited in NAHEE, *KIND Workshop Leader's Guide*, 3.

3. Cindy Milburn, "Editorial," in *Humane Education Newsletter*, no. 3 (1992), 2. Cindy Milburn is a leading humane educator in the UK. She has worked for Earthkind (UK), the International Fund for Animal Welfare and the World Society for the Protection of Animals.

4. Bob Rutter, *A Century of Caring 1893–1993: A History of the Guelph Humane Society* (Guelph: Guelph Humane Society, 1993), 11.

5. David Selby, "Humane Education: The Ultima Thule of Global Education: Part One," *Green Teacher* 39 (1994), 10.

6. The British Columbia Humane Education Society became the Education Division of the British Columbia Society for Prevention of Cruelty to Animals

in November 1996. This statement and all subsequent references were cited in the questionnaire the organization returned.

7. Lisa Koch, *Humans and other Animals* (Regina: Regina Humane Society, 1999).

8. See, for instance, Kate Kempton, "Zoos: Asking the Right Questions," *Green Teacher* 41 (1994/5), 29–31, and Annette Payne, "Animals in Jeopardy: A Schoolwide Theme on Endangered Animals for Grades K to 8," *Green Teacher* 45 (1995/6), 29–31.

9. David Selby, "Humane Education: The Ultima Thule of Global Education: Part 2," *Green Teacher* 40 (1994), 30.

10. Stephen Huddart, "What is Humane Education?" *Humane Leader* (Winter 1993), 1. Emphasis in original. This is the newsletter of the then British Columbia Humane Education Society. See endnote 6.

11. Richard Stanford, "A Simple Test of Our Morality," *The Globe and Mail*, 9 July 1991, A16. At the time of writing, Richard Stanford was directing and teaching an animal rights course at Abbott College, Montreal.

12. David Selby, *Earthkind: A Teachers' Handbook on Humane Education* (Stoke-on-Trent, UK: Trentham, 1995), 22–26.

13. Ibid., 15–16.

14. Ibid., 26–28.

15. Anne Bell and Constance Russell, "Life Ties: Disrupting Anthropocentrism in Language Arts Education," in Judith Robertson, ed., *Teaching for a Tolerant World, Grades K-6: Essays and Resources* (Urbana, IL: National Council of Teachers of English, 1999), 68–89.

16. David Selby, "Relational Modes of Knowing: Learning Process Implications of a Humane and Environmental Ethic," in Bob Jickling, ed., *A Colloquium on Environment, Ethics, and Education* (Whitehorse: Yukon College, 1996), 50–52.

17. Denis Lawrence, *Enhancing Self-Esteem in the Classroom* (London: Paul Chapman. 1987), 6–7; Selby, "Relational Modes of Knowing," 51.

18. See, for instance, Koch, *Humans and other Animals*, and British Columbia Society for the Protection of Cruelty to Animals, *The Coyote Kit: An Urban Wildlife Curriculum Unit* (Vancouver: BC SPCA, 1999).

19. Roger Hart, *Children's Participation: From Tokenism to Citizenship* (Florence, Italy: UNICEF International Child Development Centre, 1992), 4.

20. Selby, *Earthkind*, 320.

21. Pat Davis, "Dissection Issues: The Student Choice Policy," *The Humane Educator* 2 (Fall 1995), 4–5.

22. Stephen Huddart and Craig Naherniak, "Shifting Paradigms: A New Look at Animals in Classrooms," *Green Teacher* 44 (1995), 12–16; Steven Koebel, *Animals, Children and Related School Board Policy in the Elementary School* (Vancouver: British Columbia SPCA, n.d.), 9–10. Stephen Huddart is Community Relations Director and Craig Naherniak is the Education Director for the BC SPCA.

23. Huddart and Naherniak, "Shifting Paradigms," 13.

24. Craig Naherniak, "Profound Encounters: Classroom Animals — More Than Responsible Pet Care," *Humane Leader* (Fall 1993), 1–3. The guidelines include determining financial responsibility, establishing cleaning and feeding routines, constructing and situating an appropriate home and cautioning against classroom animal "honeymoon syndrome." See Huddart and Naherniak, "Shifting Paradigms," 14–16.

25. Selby, "Relational Modes of Knowing," 51.

26. Toronto Humane Society, *Classroom Pet: Delight or Disaster?* (Toronto: Toronto Humane Society Education Department, 1990).

27. Koebel, *Animals, Children and Related School Board Policy,* 14.

28. Phil Arkow, "The Relationship Between Animal Abuse and Other Forms of Family Violence," *Latham Letter* 281 (1997), 1, 6–11.

29. Stephen Kellert and Alan Felthouse, "Childhood Cruelty Toward Animals Among Criminals and Noncriminals," *Human Relations* 38 (1985), 1113–1129.

30. Alan Felthouse and Stephen Kellert, "Violence Against Animals and People: Is Aggression Against Living Creatures Generalized?" *Bulletin of the American Academy of Psychiatry and Law* 14 (1986), 55–68.

31. James Hutton, "Animal Abuse as a Diagnostic Approach in Social Work: A Pilot Study," paper presented at the 1981 International Conference on Human/Animal Companion Bond, Philadelphia, PA.

32. Elizabeth DeViney, Jeffery Dickert, and Randall Lockwood, "The Care of Pets Within Child Abusing Families," *International Journal for the Study of Animal Problems* 4 (1983), 321–329.

33. Arkow, "The Relationship Between Animal Abuse and Other Forms of Family Violence," 8–9.

34. Arkow, "The Relationship Between Animal Abuse and other Forms of Family Violence," 9–11; American Humane Association, *Protecting Children and Animals: Agenda for a Non-Violent Future* (Englewood, CO: American Humane Association, 1992). This pamphlet is a summary of the AHA conference in Herndon, Virginia, 14–15 September 1992.

35. Selby, *Earthkind,* 26.

36. Vicky Earle, "From Animals to People? Tracking Patterns of Abuse," *Rehabilitation and Community Care Management* (Winter 1997), 14; Leland Davies, "The Link Between Animal Abuse and Family Violence," *Animals' Voice* 2 (Summer 1998), 9–14.

37. Students are not restricted to a specific time or place. The program makes use of computers, video and the standard printed page, and students are encouraged to submit their assignments by e-mail and on computer disks. For more information, see <http://www.spca.bc.ca/ucc.htm>.

38. Justine Tweyman-Erez, "The Effects of a Humane Education Curriculum, Involving the Great Apes Project, on the Attitudes of Fourth-Grade Students"

(master's thesis, Department of Curriculum, Teaching and Learning, Ontario Institute for Studies in Education of the University of Toronto, 1998).

39. David Selby, "Humane Education: Challenging Anthropocentrism in the Curriculum," *Orbit* 27 (1996), 39.

40. Andree Collard with Joyce Contrucci, *Rape of the Wild: Man's Violence Against Animals and The Earth* (Bloomington: Indiana University Press, 1989); Josephine Donovan, "Animal Rights and Feminist Theory," in Greta Gaard, ed., *Ecofeminism: Women, Animals, Nature* (Philadelphia: Temple University Press, 1993); Josephine Donovan and Carol Adams, eds., *Beyond Animal Rights: A Feminist Caring Ethic for the Treatment of Animals* (New York: Continuum, 1996).

41. Bunyan Bryant, ed., *Environmental Justice: Issues, Policies and Solutions* (Covelo, CA: Island Press, 1995); Ellen O'Loughlin, "Questioning Sour Grapes: Ecofeminism and the United Farm Workers Grape Boycott," in Gaard, ed., *Ecofeminism: Women, Animals, Nature*, 146–166.

42. Craig Naherniak, e-mail correspondence with the author, February 1999.

43. Neil Burtonwood, *The Culture Concept in Educational Studies* (Windsor, UK: NFER-Nelson, 1986); David Cooper, "Animals and Cultural Traditions," *Outrage* 76 (October/November 1991), 12.

44. Huddart and Naherniak, "Shifting Paradigms," 13.

45. Selby, *Earthkind.*

46. Bell and Russell, "Life Ties," 69.

47. Stanford, "A Simple Test of Our Morality."

Chapter 11

LAW-RELATED EDUCATION

PROMOTING AWARENESS,

PARTICIPATION AND ACTION

Wanda Cassidy

LAW AND "THE EDUCATED PERSON"

It used to be, a century ago, that "the educated person" had a fundamental understanding of law — of its impact on the individual, of its regulatory power in society, of its role in shaping public policy, of its relationship with social norms and values. Indeed, knowing about law, what it is and what it does, was considered one of the hallmarks of an educated person in the western world.[1] Over the years, however, a well-rounded liberal arts education, which included law, gave way to the professionalization of law, where only those trained as lawyers had access to education about law. Public school education[2] was generally devoid of overt legal content, except for an occasional elective course often poorly conceived and accompanied by outdated material inappropriate for teaching.

If we were to zero in on a typical secondary school in Canada in the early 1970s, we would observe the following situation: a teacher with little or no knowledge of law, tackling a senior law elective with one outdated textbook based on law from the most populous province, a textbook supplemented only by a fill-in-the-blanks question-and-answer student workbook. This teacher would have had no undergraduate course in law, no exposure to law education as part of her or his teacher education, no opportunity for professional development, no support services from the community, and no other source from which to glean appropriate classroom materials. As someone who experienced that situation first hand,[3] I can attest to the frustration of being fascinated by the subject but being totally unprepared to address legal content or to engage students in law-related topics, other than to rely on help from the wider legal community and to adopt a "I don't know, but let's learn together" strategy with my students.

Fortunately for teachers across the country faced with those daunting challenges, the tide was about to turn in their favour, provoked by rumblings from the general public and from the legal profession. Across Canada, adults of the 1970s, fresh from the activism of the 1960s, began demanding that law be demystified, that legalese be abandoned and that the cloistered world of the lawyer be opened up to the average person. Running parallel to this grassroots movement, was an acknowledgement from some at the top of the legal profession that Canadians were generally ignorant of the law and that popular American television programs broadcast to Canada communicated misinformation about the law on a daily basis. Since a democratic society only functions well with a knowledgeable and engaged citizenry, and since ignorance of the law is no excuse for breaking the law, several prominent spokespeople called for something to be done, and done quickly, to foster a more legally literate public. One route, put forward by the Canadian Bar Association,[4] was to focus on the needs of the adult population, or to bring law to the people. Another route, deemed likely to be more effective in the long run, was to educate young people while they were still in school and still a captive audience.

The comment made by Bora Laskin, the former Chief Justice of Canada, in a 1977 interview for *Maclean's* magazine became a rallying cry for many across Canada who sought funding for school programing to educate young Canadians about the law:

> I'm very much concerned about the lack of education in the legal
> process in our schools, up to and including university. It's very
> important to have a citizenry which is socially literate and social
> literacy to me involves some appreciation of the legal system.
> There isn't a single act that any government can do that does not
> have to find its source in the legal system. It's just as important
> that our people have some appreciation of law as they should of
> English or French literature or economics. I hope that our edu-
> cational authorities will pay attention to this.[5]

Hugh Kindred, a Dalhousie law professor, and Ken Norman, at the
time Chief Commissioner of the Saskatchewan Human Rights
Commission, also advocated improved elementary and secondary
school education in the law. Kindred wrote extensively on the relationship between young people coming to understand the law and
youth assuming their rights and responsibilities as democratic citizens:

> It is important that students know not only their civic responsi-
> bilities, but also their freedom of action within (our) system of
> government. The measure of good citizenship is not inculcated
> conformity, but a healthy respect for the rights of others as well
> as one's own, and an allegiance to orderly process, even in diver-
> sity. The character of law encourages such critical, yet construc-
> tive attitudes.[6]

Norman argued that social studies curricula was rife with legal content that needed to be extrapolated and developed.

In British Columbia in 1993, the Justice Development
Commission, under the auspices of the province's Ministry of the
Attorney General, went so far as to undertake a study of the Law 11
elective offered in schools throughout British Columbia. The
Commission found an appalling lack of resources and support for
teachers and recommended immediate funding to counteract the
situation.

THE GROWTH OF THE LAW-RELATED EDUCATION MOVEMENT

This two-pronged demand from the grassroots and from members
of the legal professional for programs that would give Canadians an

understanding of the important role law plays in their daily life culminated in the establishment of several public legal education and information (PLEI) organizations, at least one in each province and territory, and most with an added mandate to address the needs of students in school. The schools' portion of the mandate came to be known as "law-related education," as opposed to "law or legal education," which implied a narrow focus akin to what might be learned at law school.

The term "law-related education" was imported from a parallel movement in the United States, one aimed at ensuring that elementary and secondary school students achieved literacy in the law.[7] The Canadian movement differed from the American one in that law-related education in the schools in Canada fell under the broader jurisdiction of public legal education. In the United States, most law-related education organizations were set up solely to address the needs of youth in school; in fact, there was no complementary movement in the United States for public legal education.

Although law-related education in Canada combines two fields — law and education — with the beneficiary being education, the impetus and the support for the many initiatives came almost solely from law, not from education. Funding came from provincial ministries of the attorney general, legal services or legal aid organizations, law foundations, the law courts and the federal Department of Justice, not from provincial ministries of education, teachers' federations or school districts. On occasion, small amounts of funding did come from education sources, for projects like a summer institute or regional workshop for teachers, or for the distribution of teachers' guides, case studies, pamphlets and the like, prepared by law-related education programs.

Initially, those working in law-related education saw the lack of involvement from traditional education sources as an advantage. It meant that tasks could often be completed more quickly, for they did not have to meet the expectations of several partners or work their way through the education bureaucracy to have projects approved. Topics for curriculum projects or for workshops could also be more controversial and more issue-oriented than projects or workshops likely to win approval from a cautious government.

What at first seemed efficient, and therefore more effective, would later turn out to have serious drawbacks, particularly because the relative isolation of those working in law-related education meant they could easily be written off as just another lobby group.

In the mid-1980s, however, the movement to promote law-related education in schools was flourishing. Every province and territory in Canada had programs underway.[8] In most instances, programs for schools were housed within larger public education and information agencies, or in legal aid organizations, community law offices, or court houses. Some of those organizations were blessed with a statutory mandate to address the law education needs of that province's citizenry. Other organizations cloaked themselves in their own mandate to attend to a public that needed to understand the law and its wide ranging influence on their lives. A trans-Canada network of like-minded visionaries in public and school-based law education had formed by the late 1970s, and in 1980 the First National Conference on Legal Education for Youth helped forge links between the many organizations working in schools.[9]

In general, funding for law-related activities during the late 1970s and 1980s was relatively easy to secure. There was never enough money to address the wide range of needs, and some provinces were still seriously underserved, but many funders saw law-related education for youth in schools as a priority. During the second national conference for law-related educators, held in 1988, delegates applauded a number of successes.[10] Teachers could now draw on a wide range of print and audio-visual resources for the classroom mainly for secondary school students, with some geared to younger students. There were five major textbooks, all up-to-date and more engaging than before. In some provinces, teachers and staff from law-related education organizations had successfully lobbied their ministry of education to include more law content in courses such as social studies, consumer education or business education. Faculties of education at four universities in Canada (two in British Columbia, one in Alberta, one in Ontario) also initiated programs in law education for prospective teachers and for those teachers already in classrooms who needed to update their knowledge of law and learn novel ways to teach law to students.

Many teachers were also moving away from the "black letter law" approach to teaching law — from a focus on students acquiring a myriad of facts and details about legal topics — towards a more concept-based approach where students debated legal issues and examined the law within the broader framework of society's needs, values and goals. As part of this new approach to teaching law, teachers were also beginning to consider the powerful effect of the informal curriculum on children's learning and the need for their own teaching to reflect those democratic and legal values they were espousing during the delivery of the formal curriculum. With this greater awareness of law and its role as one means of conflict resolution came an interest in other means of dispute resolution, such as quasi-judicial approaches and mediation. That new interest led to new materials and to workshops on conflict resolution, with some schools designing programs whereby the students themselves became mediators and resolved playground and various student-to-student disputes. For example, students in one school in Ontario set up a "Litter Court" to deal with the problem of littering on the school grounds.

Overall, if we were to measure law-related education by its products and its programs, we could claim considerable success. Where teachers once found almost nothing to help them put law-related education into practice, within ten years they could find materials taking a substantive, a procedure-based and an issue-based approach to learning about the law.

The substantive approach encompassed traditional legal topics such as tort law, criminal law, landlord-tenant obligations, labour law, contracts, wills and consumer transactions. The procedures-based approach centred on court procedures, a comparison between youth justice and adult criminal law processes, the workings of administrative tribunals and alternative dispute resolution processes, as well as important underlying principles such as the rule of law and right to a fair trial. The issues-based approach looked at human rights, children's rights, women's rights, First Nations' rights, poverty law, environmental law, constitutional questions and the links between the various issues.

Teachers could combine approaches and draw on videotapes,

16-mm films, comic books, role plays, simulation games, puppetry, wall charts and case studies to make the law come alive for their students. Some of the organizations promoting law-related education arranged for class field trips to the local court house and wrote mock trials based on historical or fictional cases, which students could then act out in a courtroom.

Debating contests and essay writing competitions for senior students were also promoted through various law-related agencies. Most of these agencies also produced newsletters for teachers and community groups, which usually included an update on the law, resources information, lesson ideas and articles on current legal issues. Many teachers also took advantage of available workshops to learn about law, how to teach it and where to find new resources for their classroom.

Although some provinces provided a wider range of services and resources (British Columbia and Alberta, for example, had the most extensive programs), teachers in all areas of the country, particularly secondary school teachers, could find classroom materials and find ways to improve their own knowledge. In almost every instance, law-related education agencies provided services and resources directly to the teacher. Ministries of education, school districts, teachers' federations and universities had but minimal involvement.

GRAND GOALS AND CRITICAL CHALLENGES

Fueled by heady ideals, the great need and a warm welcome from teachers, the visionaries raced ahead with several goals in mind. Generally most law-related education programs reflected the following three goals, although somewhat more attention was given to Goal 1, at least in the early years.

Goal 1: Knowledge of the law as it affects people's everyday lives, that is, practical law (family relationships, housing, the workplace, consumer issues, youth and the law).

Goal 2: Understanding the principles and premises that form the basis for Canadian society: the rule of law and the principles of fairness, equality, freedom of expression, due process, as spelled out in the Charter of Rights and Freedoms, and embedded in common law.

Goal 3: Acquiring the skills associated with law: accessing information; formulating arguments; weighing evidence; making reasoned judgements and assuming the rights and responsibilities expected of an active citizen in a democratic society.

Roland Case, in his book *On the Threshold* (the title itself suggests movement towards something grand), argued that people working in law-related education needed to address the formal, the social and the normative aspects of the law. [11] The formal aspect encompasses statute, common, and constitutional law, the workings of legal institutions, and knowledge of specific areas of law (labour, family or human rights). The social aspect examines law within the broader society; that is, how law shapes society and how society's values shape the law. Why, for example, do we have laws? What can law do or not do for society? How can people change a law? The normative aspect encompasses the complex set of values that society holds as its dominant goals or ideals, that is, the fundamental principles that underpin the law, questions around the legitimacy of authority, and the reasoning used in law.

Given the rapid proliferation of law-related education programs across Canada and the fact that many program developers had backgrounds in professions outside of education, including library science, law, community development or human rights, the Canadian Law Information Council in 1985 commissioned a study to determine what those working in law-related education believed literacy in the law to be, and, further, to describe what full and rich definition rooted in education theory should look like. [12] The study concluded that programs operated on many levels but generally aimed at competence rather than at literacy in the law. The study also found that there was still much to be done if law-related education were to move beyond the acquisition of knowledge to a critical judgement of laws and their processes, and beyond information-sharing to full exercise of citizens' rights and responsibilities. The working definition proposed by the researchers drew upon educational and literacy theory and was designed to provide a template to guide practice in curriculum development, instructional methods and program evaluation. Unfortunately the working definition, outlined in Figure 1,[13] was never fully embraced across Canada, although policy makers, funders and program developers have, from time to time, returned to it.

THE UNRAVELLING OF THE LAW-RELATED EDUCATION MOVEMENT

Although the goals of law-related education are critically important in the preparation of a knowledgeable and active citizenry, program developers made mistakes that thwarted the continued growth of the movement. Although well-intentioned and whole-hearted in their efforts, program developers could have paid more attention to successful long-term implementation strategies. For example, forming partnerships with stakeholder groups such as ministries of education, school boards and teachers' federations — partnerships that would have helped solidify the programs and entrench them in the school system. That lack of foresight, coupled with the downturn in the economy in the early 1990s, which limited the amount of money that law foundations and other funders could distribute, and changes in government policy and funding priorities, led to the elimination of many programs and the serious curtailment of the services offered by others. Today, law-related education in Canada is no longer the thriving enterprise it was in the late 1970s and 1980s. Pockets of activity still exist, but we no longer have a network of programs across the country, and the programs that have survived are much smaller and offer a more limited range of services. Much of the creative energy also waned as the struggle to survive took precedence.

In retrospect, at least five mistakes in direction contributed to the unraveling of the law-related education movement in Canada. If we can acknowledge and learn from those mistakes, we have the possibility for new growth.

1. A FOCUS ON INFORMATION RATHER THAN ON EDUCATION

Because most law-related programs for schools worked in concert with programs aimed at the general public, and because many

Figure 1. A CONTINUUM TOWARDS LITERACY IN THE LAW

FULL LITERACY IN LAW	Substance	Process	Resources
CRITICAL JUDGEMENT	Comparing the intent of the legal system with its effect in practice (for example, critically judging the morality of a given law or a process in law). Determining the desirability of preserving, modifying, or abandoning a given law or process in law.	Acting to promote, in practice, the recognition and acceptance of one's view of "best intests" in law, individually and collectively. Using the democratic process for reform (for example, voting, lobbying, citizens' action groups).	Being able to identify and gain access to power-holding individuals and groups (for example, community action groups, members of legislative assemblies, consumer-protection agencies, civil liberties associations, etc., for information and guidance in decision-making and for action aimed at reform).
UNDERSTANDING	Understanding the intent of a law or laws, in terms of the principles of justice and the concepts of guilt, innocence, liability, negligence, rights, evidence, and proof.	Understanding the effect of a law or laws, in relation to the basic principles of justice. Being able to explain how and why the legal system has different effects on different groups in society.	Understanding the purpose behind and functions of existing law resources, services, agencies, and agents.
KNOWLEDGE	Knowing one's constitutional rights (for example, the right to counsel, the right of free association). Knowing that laws exist in relation to the vaious roles a citizen assumes (for example, consumer law, tax law, marriage and family law, employer-employee law, home ownership vs renting, motor vehicle, wills, criminal law).	Knowing the law's processes as they affect the citizen in contact with agencies and agents of the law (what the ordinary person needs to know).	Knowing about resources (for example, knowing when to consult a lawyer or a notary), or how to find information on law in a library.

Information -------------------------► Action

programs were administered by those with roots in professions other than education, there was a tendency to equate the sharing of legal information with education about law. Many programs focused on spreading information about different areas of substantive law and on explaining legal procedures. The premise was that the public, including teachers and youth in school, so lacked information about the law that the "information just had to get out there." A great deal of effort went to writing pamphlets and preparing teachers' guides and the like, and to organizing short-term workshops to disseminate legal information. The focus tended to be on quantity and on the number of workshops, the number of participants, the number of pamphlets, the variety of topics, rather than on carefully strategizing about the most effective ways to influence adults', teachers' or young people's understanding of law over time and at a deeper level.

Although this approach was not followed singularly, a more carefully thought-out plan, one drawing on education and implementation theory, would have proven more effective in the long run. For example, the research shows that one-day or half-day sporadic workshops are not very effective, nor do they bring about lasting change, particularly if participants have not identified the topic as a priority for their own professional growth.[14] A more effective strategy relies on intensive courses or in-service programs where topics and issues can be addressed in depth, where participants can experiment with new approaches in their classrooms, and where participants have time to become committed to the new idea. Similarly, increasing the quantity of curriculum materials on law does not necessarily mean that teachers will use those materials. A more effective approach is to provide opportunities for teachers to help develop and field test the materials, thus creating a sense of ownership and a commitment to their use.

Interestingly, the law-related programs that have survived now tend to concentrate on the quality of their curriculum materials and the support services they offer teachers and on building educational partnerships over the long term. However, more lasting results for more players could have been achieved if we had learned these lessons earlier, during the heyday of more accessible funding and flourishing programs.

2. GOING IT ALONE VERSUS FORMING EFFECTIVE PARTNERSHIPS

Because the comfortable home for law-related education was law not education, and because most of the funding came from sources within the legal profession, those working in the field tended to stick with the familiar and to avoid the sometimes lengthy and frustrating work of attempting to set up working relationships with ministries of education, universities, school districts, or teachers' federations. While school districts and teachers' federations were generally welcoming of outside help, ministries of education were sometimes resistant and tended to see law groups as just one more powerful lobby group trying to influence the education system. Furthermore, the processes for including more overt law content in school subjects and for getting those changes approved were cumbersome and time-consuming and proved extremely unwieldy and frustrating for those who saw the great need and who wanted to help fill the gap. Except in British Columbia, where law-related educators teamed up with professors to build programs at the two largest universities (with seed money provided by the provincial law foundation), and in Alberta, where law-related education found a home within the Faculty of Extension of the University of Alberta, those working in law-related education did not generally seek out universities as partners.

This failure to build strong partnerships meant that when money dried up, there were no other sources with pre-existing educational mandates to continue the efforts. In addition, failure to work extensively with teachers' federations or school districts meant that the materials produced and the programs offered may not have been as useful as they could have been.[15] The relative lack of direct teacher involvement in preparing materials and establishing programs also meant that relatively few teachers would have a strong stake in the outcome. Implementation theory shows us that effective and long-term change comes when many different parties who have a stake in the change become committed to it.[16]

It may have been that partnerships with non-education organizations were easier to forge or that education organizations created barriers to partnerships. Whatever the reasons, deliberate or merely

neglectful on the part of law-related education agencies, this isola-
tionism thwarted the growth and entrenchment of the law-related
education movement and it affected the quality of their endeavours.
In the mid 1990s, for example, the Department of Justice public
education division invited several people from across Canada to participate in developing education strategies around youth justice.
Although education clearly was the mandate, only five of the forty-
odd delegates came from education — the others were lawyers,
judges, child advocates, psychologists, youth workers, criminolo-
gists, members of the clergy, communication specialists or directors
of public legal education and information programs. While the
discussion which ensued was provocative and engaging, it was qual-
itatively different from what would it have been had there been
greater representation from those steeped in the theory and practice
of education. Part of the problem may lie with the federal government's reluctance to deal directly and overtly with education matters — considered the jurisdiction of the provinces.

3. A FOCUS ON DOING AND PRODUCING VERSUS
REFLECTING AND ANALYZING

At the 1988 national law-related education conference, delegates
were urged during a plenary address to:

> ... share our insights, our experience and knowledge ... [to] take
> time to write ... Law-related education in Canada suffers from a
> dearth of information about what people are doing and from a
> dearth of critical reflection ... [Also] we must conduct more
> research. Gone are the days when we can just do what we think
> must be done. We need to assess the needs of the field carefully,
> develop programs based on these studies, evaluate their effective-
> ness and publish our findings.[17]

Unfortunately, the field did not heed this admonition, and very little sharing of information or actual research into programs or needs
took place. As late as 1999, staff from law-related education
programs were still citing a controversial and questionable 1981
American study which showed the positive effect of law-related
education on reducing juvenile delinquency[18] as reason to fund

law-related education in Canada. As a result of this dearth of research, those spearheading Canadian programs were at a loss to justify many of their activities or to show cause why new ideas should be funded. Redirecting some funding into research when funding was more readily available, or connecting with universities or other institutions who have the mandate and the skills to do research, would have increased the longevity of some programs, reshaped others and identified the need for new directions.

The authors of a 1995 report, which surveyed major initiatives in law-related education across Canada, made a similar observation:

> It is clear ... that there has been a limited amount of either qualitative or quantitative research done ... In many areas of the country the failure to develop a comprehensive theoretical foundation, a well-conceived plan for dealing with the problem and coherent strategies for implementation has meant a failure to address the need to make young Canadians aware of their legal rights and responsibilities.[19]

This report also identified the lack of a national perspective and the inadequate collaboration among individuals and agencies working in law-related education as contributing to the decline of the movement. Although there has been some attempt in the last five years to establish a national presence in the youth justice education field and to bring key players together to discuss common concerns, this Youth Justice Education Partnership (YJEP), as it is called, suffers from lack of funding to foster the network, a narrow mandate of youth justice and disinterest from many who should join. Canada, unlike the United States, does not have an active national bar association with a special committee, staff and designated funds to assist and foster law-related education across the country.

4. The Vocabulary of Law Education

The vocabulary of law-related education proved to be an obstacle in and of itself. Because teachers, school administrators and educational policy makers knew so little about law, many found it difficult to grasp how law is woven through science or language arts or career planning courses, or even through social studies education, apart from the study of government or the courts. Further, law was perceived as complicated and difficult to understand, which made its study seem more appropriate for the upper grades or in an elective course in law or business. To the novice, law seemed removed from the issues and topics dealt with at the elementary school level, even in social studies. Of course, knowledge about law is integral to almost every subject taught in school and is fundamental even for kindergarten children who are concerned with fairness, rule making, the right to be heard, their rights versus classroom rights, fair procedures for resolving disputes, and so on

As a result of this lack of understanding of what law education was all about, many administrators, teachers and policy makers initially reacted as though law-related education was a frill or another add-on to an already packed curriculum, rather than an important lens through which to examine sustainable development, neighbourhood strife, labour disputes, multiculturalism, children's rights or any issue current in the press. The methods of inquiry used in law studies also promotes higher-order thinking — for example, a forensic investigation in science, a mock trial of a figure in history, a case study of a human rights infringement in social studies, a mediation to resolve conflicting values in business education. Once teachers, administrators and policy makers overcame the hurdle of the vocabulary, they became excited about the possibilities of law-related education and came to see the law perspective and the skills of law as essential to several courses. Working with educators to reach that level of understanding, however, was time-consuming and energy-draining.

This vocabulary issue proved to be a contributing factor in the failure to disseminate law-related education through the school system in various grade levels and subject areas. In 1995, despite twenty years of effort to promote law-related education, researchers were unable to find any overt, planned, coherent or integrated program in law education offered in any school district in Canada — at least none that senior officials could identify when asked.[20]

Recently, law-related educators have come to realize that using a different vocabulary does not detract from the fundamental goals and that the use of complementary terms like citizenship education, human rights education, life-skills education, multiculturalism, anti-racist education or critical thinking might make law-related education more understandable and therefore more readily embraced. In some jurisdictions, the "safe school movement" of the late 1990s has subsumed part of the mandate of law-related education, focusing on the development of peaceful and sustainable school environments where principles of law and justice are taught as well as modelled.

5. GOVERNMENT CONTROL VERSUS GRASSROOTS INITIATIVES

In the early years of law-related education, the criteria for government and foundation funding was looser and relied on the initiative and creativity of applicants to propose innovative projects to meet local needs. This model encouraged diversity and tapped the energy and enthusiasm of those who were planning programs. In time, this model of funding gave way to a more controlled model, where, for example, the federal government set the topics to be funded and also designated one organization per province as the sole recipient of core funding. While this decision allowed a few organizations to thrive and plan over the long term, it relegated others to second-class stature. These changes also thwarted blossoming grassroots initiatives that rose from local needs, squelched the enthusiasm program developers had for certain pet projects and seriously curtailed the possibility that new programs with fresh ideas would gain support. Similarly, foundations, the other major funding source, established more stringent criteria and a more complicated bureaucracy for distributing funds.

Program development theory talks about successful programs being driven by visionaries with a mission who put their hearts and minds into achieving what they believe to be important and needed. Working within the framework of others usually only succeeds in disheartening those whose energy drives the programs, often causing the leaders to move on to new endeavours where their ideas are better received and where they have greater control over the outcome.

Indeed those program developers interviewed for a 1999 article in *Canadian Lawyer* spoke of the frustration they feel with the federal Department of Justice being driven by bureaucrats who come and go, who have no experience in either law or public legal education and no commitment to the concept or goals of either.[21] This, coupled with reduced funding from all sources, has demoralized those still in the field.

RENEWAL AND NEW HORIZONS

Despite all of the obstacles and frustrations facing law-related education, if we were to drop in on any classroom in Canada, we would see some law being taught — either implicitly or explicitly. Students are being exposed to the law through social studies, science, the language arts, business education, consumer education and family studies. In some instances, curriculum documents include more explicit law-related content as a result of the lobbying efforts of law-related agencies. In other instances, teachers are more comfortable addressing law-related issues because of what they have learned through courses, workshops and newsletters provided by the same agencies. More teachers are also willing to employ a broader range of law-related teaching strategies, such as a mock trial, a moot appeal, a simulated mediation or a case study because of their exposure to law-related education. Because of the efforts of leaders in law-related education and those of others who write on the hidden curriculum and democratic classroom,[22] teachers now are somewhat more cognizant of the powerful messages about law and due process communicated through the way students in school are treated, how decisions are made and how conflicts are resolved. Teachers also are more likely to look at how fairness, respect for others, privacy, individual and community rights and the common good play out in their classrooms.

In some provinces students can still take part in a mock trial at a local court house or be guided through a court visitation by law-related educators located at the site. In British Columbia (still considered the hotbed of law-related education in Canada),[23] secondary and elementary school teachers and administrators can take up to four credit courses in law-related education, offered by the two largest universities, either on campus or through distance-learning. In a few provinces, teachers can still participate in one or more workshops each year on selected law-related topics. Some teacher guides are still being produced, although the print medium is now used less often than Web-based support, which is considered more cost efficient, reaches users more quickly and permits quicker updates as the law changes.

Teachers' guides that have been produced in recent years generally reflect those national priorities set by the federal government: First Nations' issues such as treaty negotiations and Aboriginal approaches to sentencing; crime prevention; changes in the *Young Offenders' Act;* and material explaining the Canadian legal system to recent immigrants. Ontario continues to be the source of most of the commercially published textbooks on law for school use, although an edited volume on teaching law at the elementary school was recently produced by an Alberta publisher, and several smaller scale issue-based teachers' guides have been produced by a West Coast publisher.

Teachers wanting information on a broader range of legal topics, lesson ideas and discussion of controversial issues will find the best source of information on three specifically designed Web sites: the Law Connection, ACJNet and the Law Room. (For their URLs, please see the Resources listed at the end of this chapter.) For example, the Law Connection is organized around themes: women and equality; hate legislation; property law; workplace harassment; the Charter of Right and Freedoms; social responsibility; the role of the courts and the judiciary. This Web site also connects users to a legal expert who can answer questions posed by teachers or students. ACJNet provides a link to many other legal sources of information, including the Supreme Court of Canada's decisions and the services provided by each public legal education and information organization in Canada. The Alberta Legal Resource Centre and the Public Legal Education Association of Saskatchewan provide newsletters for subscribers; these include legal information, ideas for lessons and appropriate resources.

Today, the services and sources of support for teachers of law-related education and their students varies widely across Canada, with no province providing a comprehensive program and some provinces seriously lacking support. The impetus behind law-related education in the schools still lies primarily with organizations that were set up to meet the needs of the general public; with some exceptions, other education organizations do not see law-related education as a priority.[24] With funding cuts this means that only limited activity is taking place. The federal government's priorities are to fund narrowly defined projects deemed to be in the national interest but may not fit local concerns. Although teachers can find information on the law on the Web, not all teachers are comfortable using this vehicle, and the technology itself lends itself more to information sharing than to interactive learning and the practice of new strategies in the classroom. Those who run the Web sites also struggle with the funds needed to expand into new topics and to monitor and update the information on the sites. Further, because much law is provincial rather than nationally applicable, materials and services produced by one organization may not be appropriate for teachers in another region of the country. Thus it makes it more difficult to share resources without modifying them to fit other jurisdictions. In 1999, law-related educators bgan to discuss ways of better co-ordinating the development of materials through the use of templates where the core ideas are shared, but which allow provincial modifications.

Several challenges confront law-related education as we move into the new century. It has not brought about the sweeping and lasting impact on the schools that we had hoped for, but the need for law-related education remains just as great as it was thirty years ago. There is not a single thing that we do as individuals that is not influenced by law — where we live, what we do for a living, our recreational pursuits, our relationships with our children, our parents and our neighbours, our travel, our schooling, even what we eat, what we say, what we read, what we wear and how we treat our pets. Further, all important social issues facing Canada and the world today have a direct bearing on law; for law is intricately woven into the very fabric of our society and the global connections Canada has with the rest of the world. I usually ask students in my law education class on the first day to circle those articles in the newspaper before them which have something to do with law. In the end, almost everything in the newspaper is circled, from the headlines, to sports, to the fashion pages, to the classifieds — even the cartoons, the advertisements and the movie pages.

The issues facing Canada today require citizens to be knowledgeable about how to affect change and be prepared to hold elected officials accountable for their actions. The law should reflect those values we hold dear in our society: justice, fairness, respect for persons, equality, the right to privacy, freedom of speech and movement, protection of children, earned authority and caring for the less fortunate. Law-related education helps reinforce these important principles and encourages each person to play a part in seeing these values realized.

There are many important decisions that Canadians need to make: how to respond to refugees arriving on our shores; how to protect vulnerable children from abusive parents; how to resolve century-old land claims; how to regulate the Internet; how to protect Canada's natural resources; whether to support free trade and a globalized economy; how to prevent cultural genocide in various parts of the world; how to build community in an increasingly urban society; how to counteract racism and to promote respect for all people regardless of race, gender, age or background. Law-related education has an important role to play in informing Canadians about these issues and in cultivating citizenship attributes.

The need for a solid education in law is easy to justify. The challenge remains, however, as to how to package law-related education so it is embraced and how to work towards more successful implementation at the classroom level where it counts most with students. The issues that contributed to the unravelling of law-related education must be addressed if a resurgence is to occur. Program developers need to more effectively collaborate with each other — sharing resources where possible so that efforts are not duplicated and diversifying according to specialty areas rather than competing with each other for shrinking dollars. And new blood with fresh ideas and a fresh vision must be brought into the movement to restore the vibrancy, enthusiasm and energy which drove law-related education in the early years and when no obstacle seemed too large to overcome. It is time for a new generation of educators to respond to the challenge of law-related education, to work with more seasoned veterans, to build on past successes and learn from prior mistakes and take up the important mission of cultivating a responsible, proactive and compassionate citizenry who is literate in the law.

WEB SITE RESOURCES

The Law Connection, Simon Fraser University

www.educ.sfu.ca/lawconnection

This site is based on legal themes such as children's rights, social responsibility. It includes updates on court decisions and legislation, lesson plans, lists of resources, a conferencing service for teachers, and the Legal Beagle, a place where law professionals respond to questions asked by students and teachers.

ACJNet Access to Justice Network

www.acjnet.org

Offered through the Legal Studies Program at the University of Alberta and sponsored by the Department of Justice, this site contains links to the Supreme Court of Canada's decisions, federal and provincial legislation, the Canadian Bar Association, and public legal education and information organizations.

Law Room, University of Ottawa

www.uottawa.ca/hrrec/lawroom

Geared to teachers, this service offers lesson ideas and other practical resources suitable for the classroom, for example, the Lawyer Mentoring Project, which pairs lawyers with students.

CURRICULUM RESOURCES

Roland Case and L. Daniels, series eds., *Critical Challenges Across the Curriculum* (Vancouver: Pacific Educational Press, 1997, 1998, 1999). Three publications of this series of eight deal with critical questions in law and government (confederation, constitutional crisis, role of Parliament). The publications are written by teachers and based on a model of critical thinking developed by the Critical Thinking Consortium in British Columbia.

W. Cassidy and R. Yates, eds., *Let's Talk About Law in Elementary School* (Calgary: Detselig Enterprises Ltd., 1998). This anthology addresses ways to incorporate legal concepts throughout the elementary curriculum by using engaging strategies. Sample chapters include using literature to teach law, teaching law in primary classrooms, conflict resolution strategies, teaching forensics in science.

W. Cassidy and R. Yates, eds., *Storybook Mock Trials: Simulations and Role Plays for Children* (Burnaby: Simon Fraser University, forthcoming). This anthology includes several mock trials based on fairy tales for elementary-aged children. It also includes information on how to conduct a mock trial and the educational benefits of this form of learning.

M. Ferguson, M. Kooy, and R. Yates, *Just Walls: An Introduction to Learning About the Law for Middle Grade Students* (Ottawa: Department of Justice Canada, 1996). This work presents six stories about young people confronting moral and legal issues using the theme of "walls" — building walls (protection), mending walls (restitution) and dismantling walls (rehabilitation). This lesson is available through the ACJNet Web site.

G. N. Goodfellow, E. Mustache, and E. Gordon. *First Nations' Journeys of Justice* (Vancouver: Law Courts Education Society of British Columbia, 1994). This K-7 curriculum addresses concepts of justice using the oral tradition of stories from First Nations' people. This resource is geared primarily to First Nations' communities, although it is appropriate for elementary schools throughout Canada.

J. Itterman, *Legal Safari*, 3 vols. (Vancouver: Law Courts Education Society of British Columbia, 1990). This collection has practical suggestions for teaching legal concepts and skills to intermediate level elementary students. Although packaged as a teacher resource, Legal Safari also includes material for students, and is available in English and in French.

S. Yates, *Rights, Responsibilities and Respect: The Three R's of Justice Education* (Winnipeg: Gemma B. Publishing, 1995). This teacher guide addresses various issues and procedures associated with criminal law, young offenders, First Nations' legal procedures. It is a joint project of the Manitoba Community Legal Education Association, the Department of Justice and the Winnipeg School District.

ORGANIZATIONS

Centre for Education, Law and Society
Faculty of Education, Simon Fraser University
Burnaby, BC V5A 1S6

(604) 291-4570; 291-4484
Fax: (604) 291-3203
E-mail: Ruth_Yates@sfu.ca, cassidy@sfu.ca
www.educ.sfu.ca/lawconnection

The Centre's mandate is to improve the legal literacy of young people and children through a program of research, credit course offerings, graduate studies, curriculum development and consultation with school districts and teacher groups.

Educalol
C.P. 1537, Succ. Place d'Armes
Montreal, QC H2Y 3K8
(514) 954-3408
Fax: (514) 954-3493
E-mail: monik@educalol.qc.ca

This organization is active in public legal education in Quebec, and provides materials and assistance to teachers in schools.

Law Courts Education Society of British Columbia
The Vancouver Law Courts
221-800 Smithe Street
Vancouver, BC V6Z 2E1
(604) 660-9870
Fax: (604) 660-2420
E-mail: rick.craig@ag.gov.bc.ca

The society has regional offices throughout British Columbia and offers a court-watching program, curriculum materials on the courts and the justice system and provides assistance to First Nations, the Deaf, the mentally challenged and new Canadians.

Legal Studies Program
Alberta Legal Resource Centre
University of Alberta, Faculty of Extension
8303 – 112 Street
93 University Campus N.W.
Edmonton, AB T6G 2T4
(780) 492-5735
Fax: (780) 492-6180
E-mail: snk@ualberta.ca
www.extension.ualberta.ca/plena

The program offers workshops and services for teachers and other groups, produces curriculum materials, co-ordinates ACJNet and produces *Law Now*, a magazine with helpful legal information and lesson ideas.

Public Legal Education Association of Saskatchewan
#300-201 – 21 Street East
Saskatoon, SK S7K 0B8
(306) 653-1868

Fax: (306) 653-1869
E-mail: surtees @plea.org.ca
www.plea.org

Although primarily geared to public legal education and information, the association offers workshops to teachers, develops curriculum materials and produces the newsletter *The PLEA,* which provides legal information and activities for students and teachers. It is a key player in the Lawyer Mentoring Project for students (along with the Alberta and Manitoba public legal education and information groups), an on-line service available through the *Law Room.*

Public Legal Education and Information Service of New Brunswick
P.O. Box 6000
Fredericton, NB E3B 5H1
(506) 453-5369
Fax: (506) 457-7899
www.unb.ca/web/netlearn/nblaw

Although primarily geared to public legal education and information, this organization assists teachers through workshops and the development of curriculum resources and works in association with the provincial Youth Justice Ministry, which has taken some initiatives in law-related education.

NOTES

1. Stephen Arons and J. Cole, "Importance of the Study of Law and Legal Institutions to General Education." *A Report to the Ad Hoc Education Committee* (Amherst: University of Massachusetts, 1981).
2. Likewise, undergraduate courses rarely included law.
3. Wanda Cassidy, Excerpt from Plenary Panel Presentation, First National Conference on Legal Education for Canadian Youth, University of Saskatchewan, College of Law, Saskatoon, 1980.
4. Ron Ianni, "Reflections on the State of Public Legal Education in Canada," *Canadian Community Law Journal* 3 (1979), 3–11.
5. "Interview: With Bora Laskin, Chief Justice of the Supreme Court of Canada," *Maclean's* 90 (February 21, 1977), 9.
6. Hugh Kindred, "The Aims of Legal Education in High School," *Canadian Community Law Journal* 3 (1979), 20–25.
7. Mabel McKinney-Browning, "Educating for Civic Participation: Law-Related Education in the United States," in W. Cassidy and R. Yates, eds., *Let's Talk About Law in the Elementary School* (Calgary: Detselig Enterprises Ltd., 1998);

Isadore Starr, "The Law Studies Movement: A Brief Look at the Past, the Present, and the Future," in W. Crawford, ed., *Law vs. Learning: Examination for Discovery. Proceedings of the National Conference*, Vancouver, June 19–21, 1988 (Ottawa: Canadian Law Infomation Council, 1989).

8. Gail Dykstra, "Public Legal Education: The Canadian Approach," in *Understanding the Law: A Handbook on Educating the Public* (Chicago: American Bar Association, 1985), 29–38.

9. The Honourable Mr. Justice W. McIntyre, "The Rule of Law in Public Legal Education," in E. Myers, ed., *Legal Education for Canadian Youth: Proceedings of a Conference, University of Saskatchewan, College of Law, May 1980* (Ottawa: Canadian Law Information Council, 1981).

10. Wanda Cassidy, "Law-Related Education in Canada: Yesterday and Today," in Crawford, ed., *Law vs. Learning: Examination for Discovery.*

11. Roland Case, *On the Threshold: Canadian Law-Related Education* (Vancouver: Centre for the Study of Curriculum and Instruction, University of British Columbia, 1985).

12. Mike Manley-Casimir, Wanda Cassidy, and Suzanne de Castell, *Legal Literacy: Towards a Working Definition. A Report Submitted to the Canadian Law Information Council* (Ottawa: Canadian Law Information Council and the Department of Justice, 1986).

13. Ibid., 13.

14. T. Guskey, "Results-Oriented Professional Development," and D. Sparkes and S. Loucks-Horsley, "Five Models of Staff Development for Teachers," in A. Ornstein and L. Behar-Horenstein, eds., *Contemporary Issues in Curriculum* (Boston: Allyn and Bacon, 1999).

15. Law-related organizations did have a group of teachers they worked with. These teachers offered suggestions for materials, field tested the resources and were committed to the teaching of law to children. However, these teachers were not in a position to carry on the programs when funding ran out, nor were they in a position to influence policy and funding decisions within their own organizations.

16. Michael Fullan, *The Meaning of Educational Change* (Toronto: OISE Press, 1982); Walt Werner and Roland Case, *Strategies Used by Advocacy Groups to Support Implementation of Issues-Based Innovations Occasional Paper #16. Explorations in Development/Global Education* (Vancouver: Centre for the Study of Curriculum and Instruction, University of British Columbia, 1988).

17. Cassidy, "Law-Related Education in Canada: Yesterday and Today," 11.

18. Robert Hunter and Mary Jane Turner, *Law-Related Education Evaluation Project: Final Report, Year One* (Boulder, CO: Social Science Education Consortium, Law-Related Evaluation Project, 1981).

19. Sadie Kuehn, Ruth Yates, and R Mainville, *Law-Related Education Survey. Report produced for the Department of Justice Canada* (Ottawa: Government of Canada, 1995).

20. Kuehn, Yates, and Mainville, *Law-Related Education Survey*, 23.

21. J. Beaufoy, "A Plea for Better PLEI," *Canadian Lawyer* (February 1999), 27-30.

22. Philip Jackson, Robert Boostrom, and David Hansen, *The Moral Life of Schools* (San Francisco: Jossey-Bass Publishers, 1993).

23. Several organizations are still active in British Columbia: the Law Courts Education Society of British Columbia, which operates out of regional court houses in the province; the People's Law School, which primarily does public legal education; the Centre for Education, Law and Society at Simon Fraser University, which co-ordinates credit courses and does research. The Schools Program of the Legal Services Society of British Columbia, once the leader in the province, no longer exists, although the society still does some work in public legal education.

24. The Ministry of Education in British Columbia, in association with the Open Learning Agency (Open Schools), offers the senior law elective in the curriculum on-line, with links to related Web sites, and support from an experienced law teacher.

Chapter 12

MEDIA EDUCATION IN CANADA

Barry Duncan, John Pungente, SJ,
and Rick Shepherd

MEDIA EDUCATION, OR MEDIA LITERACY as it is sometimes called, is
designed to help students think critically about the media. Media
education should not be confused with teaching *through* the media,
rather it is teaching *about* the media: how the media communicate
and shape information, how audiences relate to different forms of
media, how they are organized and how they affect our culture.

Media education is, indeed, an eclectic circus. If they are following the cultural studies model, teachers need to draw from many
disciplines. They must be able to work experientially with today's
moveable texts: a block buster film, a new Calvin Klein ad, a news
item of a catastrophe or the latest celebrity gossip, an exciting new
Web site or chat line where kids can have a free exchange of opinions. The fact that many teachers may have little or no formal training in media education at the very time consultants and school
board funds are scarce makes our project especially challenging.
Nonetheless, it is heartening to know that Canada has acquired a
reputation as a world leader in media education. Today, progressive
educators recognize that media literacy is not a frill; it is a survival
skill for coping with our information environment.

The initial impulse to teach about the media often stems from a desire to "inoculate" our students against the negative effects of the media, but this approach is seriously flawed. First, it rarely works. Kicking the media — whether it be blaming it for students' poor literacy skills or their obsession with violent programs — is a sure way to turn students off. Second, this approach is neither open nor critical. It's a teacher attempting to teach students that what they like is bad and what the teacher likes is good. Our goal is not indoctrination. On the contrary, we study the media with our students to help them make sense of their culture and their relationship to that culture, and to help them become autonomous individuals who can balance enjoyment and criticism, feeling and understanding.

ORIGINS AND DEVELOPMENT

What we now think of as the first-wave of media education began in the mid-1960s and lasted, roughly, until the mid-1970s. Hindsight makes it easy to see that the courses introduced at the time were generally characterized by a desire to celebrate and enjoy the media and by a lack of critical theory. Many of these became film study courses, which tended to treat films as "high art," or film production courses, which focused on products not processes and were usually described as "screen education."

A notable exception to that trend was the publication of *City as Classroom*, by Marshall McLuhan, his son Eric McLuhan, and Kathryn Hutchon, a practising teacher. McLuhan's influence on critical thinking about the media is, of course, profound, and *City as Classroom*, with its chapters on the training of perception, the properties of the media, the effects of the media and popular culture, represented perhaps the high-water mark of the first-wave of media education.[1] Unfortunately, the book was published in 1977, when support for media education had already begun to dwindle with the general move to conservatism in education.

The Ontario of the time offered little or no post-secondary education in media literacy. McLuhan's successors carried on a small graduate program at the University of Toronto, but not one university in Ontario had undergraduate courses in media education nor was media education included in teacher training programs in the faculties of education. Nonetheless, the push for media literacy — that understanding of the media's role that was so often lacking in the early years of media studies — began in Ontario and the second-wave of media education was underway. The formation of the Association for Media Literacy (AML) in Toronto in 1978 clearly marked a turning point for media education in Canada. One of the three founding members, Barry Duncan, became the driving force behind the organization and has remained active to this day. The AML drew together those who were interested in promoting and pursuing media education as a critical discipline.

Based principally in Ontario, the AML grew slowly but steadily throughout the 1980s; its members were mostly teachers and a few media professionals. Largely as a result of the AML's advocacy, in 1986 the province of Ontario became the first educational jurisdiction in North America to make media literacy a compulsory part of all students' education from Grade 7 to Grade 12. The AML was largely responsible for writing the Ontario Ministry of Education's *Media Literacy Resource Guide,*[2] which received considerable international praise and was translated into Japanese, Spanish and Italian. A French version was also produced by the Ministry. In addition to offering workshops for members and many in-service programs for teachers and school boards, the AML also organized two large North American conferences on media education in 1990 and 1992. The latter drew more than 500 participants from sixteen countries. AML is now a leading voice in media education in Canada.

Between 1988 and 1993, media education organizations were formed in five other provinces: Nova Scotia, Quebec, Manitoba, Saskatchewan and Alberta. Each of the organizations had similar objectives and offered programs for teachers-in-training as well as for practising teachers, produced resources and worked to make media education part of provincial education. Following the 1992 conference, representatives of these five provincial organizations met and formed the Canadian Association of Media Education

Organizations. CAMEO was a co-ordinating group that fostered co-operation and communication and lobbied at the federal level, on issues such as copyright, and before federal bodies such as the CRTC (The Canadian Radio and Telecommunications Commission).

The connections made with the international media education movement during the 1980s and 1990s also proved important. British media educator Len Masterman, whose *Teaching the Media* was perhaps the first book to articulate the issues and approaches many in this field had been working towards,[3] visited Canada in 1986 and spoke with the executive of the Association for Media Literacy. He was followed by other educators from Scotland, Australia and Scandinavia. This stimulating international exchange greatly accelerated the development and refinement of theory and practice in Canada. Contacts made through the two North American conferences organized by the AML further expanded this international network. Interestingly, media education in the United States has lagged far behind the rest of the English-speaking world, although recently interest in it has become stronger.

Also significant was the publication of a number of textbooks by Canadian authors during the 1980s and 1990s: *Mass Media and Popular Culture* by Barry Duncan, Carolyn Wilson, Janine Ippolito and Cam MacPherson; *Media: Images and Issues* by Donna Carpenter, with special contributions from Bill Smart and Chris Worsnop; and *Media Works* by Neil Andersen.[4] These books offered background information on such key ideas as media forms and aesthetics, business and the commercial implications of media and the role of the audience. As well, the books' exercises and projects provided teachers with limited background in media education some practical and important in-class lessons.

Perhaps the most striking feature of the development of media education in Canada, and one which distinguishes it from media education elsewhere, is that it is almost entirely a teacher-driven movement. The pattern for media education leadership in many other countries emanates from the university or from faculties of education. In Canada, almost all who played a role in the early development, lobbying, curriculum development, teacher education and organizational work have been classroom teachers.

Although this pattern is beginning to change, it has had a strong impact on the field. Media education in Canada has been very practical and has focused on the needs of classroom teachers, with less emphasis on university-based research than is the practice elsewhere. As well, Canadian media education is highly regarded internationally.

MEDIA EDUCATION TODAY

Most new subject areas first appear at the secondary level, and media education is no exception. Secondary school teachers do specialize and their subject specialization makes new developments possible. Thus, most of the early work in media education was done at the secondary level, and so it is more fully developed at that level. Increasingly, however, the teachers and parents of elementary school students recognized the need for media education. Although many individual elementary school teachers pioneered media education, progress was hampered by the lack of teacher training and the increasingly narrow focus on traditional print resources. One choice faced by education authorities wishing to include media education in the curriculum was whether to offer it as a separate subject or to integrate it across the curriculum. Problems can arise with both approaches. It can be difficult to fit another subject into an already burdened curriculum, where established subjects are already struggling to maintain themselves against the challenge of new and high-profile subjects such as computer studies. At the secondary level, it may be difficult to find teachers with the expertise to teach full-credit courses. In these cases, media education often falls within English or Language Arts, where support may vary widely, depending on the school. At best, the subject remains a poor cousin in such situations and is seen as secondary to the real work. So while making media education part of another subject may be acceptable as a way of introducing it into the curriculum in some form, it can have serious drawbacks in the long term. At least at the secondary level, media studies should be dealt with as a completely separate subject. However, political realities at this time make that unlikely. In schools, there are always struggles over the displacement of traditional courses and the usual dilemmas over which courses, especially those that are optional, deserve to be funded.

The other route of integration also offers promise and problems. At the secondary level, we have often seen the failure of across-the-curriculum approaches, where something is everyone's responsibility, but often it is no one's. Many teachers are unwilling to give up time in "their" already crowded curriculum to teach something in which they have no training and which they consider to be someone else's responsibility. Also, this approach requires in-service training for a very large number of teachers, something school boards and ministries of education are increasingly unwilling to support. Integration offers more possibilities at the elementary level, where teachers expect to be generalists and have more experience with integration. Still, it is difficult for teachers to integrate something which they do not fully understand. Many elementary school teachers who have attempted media units at the elementary level do report that they have benefited from the experience and that subsequent efforts at integration were more successful. Our inclination is to support both integration and separate units and courses, with the emphasis on the former at the elementary level and the latter at the secondary level.

One of the most serious blocks to media education in Canada has been the widespread failure of faculties of education to respond to the needs of its teachers, even when (as is the case in Ontario) media literacy is mandatory. Many teachers recognize the need for media education and have asked for training in it. In a few parts of the country, progress in in-service training has been good, and many teachers do take summer courses offered by faculties of education and taught by practising classroom teachers. However, when it comes to teachers-in-training, media education remains sorely neglected, and each year hundreds of young elementary teachers and secondary school English teachers enter our classrooms with little background in media education. Perhaps this lack of preparation stems from the lack in the universities. In other words, that media education in Canada tends to be a teacher-driven does not necessarily mean that faculties of education will be quick to see the need for it. The place of media education in the curriculum in the various provinces and the extent to which it is mandatory varies widely.

PROVINCIAL DIFFERENCES

In the fall of 1996, British Columbia was the first of the western provinces to implement a new Language Arts curriculum with two media education components. First, media education is mandated in all Language Arts courses from K-12 through the expectation of allotting one-third of the course content for this purpose. Secondly, media education is part of the Integrated Resource Package, which is cross-curricular in all subjects from K-12.

Since the early 1960s, media education in Alberta schools has been recognized by a few innovative teachers. However, it was not until 1981 that a viewing strand was recognized as one of the five of the English Language Arts Program strands (reading, writing, speaking, listening and viewing). The Alberta Department of Education revised the English Language Arts curriculum in Grades K-12 to include media education. Implementation of the new curricula are scheduled to take place from 1999 to 2002 (Grades K to 9, September 1999; Grade 10, September 2000; Grade 11, September 2001; and Grade 12, September 2002). Media education outcomes are integrated throughout the new curricula and instructional guides and evaluation examples are under development to help teachers achieve satisfactory results.

In Saskatchewan, media education is a part of the common essential learnings and one of the supporting domains of the basic Language Arts structure. In core-content English courses, media studies require video in Grade 10, radio in Grade 11 and print journalism in Grade 12. But there is no resource plan for these courses and it will be up to teacher initiative to develop suitable resources. Besides the required credits in English, Saskatchewan Education has mandated three options for Grade 11 English: media studies, journalism and creative writing. Availability of such courses will depend upon student enrollment.

The Western Canada Protocol, a group of educators from the western provinces, created an outline of the expectations for basic curriculum components. This initiative compelled Manitoba to mandate media education in its Language Arts programs through the division of viewing and representing. All frameworks of outcomes and standards from Grades K to 12 make specific references to media and to the skills required for media education. By the end of 1998, implementation documents for all grades were completed, as well as a list of resources.

The Yukon and the Northwest Territories are members of the Western Consortium. They are including media education components in their Language Arts programs, and teachers work on their own to introduce media education into their courses.

In 1996, the Atlantic Curriculum, an Atlantic provinces initiative similar to the Language Arts Consortium in western Canada, developed a common Language Arts curriculum in which media education plays a prominent role. This curriculum was piloted in 1996 and implemented in 1997. The documents state that media education is a critical element of the language arts curriculum and is to be a mandatory part of every English course. In Nova Scotia, media literacy forms part of citizenship, communication, personal development, problem solving and technical competence — or five of the six areas deemed essential. English and social studies courses also emphasize media education. Funding, however, is limited. New Brunswick emphasized media education in its social studies curriculum and has offered elective courses in media studies as part of its Grade 12 English courses since 1992. Most secondary schools in Prince Edward Island also offer elective media studies for Grade 11 students and individual junior high schools can set up a media studies course. Newfoundland and Labrador is basing its new English Language Arts curriculun on the Atlantic Curriculum framework. It will concentrate on print, radio, television, the CD-ROM and the Internet.

Quebec's Ministry of Education developed a reformed curriculum, which was implemented in elementary and secondary schools in 1999. Media education is taught in a cross-curricular context and is considered a basic skill. Although media education is not mandatory in Quebec, it will be one of five main areas in the province's new curriculum, which is expected to be in place by September 2003. In the 1980s and 1990s, the Quebec government had approved some media literacy courses in French and English, most notably in Language Arts and in moral and religious education. In October 1999, the Ministry of Education and French-based Centre de liaison de l'ensiegnment avec le moyen d'information held a conference to raise awareness of media education among teachers, principals, school board consultants and ministry officials.

Ontario, home to one-third of the people in Canada, was the first jurisdiction in North America to make media literacy mandatory in the schools. In 1987, Ontario's Ministry of Education released new guidelines that emphasized the importance of teaching media education as part of the regular English curriculum: 10 percent in Language Arts in Grades 7 and 8; 30 percent in one course in either Grades 9 and 10; and 30 percent in one course in Grades 11 and 12. In addition, students were allowed to choose a media studies course as one of the five English credits required for graduation. In April 1995, under the New Democratic Party, the Ontario Ministry of Education issued *Provincial Standards: Language: Grades 1 to 9* and *The Common Curriculum: Policies and Outcomes: Grades 1 to 9*. Viewing and representing strands ensured that media education was to be a mandated part of the Language Arts curriculum. Under the Conservative government in 1998 and 1999, there were further revisions to Ontario's Language Arts curricula, which reiterated that media education continue to be a strongly mandated strand — in Language Arts, Grades 1 to 8, and in English, Grades 9 to 12. In addition, after vigorous lobbying on the part of the Association for Media Literacy, the stand-alone media studies credit, which was slated to be eliminated, was reinstated. It is now designated for Grade 11.

The provinces still have to develop resources to help implement these changes. There is also a major need to address the question of teacher training in media education.

ISSUES AND CONTROVERSIES

Media education typically links analytical and creative activities. Media analysis examines how meanings are constructed; how different audiences make sense of media texts; who made the text, how, why and under what circumstances. Thus, if we are examining a television text, we should be raising questions about what's on the screen and how the audience makes sense of the text. Questions about who represents whom and who is not represented at all are also critical. It is almost always wisest to start with media texts the students enjoy. Although creativity is important, critical thinking lies at the heart of media education, and teachers should steer clear of complex productions that focus on products not processes, or that simply leave students replicating existing mainstream media. Student production need not be complex; it can be as simple as sequencing a set of pictures to create a narrative or set a mood. In all cases, we should be attempting to make clear the constructed nature of all media texts, and asking questions about the intentions of the producers, whether they are students or media professionals.

North American mass media and popular culture have long been controversial. Some have been described as a window on the world, as instruments of democracy, as the foundation of modern culture. Those on the political left have accused them of communicating the social and political agendas of a powerful elite. Those on the right accuse them of leading us down the garden path to debauchery and deviltry. American presidential candidate Robert Dole succinctly denounced the media as "cesspools of depravity." Many parents who find their young children glued to the TV set watching cartoons, cop shows or afternoon talk shows, understandably find media literacy controversial.

Most of us, it would seem, have a love-hate relationship with the media: we might praise some television programs such as *Seinfeld, Fifth Estate* and *The West Wing* and despise others as being sleazy, despicable and manipulative. Not surprisingly, media theorists and media teachers have been embroiled right from the beginning in arguments over media's effects and even the meaning of "media literacy."

Until recently, our schools have taken the education of the young in traditional print literacy as their primary mandate. Despite the impact of media literacy on education in the 1980s and 1990s, for many teachers of reading or English, literacy means the printed word. Today, the corporate driven mania for computer literacy looms large, and media literacy in most schools begs for attention.

Whether the media are legitimate objects of study comes into question when popular educators like Neil Postman acknowledge television as "the first curriculum,"[5] but remain convinced that the media cannot educate us in traditional subjects that require linear thinking, logic and self-discipline. The classroom, Postman concludes, is antithetical to the ways media process information. Education is about deferred gratification, while television and popular films with their quick edits, cuts and high action give us instant gratification.

In the late 1960s, media literacy teachers believed their goal was to instill the moral and aesthetic values associated with high culture by leading the students to see the superficiality of popular culture and then revealing the elitist values of traditional, canonical culture. The Ontario Ministry of Education's *Media Literacy Resource Guide* pointed out the limitations of that approach and advised teachers to have students "explore their values and tastes that are relevant to their own immediate cultural context."[6]

In recent years, media education, especially in the United States, has been driven by moral panics and the search for protection. Fears about the proliferation of violence and pornography, objections to racial stereotypes and worries about other societal ills have been at the top of the agenda. (At the first National Media Literacy conference held at the University of North Carolina in 1995, officials from the White House were interested in media literacy because it could be used as a tool in their programs to reduce juvenile drug intake.) Media literacy as a form of protectionism has a long history. In practice, protectionism means seeing media literacy as a form of moral inoculation. The controversies over violence in the media provide the most telling examples.

Researchers are still debating the effects of violence in the media, reminding us that a correlation between viewing violence and aggressive behaviour does not mean that the former always causes the latter. That many studies are inconclusive has not stopped teachers from preparing materials to counteract the presumed harmful influences of media violence. The effectiveness of such efforts is hard to assess for the premise is that once teachers have revealed the assumptions and internal inconsistencies, students are inoculated against the harmful effects and can also avoid harm in the future.

These are naive, unsupported assumptions and much of this thinking is disputed by recent studies on audiences. More promising for the classroom teacher are programs that improve the school's climate through, for example, peer mediation and conflict resolution combined with media literacy.

Teachers also need appropriate paradigms. The paradigm that dominates media studies around the world is that of cultural studies. Cross-disciplinary in scope, it has been described as "the study of the entire range of a society's arts, beliefs, institutions and communicative practices."[7] Openly political in nature and hence too controversial for some, cultural studies looks at power, who has it and who doesn't, who gets represented in the media and by whom. The language of cultural studies weaves itself through the overall fabric of the progressive curriculum. Its insights have framed many recent debates about gender, race, multiculturalism and "political correctness." Media and cultural studies could, if combined, stimulate provocative and critical thinking about the nature and dilemmas of today's culture. This is, to quote Hamlet, "a consummation devoutly to be wished."

What is the appropriate critical pedagogy for media literacy? The influential British media educator Len Masterman points out that the egalitarian nature of the media — teachers and students sharing and processing the same or similar information — necessitates a shared investigation, an egalitarian kind of teaching.[8] That does not, however, justify loose, unfocused discussions where every opinion receives equal validation. Instead, our approach should be to examine many perspectives and to raise critical questions for which the teacher and the class may not have immediate answers. Media educator David Buckingham insists quite rightly that we must first find out what the students already know so that we can help lead them to what they do not know.[9] The most productive and dynamic media education applies analysis and inquiry to current media texts, engages in appropriate simulations and stimulates student-centred investigations and encourages the production of student media. The result: theory and practice come together.

Media education's central concern is representation. By necessity, we cross subject boundaries and the boundaries built through the representation of gender, class and race. Implicitly, we think and speak about power — who has it and under what circumstances it may be absent. We learn about and, ideally, empathize with people who find themselves marginalized because of their differences. American educator Henry Girou, an advocate of critical and border-culture pedagogy, insists that educators recognize "people moving in and out of borders constructed by the coordinates of difference and power."[10]

A key area of research in media and cultural studies is how the media industry constructs us as an audience. Work on audience offers insight into how we make sense of the media, whether we are talking about our students, our peers, our families or ourselves. Understanding the formation of audiences is especially important in understanding youth culture. Studying audiences helps to explain how and why people position themselves and others when responding to media texts. It encourages empathy with other responses and a recognition of intellectual and social complexities and contradictions. The importance of the pleasures of the text is placed in the foreground and we can see viewers as complex social subjects and see that texts convey many meanings, and hence elicit many different readings.[11]

If we accept the premises of audience studies, then the media classroom should be a place where all students learn how to make sense of a text; it should also be a place where personal media pleasures can be talked about and, when appropriate, critically examined. Media critic John Fiske popularized the idea that anyone can consent to or resist the dominant messages and ideologies of the text.[12] That we can read texts "oppositionally" should be seen as a democratic and, for many oppressed or cynical students, a liberating practice. That most students can see through most of the violent television programs is a tribute to that ability.

Understandably, the audience empowerment model is disputed by critics such as Noam Chomsky and Herbert Schiller.[13] According to Schiller, "the gigantic entertainment-information complexes exercise a near seamless and unified private corporate control over what we think and think about."[14] For educators to rule out serious discussions on the connections between business and media is irresponsible. Finally, the explorations of alternative media, from experimental films and documentaries to publications such as *Extra!* and *Z Magazine* should be part of the media teacher's essential repertoire and seen as providing the perspectives for analyzing mainstream texts.

*

We think that analysis and production should go together, for each informs the other. Theory is evident in the nature of our practices and vice versa. As media educators, we have become skeptical of teachers who offer high-profile, glossy production courses but rarely discuss critical or cultural issues arising from their work. While traditional media genres include film, television, radio, popular music and print, what about the non-electronic artifacts associated with popular culture? Shopping malls, most of which have similar stores, create an environment intimately connected with that of television. Barbie Dolls, war toys, clothing, hair cuts and popular fashion should also be essential texts in today's class-room. New and converging technologies — computers, digital media, multimedia programs — provide the opportunity for new explorations using the same key concepts already applied to under-standing traditional media. For example, teachers should examine the social and political implications of the Internet. Who benefits from this new technology? Who loses? Are we widening the gap between the information rich and the information poor? What special codes and hidden ground do these new forms hold? How are they like traditional media? How do they differ? How do we negotiate their meaning? Do we really gain power by assuming multiple identities on the Net? [15]

Kathleen Tyner, a leader in US media literacy, has made a con-vincing argument for combining visual, critical, informational and computer literacies with media literacy. Tyner asserts that "educa-tional strategies that blend critical literacy, experiential education, and critical pedagogy can do much to explain the relationship of lit-eracy, and society. Such a bend called media education, for want of a better phrase, has the potential to shape the course of modern education." [16] The question is: Are our leaders listening?

TEACHER RESOURCES

Cary Bazalgette, *Primary Media Education* (London: British Film Institute, 1989). A curriculum statement for use by elementary media literacy teachers.

David Bianculli, *Teleliteracy: Taking Television Seriously* (New York: Continuum, 1992). Examines how television can and does open up minds.

David Buckingham, ed., *Watching Media Learning: Making Sense of Media Education* (Basingstoke, Hampshire: The Falmer Press, 1990). Based on detailed classroom research, the book identifies the rewards, achievements, difficulties and contradictions of teaching about the media.

Barry Duncan, Carolyn Wilson, Janine Ippolito, and Cam Macpherson, *Mass Media and Popular Culture*, 2nd ed. (Toronto: Harcourt Brace, 1996). A secondary school book examining all aspects of media and pop culture.

Douglas Kellner, *Media Culture* (London: Routledge, 1995). Analyzes contemporary film, television, music and other artifacts to discern their nature and effects.

Jack Livesley, Barrie McMahon, Robyn Quin, and John Pungente, *Meet The Media* (Toronto: Prentice Hall, 1990). A textbook designed to introduce eleven to fifteen year olds to the mass media.

Len Masterman, *Teaching the Media* (London: Routledge, 1985). A comprehensive study of media education theory and a basic starting point in the field.

CLASSROOM RESOURCES

Videos and Kits

Buy Me That I, II, III

> **Center for Media Literacy**
> 403 – 4727 Wilshire Blvd.,
> Los Angeles, CA 90010
> 1-800-226-9494
> Three programs that serve as a child's survival guide to TV advertising.

Constructing Reality, Media and Society, Live TV

> **NFB Customer Services**
> PO Box 6100, Station A
> Montreal, QC H3C 3H5
>
> Three video packages produced by the National Film Board, complete with guides covering different aspects of the media.

Prime Time Parent

Alliance for Children and Television
60 St. Clair Ave. East, Suite 1001
Toronto, ON M5R 1V9
(416) 515-0466

A workshop kit for parents and others interested in television and its effect on children.

Scanning Television

Four hours of video excerpts from Media Television, CityTV, Warner Brothers, YTV and TVO for use in middle and secondary school classes.Includes teaching guide. (Toronto: Harcourt Brace).

ORGANIZATIONS

Alliance for Children and Television
60 St. Clair Ave. East, Suite 1001
Toronto, ON M5R 1V9
(416) 515-0466

Cable in the Classroom
350 Sparks Street, Suite 909
Ottawa, ON K1R 7S8
(613) 233-3033

Offers copyright-cleared, commercial-free, educationally relevant French and English television programs to elementary and secondary schools. Teachers are free to tape programs of interest and replay them in class.

Canadian Association for Media Organizations (CAMEO)
60 St. Clair Ave. East
Toronto, ON M4T 1W5
(416) 515 -0466
http://interact.uoregon.edu/MediaLit/FE/CAMEOHomePage

CAMEO is an umbrella group representing media literacy organizations across Canada. Contact them for the group in your region.

Centre for Literacy
3040 Sherbrooke Street West
Montreal, QC H3Z 1A4
(514) 931-8731 ext. 1415
http://www.nald.ca/litcent.htm

The Media Awareness Network
179 Rideau Street
Ottawa, ON K1A OM9

(613) 992-5380
1-800-896-3342
http://www.schoolnet2.carleton.ca/MediaNet

Media Watch
204-517 Wellington Street West
Toronto, ON M5V 1G1
(416) 408-2065
E-mail: mediawatch@myna.com

Focuses on derogatory images of women in the media and produces educational materials.

Alberta Association for Media Awareness
Sharon McCann, Film Classification Services
5th Floor, 10158-103 Street
Edmonton, AB T5J OX6
(780) 427-2006
E-mail: semccann@sas.ab.ca

Media Literacy Saskatchewan
Bob Pace
Robert Usher Collegiate
1414 – 9th Avenue North
Regina, SK S4R 8B1
(306) 791-8435
E-mail: space@cableregina.com

Manitoba Association for Media Literacy
Brian Murphy
St. Paul's High School
2200 Grant Avenue
Winnipeg, MB R3P OP8
(204) 831-2300
E-mail: brmurphy@minet.gov.mb.ca

Association for Media Literacy Ontario
Barry Duncan
SEE School
40 McArthur Street
Weston, ON M9P 3M7
(416) 394-6990
E-mail: baduncan@interlog.com

Jesuit Communication Project
John Pungente
Jesuit Communication Project
1002 – 60 St. Clair Avenue East
Toronto, ON M4T 1N5
(416) 515-0466
E-mail: pungente@chass.utoronto.ca

Association for Media Education Quebec
Lee Rother
Lake of Two Mountains School
2105 Guy Street
Deux Montaignes, QC   J7R 1W6
(450) 491-6862
E-mail: irothe@po-box.mcgill.ca

Association for Media Literacy Nova Scotia
Trudie Richards, Assistant Professor
Mount Saint Vincent University
166 Bedford Highway
Halifax, NS B3M 2J6
(902) 457-6210
E-mail: Trudie.Richards@MSVU.CA

NOTES

1. Marshall McLuhan, *City as Classroom* (Toronto: Book Society, 1986).

2. Barry Duncan et al., *Media Literacy Resource Guide* (Toronto: Ontario Ministry of Education and the Association for Media Literacy, Queen's Printer, 1989). Now out-of-print but copies may still be available.

3. Len Masterman, *Teaching the Media* (London: Routledge, 1986).

4. Barry Duncan, Carolyn Wilson, Janine Ippolito, and Cam MacPherson, *Mass Media and Popular Culture*, 2nd ed. (Toronto: Harcourt-Brace, 1996); Donna Carpenter, *Media: Images and Issues* (Toronto: Addison-Wesley, 1989); and Neil Andersen, *Media Works* (Toronto: Oxford University Press, 1989).

5. Neil Postman, *Amusing Ourselves to Death* (New York: Viking Books, 1984).

6. Duncan, *Media Literacy Resource Guide*, 8.

7. Larry Grossberg, ed., *Cultural Studies* (New York: Routledge, 1992).

8. Masterman, *Teaching the Media*.

9. David Buckingham, *Watching Media Learning* (London: Falmer Press, 1990).

10. Henry Giroux and Peter McLaren, eds., *Between Borders: Pedagogy and the Politics of Cultural Studies* (New York: Routledge, 1994), 46.

11. Barry Duncan, "Media and Audiences: Explorations in Response and Cultural Reception," *Continuum: The Australian Journal of Media and Culture* 9 (1996).

12. John Fiske, *Understanding Popular Culture* (Boston: Unwin Hyman, 1989).

13. Noam Chomsky, *Manufacturing Consent* (New York: Viking Press, 1985); Herbert Schiller, *Culture Inc.* (New York: Oxford University Press, 1989).

14. Herbert Schiller, "The Global Trust," *The Nation*, 2 June 1996, 23.

15. Sheri Turkle, *Life on the Screen: Identity in the Age of the Internet* (Toronto: Simon and Schuster, 1996).

16. Kathleen Tyner, *Literacy in a Digital World: Teaching and Learning in the Age of Information* (New Jersey: Erlbaum, 1998).

Chapter 13

MOLDED IMAGES

FIRST NATIONS PEOPLE, REPRESENTATION

AND THE ONTARIO SCHOOL CURRICULUM

Susan Dion Fletcher

> *We are what we know. We are, however, also what we do*
> *not know. If what we know about ourselves — our history,*
> *our culture, our national identity — is deformed by*
> *absences, denials, and incompleteness, then our identity —*
> *both as individuals and as Americans — is fragmented.*

> —William F. Pinar, "Notes on
> Understanding Curriculum as a Racial Text"

WHILE STANDING in line at the grocery store, I heard a voice behind me say, *Did you leave your horse back home on the reserve?* Jolted by the comment, I looked over my shoulder and realized that the remark was directed at the cashier in the next aisle. It was the day before Halloween and all the cashiers were wearing costumes. The young woman to whom the comment was made was a young white woman dressed as an "Indian Princess."[1] In response to this unsettling event, I retrieved a copy of Jan Elliot's 1991 article "America to

Indians: Stay in the Nineteenth Century" from my car and gave it to the young woman. I suggested that reading the article might help her understand why I, a First Nations[2] woman, found her attire offensive. The woman, who appeared to be in her late teens, responded apologetically, *I didn't know.*

I was not at all surprised by her response. My teaching practice involves sharing a First Nations perspective of post-Contact history with non-First Nations teachers and students. I am asked by school board consultants to do workshops with teachers and am invited by teachers to visit their classes as a guest speaker when students are completing a unit on "native peoples." Over the past seven years, I have listened to hundreds of teachers and students state their views and reveal their attitudes on First Nations people. Many of the people I speak with fail to recognize that there is more to being First Nations than furs and feathers and that being First Nations is not something that can be put on and taken off like a pair of jeans. Teachers and students who call on images of tipis, tomahawks, beads and buckskins reveal dehumanized thinking about First Nations people. Such representations can position First Nations people as the Romantic Mythical Other and reflects an understanding of history that supports the "forgetting" of past injustices and their implications for the present. I agree with Lenore Keeshig-Tobias who wrote, "non-indigenous people would rather look to an ideal romanticized 'Native' living in a never, never land than confront the reality of what being native means in Canadian society."[3] My observations are supported by social studies teacher C. Sweet, who writes:

> For many years, native studies has been presented in North American [elementary] schools from a solely European perspective ... Teachers have enthusiastically delved into the mysteries of the potlatch, the romance of the sundance, and the masks of the False Face society, as exotic traditions from another time.[4]

In the article I gave to the cashier, Jan Elliot maintains that white people love Indians as long as they're riding horse-back across the grassy plains, wearing beads and feathers and living in picturesque tipi villages. Native people are tolerated, even admired, as long as they stay within established borders. Those borders are built and maintained by and for non-Native people in their everyday lives. Native people appear as the mythical and inferior other in school textbooks, in movies, on television and in all sorts of advertisements.[5] The representation both reflects and perpetuates an understanding of history that justifies Canada's lack of response to our land claims, social issues and demand for self-government. When "real Indians" are the mythical people of the past, First Nations people advocating for the restoration of their rights become marginalized, written-off as militants and labelled as a threat to law and order.

During the past twenty-five years there has been increased attention to the field of First Nations education. Justifiably, the focus by parents, activists, teachers and curriculum planners has been on education by and for First Nations students. While that work is critical and demands our continued attention and support, it is also important to challenge what non-First Nations people are taught about First Nations issues. Transforming a relationship based on domination to one based on equality and justice cannot be accomplished unilaterally. The continuing injustices and inequality that plague First Nations people in this country are overwhelming. Our resistance alone cannot end the oppression. The non-First Nations people of Canada must accept responsibility for their role in accomplishing change. Recognizing the legacy of injustice and its implications for the present and the future is a crucial first step.

Schools are powerful social institutions and play a particularly important role in legitimating and reproducing values and knowledge:

> The choice of subject matter cannot be neutral. Whose history and literature is taught and whose ignored? Which groups are included and which are left out of the reading list or text? From whose point of view is the past and present examined? Which themes are emphasized and which are not?[6]

Whether in class, in the halls or on the playground, students take in the values, see the power relations and hear the debates of society everyday. We need, therefore, to take a critical look at how the representation of First Nations people as Romantic Mythical Other is reproduced in schools and to consider strategies for challenging that myth.

IDENTITY, POLITICS AND FRAME OF REFERENCE

My desire to challenge and to contribute to change in the representation of First Nations people is deeply rooted in my personal and professional life.[7] I am a woman of mixed ancestry, a teacher and have three children enrolled in Ontario public schools. My mother was born and raised on the Moravian of the Thames Reservation near Chatham, Ontario. When my brothers and sister and I were children, we didn't talk about being Indian. My mother had been convinced by the Canadian government's policy of forced assimilation that it would be best to forget being Indian and simply act white. But we knew that we were Indian without knowing exactly what that meant. The image presented to me at school of the Noble Savage caused me a great deal of confusion. I remember having nightmares of being chased by "wild Indians," but the Indians were my aunts and uncles and cousins. I was left to deal with my conflict over andthe challenge to my identity on my own. As an adolescent, I buried that conflict and it did not resurface until I was well into adulthood.

As a school teacher and as a parent, I am distressed to see the Romantic Mythical Other still being produced and reproduced in the schools where I teach and in my own children's classrooms. Students begin their study of Native people and suddenly a totem pole constructed out of cardboard boxes appears in the school foyer, a model of an "Indian Village" goes on display in the library and brightly coloured, fierce looking masks line the hallways. While I recognize the constraints of the classroom, I also recognize the possibilities for transforming how First Nations people are remembered and represented in the curriculum. It is no longer acceptable to portray First Nations people as primitive and savage. We insist on respect for our humanity — through our actions at Kanesatake, in books and articles, on stage, in music halls and art galleries, through Elijah Harper's defeat of the Meech Lake Accord, in our briefs to the Royal Commission on First Nations Peoples.[8]

THE CURRICULUM

The "curriculum, that array of activities used by schools to achieve its ends,"[9] expresses how "we" wish to represent ourselves to our children, the "we" being those who control the writing and circulating of the curriculum and its materials.[10] As long as non-First Nations people continue to relegate First Nations people to the past, to make us people from a make-believe world, possibilities for change remain jeopardized. For the past thirty years, political activists, parents, educators and artists have worked to change the representation of First Nations people. However, as a history teacher with twenty-five years experience told me, After teaching a certain way for such a long time, it is very difficult to do it differently. Attending to how we have come to teach what we teach about First Nations people would help us do it differently. As teachers, we are bound by our culture, our history and our experience. If we question why we teach the way we do and understand what we do when we teach, we can begin to consider other possibilities.

During the early years of public education in Canada, schooling was considered necessary for developing citizenship and a proper moral outlook. The study of geography and history, Canadian government and institutions and the principles of Christian morals were all meant to foster the "right" social attitudes.[11] The emphasis on citizenship and morality, however, provided little space for, and encouraged little interest in, the study of an "uncivilized" people. Yet, "Indians" were objects of fascination.

Traditionally, content about Indians was presented through history and social studies. The first Canadian history textbook, published in 1895, contained the following description of an "Indian":

> Master of woodcraft, he was seen at his best when hunting. Upon the war-path he was cruel, tomahawking, scalping and torturing with fiendish ingenuity. A stoic fortitude when himself tortured was about his only heroic quality. In his own village among his own clansmen he spent his time in gambling, story-telling, or taking part in some rude feast. In his domestic life the Indian was not without virtues, and his squaw and papooses were treated with somewhat rough and careless kindness. To his tribe he was unusually faithful, though to his foes false and crafty. Indian religion was purest superstition.[12]

Variations of that representation continued well into the twentieth century. The study of "Canada's Indians" focused on the geographical location of various tribes and on their pre-Contact material culture. "Indians" become worthy of study principally in terms of their usefulness to white settlers. Students still learned that during the period of exploration and during the fur trade, Indians served as "helper" to the whiteman and that while the battle for control of the continent raged, Indians were necessary allies. However, Indians almost disappear from the textbooks after the War of 1812. Even during discussions of the settlers pushing westward, Indians receive little mention. Instead, students' attention is directed to "nation-building." Progress and change happen in the world of the settlers, while Native people are frozen in time, a people of the past, a footnote in history.[13]

Just as false representations of First Nations people are produced and reproduced in textbooks, they also find reflection in the attitudes and actions of teachers and students. First Nations author/ educator Janice Acoose describes her response to the dehumanizing representation of First Nations people she experienced at school:

> I shamefully accepted that I was not only different but inferior ...
> I shamefully turned away from my history and cultural roots,
> becoming, to a certain extent, what was encouraged by the ideo
> logical collusiveness of textbooks, and the ignorant comments
> and peer pressure from non-First Nations students.[14]

Europeans have always tended to view original peoples of the lands they conquered as inferior. That ideology would foster a curriculum that portrays First Nations people as belonging to an uncivilized race and in need of salvation and protection. That representation was so securely entrenched in the curriculum that almost one hundred years later and after serious efforts to eliminate it, traces remain visible in today's curriculum. I am continually asked to speak in classrooms where bookshelves are lined with texts displaying "Indians" as warriors, lone hunters, forlorn children wrapped in blankets,[15] and as "helpers" to European explorers. Twice in the past five years, I have watched as young children present plays in which settlers who bravely tamed the wild are shown to be cowering inside log cabins while tomahawk-wielding Indians threaten the tranquillity of the settlement.

MULTICULTURALISM AND THE PONA GUIDELINES

In 1972, the National Indian Brotherhood published their policy paper *Indian Control of Indian Education* (ICIE),[16] which was adopted as policy at the federal level in 1973. The policy focused on education for First Nations students but also contributed to changes in the representation of First Nations people in Ontario schools. In 1975 and 1977, the Ontario Ministry of Education published the *People of Native Ancestry (PONA) Guidelines* and *Multiculturalism in Action*. A brief review of these two documents illustrates how they helped to establish a notably different representation of First Nations people in the curriculum.

Indian Control of Indian Education originated in the efforts of First Nations parents to reverse the continued academic failure and alienation their children experienced in federal and provincial schools.[17] The authors of the policy were critical of existing curriculum: "Where the Indian contribution is not entirely ignored it is often cast in an unfavorable light ... Courses in Indian history and culture should promote pride in the Indian child and respect in the non-Indian students."[18] The policy stated a clear call for materials that more accurately represent First Nations people, their culture and their contributions to Canadian history.

Change in education for and about First Nations people came at a time when calls for reform were also coming from within curriculum studies. The technical approach favoured by traditional theorists in the 1960s was beginning to give way to the discipline-based conceptual-empiricists. During the early 1970s, a group of educators emerged who challenged the apolitical, ahistorical and technological orientation of curriculum studies. They stressed the socio-political function of the curriculum and the role of the school in reproducing social inequality. The recognition of the school as an agent of social change and the demands that education be relevant to the student's interests and to society's needs helped lay the groundwork for the PONA Guidelines.

The guidelines would be of particular interest to teachers of Native students. Secondarily, the guidelines were also intended for those teaching about Native peoples. Teachers of non-Native students were to use the guidelines to help develop an awareness and appreciation for the heritage and distinctive traditional and contemporary cultures of the Original people and of their continuing contributions to Canadian society. The guideline for the intermediate grades advises teachers to identify and work to overcome stereotypes and prejudices: "We must move beyond the mere toleration of different heritages and perspectives towards an active commitment on the part of both the original people of our land and other Canadians to foster an understanding of the integrity of each ethnic group's cultural inheritance." Teachers were directed to achieve an appropriate balance between studying heritage and exploring issues of conflict. The PONA guidelines were premised on an understanding that "schools can play a vital role in transmitting current and valid information about Native people to the non-Native community,"[19] but that premise was secondary and would strengthen the idea that First Nations content need be taught only where there are First Nations students.

The PONA Guidelines were also part of a new focus on knowledge about and appreciation of cultural differences. With the advent of multicultural education, students would be expected to become aware of their own culture and to know about and respect the culture of others. Festivals, religious celebrations, language and customs become the subjects of discussion, writing and research. Students might be asked to take part in a multicultural feast, or in dancing, singing or other culture-specific activities. Multiculturalism sets the culture of First Nations people apart, as something distinct, something to be respected. Even if students did not actually study First Nations history as part of multiculturalism, they learned how they were expected to respond to teaching about another culture. For example students tell me, *Oh! I just love the dancing; it is so mystical!* or *How come you couldn't teach us how to chant?* These students have learned that they are required to demonstrate respectful admiration.

ANTI-RACIST EDUCATION AND NATIVE STUDIES GUIDE

In the 1990s, anti-racist education became the focus of intensive debate. In 1993, the Ontario Ministry of Education and Training published *Anti-racism and Ethnocultural Equity in School Boards* in response to the New Democratic government's amendment to the *Education Act,* in 1992. That amendment required all school boards to develop and put into practice policies on anti-racism and ethnocultural equity. The goals of anti-racist education, as described by the Ministry of Education, are to achieve the "equitable treatment of members of all racial and ethnocultural groups and the elimination of institutional and individual barriers to equity."[20] Overall, achieving the goals of anti-racist education demands a conscious examination and challenge to the Eurocentric nature of the curriculum and the inclusion of a balance of perspectives. This translates into specific directives for teaching, including:

> creating a climate in the classroom where stereotypes and racist ideas can be exposed and argued out; where sources of information can be examined; where children can be equipped to critically examine the accuracy of the information they receive; where alternative and missing information can be provided and where the historical and current reasons for the continued unequal social status of different groupings can be explored.[21]

Anti-racist education has begun to achieve some success in teaching students that judging others on the basis of racial difference is unjust and unacceptable. During the past eight to ten years, teachers have been inundated with materials that urge zero-tolerance of overt discrimination. Many history textbooks published after 1990 include a section in the chapter on Native people that deals with current issues. Residential schools, reserves and the *Indian Act* are introduced as aspects of the federal government's policy of assimilation, and publishers have made an initial effort to combat stereotypes. For example, Prentice Hall's *Canada Through Time* includes photo essays about contemporary First Nations people who work as teachers, writers and lawyers.[22]

The influence of anti-racist education is evident in the *Curriculum Guideline Native Studies Intermediate Division* issued by the Ontario Ministry of Education in 1991. Like the PONA Guidelines, it is designed for schools with a significant First Nations population but is also recommended for teaching non-First Nations students about First Nations history, culture and issues. The guideline begins with the typical focus on the pre-Contact period but also includes sample units on "Legislating Change" and "Forces of Assimilation." It offers teachers and students a means for investigating colonization and its effects on First Nations people. The guideline includes attitude and value objectives such as "willingness to analyze assumptions and attitudes underlying [a] judgment of cultural superiority and cultural equality, [an] appreciation of the effects of the interaction between Native societies and European settlers."[23]

The PONA and Native Studies Guidelines, in part shaped by multicultural and anti-racist education, reflect efforts to alter the representation of First Nations' content in the curriculum. Both have had an impact on how teachers in Ontario schools approach teaching First Nations' content. But neither multicultural education nor anti-racist education offer an opportunity to investigate the impact of colonialism. Students still learn that "real Indians" are romantic and mythical and lived a long, long time ago. What happened to them a long, long time ago was, of course, wrong and sad, but in the Canada of the 1990s we are all equal and should be treated the same. In the name of equality then, our history and culture vanish. So too does the need for change.

THE CRITICAL EMANCIPATORY APPROACH

In "After The Canon," Cameron McCarthy argues that multicultural education has been taken over by dominant humanism and is now limited to specific debates over content, texts, attitudes and values.[24] I frequently find his argument confirmed. Far too often, I visit classrooms where the study of First Nations people is limited to making dream-catchers, reading myths and legends, and colouring maps of cultural areas. Teachers argue that these "hands-on" activities appeal to students and promote "cultural understanding." It's not surprising that such activities are preferred to the hard work of investigating the history of injustice that has characterized Canada's post-Contact dealings with the First Nations. Few people welcome discussions that stir up dissension about the past. Cultural understanding and sensitivity training offer a safe approach to teaching about the relationship between First Nations people and Canadians.

In his work, McCarthy calls for "critical emancipatory multiculturalism." Proponents of critical education seek to transform the curriculum from one that reproduces inequality to one that fosters equality and justice. In *Border Crossings,* Henry Giroux describes critical education as operating from two basic premises: the need to question presuppositions and the need to raise possibilities.[25] It is not enough to replace negative, stereotyped representations of First Nations people with positive and diverse representations. If we mean to transform the power relations that sustain injustice, then teachers and students need to explore 500 years of oppression, unequal power relations and what sustains those unequal relations.

THE CLASSROOM TODAY: RECOGNIZING THE LIMITATIONS

Traditionally, the study of First Nations people in social studies involve students in cultural dissection. Students are required to study the clothing, types of shelter, religious beliefs, recreation, music and dance of the various First Nations. This approach leaves students with an understanding of First Nations people as noble savages, a primitive people of the past. The perspective is that of the European colonizers who sought and achieved domination of the land and its peoples. There is no mention of what happened to the people and their culture after European contact. No "difficult" issues are raised, let alone addressed. No information is presented that might reflect poorly on the dominant Euro-Canadian culture. There is no sense that to study First Nations people is to study real people who, despite 500 years of oppression, continue to live in Canada today. First Nations people become footnotes, to be considered only in so far as they relate to European exploration, settlement and nation-building.

The perspective presupposes that Europeans were stronger, more advanced and, therefore, more capable of making progress. First Nations people are depicted as victims of that progress, evoking pity in non-First Nations students. The elimination of First Nations peoples and their cultures is but the inevitable result of "progress." Students come away thinking that the dominant culture is superior to all others and therefore "deserves" advantages not provided to the inferior "others."

When I speak with students I tell the story of conquest and resistance, of invasion, violence and destruction. If teachers want to involve students in an investigation of the impact of colonialism on First Nations communities in Canada and its implications for today, students need to learn how the relationship between First Nations and non-First Nations people in Canada developed, including an understanding of how the attitude of superiority and the desire for power and control motivated the settlers.

The multicultural "Celebrating Our Differences" approach to teaching about First Nations people has won support from teachers, administrators and publishers. Students are encouraged to participate in making masks, constructing totem poles and building replicas of Indian villages. These activities entertain students but do not lead to any true appreciation of the complexities of First Nations cultures. Teaching about material cultures without attention to the values and philosophies of First Nations peoples reproduces stereotypes. As important as studying First Nations material cultures is, it is not enough. If students are to understand the destruction wrought by European colonization, then their investigation must extend to political and economic practices of the First Nations before contact.

Thus, while it is possible to investigate First Nations perspectives on post-Contact history from within anti-racist education and while the 1991 Native Studies Guideline does provide useful unit outlines and resource lists, my observations of many classrooms and my frequent discussions with history consultants tell me that the conscious examination of and challenge to Eurocentrism in the curriculum is not happening. Anti-racist education was taken up by teachers and by students in such a way that the emphasis on ending discrimination overshadows real challenges to Eurocentrism in the curriculum. Teachers and students are not yet asking "Who is speaking to whom, on whose behalf and in what context?"[26]

WHAT TEACHERS CAN DO?

Teachers, curriculum planners and school librarians are entwined in perpetuating a perspective that sustains the view of First Nations people as objects. This can and must change. Possibilities do exist within public education, and teachers can begin by including First Nations subject matter in all areas of the curriculum and by expanding the study from the exclusive focus on the pre-Contact period to look in depth at what happened post-contact and at the relationship between the First Nations and Canadians.

I am continually surprised by teachers who enthusiastically tell me about including a First Nations perspective in their curriculum and then proceed to tell me they did so by showing their students the film *Dances With Wolves*. I am reminded that teachers teach what they know and that most know little about post-Contact First Nations history or contemporary First Nations cultures. Furthermore, most of the materials used in Ontario schools are produced by non-First Nations people and continue to tell the story of "discovery" and domination. First Nations writers, film-makers, playwrights and musicians have produced a wide variety of works that non-first Nations teachers can draw on to educate themselves about the First Nations and to introduce a First Nations perspective into the curriculum. The works of First Nations artists such as Moses, Keeshig-Tobias, McMaster and Archibald affirm the dignity and humanity of First Nations peoples and demonstrate our active resistance to 500 years of oppression. Their works lead to an understanding of history that fosters a relationship between First Nations and non-First Nations people based on equality and justice. Only when literature written by First Nations writers and art produced by First Nations artists become part of the curriculum and are found in all subject areas will students begin to recognize that there is far more to being First Nations than beads and feathers and that our identity is not something that can be pulled on and off like a pair of jeans.

Being First Nations is about our connections to the land, family and ancestors, about our language and the power that comes from our spirituality. It is also about our shared oppression.

Collectively, the work of contemporary First Nations writers, artists and musicians affirms who we are. Politically, it manifests our resistance and our continuing struggle to transform the power relations between the first Nations and Canadians. Ideologically, it challenges the presumed superiority of the dominant society.

The use of these and other resources produced by First Nations peoples cannot in itself transform power relations. Using these materials can help set the stage, and teachers committed to equality and justice can change how First Nations subject matter is represented in the curriculum. In the fall of 1998, however, teachers in Ontario received new curriculum guidelines for Social Studies, Grades 1 to 6, and history and geography, Grades 7 and 8. Rather than moving towards a critical and emancipatory approach, the 1998 changes are disturbing and regressive.

THE CHANGES IN THE ONTARIO CURRICULUM

I started this chapter with a quote from an American curriculum specialist William Pinar:

> We are what we know. We are, however, also what we do not know. If what we know about ourselves — our history, our culture, our national identity — is deformed by absences, denials, and incompleteness, then our identity — both as individuals and as Americans — is fragmented.[27]

I was, and remain, deeply disturbed by the extent to which the new guidelines distort the history of the relationship between First Nations people and Canadians. In *The Ontario Curriculum Social Studies Grades 1 to 6 History and Geography Grades 7 to 8* guidelines (1998), the over-view of the unit on "First Nations Peoples and European Explorers" states:

> The study of Heritage and Citizenship in Grade 6 focuses on the distinct cultures, both past and present, of First Nations peoples in Canada, and on the early European explorers. Students describe the role of the environment in shaping First Nations cultures. They examine the interactions between First Nations peoples and European explorers at the time of their first contact, and they learn how the early explorers contributed to the development of Canada. They also study the origins of concerns

related to First Nations peoples and determine their present social, political, and economic conditions.

Further, the overall expectations outlined in the guidelines are that:

By the end of Grade 6 students will: identify ways in which the environment molded Canadian First Nations cultures, identify early explorers and describe their impact on the development of Canada, and demonstrate an understanding of the social, political and economic issues facing First Nations peoples in Canada today.[28]

At first glance, the overview suggests an approach which celebrates cultural diversity. But once again the emphasis is on the material aspects of culture. Specific expectations state that "students are expected to describe the relationship between First Nations peoples and their environment, e.g. with respect to food, shelter, cultural practices." Note the language that is used in the directives to teachers: students are to "identify ways in which the environment *molded* First Nations cultures" (emphasis added). The language itself reduces First Nations people to a feature of the landscape. In contrast, European explorers are portrayed as individuals having had the power to have had an *"impact on the development of Canada"* (emphasis added).[29] It is, of course, possible to reflect our knowledge of, relationship with and respect for the land in ways that affirm our humanity and dignity. That is not, however, the approach to teaching pre-Contact history suggested in the guidelines. When investigating theories about our origins, teachers are directed to consider, for example, stories of migration and settlement. No mention is made of First Nations creation stories.

After the traditional "cultural survey," the study of the First Nations quickly turns to the "interactions" between First Nations people and European explorers. The guidelines state that "By the end of Grade 6, students will: describe early explorers' perceptions of First Nations peoples' way of life."[30] A critical analysis of those "interactions" would reveal the early explorers' belief in their superiority. Unfortunately, the guidelines do not encourage that kind of inquiry.

Students are also expected to identify "current concerns" and to describe the current relationship between the government of

Canada and First Nations peoples. The social, political and economic issues facing First Nations peoples in Canada today are the result of a long and complex relationship rooted in colonial rule, and cannot be understood apart from the impact of the federal government's policy of forced assimilation. That policy included forcing our children into schools, the loss of our languages, the near destruction of our culture, the theft of our land and the forced removal of our people to reserve lands. Students in Grade 6 are eleven and twelve years old. How can these young students understand the current relationship without a comprehensive understanding of the implications of the colonial relationship? What depth of understanding can we reasonably expect from these young students and what materials are being made available to teachers to accomplish this understanding?

Removing this unit from the Grade 7 program and adding it to the Grade 6 program is not an insignificant change. At best, the understanding of these extremely complex issues will be simplistic. The curriculum planners responsible for developing the unit failed to recognize the complexity of the issues, failed to address the lack of knowledge and understanding on the part of classroom teachers and failed to compensate for the lack of curriculum materials appropriate for use at the Grade 6 level. Also, the Eurocentrism the guideline contributes to perpetuating the belief that First Nations people are the Romantic Mythical Other.

As we move into the history program in Grades 7 and 8, the focus changes to European immigration and nation-building. Again the language is revealing. In the Grades 7 and 8 unit on New France, students are expected to describe the early European and First Nations settlement patterns in North America and the economic, political and social life in New France. Students are never asked to investigate and understand the economic, political and social life of First Nations peoples. The study of New France is followed by a unit on conflict and change. One might expect to find some reference to First Nations people here, but the focus is on the rebellions of 1837.

In Grade 8 students are expected to analyze and describe current issues and their potential impact on Confederation today, for example, the demands of the First Nations peoples, Quebec issues and western issues.[31] Students are not provided with the means to understand the history behind these conflicts yet are expected to describe and analyze their manifestations today. Students are also expected to identify and explain the effects of post-Confederation immigration on the development of Western Canada but are never asked to investigate the impact of the destruction of the buffalo herds on First Nations people, nor are students asked to investigate the governments starving of First Nations people into submission and how the promise of food was used to coerce them into signing treaties to give up their lands. Students are asked to describe the everyday life of First Nations peoples, Europeans and Métis in what is now Western Canada at the time of European settlement. A description of everyday life is safe and avoids conflict. The final unit in Grade 8 is "Canada: A Changing Society." There are "specific expectations," but only one deals with First Nations people.

During the 1998-1999 school year, I spoke with a number of experienced history teachers from Grades 7 and 8 who expressed their objections to the change in the curriculum. Teachers explained that, "if there is not an explicit unit of study addressing First Nations subject matter the issues pertaining to First Nations people will not be addressed."[32] The introduction to the 1998 guideline states that "students graduating from Ontario schools require the knowledge and skills gained from social studies and the study of history and geography in order to function as informed citizens in a culturally diverse and interdependent world and to compete in a global economy."[33] That the guideline recognizes that the world students occupy is culturally diverse and interdependent is a first step, but the guideline offers no help on eliminating Eurocentrism from the curriculum.

In the 1996 report of the Royal Commission on First Nations People, the commissioners urge Canadians to attend to the past and argue that recognizing the historical relationship is the way to accomplishing a new and just relationship. The Commissioners state that:

> One of the clearest messages that emerges [from the work of the commission] is the importance of understanding the historical background to contemporary issues ... But Commissioners also concluded that most Canadians are simply unaware of the history of the First Nations presence in what is now Canada and that there is little understanding of the origins and evolution of the relationship between First Nations and non-First Nations people that have led us to the present moment. Lack of historical awareness has been combined with a lack of understanding on the part of most Canadians of the substantial cultural differences that still exist between First Nations and non-First Nations people. Together these factors have created fissures in relations between the original inhabitants of North America and generations of newcomers. They impede restoration of the balanced and respectful relationship that is the key to correcting our understanding of our shared past and moving forward together into the future.[34]

Like the commissioners, I believe that rendering non-First Nations people cognizant of our stories is a crucial first step in establishing fertile ground on which to cultivate an equitable relationship. In addition to sharing our stories of 500 years of resistance and replacing negative or stereotypical representations with positive diverse representations the discourse of the Romantic Mythical Other needs to be altered in such a way that Canadians will hear our stories and be engaged in a (re)thinking of their understanding of First Nations people, their understanding of themselves and of themselves in relationship with First Nations people. During the past thirty years there has been a substantive increase in cultural production by First Nations artists. While efforts have been made to integrate a First Nations perspective into the curriculum for First Nations students a First Nations perspective of history has not yet been introduced to the curriculum for all students.

What is remembered and what is forgotten in the "study" of First Nations people and the "study" of Canada contributes to an understanding of history that allows and encourages non-First Nations Canadians to distance themselves from and abdicate their responsibility for attending to the ongoing conditions of injustice that are a part of the day-to-day lived experiences of First Nations people in Canada. I recognize the constraints of teaching and

learning within the structure of a classroom including those constraints put in place by the provincial curriculum. I also recognize
that pockets of resistance do exist. Individual teachers committed to
accomplishing change are making use of materials produced by First
Nations artists in an effort to both educate themselves and their students. This learning is critical to the development of an equitable
relationship between First Nations and non-First Nations people in
Canada.

TEACHER RESOURCES

Hartmut Lutz, ed., *Contemporary Challenges: Conversations with Canadian Native
Artists* (Calgary: Fifth House Publishers, 1991). Interviews with First Nations
writers are particularly useful for teachers who want to explore a First Nations
perspective. This collection includes interviews with Aboriginal artists.

Canada, *Final Report of the Royal Commission on Aboriginal Peoples, Volume 1,
Looking Forward, Looking Back* (Ottawa: Ministry of Supply and Services,
1996). This volume provides an excellent and exceptionaly written account of
the post-Contact relationship between First Nations people and Canadians. A
second source detailing this critical period in the development of the current
relationship is provided by R. Gibbins and J.R. Ponting, "Historical Overview
and Background," in *Arduous Journey,* edited by J. R. Ponting (Toronto:
McClelland and Stewart, 1986).

Daniel Francis, *The Imaginary Indian* (Vancouver: Arsenal Pulp Press, 1992), and
Robert Berkhofer, *The Whiteman's Indian* (Toronto: Random House, 1979).
Both of these books investigate where the myth of the Indian came from, how
the myth has affected public policy and how it has shaped and continues to
shape how non-First Nations people understand what it means to be Canadian
or American.

CLASSROOM RESOURCES

Daniel David Moses and Terry Goldie, eds., *An Anthology of Canadian Native
Literature in English* (Toronto: Oxford University Press, 1992), and Greg
Young-Ing and Florene Belmore, eds., "Gatherings X," *The En'owkin Journal*

of First North American Peoples (Penticton, BC: Theytus Books Ltd., 1999). These volumes offer excellent short stories, poetry and essays.

Gerald McMaster and Lee-Ann Martin, eds., *Indigena* (Toronto: Douglas and McIntyre, 1992). This collection of art was created by First Nations artists in response to the hoopla in 1992 surrounding the 500th anniversary of Columbus's landing in the Americas. As editors Gerald McMaster and Lee-Ann Martin explain, we had nothing to celebrate, but we welcomed the opportunity to demonstrate that we have not only endured but lived to celebrate life and to share our work with a broader audience.

Bill Bigelo, Barbara Miner, and Bob Peterson, eds., *Rethinking Columbus* (1991). This is a special edition of *Rethinking Schools* and is an excellent collection of articles and suggestions for practical classroom activities to involve students in questioning firmly established attitudes about the "discovery" of the Americas.

First Nations: The Circle Unbroken is a Media Kit produced by Face to Face Media and Svend-Erik Erikson in 1993. This package of thirteen programs introduces First Nations' perspectives on a wide range of topics. The programs provide students with rich and complex images of the contemporary reality of the First Nations, our sense of identity and our relations with Canada.

ORGANIZATIONS

The Native Canadian Centre of Toronto
16 Spadina Rd.
Toronto, ON M5R 3M4
(416) 964-9087

Woodland Cultural Centre
184 Mohawk St., P.O. Box 1506
Brantford, ON N3T 5V6
(519) 759-2650

Mokakit Education Research Association
The University of Brtish Columbia
First Nations Longhouse
1985 West Mall
Vancouver, BC V6B 2L3
(604) 822-5023

Assembly of First Nations
47 Clarence St., Suite 300
Ottawa, ON K1N 9K1

NOTES

1. During the colonial period, two images of First Nations womanhopd surfaced. One was the pure, beautiful Pocahontas who helps the white men; the other was the sexually permissive squaw. Both these images depersonalize First Nations women and depict them as objects of male desire.

2. Jan Elliot, "America to Indians: Stay in the Nineteenth Century," *Rethinking Columbus* (Milwaukee: Rethinking Schools, 1991). Various proper names are often used to refer to the First Nations people of the Americas. I use the respectful term First Nations because it affirms our position as the original people and recognizes our status of nationhood. The term Indian or Native is used when referencing another author's work and in the context of discussing that work. It is at times a contradiction to use the term First Nations when the concept or attitude being discussed did not reflect the understanding or respect the term denotes. In these cases I use the term "Indian" or "Native." In this chapter I am describing a change in understanding from the negative stereotype of the "Indian" through the multicultural "Native" to the respectful recognition of First Nations. At times it is necessary to use each of these terms in context of discussing the different concepts and atttudes.

3. Lenore Keeshig-Tobias, "Not Just Entertainment," in B. Slapin, and D. Seale, eds., *Through Indian Eye* (Gabriola Island, BC: New Society, 1992), 100.

4. C. Sweet, "Native Studies in the North American Social Studies Curriculum," *The Social Studies* (January/February 1994), 7-10.

5. Attempts are being made to alter this representation, but it is difficult to say what impact this is having on non-First Nations people's understanding and perceptions of First Nations people, on history and on culture. My discussions with students about the television series *North of 60* suggest that such programs are yet to have a significant impact. Similarly, the portrayl of First Nations people as "savage" is declining, but still occurs.

6. Ira Shor, *Empowering Education* (Chicago: The University of Chicago Press, 1992), 14. Here Shor is drawing on the work of sociologists of education Michael Apple, Henri Giroux, and James Banks.

7. My experience with the education system is in Ontario and, therefore, this chapter focuses on Ontario. In the West and the North, there are more First Nations students and this has had an impact on the attention given to First Nations subject matter. How non-First Nations teachers teach non-First Nations students about the post-Contact relationship between First Nations and Canadians is relevant for teachers across the country.

8. During the summer of 1990 a historic confrontation between the Mohawk Nation at Kanesatke and the village of Oka, Quebec, propelled First Nations issues into the international arena. To protest the exclusion of First Nations people from constitutional talks Elijah Harper changed the constitutional direction of the country when he refused to support the 1990 Meech Lake Accord. These high profile incidents served to raise the consciousness of many

Canadians to the ongoing relationship of injustice between the First Nations and Canada.

9. E. W. Eisner, "Curriculum Ideologies," in P.W. Jackson ed., *Handbook of Research on Curriculum* (New York: MacMillan, 1992), 30.

10. William Pinar, "Notes on Understanding Curriculum as a Racial Text," in Cameron McCarthy and Warrent Crichlow, eds., *Race, Identity and Representation in Education* (New York: Routledge, 1993), 60.

11. George Tomkins, "The Social Studies In Canada," in J., Parsons, G. Milburn, and M. van Manen, eds., *A Canadian Social Studies* (Edmonton: University of Alberta,1983).

12. Daniel Francis, *The Imaginary Indian* (Vancouver: Arsenal Pulp Press, 1992), 160.

13. Deborah Doxtator, *Fluffs And Feathers — An Exhibit on the Symbols of Indianness: Teachers Kit* (Toronto: Royal Ontario Museum Education Services Department, 1988), and Francis, *The Imaginary Indian*.

14. Janice Acoose, *Iskwewak-Kah' Ki Yaw Ni Wahkomakanak: Neither Indian Princesses Nor Easy Squaws* (Toronto: Women's Press, 1995), 29.

15. See Magda Lewis, "Native Images in Children's Picture Books," in Jon Yong ed., *Breaking The Mosaic* (Toronto: Garamond Press, 1987) for a discussion of the role of picture books in constructing young childrens' understanding of First Nations people.

16. Political activism by First Nations people during the 1960s contributed to the establishment of this national organization that addresses concerns of First Nations people in Canada. The NIB was the forerunner to the Assembly of First Nations that was established in 1980-82.

17. Verna Kirkness and Sheena Bowman, *First Nations and Schools: Triumphs and Struggles* (Toronto: Canadian Education Association, 1992), 15.

18. Ibid., 34.

19. *Ontario Ministry of Education Curriculum Guideline Junior Division. People of Native Ancestry* (Toronto: Ontario Ministry of Education, 1975), 3, 5.

20. Ontario Ministry of Education, *Anti-racism and Ethnocultural Equity in School Boards* (Toronto: Ontario Ministry of Education, 1993), 5.

21. Barbara Thomas, "Principles of Anti-racist Education," *Currents* 2 (1992), 22.

22. Angus Scully, John Bebbington, Rosemary Evans, and Carol Wilson, *Canada Through Time: Book One* (Scarborough: Prentice Hall Inc., 1992).

23. Ontario Ministry of Education, *Curriculum Guideline Native Studies Intermediate Division* (Toronto: Ontario Ministry of Education,1991), 24.

24. Cameron McCarthy, "After The Canon: Knowledge and Ideological Representation in the Multicultural Discourse on Curriculum Reform," in McCarthy and Crichelow eds., *Race, Identity and Representation in Education*, 289-305.

25. Henry Giroux, *Border Crossings* (New York: Routledge, 1992).

26. Barbara Godard, "The Politics of Representation: Some Native Canadian Women Writers," in W. H. New, ed., *Native Writers and Canadian Writing* (Vancouver: UBC Press,1990), 185.

27. Pinar, "Notes on Understanding Curriculum as Racial Text," 61.

28. Ministry of Education and Training, *The Ontario Curriculum Social Studies Grades 1 to 6 History and Geography Grades 7 and 8* (Toronto: Ministry of Education and Training,1998), 25.

29. Ibid.

30. Ibid., 26.

31. Ibid., 49.

32. These comments were made during formal workshops I conducted with teachers as part of a research study and during more informal conversations with colleagues.

33. Ministry of Education and Training, *The Ontario Curriculum Social Studies Grades 1 to 6 History and Geography Grades 7 and 8*, 2.

34. Canada, *Royal Commission on Aboriginal Peoples, Final Report of the Royal Commission on Aboriginal Peoples* (Ottawa: Ministry of Supply and Services, 1996), 26-27.

Chapter 14

EDUCATING TOWARDS A CULTURE OF PEACE

Toh Swee-Hin and Virginia Floresca-Cawagas

THE UNITED NATIONS' DECLARATION of 2000 as the International Year for a Culture of Peace symbolizes the aspiration that this century be characterized by non-violence. Indeed, during the last decades of the twentieth century, nations took encouraging steps away from violent or potentially violent approaches to conflict. The ending of the Cold War, the Middle East Peace Accord, the end of civil wars in Cambodia, El Salvador, Guatemala and Mozambique, the dismantling of apartheid in South Africa, the end of authoritarian regimes in the former Soviet Union and Eastern Europe and the treaty abolishing landmines are all cause for hope that this century will be more peaceful.

Yet, life in many parts of the world remains filled with war and other violence. The ethnic cleansing in Serbia and other Balkan republics, the genocide in Rwanda, the never-ending Gulf War, the bloody civil wars in Liberia, Sierra Leone, Sudan, Congo, Sri Lanka, Angola, Afghanistan and the former Soviet republics, and the Kosovo Crisis are powerful reminders of the challenges facing us.

In 1999, the United Nations celebrated the 50th Anniversary of the Universal Declaration of Human Rights. The widespread violations of human rights worldwide remind us of the chasm between theory and practice. At the same time, international development agencies report on global poverty and the gross disparities between the rich and the poor. Even as a small proportion of humanity speeds ahead on the wings of high-tech economic growth, super-consumerism and globalization, the vast majority must struggle to meet basic needs. Despite world summits and national plans, the ecological crisis is deepening. The crisis threatens the planet even as it reveals how environmental destruction exacerbates economic and social inequalities. Nonetheless, many people, even those directly affected, have not succumbed to despair and hopelessness. There is a strong consensus that civil society can do much to make the culture of peace a reality.

Civil society encompasses communities, non-governmental organizations, individual citizens and national, regional and international networks. It is vital in sustaining peace building locally, nationally, regionally and globally. Where there is will, governments and official agencies also play constructive roles in peace building — take, for example, the land mines treaty, the Middle East Peace Accord and the International Criminal Court. Underlying the consensus is a profound recognition of the role that education can play in building a more peaceful world. The work of peace education is not as visible as participation in peace rallies, peace negotiations and other non-violent action. Still, as peace activists admit, peace education at all levels and for all sectors of society is basic to developing values, knowledge and skills vital to transforming a culture of violence to one of peace. As we shall see, what peace education means has changed as we have come to understand more about violence, conflict and peace.

EDUCATION TO END WARS

The growth of contemporary peace education has often been associated with the desire to establish and maintain peaceful relations between nation-states and with movements to end wars or to abolish war.[1] From the early peace societies and the School Peace League in the United States, associations such as the International

League for Peace and Freedom and the Société d'Education Pacifique, education has been seen as essential to the formation of citizens who abhor war, seek international understanding and thereby promote world peace. However, as far back as the Reformation and the Renaissance, peace meant not simply the absence of war but also encompassed "the improvement of life, the way to realize social justice, freedom, and development."[2]

In the aftermath of the First World War, the efforts of non-governmental organizations and peace movements were complemented by inter-governmental agencies.[3] The League of Nations, for example, through UNESCO's precursor, the International Institute for Intellectual Co-operation, worked with non-governmental organizations (NGOs) on peace building. That work included revising school textbooks. In the inter-war years, peace groups such as the British-initiated International Peace Campaign expanded worldwide, and the educator Montessori emphasized the importance of teaching based on co-operation in forming peace-oriented values, conduct and "life-giving spirituality."[4]

After the Second World War, peace education that focused on disarmament became galvanized by international protests over the atomic bombing of Hiroshima and Nagasaki and the spiralling nuclear arms race generated by the Cold War. To this day, Hiroshima remains a powerful symbol of the need to abolish weaponry and wars and is an important focus in peace education.[5] The Pugwash Conference, the International Physicians for the Prevention of Nuclear War and peace movements in Canada, the United States and Western Europe unravelled the hidden assumptions behind the doctrines of "deterrence" and "exterminism."[6] Canadian campaigners like Senator Doug Roche continue to fight to ban nuclear weapons.[7] Canadian NGOs, organizations such as Project Ploughshares, Coalition to Oppose the Arms Trade and the recently successful international campaign on the banning of land mines seek to educate peoples and governments on how the conventional arms trade fuels civil war and other conflicts.[8] Such work draws on the principles of Gandhian philosophy and practice and concentrates on seeking peaceful resolutions to international and internal conflicts through peace talks, mediation and preventive diplomacy. The growing movement for "violence prevention" and "conflict resolution," especially in North American schools, reflects a new application of disarmament education in formal education. However, as we discuss later, conflict resolution programs are not panaceas, especially when conflicts involve considerable power disparities and injustices. There are also disturbing signs that some "violence prevention" programs, which were sparked by the high-school shootings in Columbine, infringe on the rights of students.

TOWARDS A CULTURE OF PEACE

Although the roots of peace education lie in the call for disarmament, the dismantling of a culture of war and violence also means creating an awareness of violence and working to encourage all people to avert all forms of violence, whether it be social, economic, psychological, political or cultural. Peace education, like many other educations in this collection, draws on the theory and practice of other "progressive educations" — development education, human rights education, multicultural education, environmental education and global education. This holistic evolution of the concept of peace and thereby "peace education" reflects the growth of social movements over the past fifty years. Civil society remains a major catalyst for change, but international organizations like UNESCO and peace education and research bodies like the International Peace Research Association (IPRA) also provided leadership and support. UNESCO continues to build on its fifty-year old vision of peace and international understanding. In its 1974 recommendation on "Education for International Understanding, Co-operation and Peace and Education Relating to Human Rights and Fundamental Freedoms," UNESCO identified the many dimensions of peace, including intercultural respect and understanding, anti-racism, social justice, human rights, equitable development and international co-operation and solidarity. In 1995, UNESCO's Declaration and Integrated Framework in Education for Peace, Human Rights and Democracy elaborated its principles for building peace and for protecting human rights.

UNESCO's cross-disciplinary Culture of Peace project translates UNESCO's vision into all aspects of its activities, and its Culture of

Peace program works with states and civil society in international forums in both the North and the South. Other UNESCO activities include the youth-oriented Associated Schools Project (ASPnet) and UNESCO clubs, professional development for teachers, curriculum and textbook development, media literacy and independence, promoting women's empowerment, post-war programs for reconciliation and demobilization of combatants and university chairs in peace education. UNESCO has also highlighted women's vital contribution to peace-building worldwide. In sum, UNESCO is the leading agency promoting and sustaining an evolving multidimensional concept of a culture of peace.[9]

From the 1970s onwards, the actions and writings of activists have drawn attention to the need to ensure social justice, protection for human rights, ecological sustainability, intercultural respect and peace-oriented spirituality. In the United Kingdom, David Hicks and others sparked a peace education movement among teachers that led to curriculum innovations, changes in teacher education and changes in the schools. In Australia, Robin Burns and others highlighted the relationship between equitable development and peace-building. A collection of semi-autobiographical essays by Australian peace educators also reflects the many dimensions of peace-building and peace education. In the United States, Betty Reardon drew up a framework for peace education that stresses planetary stewardship, global citizenship and humane relationships, a framework that requires full respect for social justice, human rights, sustainability and democratic participation. These values are embodied in efforts of others worldwide.[10] One researcher surveyed peace education in several countries and summarized their goals for peace education as preparedness for non-violence, taking responsibility as a citizen of the world, egalitarian attitudes and a readiness to search critically for alternatives.[11] A review of a hundred years of peace education also reveals why disarmament alone is inadequate.[12]

In our own work with peace educators in the Philippines, we have drawn up a holistic framework for peace education based on demilitarization, ending structural violence, protecting human rights, fostering cultural solidarity, environmental care and personal peace. In a presentation at UNESCO's International Forum on

Governance and a Culture of Peace in Maputo, Mozambique, Toh expanded on these principles:

- Dismantling the culture of war means ending militarism, whether nuclear or conventional, and ending other manifestations of violence, including the symbolic media violence, war toys, and including violence in the home.

- Living with compassion and justice means calling on all peoples and all nations, especially in the industrialized North, to work for just and participatory development to overcome the wide disparities between the North and the South and the wide disparities within nations, and to challenge globalization and the power of elites (transnational corporations and international financial institutions).

- Lighting the candle of dignity stresses the courage demanded of those who uphold and promote human rights in the face of continuing violations by governments and by powerful elites.

- Harmony among cultures calls for deep understanding and respect for and the sharing of wisdoms, identities and knowledge between and among different cultures. At the same time, it acknowledges that conflicts between cultures can have strong roots in political and economic injustices and require redress as well as healing and reconciliation.

- Caring for the seven generations reminds us of the profound indigenous wisdom of indigenous teachings on the importance of living in peace with Mother Earth, and hence of the need for development that promotes sustainability not environmental destruction.

- Renewing the roots of personal peace emphasizes the synergy that arises from profound inner peace and gives strength to peace-building and to a spirituality that transcends the alienation caused by consumerism.[13]

These principles are linked to one another and remind us that efforts to resolve conflict must always consider the roots. In schools, the preferred strategy would be to weave peace education throughout the curriculum, not make it a separate subject. Nor is it enough simply to educate about peace. Teaching itself needs to be consistently peaceful, participatory and empowering so that students become motivated to translate their critical understanding into action for social and personal transformation.[14]

Peace education's widening focus clearly has implications for the theory and practice of education. However, as the next section reveals, the field is not without its tensions. Advocates of a comprehensive approach to peace education tend not to be bound by nomenclature. A 1988 survey of Canadian teachers found that those identified as working in peace education were addressing global understanding, current global issues, human rights and social justice, world hunger and development, peacemaking and non-violence, multiculturalism, ecological balance, international law and international organizations, and religious perspectives on war and peace. Nearly all these topics are noted in existing provincial curriculum guidelines, often in social studies. The curricular conditions for a comprehensive peace education are at least partly in place and teachers and parents need not feel that educating for peace is a new initiative or that peace education need be a separate subject.[15]

PREVENTING, REDUCING AND RESOLVING VIOLENCE IN THE SCHOOLS

In recent years, a growing movement has sought to make schools and other educational institutions peaceful environments. Particularly in the United States, Canada, Australia and parts of Europe, schools are being asked to respond urgently and creatively to the violence within their own walls. Teachers, administrators, parents, students and other community members, government and non-government agencies express fear over reports of mounting violence within schools. The literature is clear that the the forms of violence receiving the most attention include physical homicides, gang fighting, sexual attacks, bullying, physically abusive discipline, hazing, arson, vandalism and possession of a deadly weapon. However, the literature on violence in the schools also examines insults, initiation rituals, sexual harassment, drug addiction, intolerance, racism and discrimination. Any behaviour that demeans can lead to physical violence. Furthermore, students are not the only focus of the violence, whether as perpetrators or victims. School personnel, especially those who administer discipline, as well as parents and community members, as in the case of students hurt by domestic violence, are also accountable.

In response to the public and private fear about the perceived rise in violence in the schools, boards of education are preparing policies and setting up programs to help prevent, reduce and resolve the problem. Referred to as "anti-violence," "violence-prevention" and "conflict-resolution" programs, these efforts often include the following components:

- Educating about the nature, causes and consequences of violence.
- Building confidence to overcome the "code of silence" or "denial."
- Setting guidelines that encourage reporting and that ensure an appropriate and timely response.
- Integrating the teaching of conflict resolution and related skills in conflict-management conflict-intervention, conflict resolution and peer mediation throughout the curriculum.
- Integrating the principles of non-violence throughout extra curricular activities.
- Setting up and carrying out appropriate, fair and assertively implemented violence-free policies and codes of behaviour and discipline.
- Requesting school staff to model appropriate behaviour (respect for all, non-violent language, no stereotyping).
- Responding effectively and appropriately to victims of violence.
- Finding ways to rehabilitate offenders.
- Helping students face and challenge marginalization and discrimination, especially in conflicts arising from discrimination.
- Strengthening student and staff participation in the school and in the wider community.
- Legislating safe schools.
- Supporting teachers who exercise legal remedies.

- Co-ordinating efforts to end school violence with the police, social services, counsellors and youth community associations.
- Strengthening the social commitment to a non-violent environment (in homes, at sports arenas, in the malls, in the media).

These programs show that building a non-violent culture within schools needs to take into account the multiple dimensions of a school community. The curriculum, whether formal, extra (sports, recreation) or hidden, needs to integrate peaceful values, knowledge and skills. Administration procedures should consistently uphold non-violence. A culture of peace also needs to underpin relationships between schools and other communities.

In the United States, Educators for Social Responsibility co-ordinate the nationwide Resolving Conflict Creatively Program, which reaches 150,000 children in grades K through 12 and 5,000 teachers in 325 schools. Activities include training, preparing teacher's guides and curricula resources, extensive support for staff development, workshops for parents and leadership training for school administrators. In Canada, parallel efforts include the Safe and Caring Schools Project co-ordinated by the Alberta Teachers Association, and the education of youth in Gandhian principles co-ordinated by the Mahatma Gandhi Foundation for World Peace. Many schools in British Columbia have peer mediation and conflict resolution programs as part of the vision of safe school communities. Nova Scotia's League of Peaceful Schools was formed in January 1998. The League includes over fifty schools and demonstrates a "commitment to ensuring that students are taught attitudes, knowledge and skills needed for the peaceful resolution of conflict."[16] In Ontario, school systems and boards formulated and implemented policies to promote non-violence.[17]

Australia, New Zealand, Japan, Israel and some European countries also include conflict resolution and anti-violence education as part of formal schooling. In South Africa, the Centre for Conflict Resolution offers training in conflict resolution and peer mediation and works to integrate conflict resolution into the curriculum. The Centre also encourages parental and community participation in South African schools. Educators in India continue to draw inspiration from Gandhi, and in the Philippines, some teachers and NGOs are working to bring conflict resolution into the schools. The recently funded and Austrian co-ordinated international school network on Peace Education and Conflict Resolution includes schools in Argentina, India and Nigeria. UNESCO's culture of peace projects in El Salvador, Mozambique, Burundi and Nicaragua include, or plan to include, school-based programs in non-violent conflict management.[18]

Despite increasing popularity of these violence-prevention and violence-reduction programs, it is still important to ask if they can effectively build a culture of peace. Peace means more than the absence of physical violence, more than the ending or at least the prevention of war, more than the abolition of weapons, more than the end of physical violence at school, in the home or on the street. Building peace means working to redress injustice within and across societies. It means ending ecological violence. It means protecting human rights and freedoms. It means being moved by active non-violence, as Gandhi firmly asserted, in grounding *ahimsa* and *satyagraha* in social justice and human rights.

BEYOND VIOLENCE PREVENTION

A non-violent school needs to simultaneously build a culture of peace from local and community to national, regional and global levels. The following seven themes are possible bridges we can use to extend violence prevention education into more holistic projects that serve not only the interests and needs of participants in one site or community or region, but ultimately the interests of our common humanity.

ENDING STRUCTURAL VIOLENCE

A more peaceful world cannot be built on flawed foundations. Unsuccessful efforts to redress social and economic injustices have led to war. Schools should be strengthening students' capacity to work for justice. Throughout the world, however, schooling itself helps to maintain inequality. Building non-violent schools also means reforming schools so that the influence of social class is minimized. Schools committed to a culture of peace must also become part of ending structural violence in the wider community, society and across the world. Violence prevention programs need to be as concerned about the marginalization that results from social and economic injustices within and between nations. Development education and world studies are indispensable to peace education and help students develop a critical awareness of the roots of poverty and hunger. From that awareness, the students may be moved to redress injustice on a local, national and global level.

In 1995, Craig Keilburger, a twelve-year-old Canadian, began to mobilize other children to end the exploitation of child labour. The Free the Children campaign calls on governments and transnational corporations to take a stand on child labour and to protect workers' rights. Free the Children reminds us, "It is not enough to remove children from factories; alternatives must be found for children and their families to provide food, shelter, and education."[19]

In the Philippines, some schools integrate programs of immersion or outreach in rural and urban poor communities. It is hoped that as students personally experience the realities of poverty and social injustice, they will be moved to support social justice movements in Filipino society.[20]

UPHOLDING HUMAN RIGHTS

Building a school-based culture of peace complements the diverse efforts in human rights education worldwide. Respect among all school members for each others' rights helps to reduce conflicts that can lead to violence. Fair policies and codes of conduct promote basic principles of human rights thinking and practices.

Schools can and should work to protect human rights. Building a culture of peace includes engaging students in activities that challenge human rights violations (Amnesty International clubs), promoting the rights of children everywhere (the campaign to protect child labourers, supporting grassroots development projects, programs to help street children) and upholding the rights of women. Such activities help youth adopt values and practices that support a peaceful culture within schools and in the world at large.

DISARMAMENT EDUCATION

Many millions of children go, or try to go, to school amidst situations of armed conflict. Hundreds of thousands suffer physical and psychological trauma, become refugees or, increasingly, become foot-soldiers in the armies and paramilitary forces. Once a war ends, national reconciliation is needed to overcome the legacy of enmity, distrust and bitterness in the regions.[21] Building a culture of peace in schools in such situations means addressing violence and militarism in the wider society. Programs in these schools must include help for war-traumatized children and encourage participation in community efforts towards peace-building, such as the zones of peace and the peace process in the Philippines. They must also include national commissions on truth and reconciliation, such as those in South Africa, and address the issue of gun control, an increasingly controversial public issue in the United States.

Violence prevention programs in schools can also raise student awareness and encourage action to end militarism by focusing attention on the value of war toys and through joining campaigns to end the arms trade. Recently, many school children in Australia, New Zealand, Philippines and the island nations of the South Pacific took part in the protest against French nuclear testing. The challenge of demilitarism is also significant at the level of families and communities. In many countries, there are increasing efforts to educate and overcome the problem of domestic violence that especially harms women and children.

CULTURAL SOLIDARITY

Some violence prevention programs do address racism, ethnic stereotyping and the depreciation of Indigenous cultures and peoples. Such programs need to be grounded in a keen awareness that cultural influences have on conflict resolution, especially in culturally diverse schools. Multicultural education offers many insights into differences between cultures, but if it is to avoid reducing culture to dance, diet, dress and dialect, it must look deeply into the causes of conflicts between cultures. Anti-racist education, including working within the community, is also vital in building a school-based culture of peace.[22] All students need to learn to live with each other in a spirit of trust, respect and sharing. In the Philippines, work continues on bridging many decades of distrust and violent conflict between Muslims and Christians. In Canada and the US, Australia and New Zealand, the displacement and marginalization of First Nations peoples must end. First Nations schools themselves face serious challenges in building a culture of peace amidst the legacy of colonialism.[23] Elders who are well-grounded in the culture play a vital role in educating for a culture of peace. Similarly, UNESCO's culture of peace program emphasizes drawing on traditional means of conflict resolution. Speaking from "the power of Aboriginal traditional ways," Graveline advocates a medicine wheel metaphor of knowledge worldviews and pedagogical practices. She suggests a "model-in-use" which, in the first place, encourages learners to "present their classroom and life experiences in the form of a story, making connections between their personal experiences and the cultural and structural realities that frame our individual/family/community lives." A holistic and healing consciousness of self, others and communities can be developed through the use of "talking circles" and personal journals.[24]

LIVING IN PEACE WITH THE EARTH

The literature on violence prevention programs mentions the violence that humanity inflicts on the natural environment. Yet, unless we learn to live in peace with the Earth, humanity is not likely to survive. Conflicts over resources and ecological destruction have led to structural violence and human rights violations, such as the execution of Nigerian poet Ken Saro Wiwa, the displacement of peoples from ancestral lands, pollution and the depletion of resources required for subsistence. Logging interests have resorted to the armed repression of environmentalists. Nations have gone to war over environmental wealth. Programs that foster an environmentally friendly school can help build a culture of peace by teaching to respect the right to a clean and safe environment and the humane treatment of all species. Environmental education also contributes to a culture of peace. The social action that environmental education encourages — campaigns to save the rainforest and ban toxic dumping, recycling programs, promoting "green justice" and an awareness of over-consumption — gives students the skills and the confidence needed for building a culture of peace.[25]

FOSTERING INNER PEACE

As those working for peace over the centuries have stressed, equilibrium and inner peace are vital in sustaining peace.[26] We have many traditions to draw on. In Edmonton, Alberta, a world-renowned physician specializing in alternative healing and medicine conducts *chiqong* relaxation exercises with high school students so that they become better equipped to maintain calm at school and elsewhere. As Graveline advocates, "traditional healing and learning methods, which are meditation, rural-based and earth-based," can help students be "more in touch with their physical selves, release accumulated tensions and stresses, and enhance their earth connection."[27]

The world's religions and spiritual traditions can remind believers of their role in upholding a culture of peace. Youth can also think critically about the positive and negative roles religion and traditions play locally, nationally and internationally. Highlighting the need for inner peace, however, does not imply that this alone will accomplish our goal.

ENVISIONING PEACEFUL FUTURES

Increasingly peace education calls on teachers and learners to imagine a better world. Unless the youth feel empowered to consider possibilities which meet their needs for security, safety and peace, they can fall prey to cynicism, despair and hopelessness. Encouraging students to reflect critically and openly on the future is to present them with opportunities to deal constructively with fears, insecurities, biases, misperceptions, anger, alienation and hopelessness. There is some consensus that alienated youth constitute a potent source for current and future social violence, including gangs. Alienated youth can come to see that they have some power over their lives, and can find inspiration in the stories of ordinary peoples' struggles to build a just and peaceful world.[28]

CHALLENGES AND HOPES

Modern schooling in almost all societies is rooted in the ideology of intense competition and individualism.[29] From the selection and the reward system (evaluation, grading, testing) to the hidden curriculum of classroom interactions and sports, modern schools are very effective at socializing future adults to compete excessively and egoistically. Indeed, as part of the push towards globalization and its concomitant restructuring and other neoliberal policies, schools are being even more pressured to serve the imperatives of maximum growth, commercialization, and global competitiveness.[30] This is the first challenge.

The second challenge lies in the opposition from some parents and some interest groups. Indeed, in the 1970s and 1980s, when peace education was taking root in the schools, a vigorous movement against peace education emerged in the United Kingdom, Australia and the United States. These often well-organized and well-funded attacks reflect a conservative ideology, which sees peace education as anti-western, anti-capitalist, pro-Marxist, or to use the religious right's language, as "secular humanist" efforts to indoctrinate youth in the "political correctness" of feminism, environmentalism, human rights, multiculturalism and anti-racism.[31] There is less opposition to peace education that focuses on conflict resolution and violence prevention. This should not be surprising since conflict resolution and violence-prevention programs do not necessarily address controversial political, social, economic and cultural issues. Thus conservatives can welcome anti-violence programs, oppose gun control and favour an aggressive foreign policy.

A third challenge lies in teacher education. Teachers are vital to building a culture of peace. Conflict resolution and violence prevention programs are not enough to prepare teachers who want to take up that task. In our work with student teachers we often notice that some who are committed to and skilled in conflict resolution and violence prevention need sustained and sensitive education about racism, social injustice and ecology. This should not be surprising. None of us receives much encouragement to examine our assumptions, values, preferences and habits of action.

To ensure that future teachers are committed to and able to encourage learning in ways consistent with a culture of peace, teacher education programs need to promote the following aspects in teacher education:

- Make non-violence and comprehensive peace education part of the entire curriculum and of teaching itself.
- Stress classroom management that endorses conflict resolution.
- Foster teacher commitment to help students take appropriate and non-violent action based on critical analysis (project assignments, student associations, school-led campaigns).
- Work with parents, community groups, social agencies and political bodies to design and carry out culture of peace programs.
- Challenge injustices, human rights violations, ecological destruction and manifestations of violence.
- Engage in research on education and schooling that seeks ways to promote violence prevention and peace-building programs.
- Encourage professional autonomy among teachers, including the freedom to challenge measures that undermine peace-building (narrowing the curriculum, excessive testing, "tough" discipline). Where teachers have low status, however, it is very difficult for them to contribute what they might to building a culture of peace, no matter how appropriately educated they are.
- Work with other faculties and colleges of education to ensure that student teachers understand how to make peace education part of history, literature, language, social studies, civics, cultural studies, mathematics and the sciences.

*

Those of us who work towards building a culture of peace within individuals, families, schools, communities and the wider world can draw inspiration from metaphors that challenge the old world order: healing Mother Earth; a global civilization; awakening the non-violent "warrior" who lives with compassion, courage and discipline; planetary theology; green justice; science for liberation; freedom of simplicity; the bodhisattava ideal; the preferential option for the poor; resolution from within; reweaving the web of life. These metaphors speak to a commitment of creating a culture that nurtures non-violence, justice, sharing, compassion and living in harmony with Earth.

TEACHER RESOURCES

Robin J. Burns and Robert Aspeslagh, eds., *Three Decades of Peace Education around the World* (New York: Garland Publishing, 1996). This collection summarizes the rich theory and practice of the Peace Education Commission of the International Peace Research Association. It includes a chapter on the background, concepts and theories of peace education as it has evolved.

UNESCO, *From a Culture of Violence to a Culture of Peace* (Paris: UNESCO, 1997). This collection includes articles by peace researchers, philosophers, jurists and educators on the universal nature of a culture of peace and how it can be achieved. It also looks at the role of education, media and intercultural dialogue in bringing about a culture of peace.

David C. Smith and Terrance R. Carson, *Educating for a Peaceful Future* (Toronto: Kagan and Woo Limited, 1998). This book discusses the background to peace education and ways of making peace education part of the curriculum and practice in schools. The twenty-six learning activities drawn up by Graham Pike and David Selby are particularly useful.

Joanna Macy and Molly Young Brown, *Coming Back to Life* (Philadelphia: New Society Books, 1998). This guidebook provides inspiration for personal action and group reflection and offers teachers powerful strategies for community-building and for engaging both young and old in dialogue.

European Platform for Conflict Prevention and Transformation, Prevention and Management of Conflicts. An International Directory (Utrecht: European Platform for Conflict Prevention and Transformation, 1998). This directory profiles 475 organizations and institutions working on conflict prevention and conflict management worldwide. It includes surveys on prevention efforts in fifteen conflict-ridden areas and notes the main actors, programs, publications, resource persons and Web sites. There are essays on the theory and practice and on trends in armed conflict.

CLASSROOM RESOURCES

Peace Magazine
(Published by Canadian Disarmament Information Service)
736 Bathurst St.
Toronto, ON
(416) 533-7581
Fax: (416) 531-6214

This magazine is very useful for teachers, journalists and activists. Published six times a year, it features news stories, book and film reviews, letters and a calendars of events. It covers disarmament, conflict resolution, non-violent sanctions, profiles of activists and researchers, controversies about development, population and environmental protection.

Patricia Occhiuzzo Giggans and Barrie Levy, *50 Ways to a Safer World* (Seattle: Seal Press, 1997). This book is a collection of actions that prevent violence at school, in the neighbourhood and in the community. While the book describes concrete actions, it also provides a peace education dimension for violence prevention.

Carol Miller Lieber, *Making Choices About Conflict, Security, and Peacemaking Part I: Personal Perspectives* (Cambridge, MA: Educators for Social Responsibility, 1994). This 400-page book has hands-on activities, role-plays, ideas for group brain-storming sessions and other projects that can help high school students develop a "conflict toolbox" to help them resolve differences without resorting to violence.

Carol Miller Lieber, *Making Choices About Conflict, Security, and Peacemaking Part II: From Local to Global Perspectives* (Cambridge, MA: Educators for Social Responsibility, 1996). High school teachers interested in infusing conflict resolution will find this collection extremely useful. It features co-operatively structured, highly-interactive role-plays, case studies and simulations on the global economy, arms proliferation, environmental conflicts and international trade negotiations.

Toh Swee-Hin and Virginia Floresca-Cawagas, *Peaceful Theory and Practice in Values Education* (Quezon City: Phoenix Publishing House, 1990). This book is both theoretical and practical. It offers more than thirty activities dealing with structural violence, environmental care, human rights, cultural solidarity, militarization and personal peace. For copies, contact the authors at Educational Policy Studies, University of Alberta, Edmonton, AB T6G 2G5.

ORGANIZATIONS

Canadian Council for International Peace and Security
1 Nicholas Street, Suite 300
Ottawa, ON K1N 7B7
(613)562-2763
Fax: (613)562-2741
E-mail: ccips@web.apc.org
www.web.net/~ccips

The Council promotes public debate and discussion on matters of international peace and security. Activities of the Council provide useful lessons on Canada's peace-keeping operations and other peace efforts throughout the world.

Canadian Catholic Organization for Development and Peace
10 St. Mary Street, Suite 420
Toronto, ON M4Y 1P9
(416) 922-1592
1-800-494-1401
Fax : (416) 922-0957

The CCODP helps to improve living and working conditions in seventy countries around the globe, and provides funding for human rights, community development and humanitarian aid in Africa, the Middle East, Asia, Latin America and the Caribbean. This organization provides educational materials and resource people on justice, peace and development issues. Their materials and workshops are appropriate for both teachers and students.

Canadian Institute for Conflict Resolution
Saint Paul University
223 Main Sreet
Ottawa, ON K1S 1C5
(613) 235-5800
Fax: (613) 235-5801

The Institute provides training in conflict resolution in a multicultural and multiethnic society. It offers a series of workshops on conflict resolution, negotiation and facilitation skills throughout the summer and autumn.

Canadian Peacebuilding Co-ordinating Committee
145 Spruce Street
Ottawa, ON K1R 6P1
(613) 233-8621
Fax: (613) 233-9028

The CPCC is a network that draws up policies and guidelines on peace-building for NGOs. Participants work in humanitarian assistance, development, conflict resolution, peace, human rights, or in universities or research institutes.

Peacefund Canada
145 Spruce Street, Suite 206
Ottawa, ON K1R 6P1
(613) 230-0860
Fax: (613) 563-0017
E-mail: pfcan@web.net

> Peacefund Canada supports educational programs and projects focused on understanding causes and seeking answers to conflicts, building a culture of peace, and finding methods of preventing and resolving conflict.

Project Ploughshares
Institute of Peace & Conflict Studies
Conrad Grebel College
Waterloo, ON N2L 3G6
(519) 888-6541
Fax: (519) 885-0806
E-mail: plough@watserv1.waterloo.ca
http://watserv1.waterloo.ca~plough/index

> A project of the Canadian Council of Churches, Project Ploughshares undertakes policy research, education and advocacy to promote the peaceful resolution of conflicts, demilitarization and security based on equity, justice and sustainability. Since its founding in 1976, Project Ploughshares has promoted the concept of common security, which is a product of mutuality, not competition.

TEN DAYS for Global Justice
77 Charles Street, Suite 401
Toronto, ON M5S 1K5
(416) 922-0591
Fax: (416) 922-1419

> TEN DAYS for Global Justice is a Canadian inter-church coalition and a network of community-based ecumenical groups that works for global justice. Through education and action, TEN DAYS challenges dehumanizing and destructive forces and promotes alternative models of society that put people and creation first.

NOTES

1. See, for example, Robin Burns and Robert Aspeslagh, eds., *Three Decades of Peace Education around the World* (New York: Garland, 1996), and David Smith and Terry Carson, *Educating for a Peaceful Future* (Toronto: Kagan and Woo, 1998).

2. I. Kende, "The History of Peace: Concept and Organizations from the Late Middle Ages to the 1870s," *Journal of Peace Research* 26 (1989), 233-747.

3. E. Hermon, "The International Peace Education Movement, 1919-1939," in C. Chatfield and P. van den Dungen, eds., *Peace Movements and Political Cultures* (Knoxville: University of Tennessee, 1988), 127-142.

4. Smith and Carson, *Educating for a Peaceful Future*.

5. T. Araki, "The Spirit of Hiroshima," in T. Perry and J.G. Foulks, eds., *End the Arms Race: Fund Human Needs* (Vancouver: Soules, 1987); and T. Murakami, "Peace Education in Britain and Japan: A Comparison," in Ake Bjerstedt, ed., *Peace Education: Global Perspectives* (Stockholm: Almqvist and Wiksell Internation-al, 1993), 79-83.

6. New Left Review, ed., *Exterminism and Cold War* (London: Verson, 1982); Joseph Rotblat, ed., *Scientist, the Arms Race and Disarmament* (London: Taylor and Francis, 1982).

7. Doug Roche, *A Bargain for Humanity* (Edmonton: University of Alberta, 1993).

8. Project Ploughshares, *The Armed Conflict Report* (Waterloo: Project Ploughshares, 1999).

9. See, for example, David Adam, ed., *UNESCO and a Culture of Peace* (Paris: UNESCO, 1995); and I. Breines, D. Gierycz, and Betty Reardon, *Towards a Women's Agenda for a Culture of Peace* (Paris: UNESCO, 1998).

10. David Hicks, ed., *Education for Peace* (London: Routledge, 1988); Burns and Aspeslagh, *Three Decades of Peace Education around the World*; Swee-Hin Toh, ed., *Journeys in Peace Education: Critical Reflections from Australia* (Sydney, AUS: Earth, 1991); Betty Reardon, ed., *Education for Global Responsibility* (New York: Teachers College Press, 1988); Birgit Brock-Utne, *Feminist Perspectives on Peace and Peace Education* (New York: Pergamon, 1989).

11. A. Bjerstedt, ed., *Peace Education: Global Perspectives* (Stockholm: Almqvist and Wiksell International, 1993).

12. Burns and Aspeslagh, eds., *Three Decades of Peace Education around the World*.

13. Toh Swee-Hin, "Bringing the World into the Classroom," *Global Education* 1 (1993), 9-17. See also, Toh Swee-Hin and Virginia Floresca-Cawagas, *Peace Education: A Framework for the Philippines* (Quezon City: Phoenix Publishing House, 1987).

14. P. Freire, *Pedagogy of Hope* (New York: Continuum and Shor, 1994); I. Shor and P. Freire, *A Pedagogy for Liberation* (South Hedland: Bergin and Garvey, 1987).

15. W. Brouwer, "A Survey of Peace Education in Canada," in C. Alger and M. Stohl, eds., *A Just Peace Through Transformation* (Boulder, CO: Westview Press, 1988), 233-245.

16. S. Bareham and J. Clark, *Safe School Communities: An Information and Policy Guide for the Prevention of Violence* (Vancouver: The British Columbia School Trustees Association, 1994); British Columbia Teachers' Federation, *Task Force on Violence in Schools: Final Report* (Vancouver: BCTF, 1994). See the League of Peaceful Schools Web site for further information: <www.leagueofpeacefulschools.ns.ca/>.

17. Ontario Ministry of Education and Training, *Violence-Free Schools Policy* (Toronto: Ministry of Education and Training, 1994).

18. G. Graham, H. Cornelius, S. Faire, and S. Hall, *Conflict Resolutions Skills for the School Community* (Australia: Conflict Resolution Network, 1991); Valerie Dovey, ed., "Focus: Conflict Resolution in Education," *Track Two* 4 (December 1995); Mabel Aranha, "Some Experiences in Education towards Peace in India," *Peace, Environment and Education* 5 (1994), 43-44; Adam, *UNESCO and a Culture of Peace.*

19. Craig Keilburger, *Free the Children* (New York: Harper Collins, 1998).

20. Ellen Dionisio, "TAGASAN: Student Organizations as Alternative Education," in Burns and Aspeslagh, eds., *Three Decades of Peace Education around the World,* 273-290.

21. FLACAT, *War, Genocide, Torture: Reconciliation, at What Price?* (Montreal: Editions Marcel Didier, 1998).

22. George Dei, *Anti-Racist Education: Theory and Practice* (Halifax: Fernwood Books, 1996); "Information Page," *Artists Against Racism.* <www.vrxnet/aar/prelease.html>. 1999.

23. A. M. Battiste and J. Barman, eds., *First Nations Education in Canada: The Circle Unfolds* (Vancouver: UBC, 1995).

24. F. J. Graveline, *Circle Works: Transforming Eurocentric Consciousness* (Halifax: Fernwood Books, 1998), 73.

25. Betty Reardon and Eva Nordland, eds., *Learning Peace* (Albany, NY: SUNY, 1994). See also Environment Canada/Canada Schoolnet, Teacher's Place on their Web site: <www.ec.gc.ca/~ta/default.html>.

26. Gordon Haim and Lenard Grob, eds., *Education for Peace: Testimonies of World Religions* (Maryknoll: Orbis, 1987); Joanna Macy and Molly Young Brown, *Coming Back to Life* (Philadelphia: New Society Press, 1998).

27. Graveline, *Circle Works,* 184.

28. David Hicks and C. Holden, *Visions of the Future* (Stoke-on-Trent, UK: Trentham Books, 1995); Frank Hutchinson, *Educating beyond Violent Futures* (London: Routledge, 1996).

29. Maude Barlow and Heather-jane Robertson, *Class Warfare* (Toronto: Key Porter, 1994).

30. Heather-jane Robertson, *No More Teachers, No More Books* (Toronto: McClelland and Stewart, 1998); T. Harrison and Jery Kachur, eds., *Contested Classrooms: Education, Globalization and Democracy in Alberta* (Edmonton: University of Alberta and Parkland Institute, 1999).

31. Toh Swee-Hin, "Neo-Conservatives and Controversies in Australian Peace Education: Some Critical Reflections and a Counter-Strategy," in Alger and Stohl, eds. *A Just Peace through Transformation,* 211-232.

AFTERWORD

Tara Goldstein and David Selby

DAVID: In this concluding discussion, let's focus upon change processes within and beyond the classroom. I'd like to begin by suggesting that the different educations discussed here share much in common in what they have to say about the ways in which people learn for personal and social change. Mahatma Gandhi said, "There is no road to peace; peace is the road." Marshall McLuhan said, "The medium is the message." These celebrated champions of social and political change are signalling that the processes of change need to harmonize with, and matter as much as, the goals to which change is directed. All the contributors have, to a greater or lesser extent, taken these famous quotations on board and have recognized that, while each of their fields has a distinct content to be addressed, the characteristics of learning need to be congruent with, and indeed, model the overarching values of their fields. If we are educating for peace, the quality of interactions in learning needs to embody the values of peace such as co-operation, inclusivity, sharing and participation. If we are educating for human rights, the learning processes and quality of relationships in the classroom need to be respectful of rights. If we are educating for environmental awareness, learning should reflect aspects of an ecosystem such as diversity, multi-directional interactions and multiple forms of partnership. It is not surprising that our writers are at one in calling for participatory, critical and democratic learning processes, horizontal (as opposed to vertical) power relationships between teacher and learner, combined with inner journeying, and a shift away from teaching in the traditional sense to teaching as facilitation.

TARA: What do you mean by "inner journeying"? How does it relate to critical learning?

DAVID: I believe that learning for social change needs to be inner- as well as outer-directed. Deeper understandings of our own assumptions, motivations, biases, prejudices and worldviews are essential for making an effective contribution to social change. Social change includes us personally. Our commitment to it has to be authentic and internalized. Toh Swee-Hin and Virginia Floresca-Cawagas write that personal equilibrium and inner peace are vital in sustaining a culture of peace in the world. In his book *Person/Planet,* ecopsychologist Theodore Roszak tells us that "the needs of the planet are the needs of the person ... (the) adventure of self-discovery stands before us as the most practical of pleasures."[1]

TARA: bell hooks talks about learning and teaching for social change as the "practice of freedom."[2] Drawing on memories of her own school days, hooks writes that the all-Black grade schools she went to were places where learning itself was revolution. "We learned early that our devotion to learning, to a life of the mind, was a counter-hegemonic act, a fundamental way to resist every strategy of white racist colonization." With racial integration, school changed for bell hooks. She writes that she no longer learned in a world where teachers believed that educating Black children required a political commitment. "Now we were mainly taught by white teachers whose lessons reinforced racist stereotypes. For black children, education was no longer about the practice of freedom. Realizing this, I lost my love of school."[3] For hooks, learning and teaching for social change needs to be rooted in anti-racist, anti-colonial, feminist struggle.

DAVID: I agree with hooks and want to link our discussion to change beyond the classroom. Proponents of the educations discussed in this collection are at one in asserting that what they are advocating has implications beyond curriculum and classroom learning and teaching. As you mentioned in our introduction, whole-school policies and procedures are essential for combatting sexual harassment. They are also needed for every field covered in this book. We need to ask ourselves what, for instance, development, peace, anti-racist, environmental and humane education have to say about relationships between people in the school, decision-making processes, administrative and management styles, school-community relations, and the very climate or ethos of the school. It goes without saying that I am not talking here about the whole-school implementation of one of the fields but rather about folding the implications of all the fields into the single learning community. Graham Pike provides an example of how this can work when he describes the efforts in Newfoundland to use global education as a vehicle for school improvement.

TARA: Yes, that's true. But the school is only one element within our educational system. Democratic, environmental and equity oriented changes in individual schools can certainly make a profound difference in the lives of the students, teachers and staff who work there. However, to challenge discrimination across provincial school systems, what is needed is the development and implementation of government policies. In the early and mid-1990s, under the leadership of the New Democratic Party government, Ontario education policy makers made a bold attempt to challenge systemic racism and sexism in schools with the publication of two policy documents: the 1993 *Antiracism and Ethnocultural Equity in School Boards Guidelines* and the curriculum support document *Engendering Equity: Transforming Curriculum*. With ten areas of focus for policy development and implementation, the Guidelines reflected a commitment to addressing the racism issues raised in our introduction. As a support document, *Engendering Equity* was designed to help teachers address gender equity issues through *The Common Curriculum*. With the election of the Progressive Conservative government in 1995, implementation of these policies came to a halt. How can we challenge systemic racism and sexism in a thorough and ongoing way without broader political commitment?

DAVID: Or when we have made such significant systemic advances, how can we best prevent the carpet from being rolled back again? We need to be vigilant and strategic about preserving our gains.

TARA: How can we work in strategic ways? Barry Duncan, John Pungente and Rick Shepherd talk about the possibility of teacher-driven change. Wanda Cassidy, drawing on past experience, writes about the importance of forming effective partnerships with ministries of education, school boards, teachers' federations and universities. Tim McCaskell and Vanessa Russell tell us that the force for change lies in marginalized communities. Ouida Wright traces the implementation of anti-racist education in schools to parents of colour who began to use the word "racism" to explain their children's poor academic performance. Susan Fletcher believes teachers must use materials produced by First Nations artists to educate themselves and their students. Preserving our gains involves looking for leadership from oppressed communities themselves.

DAVID: Yes, and one thing we should not overlook is that the contributors to this collection are presenting educational expressions of social change movements that have risen to prominence in Canada in the last fifty years, and especially since the 1960s. Social movements have affected educational thought, philosophy and instruction in a number of ways. For example, in the last twenty years, the humane education movement has been inspired by animal rights activism. As Connie Russell, Anne Bell and Leesa Fawcett write, the environmental and sustainablity movements have led to a variety of environmental education initiatives.

TARA: Lyndsay Moffatt writes that workers in the women's movement began to examine the ways sexism played out in a variety of educational settings that ranged from daycare centres to universities. In the early years, teachers and parents looked at the ways school textbooks and children's picture books reinforced gender stereotypes. They also began to examine the role models that students encountered every day at school.

DAVID: While there are "conservative," "liberal" and "radical" tendencies or strands within each of these social movements and also areas of tension between the movements, they each embrace, more or less, the values of non-violence and social and environmental justice we've been considering. They also have a number of common features. They tend to cut across traditional political or institutional boundaries in terms of adherence. In any community, these movements tend to be embraced by a diverse range of pressure groups and lobbies; for example, local branches of the United Nations and other international organizations. Charities, loose networks, religious groups as well as overtly-campaigning or direct-action groups are also involved. All are characterized to a significant extent by grassroots politics as well as the micro politics of the home and interpersonal relationships. The degree to which they have become institutionalized in terms of local, provincial and federal government legislation and action is in large measure due to both concerted action and organization at grassroots level as well as conscious and deliberate choice at the micro political level. It is evident, too, that each movement began life at the political periphery and, as it has gained profile and momentum, has moved into mainstream political consciousness (though some have been more successful than others in this regard).

TARA: So social movements can draw in a wide range of support and advocates and as they gain momentum, they move into the public and political realm. All the educations that are written about here can be considered as part of a contemporary Canadian progressive educational movement that is trying to challenge school reforms that ignore issues of social and environmental injustice. As Susan Fletcher says, possibilities still exist in public education. They exist in the use of the resources and learning activities recommended in each of these chapters and they exist in the everyday educational activism of teachers who continue to teach for justice, equity and peace.

DAVID: With the strongly rightward shift in the Canadian political landscape, the 1990s and the beginning of the new decade have not generally been a good time for Canada's progressive educational movement. However, the concerns and issues it represents have in no way been pushed aside within political debate on education.

They have become an irrepressible part of the political agenda. We need to view their concrete advance over the long term and see the setbacks of the last decade in perspective. Given the focus of this anthology, it needs to be added that, without exception, the educations described here have fired the imagination and idealism of many people and engaged their activism. Individually and collectively, our authors offer a vision for the new century that, when addressed and expressed within schools and classrooms, can speak to students.

TARA: Yet, educators who teach for social and environmental justice in Canadian schools often walk a difficult line between education and activism, an issue raised by many of our contributors. Connie Russell, Anne Bell and Leesa Fawcett discuss the dilemmas facing environmental educators who are also activists. They ask to what extent teachers should bring their roles as advocates to their classrooms. Teachers are often expected, given their perceived authority, to take a "balanced" stance on controversial issues. Gale Smith and Linda Peterat highlight the need for health educators to be well prepared in dealing with sensitive topics such as sexuality, abortion, contraception and death. Tim McCaskell and Vanessa Russell remind us that changing the way systems operate is seldom easy, but anti-homophobia educational programs present special problems. For example, while teachers and administrators worry about the impact of homophobic incidents on their students, they also fear parental response if they begin doing direct anti-homophobia work in their classrooms. Tim and Vanessa end their chapter by saying that for any community to mobilize, it must believe that social justice is worth the fight and that positive change can be won. Even though this belief is being eroded across the country, they draw comfort from the fact that Canadian students still find the courage to be themselves and that they still take up community activism in the way Wanda Cassidy, Mark Evans and Ian Hundey write about.

DAVID: I think that we can also draw both comfort and new resolve from ancient and modern thinking on the nature of change. Traditional Chinese philosophers have influenced many in the West. They see reality ("Tao") as a continual process of fluctuation between two complementary qualities called "yin" and "yang." These terms have been somewhat distorted by their over-association with, respectively, the feminine and masculine. However, they do provide a way of conceiving change at both individual and societal levels. "The yang having reached its climax retreats in favour of the yin; the yin having reached its climax retreats in favour of the yang."[4] This philosophy tells us that there are limits to cycles of change and that the current cycle, which we might describe as aggressive, unyielding and unresponsive ("yang-like"), will eventually give way to something more humane, caring and nurturing ("yin-like").

Some writers warned us before the rightward shift started that the more successful we were in effecting change towards a more eco-responsive and egalitarian world, the greater and more sustained would be the counter-challenge but that the counter-challenge would in time become unsustainable and weaken.[5] They also anticipated further waves of change each followed by a further wave of (progressively weaker) reaction. Similarly, some modern change theorists have also identified setback as an inevitable element within a spiral of change.[6] They see it as a helpful and healthy, if at the time, a distinctively uncomfortable and unwelcome feature of the change processes. Those seeking change in themselves and in society emerge from the despondency, despair and disillusionment of setback having rethought their views, goals and strategies. Hence, they are more effective. What is now will not be in ten or twenty years time. We need to take a longer-term perspective and work from the backcloth of optimism that such a perspective brings.

TARA: Optimism around the possibility of continuing the struggle for peace, environmental and social justice is reflected in all the chapters collected here. It shines through in Toh Swee-Hin's and Virginia Floresca-Cawagas's idea of having students envision peaceful futures. Maxine Bramble talks about rethinking current approaches to Black education since many of the strategies used to address the problems Black students face in schools have not been effective. Such work includes challenging our tendency to think of Black students as a homogeneous racial group in a way that overlooks their multiple and different realities and experiences at school.

Louella Cronkhite writes about teachers keeping up to date on global issues and provides us with ideas on how to analyze global economic, political and social trends in our classrooms. And Ouida Wright reminds us to be "justly proud" of our achievements even while we acknowledge that there is still much work to be done. "We have the blueprints," she tells us, "the execution remains."

DAVID: The writers in this book have shown us that education can help us to remember and realize our better dreams. Those dreams are not about "living in utility." Acquiring more wealth, faster technology, more output are dreams that government, big business and the media foist upon us but that leave us asking "For what purpose?" The better dreams are about realizing all our human potentials in harmony, joy, love and social justice and in communion with our inner self, each other and the planet. Here lies a truly human vision for education in a new century.

TARA: Like bell hooks, the writers in this collection have shown us that the classroom has the potential to be the most radical place of possibility in the education system. It has been a place where many teachers and students have pursued better dreams. With these essays, our writers keep the momentum going by adding their voices and experiences to a collective call for renewal and rejuvenation in teaching practices for peace, environmental and social justice. With the publication of these essays, we celebrate what hooks calls "transgressions" — movement against and beyond current boundaries. It is that movement that makes education the practice of freedom.

NOTES

1. Theodore Roszak, *Person/Planet* (London: Granada, 1978).

2. bell hooks, *Teaching to Transgress: Education as the Practice of Freedom* (New York: Routledge, 1994).

3. Ibid, 2, 3.

4. Fritjof Capra, *The Tao of Physics: An Exploration of the Parallels Between Modern Physics and Eastern Mysticism* (London: Flamingo, 1983), 17-18.

5. Fritijof Capra, *The Turning Point: Science, Society and the Rising Culture* (London: Flamingo, 1983); and Marilyn Ferguson, *The Aquarian Conspiracy: Personal and Social Transformation in the 1980's* (London: Granada, 1982).

6. For example, see James Prochaska, John Norcross, and Di Clemente, *Changing for Good* (New York: Avon, 1994); and David Selby, "Schooling in Sustainability: Towards Education that Sustains and Educational Change that Can be Sustained," in Jiri Kulich and K Sobotkova, eds., *Five Fingers to Touch a Sustainable Way of Life: Proceedings of the International Conference on Environmental Education* (Rychory, Czech Republic: SEVER, Centre for Environmental Education and Ethics, 1998).

CONTRIBUTORS' NOTES

ANNE BELL is a doctoral student in the Faculty of Environmental Studies at York University. A keen amateur naturalist, gardener and outdoor enthusiast, she considers nature study a focal point of her work in environmental education and advocacy.

MAXINE BRAMBLE is a PhD student in the Faculty of Education at York University. Her doctoral research looks at the biography of second-generation Caribbean Canadian teachers and its relation to their work with students of Caribbean heritage. She worked as a high school teacher in St. Vincent where she taught French and Spanish for one year before immigrating to Canada.

WANDA CASSIDY is Assistant Professor of curriculum, social studies and law education in the Faculty of Education at Simon Fraser University, and Director of the Centre for Education, Law and Society, an endowed centre which she established with a colleague in the early 1980s. She has a long-standing commitment to law-related education, beginning as a high school teacher of law and then as director of the Schools Program of the Legal Services Society of British Columbia.

LOUELLA CRONKHITE has been a development educator for over twenty-five years. Her work with CUSO in Botswana and with the Mennonite Central Committee in Burkina Faso and Louisiana provided her with the background for over a decade of work with the World citizens Learner Centre in Lethbridge and the Alberta Global Education Project. Louella is currently the Alberta Provincial Co-ordinator for USC Canada, an international NGO based in Ottawa.

BARRY DUNCAN, a founder and former president of the Association for Media Literacy, is a part-time teacher of secondary English and media at the School for Experiential Education in Etobicoke, Ontario.

MARK EVANS is Senior Lecturer in the Department of Curriculum, Teaching and Learning and Co-ordinator of the School, Community and Global Connections alternative teacher education program at OISE/UT. Mark has worked extensively with teachers and schools and has been involved in a broad range of curriculum and teacher education reform initiatives both locally and internationally.

LEESA FAWCETT is a professor in the Faculty of Environmental Studies at York University where she teaches courses on environmental education and nature, technology and society. Her current research interests include childhood experiences with animals, animal consciousness, eco-feminism, biological conservation, natural history and organic gardening.

SUSAN DION FLETCHER is a PhD candidate in the Department of Education at the University of Toronto. Susan's work both as a practising teacher and an academic derives from her desire to contribute to accomplishing change in the ways in which Aboriginal people are represented in the curriculum.

VIRGINIA FLORESCA-CAWAGAS is Adjunct Professor in Educational Policy Studies at the University of Alberta. She has extensive experience as a teacher and an educational administrator. Her teaching, research and professional development interests include education for peace, human rights and people-centred development.

TARA GOLDSTEIN is an Associate Professor at OISE/UT where she works in the pre-service teacher education and graduate education programs.. Her research interests include the education of immigrant adolescents, schooling in multilingual communities, playwriting as critical ethnography and applied theatre research. Tara is also the Academic Director of Student Services, which offers a range of co-curricular teacher development programing for students at OISE/UT. Her first play, *Hong Kong, Canada*, was performed in July 2000.

IAN HUNDEY is Senior Lecturer and Co-ordinator of Secondary Pre-service Programs at OISE/UT. He has taught in Canada, Britain, Pakistan and Sweden, and has published or contributed to many books, teacher resources and articles in areas such as Canadian Studies, history, history teaching, careers and citizenship education.

TIM MCCASKELL has been a Student Program Worker for the Toronto Board of Education since 1982, working with youth around issues of racism, sexism and homophobia. He co-facilitated the Board's Lesbian and Gay Students' support group from 1989 to1 996 and has been active in a number of different gay and lesbian community organizations since coming out in 1974.

LYNDSAY MOFFATT is a teacher-librarian in an inner-city elementary school in Toronto.

LINDA PETERAT is a Professor in the Faculty of Education at the University of British Columbia where she is the co-ordinator of social studies, business education, physical education and home economic education. She was instrumental in developing the Diploma Program in Health Education at UBC.

GRAHAM PIKE is Assistant Professor and Director of International Education at the University of Prince Edward Island. From 1992 to 1998, he was co-director of the International Institute for Global Education at the University of Toronto. He runs pre-service and graduate courses in global and international education at UPEI and is a consultant for UNICEF, ministries of education and non-governmental organizations in many countries. He has published widely on global education, including co-writing ten handbooks for teachers.

JOHN J. PUNGENTE, SJ, is director of the Jesuit Communication Project, a Canadian resource centre for media literacy, and president of the Canadian Association for Media Education Organizations.

CONSTANCE RUSSELL works for the International Institute for Global Education at OISE/UT and for the Faculty of Environmental Studies, York University. Her recent research has found her on whale watching boats studying the educational experiences of tourists and tromping about the Niagara escarpment with secondary school students who are enrolled in an integrated environmental studies program.

VANESSA RUSSELL worked as a Student Program Worker at the Toronto Board of Education from 1991 to 1997, with special emphasis on sexual harassment, body image and homophobia. For the past three years, she has been the full-time teacher and co-ordinator of the Triangle Program of Oasis Alternative Secondary School, Canada's only high school classroom for lesbian, gay, bisexual and transgender youth.

DAVID SELBY is Professor and Director of the International Institute for Global Education, OISE/UT. He frequently lectures and facilitates workshops on global, humane and related educations across Canada and internationally. His recent publications and co-publications include *Global Education: Making Basic Learning a Child-Friendly Experience* (UNICEF, 1999); and *In the Global Classroom Book One* and *Book Two* (Pippin, 1999/2000). He is a keen gardener, hiker and photographer of wild orchids.

RICK SHEPHERD teaches secondary school in North York and is vice-president of the Association for Media Literacy.

GALE SMITH is currently a home economics teacher in Surrey School District in British Columbia. She holds a PhD in Curriculum Studies with research interests in curriculum theory, action research and professional practice.

SWEE-HIN TOH is a professor in International/Intercultural Education at the University of Alberta. He has helped to pioneer the development of peace education in countries of both the North and the South and has been a consultant for UNESCO's Culture of Peace Program. Dr. Toh was awarded the UNESCO Prize for Peace Education for the Year 2000.

DR. OUIDA WRIGHT, now retired, has taught and provided leadership in elementary, secondary and post-secondary education. As Assistant Superintendent and later Superintendent for the Toronto Board of Education, she participated in the development and implementation of a wide range of equity policies. She received the Colonel Watson Award of the Ontario Association for Curriculum Development for her outstanding work in curriculum development. Dr. Wright was Assistant Deputy Minister of the Division of Anti-Racism, Access and Equity in the Ontario Ministry of Education and Training from 1993 to 1995.